GENERAL JO SHELBY

MAJOR GENERAL JOSEPH ORVILLE SHELBY,
Commander, Cavalry Division of the Confederate Army of the
Trans-Mississippi (Confederate Museum, Richmond, Va.)

General Jo Shelby

UNDEFEATED REBEL

Daniel O'Flaherty

Foreword by
Daniel E. Sutherland

The University of North Carolina Press
Chapel Hill and London

The paper in this book meets the guidelines for permanence and
durability of the Committee on Production Guidelines for Book
Longevity of the Council on Library Resources.

Library of Congress Cataloging-in-Publication Data

O'Flaherty, Daniel.
General Jo Shelby: undefeated rebel /
by Daniel O'Flaherty; foreword by Daniel E. Sutherland.
p. cm.
Originally published: 1954.
Includes bibliographical references (p.) and index.

ISBN 0-8078-4878-6 (pbk.: alk. paper)

1. Shelby, Joseph Orville, 1830–1897.
2. Generals—Confederate States of America—Biography.
3. Confederate States of America. Army—Biography.
4. United States—History—Civil War, 1861–1865—Cavalry operations.
5. Missouri—History—Civil War, 1861–1865—Cavalry operations.
6. Texas—History—Civil War, 1861–1865—Cavalry operations.
7. Mexico—History—European intervention, 1861–1867.
I. Title.

E467.1.S53 O3 2000
973.7'42'092—dc21
[B]   99-089857

04 03 02 01 00   5 4 3 2 1

For
NELL AND WALTER DREW

Contents

Foreword

D ANIEL O'FLAHERTY's biography of Joseph O. Shelby could easily have been lost in the shuffle when it first appeared in 1954. It was one of at least two dozen biographies of Civil War generals published from the late 1940s to the late 1950s, roughly five years on either side of his own book. Burke Davis published a notable biography of Thomas J. "Stonewall" Jackson in that same year, as did Joseph H. Parks of Edmund Kirby Smith. The longer span of ten years brought the appearance of such classic works as T. Harry Williams's biography of Pierre G. T. Beauregard, Hans L. Trefousse's of Benjamin Butler, Jay Monaghan's of George A. Custer, Millard K. Bushong's of Jubal A. Early, Lloyd Lewis's of Ulysses S. Grant, Manly Wade Wellman's of Wade Hampton, John P. Dyer's of John Bell Hood, books by both Lenoir Chambers and Frank Vandiver on Jackson, the Gilbert E. Govan and James W. Livingood biography of Joseph E. Johnston, Earl S. Miers's biography of Robert E. Lee, books by Burke Davis on both Lee and James E. B. Stuart, the Donald B. Sanger and Thomas R. Hay biography of James Longstreet, Warren Hassler's biography of George B. McClellan, Elizabeth J. Whaley's of James B. McPherson, Richard O'Conner's of Philip H. Sheridan, and W. A. Swanberg's of Daniel Sickles. An impressive list, to say the least, and all of this even before the explosion of Civil War books that accompanied the war's centennial celebration.

Reviewers divided over the merits of O'Flaherty's portrait of Shelby. Virtually all acknowledged that O'Flaherty had produced a dramatic, fast-paced story that kept readers turning the pages. "Mr. O'Flaherty is fortunate in his subject," observed Harnett T. Kane, the popular southern writer and novelist, "and the general is lucky to have so lively and appreciative a biographer." Of course, he added, O'Flaherty's "occasionally over-enthusiastic, over-lush . . . style" would not suit everyone, and "professional historians," Kane warned, might "quarrel with some of his points." And indeed some did. They picked at some factual errors, complained about a lack of analysis, and questioned O'Flaherty's use of sources. O'Flaherty, a writer for magazines and radio, had produced "an interesting story for popular consumption," they said, but he had fallen short of writing a definitive biography of the Confederate cavalryman.[1] O'Flaherty would not have gainsaid most of his critics. He confessed to being "neither a military expert nor a scholar." His purpose, O'Flaherty maintained modestly, had been only to "trace the thread of Shelby's life through the kaleidoscopic pattern of American history between the 1840's and 1890's" (p. xviii).

Yet, some fifty years on, O'Flaherty's work has clearly held its own within its generation of Civil War biographies. Newer books about Custer, Grant, Hood, Jackson, Joe Johnston, Lee, Longstreet, McClellan, Sheridan, and Stuart have nudged aside earlier interpretations of their subjects, but O'Flaherty's remains the only biography of the man he called the "greatest cavalry chieftain" of the war (p. xvii). And it is more than a biography. O'Flaherty also intended that his book should attract attention to the war in the Trans-Mississippi—then, as now, a badly neglected subject—and here, too, it continues to serve as a standard source. O'Flaherty might have cited his sources more precisely, researched more thoroughly some features of Shelby's prewar and postwar careers, double-checked a few more dates, scrutinized his maps more closely, and dealt with Shelby's wartime reputation more satisfactorily; but given the sources available to him, and considering historical interpretations of the war at the time he wrote, there remains good reason to admire the finished product.

1. Quotes are from Harnett T. Kane, "A Flaming Spirit," *New York Times Book Review*, July 4, 1954, 6, and Bernarr Cresap, review in *Journal of Southern History* 20 (November 1954): 560. For a variety of other reviews, see John W. Payne in *Arkansas Historical Quarterly* 14 (Summer 1955): 185–86; W. Francis English in *American Historical Review* 60 (October 1954): 195–96; Frank Vandiver in *Mississippi Valley Historical Review* 41 (September 1954): 341–42; and David J. Eicher, *The Civil War in Books: An Analytical Bibliography* (Urbana: University of Illinois Press, 1997), 108.

The real question in judging any biography is this: Has the author captured the essence of the subject? In the case of O'Flaherty, the answer must be yes. Even his initial critics acknowledged as much. "Mr. O'Flaherty has done a creditable job in reconstructing Shelby's early life," announced one reviewer, "and he does present a convincing picture of Shelby as a man and as a soldier."[2] To O'Flaherty, Shelby was "a man of savage temper" (p. 45). "He fought like a man who invented fighting," added the biographer, "and the men of the Missouri Cavalry Brigade looked on him as the perfect commanding officer: colorful and dashing, but with a recklessness so shrewd that it amounted almost to caution" (p. 163). This accords with everything his contemporaries said about Jo Shelby. "*He looked liked somebody*," submitted an Arkansas soldier. "He looked like someone who had something to him" (p. 28). Or, somewhat metaphorically, a former Union army officer offered this appraisal: "He was not what might be termed a round man, uniform and regular in his mental and moral composition. On the contrary, he was angular to acuteness. It was the sharp angles, the abrupt curvatures in his character that created the constant surprises in his career and lent to his life its singular attractiveness and picturesqueness" (p. 400).

Born in Lexington, Kentucky, in 1830, Joseph Orville Shelby was a rope manufacturer, not a soldier, by trade. Having been educated at Transylvania University in his hometown and in Philadelphia, the twenty-one-year-old Shelby moved to Missouri, where he became a planter. Shelby's civil war, like that of many Missourians, began in Bleeding Kansas during the 1850s. Shelby was a hardened "border ruffian" long before he accepted a captain's commission in the Missouri State Guard. He was a colonel before the first year of the war had passed, a general by the end of 1863, and a participant in every major engagement of the war in Arkansas and Missouri. Like Sterling Price, a native Virginian who had also moved west in his early twenties, Shelby considered Missouri his home and spent the war trying to win it for the Confederacy. His most notable effort came when he led his "Iron Brigade" of Missouri volunteers on the longest cavalry raid of the war. From September 22 to November 3, 1863, Shelby and his men romped 1,500 miles through the state, inflicted more than 1,000 casualties on Union forces, and captured or destroyed $2 million worth of enemy supplies and property.

2. *Journal of Southern History* 20 (November 1954): 560.

The surrender of the Confederate States did not mean the end of the rebellion for this "undefeated rebel." Shelby, along with Price and many other western Confederates, fled to Mexico after the war, an episode to which O'Flaherty devotes one-fourth of his narrative (about half the book covers the war years). Upon hearing of the Confederate capitulation in Virginia, Shelby announced that he would never live under Yankee rule. "No! no!" he exclaimed to his men. "We will do this: we will hang together, we will keep our organization, our arms, our discipline, our hatred of oppression, until one universal shout goes up from an admiring age that this Missouri Cavalry Division preferred exile to submission, death to dishonor."[3] He and what remained of the Iron Brigade crossed the Rio Grande and offered their services to Maximilian. Political expediency forced the French puppet to refuse their assistance, but he generously offered free land in the Cordoba Valley to the hundreds of ex-Confederates then pouring across the border. Shelby's family soon joined him, and he did not return to the United States until the fall of Maximilian in June 1867.

Shelby lost much of his feistiness over the next three decades, but not his reputation as a Confederate hero, and he never abandoned his adventurous style of living. He became involved in Democratic politics (although he consistently refused to run for public office), tried several business ventures (with only modest success), assisted former rebel soldiers (including Frank James, the outlaw), and, having accepted an appointment as federal marshal for western Missouri from President Grover Cleveland, helped break the Pullman Strike of 1893. His appointment as marshal also forced him finally to take a postwar oath to uphold the Constitution of the United States. But, then, after he returned to Missouri in 1867, Shelby never showed signs of bitterness toward the North. In that sense, O'Flaherty's portrayal of him as an undefeated rebel masks an important subtlety. Shelby's refusal to admit defeat in war did not imply blind devotion to rebellion. Rather, he was undefeated in the sense of remaining undaunted, capable of rising above the ruins of the Confederacy, maintaining his personal dignity, and accepting the political and economic necessity of sectional reconciliation.

3. Quote from "Confederate Persistency," *Confederate Veteran* 5 (April 1897): 166.

It is an interesting distinction, and one only partially realized in O'Flaherty's biography, but an important one for understanding Shelby's postwar years—and perhaps something about his character. Certainly Shelby repented his role in Bleeding Kansas. "I went there to kill Free State men," he confessed in 1897. "I did kill them. I am not ashamed of myself for having done so, but then times were different from what they are now. . . . No Missourian had any business there with arms in his hands. The policy that sent us there was damnable and the trouble we started on the border bore fruit for ten years." The passions aroused by the debate over slavery made men "irresponsible," and, Shelby concluded, "I now see I was so myself" (p. 44).

Yet, like most old Confederates, Shelby could not—or would not—fully reject the cause of his youth. "We failed but we (the South) have the satisfaction of Knowing that no people on Earth endured or fought more from patriotic desires," he wrote to a former comrade in 1885. "It is over, and as we all surrendered it behooves us all to abide by the terms imposed" (p. 353). Shelby became active in the United Confederate Veterans, which kept him and his reputation firmly tied to the Lost Cause. He served as the commander of the Missouri Division of the UCV in the years before his death, and just months before his passing in 1897, he attended a grand Confederate reunion in Richmond. Speaking briefly to the convention, which had gathered to lay the cornerstone of a monument to Jefferson Davis, Shelby remained a symbol of the Confederate Trans-Mississippi: "We are here, as ex-Confederates, . . . and I stand here as a representative of the Confederate cause west of the Mississippi, and I speak for the Missourians when I say that this for all time shall be our Mecca" (p. 393).

Was Shelby, as O'Flaherty insists, the greatest cavalryman of the war? Gen. Alfred Pleasonton, who had fought for three years against Jeb Stuart in Virginia before vainly crossing swords with Shelby, apparently thought so. "Shelby was the best cavalry general of the South. Under other conditions, he would have been one of the best in the world," attested the Union commander (p. xvii). Sterling Price knew Shelby's worth, too, going so far as to call him a "brilliant and heroic officer" and the "best cavalry officer" he had ever seen. Even more modest historical estimates rate Shelby as the "finest [cavalry commander] of the Trans-Mississippi." Clearly his men idealized him. "You've heard of Shelby's Raid?" asked aging veterans. "Jeb Stuart's Ride around McClellan? Hell, brother, Jo Shelby rode around MISSOURI!" And they composed songs to glorify his feats:

Ho Boys! Make a Noise!
The Yankees are afraid!
The river's up, hell's to pay—
Shelby's on a Raid! (p. 189)

And if men are worthy of their leader, then we cannot discount one historian's judgment that the Iron Brigade was "perhaps the best cavalry unit in the West."[4]

Any estimation of Shelby and his reputation must also include an evaluation of Shelby's Boswell, John N. Edwards. Edwards first met Shelby in the mid-1850s, served as his adjutant for most of the war, and developed an admiration for his commander that bordered on hero worship. He wrote most of Shelby's after-action reports and became his alter ego. Most important, Edwards wrote three books about the war, two of which, *Shelby and His Men* and *Shelby's Expedition to Mexico*, chronicled the wartime and early postwar history of the Iron Brigade.[5] A prominent Missouri newspaper editor, columnist, and editorial writer, Edwards was notorious for his purple prose and his romanticized view of all things Confederate. Still, his books tell us most of what we know about Shelby's personal life during and immediately after the war. Historians dealing with Shelby must come to terms with Edwards, and while virtually all warn about the need to proceed with caution, they concede the general accuracy of his accounts. O'Flaherty, with his own penchant for colorful language, ac-

4. U.S. War Department, *War of the Rebellion: Official Records of the Union and Confederate Armies*, 130 vols. (Washington, D.C.: Government Printing Office, 1880–1901), ser. 1, vol. 41, pt. 1, p. 639; Dallas Cothrum, "Jo Shelby: Reluctant Guerrilla" (Ph.D. diss., Texas Christian University, 1999), 269; Albert Castel, *General Sterling Price and the Civil War in the West* (Baton Rouge: Louisiana State University Press, 1968), 153.
5. The full titles of these two books are *Shelby and His Men: Or the War in the West* (Cincinnati: Miami Publishing, 1867), and *Shelby's Expedition to Mexico: An Unwritten Leaf of the War* (Kansas City, Mo.: Kansas City *Times*, 1872). Edwards's third book, *Noted Guerrillas: Or the Warfare of the Border* (St. Louis: Brand Publishing, 1877), is not as highly regarded as the first two works, being generally seen as a veiled defense for the worst excesses of Confederate guerrillas in Missouri. On the historical accuracy of Edwards, see Castel, *General Sterling Price*, 160–61, 174 (n. 17), 269 (n. 34), and the introduction by Conger Beasley to the newly edited *Shelby's Expedition to Mexico* (Fayetteville: University of Arkansas Press, 2000). Beasley's introduction also provides an excellent biographical sketch of Edwards.

knowledged that Edwards seldom missed an opportunity to "gild the lily," but he joined with other historians in defending Edwards's books, especially *Shelby's Expedition to Mexico*. "It is a matter of sober fact that Shelby's whole career was one long sequence of highly improbable, but well authenticated, historical events," explained O'Flaherty; "and it is equally probable that Major Edwards strayed no further from the truth than was considered permissible in his time for a Southern officer and gentleman" (p. xix).

Of course, there is very likely more to Shelby's story than Edwards revealed or than O'Flaherty could have appreciated in the 1950s. Any future biographer will have to ground Shelby more securely in the social, economic, and, yes, even the military history of the period. O'Flaherty interpreted Shelby's life through the "kaleidoscopic pattern of American history between the 1840's and the 1890's," but kaleidoscopes are notoriously vulnerable to the least shift or tremor. Research in areas important to our understanding of Shelby has enhanced our knowledge of Shelby's world in ways that must change old perspectives on him. Post-1950s research on the American economy, slavery, the territorial issue, wartime military strategy, wartime political strategy, guerrilla warfare, postwar Confederate emigration, Reconstruction, sectional reconciliation, and any number of more narrowly defined themes has altered historical assumptions that O'Flaherty would have taken for granted.

But the incorporation of these new insights into Shelby's story lies in the future, and any new search to understand Shelby must begin with O'Flaherty. His Shelby is as real and vital a force as one can hope to find in the world of biography, and his skillful description of the Civil War in the tumultuous and ferocious Trans-Mississippi is powerful. Reading O'Flaherty, it is easy to understand the devotion and enthusiasm Shelby's men felt for this Confederate warrior: "Ho Boys! Make a Noise! . . . Shelby's on a Raid!"

DANIEL E. SUTHERLAND

December 1999

Preface

M AJOR GENERAL Alfred Pleasanton, the creator of the Cavalry Corps of the Army of the Potomac, who fought Stuart in Virginia and led the pursuit of Price's raiders in Missouri in 1864, said of Major General Joseph Orville Shelby, C.S.A., "Shelby was the best cavalry general of the South. Under other conditions, he would have been one of the best in the world." The brilliant Union cavalry leader was himself on his death bed in a Washington, D. C., hotel when the news was brought to him of the passing of Shelby at Adrian, Missouri, in February, 1897, and his generous tribute to the memory of an old foe was almost Pleasanton's last conscious utterance.

Yet today the dust of Joseph Shelby, the only ranking Confederate commander on active duty in 1865 never to surrender, and the greatest cavalry chieftain of them all, in the opinion of those who should have known best, his enemies, lies almost forgotten beneath a modest marker at the foot of the Confederate Monument in Forest Hill Cemetery, Kansas City, on the Battlefield of Westport, where he saved the last Confederate army of the West from destruction, with Pleasanton in vain pursuit. Not another stone has been raised to his memory either in Kentucky, his birthplace, or in his adopted state of Missouri, where in the closing years of the last century he was elevated almost to the status of a folk god by the people of the state. In all the glittering constellation of the South's cavalry leaders, Shelby alone remains a dim and almost invisible star, for reasons which will appear; no single reason alone is responsible for the obscurity which his fame has suffered. It has been a fortuitous combination of circumstances such as the chronicler seldom confronts; and it is the story that has never been told, in all of the millions of words written on the Civil War, despite the fact that the story of Shelby's life, over five tumultuous decades, is one of the great American epics. During those decades he lived more lives than half a dozen other notables of history put together, and even without his whirlwind passage through the Civil War, in which he marched and raided more miles than any other Confederate cavalryman, his life was one of high adventure never matched by any of his countrymen before or since. It was a Wagnerian opera of the West, in which there are thunderous overtones of Missouri River steamboats loaded with hemp, the crack of John Brown's well-oiled rifles, the drumfire of Confederate cavalry hoofs, the Marseillaise played by French bands in the plazas of Maximilian's Mexico, the hammer of railway track being laid to the Golden Gate, and the "Stars and Stripes Forever" played by a Missouri brass band at a Fourth of July courthouse celebration.

Shelby was as American as Jeb Stuart, Mark Twain, or P. T. Barnum, but in his many-faceted character there was more of the Chevalier Bayard than of the Showman or the Soldier of Fortune. He was the archetype and idol in Missouri of those who called themselves the Chivalry; he was, as George Creel has called him, the Last of the Cavaliers.

No attempt has been made in this book to cover the whole operation of the War in the West, except insofar as Shelby played a part in it, and there has not been space for detailed attention to the functioning of the Confederate Department of the Trans-Mississippi, in which the Missourians chiefly fought; those are fields still awaiting the historian. The writer is neither a military expert nor a scholar, and has been content simply to trace the thread of Shelby's life through the kaleidoscopic pattern of American history between the 1840's and the 1890's. A word is necessary, however, on the author's source of material on Shelby's expedition into Mexico. There is only one source, the works of Shelby's adjutant, Major John Newman Edwards. Edwards had a gift for exaggeration, and no ear for contemporary conversation; his characters spoke a language never heard on land or sea outside the pages of Sir Walter Scott, his literary model. Though it would be pleasant to be able to make the claim that all quotations are actual transcripts from an indubitable record, it has been necessary to recast these conversations along more probable lines; but as George Creel says, in a letter to the writer, "Major Edwards never failed to gild the lily, but from what Colonel Elliott (Shelby's Marshal Ney) and others told me . . . he usually had a basis of fact."

Mr. Creel can speak with more than usual authority, for he was a young reporter covering the Federal Building in Kansas City when Shelby was United States Marshal for the Western District of Missouri. In his autobiography, *A Rebel at Large*, Mr. Creel says:

"The Federal Building was on my beat, and when I dropped in to see the General, it was usually an hour before I could get away. As a rule, members of his old command sat with him, and when dispute occurred as to a date or incident, they turned to their Bible, Major John N. Edwards' chronicle of the expedition."

This testimony that the men who went to Mexico with Shelby regarded Edwards as Holy Writ, coming as it does from one of America's most distinguished writers and Woodrow Wilson's chief of information during World War I, would seem sufficient reply to those historians who have felt, quite pardonably, that some of Major Edwards' "gilding of the lily" almost passes the boundaries of credence; but Edwards wrote in the extravagant style of the day, with the Southern historian's proverbial tendency to exaggerate the casualties, and the villainy, of the enemy; and a grain of salt, plus a little intelligent discrimination, are all that is needed to separate the wheat from the chaff in the boisterous works of Major John Newman Edwards. It is a matter of sober fact that Shelby's whole career was one long sequence of highly improbable, but well authenticated, historical events; and it is equally probable that Major Edwards strayed no further from the truth than was considered permissible in his time for a Southern officer and gentleman.

Because of the scarcity of primary data on Shelby's private life, the author is more than usually indebted to a large number of persons who have assisted in the search for material. He is especially in the debt of Mr. C. Frank Dunn and Mr. Charles R. Staples, of Lexington, Kentucky, and Miss Ludie J. Kinkead, of the Filson Club, Louisville, for their devoted interest to the cause of unearthing data on the Lexington of Shelby's boyhood; to Mrs. H. H. Gratz, of Lexington, widow of Shelby's partner, for her recollection of Betty Shelby; to Mr. J. W. Motte of Waverly, Missouri, for his vivid reconstruction,

for the author, of the town of Waverly in the fifties; and to Mr. A. L.
Maxwell of Lexington, Missouri, who knows more history of the
Missouri River Valley than has been, or ever will be, written. Ac-
knowledgment is made elsewhere of the author's heavy obligation to
Messrs. Cass K. Shelby of Hollidaysburg, Pennsylvania, and Edward
F. Shelby, of Uniontown, for genealogical data on the Shelby family;
and at the top of the list belongs an expression of heartfelt appreciation for the day-by-day assistance, for a year and a half, rendered
by Mr. Milton C. Russell, of the Virginia State Library, and Mrs.
Bertie Craig Smith, Mrs. Margaret Causby, Mrs. Susan Seaboyer and
Miss Eudora Elizabeth Thomas, members of the staff, assistance which
included not only research within the library but a continuing correspondence with other libraries throughout the country. In addition,
the Virginia State Library provided the author with a private office,
with the compliments of the Commonwealth, into which no noise
louder than the distant hum of an elevator could penetrate—a boon
the enjoyment of which has to be experienced to be appreciated, but
the nature of which any writer will understand.

In addition, equal thanks are due to all of the following, in the
search for Shelby material, which led from Pennsylvania to Mexico
City, vertically, and from Vera Cruz to California, horizontally:
Donald G. Patterson, Acting Chief of the General Reference and
Bibliography Division, Library of Congress; David C. Mearns, Chief
of Manuscript Division, Library of Congress; Emerson Greenaway,
Librarian, Free Library of Philadelphia; Paul North Rice, Chief of
Reference Department, New York Public Library; M. E. Kekker,
Book Editor of *Armor*, formerly the *United States Cavalry Journal*,
U. S. Armor Association, Washington, D. C.; John R. Wallace, presi-
dent of the Public Library and Historical Association, Lexington, Mis-
souri; Miss Sarah Guitar, Reference Librarian of the State Historical
Society of Missouri, Columbia, Mo.; Miss Roemol Henry, Librarian,
Transylvania College, Lexington, Kentucky; W. B. McDaniel II,
Librarian, The College of Physicians of Philadelphia; Dr. Harry E.
Pratt, Historian of the State of Illinois; Ralph H. Parker, Librarian,
University of Missouri, Columbia, Mo.; R. N. Williams 2nd, Director
of the Historical Society of Pennsylvania; Gilbert Knipmeyer, Archi-
vist of the State of Missouri, Jefferson City, Mo.; Mrs. Frances Biese,
Archivist of the Missouri Historical Society, St. Louis; Miss Barbara
Kell, Reference Librarian of the Society; Joseph H. Thom, Chief of

the Reference Department, Washington University Libraries, St. Louis; Miss Helen M. McFarland, Librarian, Kansas State Historical Society, Topeka; Dr. Floyd C. Shoemaker, Secretary of the State Historical Society of Missouri at Columbia; Dr. James N. Primm, Assistant Director of the Western Historical Manuscripts Collection, University of Missouri, Columbia; Miss Norma Cass, Reference Librarian, University of Kentucky, Lexington; Thomas C. Morelock, Director of Public Information, University of Missouri; Mrs. Viola A. Perrotti, Curator, Snyder Memorial Library, University of Kansas City; William Ainsworth Parker, Secretary for Fellowships of the American Council of Learned Societies, Washington, D. C.; Warren C. Stewart, American Consul, Vera Cruz, Mexico; Edward F. Lane, Assistant to the Vice President of the University of Pennsylvania; George A. Harris, Alumni Secretary, Villanova College; Thomas F. Shannon, Alumni Secretary, St. Joseph's College, Philadelphia; Bennett S. Cooper, Alumni Secretary, Haverford College, Haverford, Pa.; John E. Kramer, Registrar of the Philadelphia College of Pharmacy and Science; Miss Henrietta Lynch, Secretary of the Troost Avenue Cemetery Corporation, Kansas City; Miss Minnie B. Cameron, Librarian, San Antonio Public Library; Robert E. Hickman, of Benton, Ill.; Mrs. Shelby Grove Steger, Van Buren, Mo.; John F. Shelby, Butler, Mo.; Henry A. Bundschu, Referee in Bankruptcy, U. S. District Court for the Western District of Missouri, Kansas City; Mrs. Lee Redd Nally, Bronxville, N. Y.; Drury T. Boyd, Joplin, Mo.; Bryan Lacy, Postmaster, Adrian, Mo.; John Bakeless, Seymour, Conn., Historian of the Missouri Pacific Railroad; Rev. Wade Safford, Washington, D. C.; Mrs. Irwin Donovan (Mrs. Laura Edwards Donovan) of Muskogee, Okla.; Maurice J. Schwab, Recorder of Deeds, Lexington, Mo.; Miss Elizabeth Corder, Marshall, Mo.; Dr. James Welch Patton, Director of the Southern Historical Collection, University of North Carolina, Chapel Hill; Mrs. Lutie Gordon Jordan of Waverly, Mrs. Louise Davis Brown of Waverly, Mrs. L. N. Morgan of Norman, Okla., and Mrs. Adrianna Kuyk Ludwig, in whose home the first half of this book was written, and who as a musician is more of an artist than any biographer.

DANIEL O'FLAHERTY

Richmond, Virginia
September, 1953

General Jo Shelby

I saw, or imagined I saw,
a great empire beyond the Rio.
This river they call the great river.
Joseph Orville Shelby

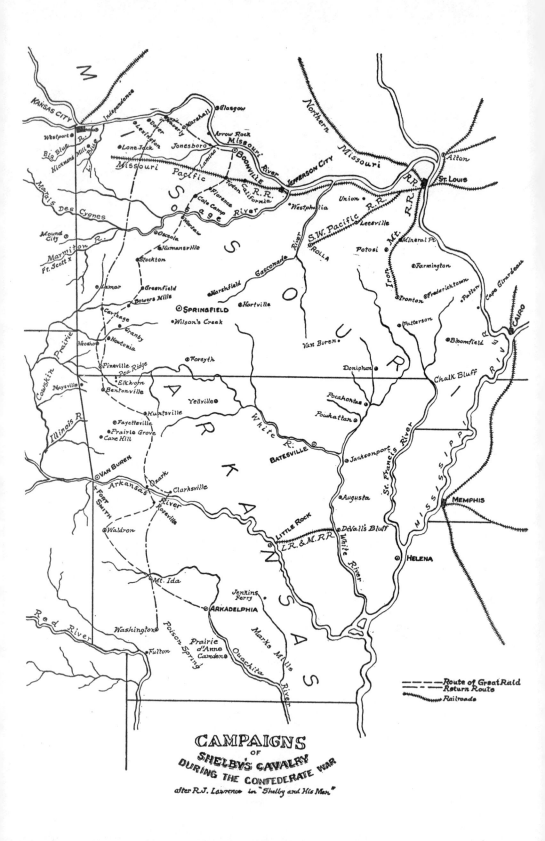

CAMPAIGNS
OF
SHELBY'S CAVALRY
DURING THE CONFEDERATE WAR

after R.J. Lawrence in "Shelby and His Men"

PART ONE

The Sign of the Centaur

◆●◆

1. *Lincoln's Confederate General*

AFTER the American Civil War, when the heavy hand of military defeat lay upon the South, thousands of ex-Confederates looked longingly across the border into Mexico, which was still a white man's country under the reign of the Emperor Ferdinand Maximilian. The *opéra bouffe* empire of the blond-bearded, thirty-two-year-old Austrian Hapsburg, supported by French occupation troops, still had two years to go, and the broad vistas of an ancient and romantic land beckoned invitingly to all those Southerners footloose enough to follow the sun.

True, the Mexicans had a civil war of their own, and there was a Juarista behind every boulder in the north, but hundreds of disbanded Confederates, seeing it as the promised land, slipped across the border either to join Juárez or to seek service with the Emperor. The pickings were good from the beginning, but it was not until June 2, 1865, that there was any concerted movement southward.

On that day Major General Joseph Orville Shelby,[1] late commander of the Missouri Cavalry Division of the Confederate Army of the Trans-Mississippi, marched south from Corsicana, Texas, with a band of a few hundred men, soon swelled to a thousand, and began a triumphal march to Mexico City which was one of the strangest military excursions in history.[2]

It was not an invasion, nor a raid, though all were armed to the teeth and angry as only men can be who have lost a war. It was a trespass, pure and simple; but in the unsettled state of the country there was none to forbid them entry. When General Jeanningros, the French commander at Monterrey, heard about it he promised to hang them all, for it was the conviction of Jeanningros and his master in Mexico City, Marshal Bazaine, that Shelby's expedition was but the spearhead of another gringo invasion such as Mexico had suffered in the 1840's. In this they guessed better than they knew. Although even his soldiers did not know it, General Shelby had the unofficial blessing of Abraham Lincoln in this venture; and if Lincoln had been alive this June day Shelby could have said to his men, "Boys, I have the word of the President of the United States that if you join Juárez and oust the French, thus saving Washington the trouble, you may have anything you like in Mexico." [3] With Lincoln dead, he kept silent, for no one any longer knew what Washington would do; the South-haters were in the saddle; they might even demand the return of the exiles as traitors. And yet—and yet, old Abe had picked him for the mission. It was another in the long list of distinctions which Jo Shelby could wear and no other man could—he was Abraham Lincoln's Confederate General.

At Piedras Negras, opposite Eagle Pass, Shelby and his men received a magnificent offer to join the Republicans under Juárez, which would have made them military masters of the Mexican states of Tamaulipas, Coahuila, and Nuevo León. The fame of the Missouri Cavalry Division had preceded them. Perhaps a message from Lincoln, through Juárez, now in the United States, had also preceded them. Governor Biesca, Juárez' right-hand man in the north, proposed to abdicate all but his civil authority in Coahuila in favor of Shelby, making him military commandant of the district in return for the services of his brigade and his ten Napoleon howitzers. Shelby was to be commissioned a major general, with absolute authority from Juárez to recruit fifty thousand Americans. [4]

A vote was taken, since Shelby's was a democratic organization, and the men voted unanimously to reject Biesca's offer. After all, Juárez commanded only greasers, in their view, and the gray coats of the Juaristas, coupled with their obvious economic distress, reminded the Confederates unfavorably of the war they had lost at home. Furthermore, the glittering braid of Empire had an irresistible attraction for them and they plumped for the Emperor, although it should have been obvious to rational men that Maximilian's days were numbered and that they were allying themselves with another Lost Cause.

Rational men, however, would have had no place in an expedition such as Shelby's. He and his vagabonds were possessed by a dream, and the dream confused reality, as it always does on such elysian argosies; it was the dream of a truant race. Their dream was to become an elite guard of cuirassiers in the service of an Emperor, with brilliant uniforms, flying scarves, silver spurs, and jeweled pistols, with gold for gaming and sloe-eyed señoritas for dalliance in the tropic dusk. This was to be their compensation for their rags of butternut and the victory so often snatched from their grasp—for their poverty and their exile.

They had been too long on Confederate army rations and quartered too long in hellfire Baptist towns in Texas, where the townspeople sniffed at them and the girls sang psalms on Mondays and it was Sunday every day of the week. They were headed now for a warrior's heaven in the "land of garlic, stilettos, and straw hats." They had charted their course for Hi-Brazil, for Fiddler's Green, and the Gates of El Dorado, with Jo Shelby up in front. Their goal was simple: loot, liquor, and women in the sinful cities of Cortez, with good horses to ride, bright lances to flash, and fine feathers to preen. The Emperor would not want them as a bodyguard—fearing the wrath of the United States—and would offer them only lands to homestead, but at Piedras Negras they could not know that.

In Jo Shelby they had the right leader. Descendant of a family which had fought at King's Mountain and produced the first governor of Kentucky, for four years he had been to the Confederate Army of the Trans-Mississippi what Jeb Stuart was to the Army of Northern Virginia—its cavalry arm. And lest the Army of the Trans-Mississippi be thought of as only a few small brigades in unimportant territory, let it be remembered that it stood at sixty thousand men at its peak—more than Lee had after Gettysburg—and its tragedy was that it had never been used to assist the eastern armies.

Like Stuart, Shelby was young, a brigadier general at thirty-three and a major general at thirty-five. Unlike Stuart, he was handsome. Both had the quality of inspiring adoration in men and women alike. But here the comparison with Stuart ends—save in the matter of cavalry genius—although Shelby was the Stuart of the West, for Stuart was a bluenose in his private life, while Shelby could drink, fight, and court with the best of them.

We have no fine paintings and murals of Shelby on horseback, as we have of Stuart and Mosby, gallant with plumes in the moonlight. Nor is there a single equestrian monument honoring him in all the

South. He avoided having pictures taken as he avoided writing official reports when he could—to the distraction of the historian. A friend had to drag him into a picture gallery in Kansas City for one of the two postwar photographs we have of him. The earlier picture shows him with a beard like the waved mane of a circus horse, fine gray eyes with deep wrinkles of intelligence about them in a square and massive face, and hair combed as flat as a New Orleans bartender's.

This last, too-slick touch is obviously the result of an effort to tame his locks for the ambrotype man, and he was forty years old when it was taken. In battle, with the shock of brown hair matted beneath the brim of his dark slouch hat, and his black plume flying, he must have resembled a curly wolf in butternut. In addition, he had the fine figure of the Confederate cavalryman, a resounding voice capable of the most dulcet and persuasive oratory, and he was a ladies' man of distinction in a country full of ladies' men.

Though pictures of him are hard to find, the men of the Missouri Cavalry Division, those who survived, carried with them a picture in their minds that never dimmed with the passage of three score years and more. It was the picture of Shelby as a scourge in the saddle, a cavalry leader who never made a mistake; who could hold off fifteen thousand men with only one thousand throughout one bloody, live-long day; who harnessed his men to the guns of the artillery when the horses gave out—and the men were glad to take their places; who smote the enemy hip and thigh, and won the last battle west of the Mississippi for the Confederacy; and whose flag, in the end, was not lowered in the presence of the enemy.

Before the war Shelby had been a leader of the Missouri border ruffians in Kansas and had killed his share of abolitionists in the border warfare. Far from being a bushwhacker, however, he was one of the richest and most elegant young planters in Missouri at the time, own-ing land, slaves, steamboats, and a hemp factory in the romantic old river town of Waverly. During the war itself, he carried the conflict to the enemy so fiercely that his name was either a talisman to conjure with, or a hissing and a byword, depending upon which side you were on in that fight. In the very first reports in which his name appears in the Official Records, he is already being referred to by the Federals as "the notorious Shelby."

There is never a hint, however, that he is not an honorable soldier. His notoriety with the Federals derived from his slashing prairie style of attack, which he had learned in Kansas. Shelby was, by temperament, a freebooter first of all. An understanding of this fact is essential in forming an estimate of his character. It was Shelby's fate that his cavalry genius was used over and over again merely to save Confederate armies from the destruction invited by the military incompetence of his superiors; he failed not once to smash the will of the enemy to follow up an advantage, but to a man like Shelby, whose most modest plans would have called for an invasion of the United States clear up to Canada, this was frustration of the most punishing kind.

The Missouri Cavalry Division, which he commanded throughout its life, was composed first to last of volunteers, mostly boys. The Confederacy sent Shelby not a squad during the four years of the war, nor did he want any of their "conscript trash." He foraged for good men the way some generals foraged for the good beef cattle and the giant sweet potatoes of the region, and he kept his division at full strength throughout the war despite the fact that its casualties ran so high in such slaughters as Westport, Independence, and Newtonia, that in any other division they would have discouraged enlistments. He was fond of his men, but he did not spare them—or himself.

He was not above annexing whole regiments by invitation, which flattered them into fighting with a ferocity and an élan equaled in this war only by the Louisiana Tigers under Stuart in Virginia, and he maintained an "underground" into Union-held territory through which streamed thousands of volunteers—bushwhackers, some would call them—to the Missouri Cavalry Division. Most of them were boys with memories of enemy outrages seared in their brains, who wanted to join Jo Shelby and carry the war back to their own firesides.

"Boys for war" was Shelby's motto. He knew that a boy of eighteen who volunteers is worth a whole company of conscripts. The reason that old soldiers never die is that they have sense enough to lie down when they are hit. Young volunteers never lie down except for good. Shelby once dallied with the idea of a regiment composed wholly of boys, with boys as officers, but inasmuch as the outfit would have included nearly every man in his division at the time, he never put the idea into effect. The average age at which he preferred to recruit his spur-jingling cavalrymen was not much above twenty, and in the terrain over which they fought in Missouri and Arkansas they were practically an amphibious breed, "half alligator and half horse."

Mounted, they swept over the plains like a plague of locusts; dismounted, dragoonwise, they could fall upon a campfire as silently as Indians, or fight with bowie knives waist-deep in a swamp. As Shelby's biographer and fellow soldier, Major John Newman Edwards, says, in their long and bloody career the Missouri Cavalry Division fought "Yankees, Dutch, Indians, Negroes, ironclads, alligators, fever, small-pox, starvation, and wintry blasts, and never once retired from any of these without defiance on their battered crest, and ranks closed up and serried."

If Shelby had been nearer the seat of war and government in Richmond, he would have demanded for his division all the accoutre-ments and panoply of war with which the plush-collared cavalry was surrounded in Virginia; as it was, he was in continual short supply of uniforms and equipment, and to dress up appearances he had to be content with issuing a few John Brown pikes to serve as lances. The rest was butternut, or homespun Confederate gray. Or calico.

Because of the volunteer nature of his organization, Shelby permitted a laxity of behavior and discipline which would have demoralized a lesser command. A Kentuckian by birth and a Missourian by adoption, he knew that he commanded Southerners with Western ideas of chivalry. He respected their code, which was based upon a sense of personal honor exaggerated to an extreme degree. Dueling was recog-nized, without regard to rank, and many an officer who "insulted" a private found that he had either to fight or resign. On the other hand, Shelby's brand of discipline, though unorthodox, was strict, and no man of his division would have faced his wrath willingly.

As a result of this shrewd estimate of the character of his men, Shelby was rewarded with a devotion not exceeded anywhere in the army. He could, and did, take liberties with the lives and persons of his men which would have raised a mutiny anywhere else, and he could fraternize with both officers and men more freely, without losing dignity, than any other general in the Confederacy. No one presumed upon his affability. A thing was right if Jo Shelby did it. That was all.

Following this pattern to its logical conclusion, Shelby sometimes conducted himself with his superiors in a manner which would have got him courtmartialed in the eastern armies. His insubordinate habits were tolerated, however, by his superiors, who were under no mis-apprehension as to his genius, though they regarded him as a "boy" and persistently refused to give him the rank to which he was entitled by virtue of the number of men he commanded.

In such a free and easy fraternity it was natural that Shelby did not deplore too much the activities of bushwhackers such as Quantrill as long as they were on the Southern side. (Quantrill and the James Boys, Frank and Jesse, were attached to his command as an independent company of partisan rangers.) It was Shelby's theory of the war, which he regarded as a struggle between the Puritan and the Cavalier, to "dig the gulf between the two sections so deep that it could not be bridged except by the bodies of the conquered." [5] He was to change his views after the war, and he did as much as any man to restore the Union, but in the heat of the conflict he was as bitter as Jeb Stuart, who wrote his wife never to permit his children to go north of the Mason and Dixon line after the war.[6]

Quantrill he at first regarded as a good man driven to desperation by the unceasing persecutions of the Federals, who had murdered his brother before the war—so Quantrill said—and had hunted Quantrill himself like a rabid animal. Shelby used Quantrill's scouts and guerrillas wherever they could be of use to the army and it was largely through such partisan organizations, after 1862, that he maintained his service for recruiting volunteers in Union-held territory.[7]

As a result of the nature of his cavalry operations—over thousands of miles of territory—Shelby was frequently criticized in bitter fashion by the natives of the regions through which he passed, the complaints reaching even to the ear of Jefferson Davis in Richmond. Nothing came of them, however, and Shelby ignored the critics, as did his superiors in the Trans-Mississippi Department. It is hardly necessary to point out that the Confederate cavalryman, throughout the war, was hungry and necessitous, and from the Potomac to the Gulf there were the same continual complaints from loyal Secessionists that they would rather see the Yankees any day than their own horsemen.

Actually Shelby was very jealous of his men's reputation and did all he could to restrain looting, though he admitted unofficially that it was a hopeless task sometimes. Furthermore Shelby knew that most of those who complained the loudest, in the territory in which he operated in Missouri and Arkansas, were doing a brisk trade with the enemy and objected only to the interruption of their business, though they cheered mightily for the Confederacy when Shelby was in the neighborhood.

To Shelby these weathervane patriots seemed as useless as prairie dogs, which are said to have a strange preference for living in the same burrow with owls and rattlesnakes. He drove them from his camp in Texas after Appomattox when "committees" called on him, suggesting that he surrender. The thought of surrender was anathema to him, and he would have hanged cheerfully all those who did surrender.

He himself never surrendered. He marched to Mexico instead—restoring order in Texas as he went. Bushwhackers were as numerous as coyotes in the eastern part of the state after the breakup of the Confederate armies, and no one's life or property was safe.

At Austin Shelby's column surprised a band of renegades in the act of looting the sub-treasury of the last gold and silver of the Confederacy. He gave them no chance to surrender or plead for mercy. He shot them down to the last man, and turned the money over to Governor Murrah of Texas, refusing to touch a penny of it for himself or his men, though none of them had been paid for years.

At other places he scattered bands of outlaws as he caught up with them, and as the news of his coming preceded him, the bushwhackers and borderers lit out for other parts of the country. Mayors and town officials sent messengers to Shelby begging him to pitch camp near their communities and insure tranquillity merely by his presence. For a few weeks, until General Philip H. Sheridan took over in Texas with 50,000 men, Shelby's was the only force for law and order in the eastern counties of the state. He also recruited as he went, and some very bad eggs joined up, as later events proved. Major Edwards, the Boswell of the expedition, says in his memoirs, "Some he hung and some he recruited, the last not always the best." [8]

Their progress through Texas lasted for twenty-nine days, ending on the American side of the border, across from Piedras Negras, on July first. On the Fourth of July, the men of the former Missouri Cavalry Division lowered their colors reverently for the last time. They sank their flag into the Rio Grande, weighted with stones till the Judgment Day, and then they marched south into Mexico as a mounted regiment in full battle dress—iron, defiant, and unreconstructible, clanking with artillery, carbines, bowie knives, and four Colt dragoon pistols apiece. [9]

At the bottom of the Rio Grande also rested Shelby's famous black plume, wrapped in the folds of the flag forever.

2. *Boyhood in Kentucky*

ONLY THE Lees of Virginia can match the record of the Shelbys of Kentucky in giving great men to the South from the time of the French and Indian War down to the Civil War. The Shelbys, like the Lees, were large landowners, wealthy and aristocratic; also like the Lees they were linked closely by ties of blood and marriage to the most distinguished families of their respective states.

A list of the Shelby family connections in Kentucky reads like a Who's Who of the Golden Age of the Bluegrass State before the war: the Gists, the Gratzes, the Boswells, the Browns, the Harts, the Bentons, the Bledsoes, the Henry Clays, and the Francis Preston Blairs. Most of these families, except the Gratzes, boasted Virginian ancestry, and the Gratzes had been merchant princes in Philadelphia for two generations before Benjamin Gratz, who became the stepfather of Joseph Orville Shelby, settled in Lexington, Kentucky, in 1818.

For a hundred years or more there were Shelby fighting men everywhere in American history, from the Kanawha in Virginia to the Thames in Canada, and from the Missouri to the Rio Grande. There were at least three Shelbys at the Battle of King's Mountain, and one of them, Colonel Isaac Shelby, who proposed the expedition, became first governor of Kentucky and a distinguished soldier in the War of 1812, commanding twelve Kentucky regiments at the Battle of the Thames. It is for Isaac Shelby that cities and counties all over the United States are named—wherever his fellow Kentuckians pushed on to build new homes and found new communities.[1]

Some genealogists assert with confidence that David Shelby, cousin of Isaac and grandfather of Joseph Orville Shelby, also was present. If so, he was one of the youngest soldiers in the battle—only seventeen years old.[2] Altogether the number of Shelbys taking part, according to the conflicting records, may have been an even half dozen; and this seems not unlikely since whole families responded to the clarion call that rang through the hills as the Tories and the British regulars under Ferguson marched up through South Carolina to the battle that has been called the turning point of the American Revolution.

The Shelby clan in America had a common ancestor, Evan Shelby, who emigrated to Pennsylvania from Wales in 1735, bringing with him his wife Catherine and four small sons. All of Evan's sons set out eventually to seek their fortune in the wilderness. They were a hill people, the Shelbys, with an inborn memory of the steep, comforting horizons of Wales; and they were drawn as by a magnet to the mountain wall of the Appalachians, where the frontier promised wealth for those who could endure the hardships and fight off the Indians. The Shelbys could. They left their indelible stamp, as well as their numerous progeny, in all of the country through which they passed, and they were not only fighters and landseekers, but builders, educators, and canny business men, as an examination of the record attests.[3]

The line of Joseph Orville Shelby comes down through John, one of the sons of the original Evan.[4] This John was the great-grandfather of Joseph Orville Shelby, and father of the David who was reputedly one of the youngest soldiers at King's Mountain. Of David Shelby little is known except that he owned broad acres, as did all the Shelbys, that he represented his county in the Tennessee Constitutional Convention at Knoxville in 1796, and that he was clerk of the Sumner County Court for thirty-five years until his death in 1822. David married Sarah Bledsoe, of a Tennessee Virginian family, and by her had eleven children, of whom Orville Shelby, father of Joseph Orville Shelby, was the ninth. Orville Shelby was born on January 21, 1803, at "Spencer's Choice," the family home in Sumner County. He was married twice, lived in Mississippi, Tennessee, and Kentucky, and died young.

Orville's first wife was Caroline Winchester, daughter of General James Winchester, a Tennessee general of the Revolution and of the War of 1812. He is described in Robert B. McAfee's *History of the Late War in the Western Country*, as "a wealthy citizen of Tennessee, where he lived for many years in a degree of elegant luxury and ease." [5] Caroline Shelby died several years after her marriage to Orville, leaving him with two small children, Caroline and Isaac, and also with a large fortune inherited from her father.

On July 27, 1829, Orville remarried. His second wife was Anna Maria Boswell, of Lexington, Kentucky, daughter of a well known physician of the community. Orville took his new bride back to Mississippi, but aside from the fact that they lived in Vicksburg, nothing is known of their life there. Fifteen months after their marriage they were back in Lexington for a visit, and it was during their stay that little Jo was born.

Appropriately enough, Joseph Orville Shelby was born on December 12, 1830, under the sign of Sagittarius, the Centaur. The great event took place at the home of his grandfather, Dr. Joseph Boswell, on Short Street, and he was named Joseph for his grandfather and Orville for his father.

Jupiter rules in the constellation of Sagittarius, and the ancients said that Jupiter is the Greater Fortune, the patron god of wealth and power. Whether the stars rule in human affairs or not, certain it is that the good fairy who stood by the cradle of little Jo Shelby gave him every good thing. She gave him wealth, good looks, buoyant health, boundless optimism, and the golden quality which, for lack of a better word, is called magnetism. All his life he would have the power of making men and women fall in love with him on whom he bestowed no more than a passing glance. And finally, as if to empty her bag of treasures, the same good fairy gave him intuition, the priceless power which is worth all the logic in the books. It is the green ace, the ace of hippogriffs, which outranks all other cards in the deck and takes everything in sight: and it is another word for cavalry genius.

Like his boyhood friend, John Hunt Morgan,[6] who was also destined to become a great Confederate raider, Shelby was born to the tradition of the Kentucky Bluegrass, with all its extravagance of living and all its graciousness, as well as all its faults. As Shelby's biographer, Major Edwards, says, "Shelby's renown belongs to Missouri, but Lexington should feel honored that from her good old shades were launched forth upon the military firmament two comets of such intense brilliancy."[7]

None of this could be known to the parents of the rather chunky, friendly baby as he was admired in his crib on that December day in 1830, and it may be imagined that the good physician of Lexington, Dr. Boswell, had to shoo the proud Orville Shelby out of the room; Orville then sat down to write a will in which he created a trust fund for his son to be paid to him in fee simple on his twenty-first birthday. Orville Shelby remains a shadowy character at the distance of a century and a quarter, for he died at thirty-two and the newspapers of the time did not even carry a notice of his death. That he was a man of substance, however, is clear, for the trust fund he created amounted to $80,000 when Joseph Orville Shelby came of age in 1851.[8] We also know that Orville Shelby owned blooded horses; in the Lexington *Reporter* in February, 1826, T. Watson announced for Orville Shelby that "the celebrated horse Stockholder will stand the ensuing season at my stable one mile south of Gallatin, in Tennessee . . . mares sent from Kentucky will be returned to Shelbyville, Ky. or the neighborhood by Lewis Sherley, who will keep the horse during the season." [9]

Like many well-to-do Kentuckians of the time, Orville Shelby was also attracted by the possibilities of hemp farming. It is little remembered now, but the hemp industry was Big Business in the South in the decades preceding the Civil War, and as a money crop hemp ranked not far below cotton. In the 1830's Kentucky produced three-fourths of the hemp used in the United States,[10] and as long as Cotton was King, the demand for baling rope was inexhaustible. The United States Navy, too, in the days of sailing ships, used an astronomical amount of Kentucky hemp, for the rich limestone soil produced a tough, silky fibre which was unexcelled as cordage for canvas in all sorts of weather and all sorts of climates. Kentucky hemp was superior not only for rope, but for bagging,[11] and the market for that, too, was world-wide. A planter with even a modest investment in Kentucky hemp could easily lay the foundations of a fortune.

The records of the time show that in November, 1833, when little Jo was a month less than three years old, Orville Shelby bought from John C. Richardson, Jr., 257 acres of farmland on North Elkhorn Creek in Fayette County. The price paid was $8,594.55, and the deed states that the farm was bounded "by nine poles on the Winchester Turnpike." [12] At this time Fayette County, of which Lexington is the county seat, was the leading cordage-making county in Kentucky, and boasted twenty-one ropewalks, as the hemp factories were called, nine of them in the town of Lexington.

The Orville Shelbys lived for less than a year on the Elkhorn plantation, however. In September, 1834, perhaps because of Orville Shelby's health, they sold it to Dr. Nicholas Warfield of Bourbon County for $8,279.33, three hundred dollars less than they had paid for it. The deed, dated September 23, discloses that Ann and Orville Shelby had moved back to Tennessee, and were residing in Tipton County. The following year Orville Shelby died, and Ann Shelby returned eventually with little Jo to the Boswell home in Lexington.

It is not likely that Jo Shelby had any but the vaguest recollection of his father or any of his early homes other than that of his grandfather on Short Street. Dr. Boswell was a popular and busy physician, who owned a farm outside of Lexington, and his practice took him frequently into the country, sometimes on horseback, as was often necessary to negotiate the back-country roads. It was on one of these trips, during the great cholera epidemic in Lexington,[13] that he was stricken and died, so that little Jo early in life was deprived of both father and grandfather. The circumstances under which the cholera struck Dr. Boswell down—as it did fifteen hundred of Lexington's forty-two hundred inhabitants during the plague—were tragic.

As Dr. Boswell was returning from his farm on June 13, 1833, he became violently ill. In great pain, and able to diagnose his own condition, he tied his horse to a fence rail, walked up onto the porch of a farmhouse, and knocked. The farmer's wife answered the door.

"I am going to die," Dr. Boswell told the startled woman. "Here is my wallet. Please notify my family." Having spoken these words, he collapsed on the porch.

The farmer's wife called her husband, but the two of them, realizing that their visitor was dead, and fearing contagion, dragged the body some distance from the house and buried it. The spot was marked with a stake, but a search for the body was not made until some months later—Lexington being in a state of turmoil—and by that time pigs or other domestic animals had displaced the marker, so that the impromptu grave dug for Dr. Boswell was never found.[14]

Ann Shelby was a beautiful and vivacious young woman who had been a reigning belle of Lexington before her marriage, and as a wealthy young widow she did not lack suitors, but she turned them all away steadfastly until July 6, 1843, when she married Benjamin Gratz, whose first wife had been her aunt, one of the celebrated Gist beauties.[15] Thus little Jo's new father was no stranger to him. He was, in fact, "Uncle Benjamin," and between the two there was already a strong bond of affection which was to survive many years and vicissitudes, for Benjamin Gratz lived to be ninety and was blind in his old age. Because of this close relationship, which was that of father and son rather than of stepfather and stepson, Benjamin Gratz must be rated foremost among those who by precept and example shaped the character of the youthful Jo Shelby.

Gratz ranked easily among the most distinguished citizens of Lexington—a friend of Henry Clay and heir to one of the first great

American fortunes, that of the Gratz family of Philadelphia. His portrait by Sully shows him to have been as handsome as Sir Walter Scott, with whom his family name is associated in an immortal literary legend.[16] He was the son of Michael Gratz, who, with his brother Barnard, had migrated to America in 1755 from Langensdorf, in Upper Silesia, Germany. Michael and Barnard Gratz became rich beyond the wildest dreams of immigrant boys. Michael married Miriam Simon, daughter of Joseph Simon, a wealthy landowner of Lancaster, Pennsylvania, and with the financial assistance of Michael's father-in-law the Gratz brothers soon loomed large in the commercial life of Philadelphia. In the latter half of the eighteenth century they and other "merchant venturers" opened up vast tracts of land in the wilderness to trade and exploration. From the forks of the Ohio River their keel boats penetrated into the Indian country, bringing back furs from the territory which is now West Virginia, Ohio, and Kentucky. Later their holdings were extended to the Great Lakes and as far west as Vincennes, Indiana. The land on which the Mammoth Cave of Kentucky was discovered was part of the Gratz empire.[17]

During the quarrel with England, the brothers, along with other merchants of Philadelphia, were signers of the Non-Importation Act passed in 1765 as a protest against the Stamp Act.[18] The Gratzes, like Haym Salomon and other wealthy Jews of Philadelphia, contributed heavily to the war chest of the Continental Congress, and Barnard Gratz, who remained in Philadelphia while Michael moved to Lancaster, is mentioned in a letter of Benjamin Franklin to the Governor of New Jersey as a man important in the Revolutionary cause.

Benjamin Gratz, Jo Shelby's stepfather, graduated in law from the University of Pennsylvania in 1811. In 1818 he was commissioned by his older brothers to go west and look after the landed possessions of the family. Traveling by stage and horseback to Vincennes, Indiana, he spent a year on the western frontier. Returning eastward, he stopped at Lexington, then as now one of the most charming cities of the South, to visit Maria Cecil Gist, a Lexington belle whom he had met in Philadelphia and member of a distinguished colonial family. When Maria Gist consented to marry him, Benjamin Gratz gave up plans to return to Philadelphia and the law. He was a man of cultivated interests and in Lexington he found a combination of breeding and wealth which was irresistible. Upon his marriage to the lovely Maria, he settled down in a brick Georgian mansion opposite the park,[19] a block from Transylvania University, and devoted his time, not principally to the law, but to the business of manufacturing hemp. For the rest of his life, until his death in 1884, he was one of the leading citizens of Kentucky and an exponent of the aristocratic way of life.[20]

This was the man, worldly-wise, wealthy, and cultured, under whose influence Jo Shelby was placed at the most impressionable age of his life, as he was entering adolescence.

The dark and patrician Maria Gist Gratz, whose portrait still hangs over the mantel in the parlor of the mansion on Mill Street, died in 1841, leaving her husband and four sons a lonely family of males in the big house with the Negro servants. The boys were Michael Barnard Gratz, now going on twenty-one; Henry Howard Gratz, nineteen; Hyman Cecil Gratz, sixteen; and Cary Gist Gratz, fourteen, one year older than Jo Shelby.

Although Cary Gratz was nearest his own age, it was Howard Gratz, an enviable nineteen, whom Jo found the most congenial of the brothers, and it was Howard Gratz with whom he went into business when he became of age, and for whom he named one of his sons. Of Howard and his coterie of friends he became a devoted follower. And among Howard's friends were three young men, vastly different in outlook, who had one thing in common. All were to write their names in American history to a greater or less degree. They were John Hunt Morgan, who, like Shelby, was to become a great Confederate raider; Benjamin Gratz Brown, a cousin, who was to become a political power in Missouri and a postwar governor of the state; and Francis Preston Blair, Jr., another cousin, who, next to Shelby, wrote his name largest in history of all the Gist descendants. He became a member of Congress, a brigadier general for the Union during the Civil War, the friend and confidant of Lincoln, and the man whose energetic action in 1861 kept Missouri from falling into the hands of the Secessionists.

John Morgan was a strapping six-footer, with the striking blue eyes, high cheekbones, and wide forehead of his Welsh ancestry, a dashing and handsome figure, a reckless horseman and a town beau. At present he was at liberty, having recently had the distinction of being suspended from Transylvania University for an undergraduate prank.[21] He lived with his mother just down the street from the Gratzes, at "Hopemont," another magnificent Southern mansion on the corner of Mill and Short streets.[22]

Gratz Brown, as he was always known, was the son of Mason Brown of Frankfort, a close friend of Benjamin Gratz, for whom Mason Brown named the first son of his second marriage.[23] Young Gratz Brown was studying law and aiming for a political career, and although he lived in Frankfort he spent much time at the Gratz home in Lexington.

Frank Blair was a son of the famous Jacksonian editor of the Washington *Globe* and Eliza Violet Gist. At this time he was a student at Princeton, having completed an earlier course at Transylvania. Like Gratz Brown he was a frequent visitor at the Gratz home. Jo had known him ever since he could remember, for Frank had lived with Uncle Benjamin and Aunt Maria while attending Transylvania. Frank was dark, intense, and handsome. He had the same quick temper and quick resolution which were the outstanding characteristics of his cousin Jo, of whom he was passionately fond. It is on record that he helped young Jo over the rough spots in his lessons, for at this time the younger cousin was "struggling," so we are told, for an education.[24] The friendship of Jo Shelby and Frank Blair survived the test of the Civil War, and continued until Frank's death in 1875.

As the Lexington *Morning Herald* said many years later, "It was a remarkable trio of cousins, the three young fellows who lived under the hospitable roof of that noted gentleman, Benjamin Gratz, and started life in Missouri. It was a rich gift from mother to daughter when Kentucky sent Frank Blair, Gratz Brown, and Jo Shelby to Missouri." [25]

The influence of such young men as Morgan, Blair, Gratz Brown, and Howard Gratz over the youthful Jo Shelby is inestimable. Morgan set him the example of the *beau sabreur*, the knight errant of Lexington and the darling of the fair sex. Blair was the diplomatic and polished man of the world, reared among statesmen and politicians in Washington who were deferential to his father as the powerful editor of the *Globe*. Gratz Brown was the typical young Southerner who had picked the law and politics for his profession. (He is remembered chiefly today for the fact that as a Liberal governor of Missouri he led the state out of the chaos of Reconstruction.) And Howard Gratz was Jo's favorite brother and mentor.

In this company, despite his junior years, Jo Shelby conducted himself with aplomb. He had led a pampered existence, with private tutoring instead of public schooling, and at fourteen he was growing into a romantic-looking lad with chestnut hair and deep gray eyes. In after years he was described frequently as tall and dark, but he was neither. In fact he was well under average height and his gray eyes flashed brown only when his temper was aroused; but his bearing, even as a youth, was remembered by all who saw him. The same Lexington *Morning Herald* said of him affectionately in 1897, "He was a manly boy in our streets and he went out into the conflicts of life from this dear old town." [26]

In the streets he was accompanied by his faithful shadow, a Negro boy of his own age named Billy Hunter, who belonged to him and was his personal servant. Shelby's adoring mother had bought Billy Hunter for her only son when both were eleven years old, paying the unheard-of price of $2,000 for him in the Lexington slave market. [27] Thus, when the aristocratic Jo fared forth upon the streets of the town, with Billy Hunter in attendance, his progress was something in the nature of a triumphal procession, and as the *Morning Herald* noted, was long remembered by the oldest inhabitants.

As Jo grew older, he frequently took part, with Billy Hunter discreetly in the background, in the many amusements, sports, and diversions which Lexington afforded for those not handicapped by female companions. Lexington was a rough-and-tumble town behind the façade of elegance and culture which it had erected for itself as "the Athens of the West," and F. Garvin Davenport in his *Ante-Bellum Kentucky* describes it thus:

"Pistol galleries and gaming tables were popular and ten-pin alleys were supported by steady patronage. Billiard rooms were well patronized and the suburban cockpit was approved by the sports-loving poor man as well as by his rich neighbor. A type of football, usually played in the streets, was popular with the more rugged element. In Lexington, the game became a nuisance, especially on Sundays and holidays, so that the City Council passed an ordinance declaring that 'no person shall roll or kick a football in any of the streets or alleys of the city.'" [28]

When sidewalk adventure palled, there were the rolling fields of the Bluegrass country, the winding creeks and the broad rivers, calling to a young man who could ride, hunt, shoot, and had a Negro boy to help him do it. By the time he was of college age, Shelby could sit a horse as well as John Morgan, and long before that the girls were casting sidelong glances at him. In summer there were picnics and barbecues, and in the fall and winter months life in Lexington was one round of parties and dances. On the occasions when the winds north of the Ohio River bore in a blanket of snow for the Bluegrass, there were sleighing parties and a hot drink on the hearth at home afterward.

The Gratz household was as hospitable as any in all the Bluegrass, but with a difference. At home the young men listened respectfully to some of the most significant conversations of nineteenth-century America, for around the Gratz fireside assembled such men as Henry Clay, John J. Crittenden, and Frank Blair, Sr. The elder Blair, at the time of Shelby's young manhood, was passing from control of the administration organ at Washington and spent much time in the Gratz household. In the same parlor where they gathered, the older generation and the younger, the Marquis de Lafayette twenty years before had dandled young Howard Gratz on his knee.[29] Outside of Virginia, seldom have so many great men been at home in a private residence as in the home of Benjamin Gratz at Lexington.

Most Kentuckians were men of action, however, rather than scholars or philosophers, and it is not surprising to find that even in this atmosphere of culture and learning there could be found those who, like Morgan and Jo Shelby, cared nothing for books and did not like to study. Young Jo was precocious in a worldly sort of way, but he had no academic leanings. He would much rather be riding across the fields after rabbits with Billy Hunter than studying Latin, or standing with Morgan and the other young bucks on the street corners near Transylvania, making sarcastic remarks on the appearance of passers-by.[30]

From the time that Shelby came to live with him, Benjamin Gratz assumed personal charge of his education, and from his stepfather young Jo learned much besides the fundamentals of language and mathematics. Gratz was a cosmopolite, a citizen of the world, and like Montaigne he considered urbanity the most essential of all qualities for success. He drilled into Shelby the fundamental truth that the man who sits on top of the world is there because he will not let the world sit on top of him; in short, because he is master of every situation. "I have lived long enough to discover," Gratz said in a letter to his son Howard, "that those who get along best in the world are those who conduct themselves with amiability, urbane in their manners, and perfectly honorable in all their transactions. With these requisites, one can make his way anywhere." [31]

Though not an enthusiastic student, Jo Shelby was what the actors call "a quick study," when he wanted to be, which was seldom, and under the tutelage of his stepfather he was kept at his books; but soon the time came for him to go to school "in the East," as was fashionable at the time, and prepare for Transylvania. In 1846 he was packed off to the effete East, probably to Mr. Wilson's School at Hartsville, Pennsylvania, where Howard Gratz had finished in 1840.[32] The letters of Rebecca Gratz, whom he visited, would throw more light on this period, except that they have been edited before publication to delete "such portions as are of too intimate a family nature to be paraded before the public eye," [33] but one of them, written on March 24, 1846, shows that Jo had been at school in Pennsylvania and was going home for a spring visit.

The letter, written to her sister-in-law Anna Gratz, shows the warm and deep affection which had sprung up between the two women, and also the affectionate esteem in which young Jo was held in the Gratz home on Walnut Street in Philadelphia. Rebecca, who was the homemaker for her unmarried brothers and the orphaned children of her sister Rachel Moses (she never married) had welcomed Jo into the family circle as one of her own. To Anna Gratz she wrote:

"Your heart will rejoice in the presence of your son, and I think you will find him greatly improved in health as well as in his studies —the Boys have been here only a few days & I should be glad to keep them a week longer if I did not find they were yearning to be home. I shall give this to Jo with a charge that he does not deliver it until two days after his arrival, that you may enjoy his company first without the intrusion of even a letter. Jo seems to have the spirit of mirth inborn in him, for he is as merry as a bird, or rather as a boy let loose from School, which he illustrated in a way to justify the adage." [34]

That Jo was a bird, and a merry one at that, the neighbors in Lexington would have agreed, although in them he did not always arouse a spirit of mirth, as sometimes his pranks tended toward the smart-alecky. For example, a reigning Kentucky belle whose name has not come down to us through the coyness of a contemporary chronicler, was often a visitor at the Morgan home, probably being a relative, and on her visits to Lexington she was the subject of much admiring attention by a very important personage, a General of the U. S. Regular Army, whose name also is unrecorded. Little Jo, then about ten, regarded this dignitary as a stuffed shirt, and the frequency of the visits caused him to improvise a sign and hang it on the doorknob of the Morgan home. The sign, in bold lettering, read, "Headquarters of General ———, U.S.A." [35]

In the retelling, the legend had it that this anonymous General later commanded Federal occupation troops in Lexington during the war, and that "when the owner of the house offered him a room for an office, he positively refused, saying instead (recalling the practical joke), 'I will send a guard to protect you as long as you stay here.'" According to the narrator, Mrs. T. J. Henry, who recalls the incident in *Five Famous Missourians*, "the lady of the house often told this story and said little Jo's daring piece of fun—showing the gushing fountain at ten years, saved her home from destruction, for she was the mother of the great Southern raider John Morgan." [36]

Someone has tried to make a good story better here, for the Morgan home was never in danger of destruction by the Federals, and the only private home commandeered by the occupying forces during the war was the Bodley home, across the park, whose chief charm was its fine furnace and central heating system. [37] All of the commanders of the Federal forces in Lexington during the war—they were not always generals, sometimes merely colonels—had their headquarters at the Phoenix Hotel. Furthermore, Lexington was such a redhot Confederate center that Mrs. Morgan would have needed no Federal guards to protect her. If they were there, it was for a different reason. [38] Nevertheless, Jo Shelby's reputation in Lexington as a kind of aristocratic Tom Sawyer seems fully justified, and the pastiches which the local storytellers have added to the edifice of the legend are, if somewhat embellished, at least wholly in character.

With the Pennsylvania schooling under his belt, Jo Shelby entered Transylvania, probably in the fall of 1847. The qualifying adverb is necessary here, for the records of the institution are incomplete, and Jo Shelby's name is among the missing. [39] He is not listed at the university as having attended Transylvania, but according to members of the family and all the biographical sketches of him which exist, he spent several years at that institution.

One of the family legends concerns Jo's college days at Transyl-

vania. Apparently he was following gaily in the footsteps of his idol, John Morgan, and taking part in any undergraduate pranks that might be going. The medical department of Transylvania, in common with other medical schools of the era, had to obtain cadavers surreptitiously. It was against the law to buy bodies for dissection, and the common practice was to obtain them from professional grave robbers who kept an eye on new graves in the paupers' sections of the cemeteries. One morning early, before classes, young Jo and several others dispossessed one of these bootleg cadavers from a pine box in the dissecting room, and one of the students took its place. When Negro attendants came to remove the body, the "corpse" remarked, "Lift me gently, boys." The ensuing panic, of course, came to the attention of the authorities.

Whether the "corpse" was Jo Shelby and whether he suffered punishment, like Morgan, for this practical joke, we shall never know. The record does not exist. Like nearly all other records of Jo Shelby in Lexington, except those of the most fragmentary nature, it has found its way into a limbo of its own. The record has been sponged as clean by the hand of time as if it had been written in chalk upon a blackboard at Transylvania University. Even when Shelby engaged in a lawsuit in later years in Lexington, the testimony somehow manages to absent itself from the records of the Fayette County Court; the newspapers of the period have little to say about him; and except for the letters of Rebecca Gratz, which were published in part and thus preserved, there are no other Shelby letters or documents available of any period of his life in Lexington. Except for a few old-timers, Lexington has forgotten him.

3. Waverly: The Golden Years

THE YEAR 1849, the year of the great westward migration to California, found two future Confederate cavalry chieftains in Lexington in the prosaic business of making ropes and bagging out of hemp. John Morgan, having returned from a brief and uneventful career as a volunteer in the Mexican War in 1846,[1] had been employed since 1847 in his family's ropewalk[2] and was now factory manager. Jo Shelby at that time was still at Transylvania, but as soon as he could make good his escape from the ivied halls, he turned with enthusiasm to his step-father's business—the natural and almost inevitable thing for him to do. Although he had not graduated, his school days were over when he left Transylvania.[3]

The ropewalk of Gratz and Bruce was one of the most imposing establishments of its kind in Lexington. The main factory was two stories high, 195 feet long, and 25 feet deep, with a hacking house, a weaving house, and a "calender and hemp house" adjoining.[4] These divisions had storage space for 260 tons of hemp, and on each of the two stories of the main factory were rows of spindles and looms. The ropewalks were so called because the spinners, usually slaves or freed Negroes, tied the hemp about their waists, hooked one end to a spin-ning wheel, and walked back and forth, thus spinning out the strands of hemp like a spider making a web. The yarns thus made were twisted into strands, three or more strands making a rope.[5] One of Jo Shelby's duties as a supervisor was to see that the spinners walked with more or less regularity.

Benjamin Gratz advised his stepson to learn the business thoroughly, since he would soon be coming into a sizable fortune and would be able, if that were his inclination, to set up his own ropewalk. This was precisely what Jo Shelby had in mind, but in the fall of 1849 he was not sure that he wanted to settle permanently in the small town atmosphere of Lexington. Frank Blair and Gratz Brown had already gone to St. Louis, and in Philadelphia he had had a taste of big city life. It would be exciting to move to St. Louis, the biggest steamboat town north of New Orleans, with all of its cosmopolitan gayety. Young Jo was eager to go to St. Louis for a visit, at least, and he seems to have been talking glibly at home of the greater opportuni-ties there, for on November 18, 1849, Rebecca Gratz was writing to his mother in Lexington:

"You must have difficulty in consenting to Jo Shelby's departure for St. Louis, he is so amiable affectionate & clever that his society to you was of great consequence, but it was entirely right, it is such a thriving place and he has so many friends. You must give my love to Jo when you write him and tell him to go unceremoniously to Gratz Moses',[6] and make himself at home in the family. When they know each other it will be mutually agreeable, and there are so many connections there that there may be quite a family gathering."[7]

In St. Louis Shelby found Gratz Brown and Frank Blair hip-deep in Missouri politics. With the assistance of backers, they had bought the *Morning Signal*, changed its name to the *Missouri Democrat*, and with Frank Blair as editor-in-chief were advocating a policy of Free Soilism which was earning them the undying enmity of the old-line Southern politicians.[8]

At this stage of the game young Jo probably did no more than disagree goodnaturedly with Frank Blair on his radical ideas, over their punches at the Planter's House in St. Louis. In the uncomplicated lexicon of Jo Shelby abolitionists were cranks, foreigners, or New Englanders—which came to the same thing—and he could not imagine the patrician Frank Blair seriously allying himself with such riffraff. As far as he was concerned, none of the nonsense being talked by the "emancipationists" had anything to do with the South, of whose beautiful earth he would soon be one of the inheritors. The South's representatives in Washington would see to that, for the Slave Power ran the government. Furthermore, it was difficult for a youth of nineteen, who would soon inherit a fortune, to be seriously alarmed about anything. Visiting Frank Blair had no discernible influence over Shelby's future, since Blair talked only politics, and the wrong kind of politics at that. Jo enjoyed himself in St. Louis without coming to a definite decision as to his plans, and in a short time returned to Lexington.

There was considerable local excitement in Lexington just then, for two of the largest ropewalks in town, those of L. C. Randall and Co. and John McCauley, had been burned down, probably by Negro slaves, and the Columbia Rail Road had imported a 6,000-foot tow rope to be used on the Incline Plane outside of Lexington to haul locomotives to the station. The immense cable was nine inches thick and required fourteen tons of Italian hemp. It had been manufactured in Philadelphia, apparently because there was no ropewalk in Kentucky capable of turning out such a giant piece of cordage.[9] Young Jo and the rest of the town went out to see this new civic improvement in action.

In the end, it was Howard Gratz who nipped in the bud any plans Jo may have had for moving to St. Louis and cutting a wide swath in the life of the river capital of the mid-South. Howard, who was courting Minerva Campbell Anderson of Lexington, had a scintillating scheme of his own. He and his prospective father-in-law, Oliver Anderson, saw great possibilities in the cultivation and processing of hemp in western Missouri. Out there, land was fertile and cheap, and a man could grow rich in no time. Howard pointed out enthusiastically that this very year Missouri's hemp production had come close to the record set by Kentucky—within 20,000 tons of it, in fact [10]— and in such a thinly settled territory as Missouri this was only a beginning. He and his father-in-law had already picked as a likely spot the up-and-coming town of Waverly on the Missouri River, 346 river-miles west of St. Louis in the heart of the rolling prairie. As soon as he and Minerva were married, young Jo could come in with him, when he was twenty-one, and the firm would be Gratz and Shelby.

It is likely that the two young Kentuckians made a trip to Waverly and that Jo was fired with enthusiasm for the venture. He put aside his plans for moving to St. Louis and buckled down in Lexington for the next two years to learn all there was to be known about the processing and merchandising of hemp. Shelby was never lazy; he liked meeting people, and in the world of the hemp industry in Lexington he met his own kind. When he was not clerking behind the counter, or acting as floor manager for the ropewalk, he rode out to the plantations of Fayette County to look over the crops and pass the time of day with the planters, an occupation which he enjoyed. On the social side he continued to attend the numerous balls and parties which had become an almost daily feature of Lexington life ever since the town had gone overboard with its grand dinner and ball for Lafayette twenty-five years before.

As to the ladies, he was completely heart-whole and fancy-free. To one who loved a pretty face as much as Jo Shelby, the thought of confining his attention to a single charmer was too much like starving in the midst of plenty. He was a ladies' man, and he squired the Lexington belles to social functions impartially, with nothing more serious than a few stolen kisses in the moonlight.[11] Soon he was the despair of the Lexington mamas, as a young man of obviously no matrimonial intentions. *"Just think of it!* The most eligible boy in town, *with all that money*, and talking about going off alone to some outlandish place in Missouri to farm!" Efforts to provide him with a wife for the journey, however, were met with bland, courtly inattention.

Early in 1852, then, having come into his inheritance,[12] Shelby was off to join Howard Gratz in Waverly, with the blessings of the family. He was now one of the wealthiest young men in the state, and it is conclusive evidence of the soundness of his character that he did not stay at home to devote himself to women, foxhunting, and whiskey, as many another young Kentucky blueblood would have done. Instead, he set out to increase his fortune. Unlike John Morgan, he did not have an overwhelming interest in military matters,[13] and ten years before the war the thought of organizing a cavalry company was the farthest thing from his mind. That mind was set on creating for himself an industrial empire in hemp, and with cash money he could do it. As his steamer nosed into the shallow Missouri west of St. Louis, his head was spinning with plans.

The town of Waverly, on the south bank of the river where the deep water is, was as new as the shiny boots Jo Shelby was wearing when he stepped down the gangplank of the steamboat at St. Thomas's Wharf. From the wharf by the cottonwoods he could see an iron foundry, a flouring mill, several large warehouses, a ropewalk—his and Howard Gratz's—a blacksmith shop, several stores, and clusters of sturdy dwellings. There was about the town the air of bustle and progress which characterized all of the river towns of the West, and as Jo Shelby looked about him, he was more than ever convinced that he had come to the right place. As J. M. Motte says in his monograph on the history of Waverly, "The Waverly of the Fifties, when hemp was king—before Mr. Lincoln had issued his proclamation—when there was no convenient rail road, when boats used the only steam whistle that was heard in the land, Waverly, then, was a town of real importance." [14]

There had been a settlement of sorts on the site of Waverly since 1818. In that year, when James Monroe was president, a man named Notley Thomas had built a house on one of the bluffs overlooking the river, where he could see the keelboats of the fur traders through the interlacing branches of a primeval forest, and had cleared enough land to raise a hemp crop which he had sold for seven dollars a hundred at Old Franklin.[15] That was the beginning of the hemp industry at Waverly.

Soon the keelboats had given way to the steamboats—the first of these, Major Long's *Western Engineer*, having a prow carved to resemble a gigantic serpent with smoke pouring from its nostrils to frighten Indians [16]—and when the steamboats came they were mostly carrying restless people to the settlements of Independence and Lex-

ington, Missouri, farther west. Two distinct villages had grown up
around the hilltop house of Notley Thomas, however. One, laid out
by Washington Shroyer, was known as Middletown because it was
halfway between Lexington and Marshall. The other, St. Thomas,
had been founded by Colonel John Dennis Thomas of Virginia, a
veteran of the War of 1812. In a few years the two communities
were practically one, and in 1845 Middletown and St. Thomas became Waverly, named for Waverly, Illinois, whence some of the new
citizens of the town had come.[17]

The Missouri River at this point was three quarters of a mile wide
—a broad, if treacherous highway leading to the Mississippi. There
was a wooded island offshore, as pretty as a picture, and as Jo Shelby
looked up at the bluffs in back of the town, his fancy was caught by
one hilltop, covered with maples, which stood out above the others.
This eminence was known as Mount Rucker, named for an early physician of the place, and here, Jo Shelby knew, he would build his house,
a great mansion with dormer windows, overlooking the ropewalk
and the flatlands below. The establishment he envisioned was one in
which a capable Negro woman would keep house, abetted by half a
dozen blackamoors of various ages, and in which he and Billy Hunter
would live in the Missouri equivalent of Oriental splendor. No fiancée
back in Lexington was awaiting the call to join him; no scenes of
domestic bliss were more enchanting than the ones he conjured up
that morning, as he stepped off the steamboat.

Within a few months after the formation of the firm of Gratz
and Shelby, the bachelor mansion was a reality. It was a white frame
house, halfway up Mount Rucker and facing the northeast. The early
morning sun caught its dormer windows in blazing squares of orange
light which flashed like a heliograph as far away as the bend in the
river; it dominated the town by day, and at night, when the lamps
were lit, it served as a friendly, twinkling beacon for the steamboats.
From his porch Jo Shelby could see a solid line of green forest on
the banks across the river, extending for miles to a point where the
sky and the Carroll County bluffs merged, so that you could not tell
where one began and the other ended; and a quarter of a mile offshore, the usually monotonous and muddy expanse of the Missouri
was broken by a five-hundred-acre island, known as Willow Bar,
covered with giant trees.[18]

On the east lay the timber-covered bluffs of Lafayette County, dropping into wide lowlands where the Missouri takes a bend and travels due north for a few miles, and where, from Mount Rucker, the settlers' homes resembled pygmy dwellings. On the west was another bluff, also timber-covered and known as Mount Ennis, broken by a ravine of flatland, onto which the business district of Waverly was edging. Down this bluff from the prairie wound two roads where, in good weather, one could see teams of oxen hauling hemp, corn, and other farmland products into town. At the steamboat wharf downriver, likely as not, there would be a steamboat tied up, a great floating hotel with double smokestacks. Nowhere in the river country of the rural South could the young hemp baron have picked a finer view.

The firm of Gratz and Shelby, too, was a going concern in every department. Besides the ropewalk, the two young men owned 700 acres in Lafayette County, a farm which was one of the showplaces of the countryside. Here they raised wheat, hemp, cattle, corn, hogs, and blooded horses. Since the land hereabouts was heavily wooded to the prairie's edge, they soon built a giant sawmill at Dover, five and a half miles east of Waverly, to reap a harvest of dollars from the felled timber of the region. At Dover they also had plans for a big new town to be called Berlin. In 1853, a year in which Missouri hemp was selling for $120 a ton, and Gratz and Shelby were delivering it in lots up to 400 tons, they laid out the town, holding a gala auction at which fifty-nine lots were sold for $98.50 each.[19]

The interests of Gratz and Shelby, in fact, extended in every direction in Lafayette County. The extent of their prosperity can be gauged partly by the number of lawsuits on record at the county courthouse in Lexington in which they were either suing or being sued over damage to goods in transit, and as a result of which, naturally, Gratz and Shelby soon bought a steamboat of their own.[20] Jo Shelby had a passion for steamboats and would never allow one to be damaged, even during the war when he captured them with cavalry; but on the treacherous Missouri, with its snags, shifting sand bars, caving banks, and rapid currents, steamboats had a difficult time, especially in the hands of reckless pilots who were more concerned with making time than with safeguarding their cargoes. Also, in the piratical, unregulated manner in which they were operated, the steamers frequently blew up.

But this was the golden age of steamboats on the Missouri—an aver-

age of 355 a year reached St. Louis on its shallow, muddy waters [21]
—and the great cotton export centers of New Orleans and Mobile
were crying for baling rope. In his broadcloth coat and broad-
brimmed hat, with fawn-colored trousers, fancy waistcoat, starched
shirt front, and hips of a cavalryman, young Jo Shelby, now filled
out with the manhood of his early twenties, cut a fine figure as he
directed the hands in the loading of hemp at St. Thomas's Wharf.

Every account we have of him—as a youth growing up in Kentucky,
as a beau of the countryside in Waverly, as a cavalry leader during
the war, and as a soldier among soldiers at the court of Maximilian—
stresses the fact that Jo Shelby made an electrifying impression on
all who saw him. An Arkansas sergeant who served in the infantry
when Shelby's cavalrymen were the heroes of the whole army summed
it up when he said, "He was the finest looking man I ever saw, black
hair and handsome features. *He looked like somebody.* He looked
like someone who had something to him, like he was a fine strong
man, which no doubt he was." [22] The Arkansas footsoldier saw beneath the handsome façade the indomitable character and the iron
will; it was obvious to all that there was "something to" Jo Shelby.
He was by now a leading citizen of the town and one of its chief
prides, though the local belles, like the Lexington beauties, found his
gay bachelorhood downright provoking.

As soon as Jo discovered that his father's first cousin, William
Shelby, was living on a large plantation only six miles from Waverly,
he saddled a horse and rode out to see him. William Shelby was an
old settler hereabouts, having come from Marion County, Kentucky,
in 1836. He greeted his young kinsman cordially, and said to a little
dark-haired girl who was walking on top of a fence rail, "Betty, come
here and meet your cousin." [23] It was Jo's first meeting with his future
wife. What Betty thought of the romantic-looking Jo is not known,
and to him she was just another pretty little girl; but Elizabeth
Shelby was to be the only woman who was ever to excite in him
anything more than a passing interest. It may have been that her
delicate, doll-like beauty at seventeen, when he married her, forever
aroused his protective and chivalrous instincts, but, whatever the
cause, all his life Betty was the only one who could influence him,
or "do anything with him," as they used to say, when he was on a
rampage, and theirs was to be a lifelong romance.

While Betsy, as she was often called, was still in pigtails, however, her husband-to-be continued to live the busy life of a wealthy bachelor planter and manufacturer in the Missouri River Valley of the early fifties. As a man of substance and the owner of slaves he was soon acquiring the friendship of such powerful proslavery leaders as Claiborne Jackson and General David R. Atchison, who, some said, had once been President of the United States for a day;[24] and on his front porch, over Billy Hunter's mint juleps, he sat with his neighbors and discussed the inflammatory proposal to create a new Territory over in Kansas which would be overrun by the damned abolitionists.

Social life in Waverly was far different from that of Kentucky, where stuffy dowagers ruled, and Jo Shelby found it vastly more to his liking. His neighbors, transplanted Virginians and Kentuckians for the most part, foxhunted and visited, when they were not talking politics, just as their families did back home,[25] but their relaxation was more exuberant and informal, heavily influenced by that broad highway of commerce, the Missouri River, at their front door.

The steamboats, with their luxurious appointments, their good food and wines, and the splendor of their salons, were ideal for "river parties," and the young people flocked aboard them at every landing. Whenever a steamboat tied up at Lexington or Dover, the younger generation would invade and take over. As soon as the evening meal had been served, chairs and tables would be cleared away, the musicians tipped—every steamboat had its fiddlers—and the young couples from the town would organize a dance which lasted until the next stop was reached. In their eighteen-foot hoopskirts the girls were bewitching, and if the night was moonless, perhaps the captain—Captain Woolford, say, of the *Sioux City*—could be persuaded to tie up at Waverly, "and the gay young people were in for an all night dance." [26]

Jo Shelby was much in evidence at these festivities. He frequently danced all night and worked all day, just as he later rode all night and fought all day, and fresh as a daisy with it all. His name has survived as a participant in some of these river parties long after the other guests have been forgotten, for Charles P. Deatherage in his *Steamboating on the Missouri River in the Sixties* says, "General Shelby and many others who were hemp raisers in Missouri before the war, being of that extreme hospitality characteristic of the early settlers, joining with the others up the river kept that boat in a quiver until the approaching dawn compelled the captain to call a halt, and the young people took the stage back to their homes or caught the next boat going up the river." [27]

One wonders if he ever drove the sleepy Betsy home from one of these parties in a rig in the Missouri dawn, with her head on his shoulder; likely he did, though she was only sixteen when he started courting her; and when he married her, they had a steamboat all to themselves and their party for the wedding trip to St. Louis. Jo Shelby never did anything by halves.

It was a gay town, Waverly in the fifties. And to the young people at least, war's alarms seemed far away.

4. *The Border Wars*

IN THE SPRING OF 1854 Congress passed the Act to Organize the Territory of Kansas, and Jo Shelby found himself becoming one of the wealthiest hemp processers and planters in Missouri. These two facts, seemingly unconnected, actually bore an intimate relationship to each other.

The opening up of Kansas to colonization would bring a flood of immigration from the North and East, and such immigration would constitute a long-range, deadly threat to the prosperity of the slave-holding South, in which Jo Shelby was a blue-chip stockholder. The steps he would take to defend that prosperity were to shape the course of his life for thirteen years, through the Border Wars, the Civil War, and the junket to Mexico, from which he was to return in 1867 a penniless wanderer.

The prosperous condition of Missouri in the spring of 1854 was due in part to the bad luck that had plagued farmers east of the Mississippi. A great drought during the previous season had ruined the crops in Kentucky; and the demand for Missouri hemp, which had been rising steadily with one or two setbacks since 1849, was at a peak. The boom which was to last until the Civil War was in full swing. Corn was also selling at five dollars a bushel, and Jo Shelby remarked to Howard Gratz that they'd be better off to butcher their hogs and sell their corn, rather than keep the hogs and let them eat the corn. He and his step-brother had 5,000 hogs on the farm near Berlin, and 1,000 head of cattle.[1] Four years of solid prosperity lay ahead for the Waverly Steam Rope Company, as their ropewalk was now called, and it was a period of boom prosperity such as Missouri had not dreamed of back in the 1840's.

Across the river and plains in Kansas, however, that other boom was going on which was to menace, and ultimately to overthrow, all of the slave-supported industries of the South. Antislavery men, with their families, were pouring into Kansas from the New England states and from their sister states of New York, Ohio, and Illinois. Although Missourians had rushed across the border and staked their claims to the best lands as soon as the Territory was opened, there was no possibility of matching the emigration from the North, family for family; Missourians were doomed to remain a minority in Kansas, and under these circumstances a clash with the Free State Yankees was as inevitable as sunup.

Before the opening up of the Territory, the greater part of the eastern border of Kansas was an Indian reservation from which the Indians had all but disappeared. There were only a few white settlers, of an impermanent character, in any part of the vast and rolling prairie. Until the discovery of gold in California, the area had been believed to be a barren waste which might as well be left to the itinerant "squatters" and the remnants of the Indian tribes. In fact the Indians had been resettled here on the promise that they would never be disturbed.[2] The Gold Rush changed all that. Travelers returning from the West saw that the fertile lands of Kansas and Nebraska held greater riches than all the gold in the creek-beds of the West, and they spread the news all up and down the eastern seaboard.

Under its mat of buffalo grass, they reported, the Kansas soil was deep and black, a virgin loam lying on a bed of porous clay and limestone; whether farmed for wheat or corn, or stocked with cattle, it could make a man rich; and the climate was said to be peculiarly invigorating, as favorable for pulmonary diseases as the tablelands of Mexico. Furthermore, on the banks of the rivers, the Missouri and the Osage, the Arkansas and the Kaw, were heavy stands of timber, and along the banks of the streams settlers had discovered coal, the fodder of the iron horse. One enthusiastic traveler called Kansas "The Italy of America," and the name fired the imagination of the adventurous back East.

When the Indian title expired in 1854, Missourians considered that the region, being but an extension of their own prairie, belonged to them. And indeed there was some justifiable basis for their claim. The Missouri River is the natural boundary in this part of the country. As it wanders from its headwaters, up Montana way, it cuts diagonally across Missouri, and physically the prairies of Missouri and of Kansas are the same. There was by now enough population in Missouri to colonize Kansas gradually, as settlers from Kentucky had colonized Missouri: it was the logical place for Southern expansion, and Missourians had always taken it for granted that they would move in, bag and baggage, when the time came, and take over, carrying their slaves, their customs, and their institutions with them.

Back East in New England, however, were men with an entirely different set of ideas. In New England, Kansas had long since replaced California as a topic of conversation. From their rockbound farms the New Englanders looked longingly at the plains of Kansas, and as soon as the Territory was opened they headed westward by steamboat, down the Ohio and up the Missouri, past Jo Shelby's ropewalk under the bluff at Waverly, bringing their families and their New England ideas with them. They were an evangelical, hardbitten lot, these descendants of the Puritans, and they regarded slavery as an abomination and the loose-living South as a Scarlet Woman. Abolitionists to the core—most of them—they were as strongly committed to destroy "the peculiar institution" as to slay a Beast of the Apocalypse.[3]

The Emigrant Aid Society of New England had been set up to assist these people to settle in Kansas, and no act of the abolitionists in years had so infuriated the South. First of all, under the Kansas-Nebraska Act, which was now in effect, the people of a Territory could decide, through their elected representatives, when the time came, whether they wished to apply for admission to the Union as a slave state or a free state; and there was no doubt which way Kansas would go if the Emigrant Aid settlers had their way. Second, the Massachusetts legislature had granted a charter to the Society in that state authorizing a capital of $5,000,000. With this staggering sum every pauper in New England could be transplanted to Kansas to vote, or so the Southerners believed, and thunderous protests began to go up south of the Mason and Dixon line.

It was by now well understood, both North and South, that the fate of slavery in the nation was to be decided in Kansas. It was no mere local issue. The debates in Congress, the editorials in the press, and the pronouncements of leaders on both sides, all trumpeted the fact that from here on, under the right of self-determination as guaranteed by the Kansas-Nebraska Act, it was to be a neck-and-neck race between the two factions to control each new state as it came into the Union. If the abolitionists won in Kansas, the West would be flooded with Free State settlers from the North, and the hold of the Slave Power on the government at Washington, which it had dominated for so long, would be at an end.

A storm of anger swept the Missouri border, and Jo Shelby and his friends took direct, characteristic action. The rich slaveholders of the Missouri River Valley realized that they could do nothing to halt the Free State immigration, nor could they match it; their own people were not anxious to take their slaves into a territory which might become a free state. Furthermore, such an academic solution had little appeal for the violent-tempered Missourians. There was but one thing to do: control the elections in Kansas, at pistol point if necessary, and they were fully resolved to do it.

This cool proposal to rob the Kansas settlers of the right to elect their own representatives may sound today like the harebrained scheme of irresponsible roughnecks: it was nothing of the sort. It was the product of the brains and scheming of men in whose veins ran the best blood in Missouri, men like Jo Shelby, David Atchison, General Benjamin F. Stringfellow, and Claiborne Jackson, and it was carried into effect with all the ruthless efficiency of which they were capable.

Being Missourians, they had a natural aptitude both for politics and for military organization, and they set to work at once to forge a weapon with which to take over in Kansas. Almost overnight a kangaroo organization—the Blue Lodge—sprang up, which was modeled along Masonic lines. The Blue Lodge, which had for its sole purpose the domination of the Kansas elections, was also known as "The Sons of the South," "The Social Band," "The Friendly Society," and by other names; but these did not stick. The Blue Lodge was the title which captured the fancy of most Missourians.[4]

It was natural and inevitable that Jo Shelby should be in the forefront of this movement. No man in Missouri had a greater stake in the future of Kansas: he was young, he was rich, he owned slaves

who were the backbone of his hemp business, and he was a Kentucky
blueblood. Furthermore, he had a hair-trigger temper, and no man
among the slaveholding autocrats would more greatly enjoy rough-
ing up the abolitionists. From the day that Congress passed the Act
to Organize the Territory of Kansas, he was deep in conferences
with Atchison, Jackson, General Stringfellow, Colonel Sam Young,
and all of the other proslavery leaders; and he organized the Blue
Lodge at Waverly. No records of its meetings have come to light,
but it is possible, from other records, to trace Shelby's part in the
early Border Wars minutely.

The first election in Kansas took place in December, 1854, for a
Territorial delegate to Congress, but there is no evidence that Shelby
took any hand in it. The Missouri "ringers" triumphed in their first
visit to the Kansas polls: a proslavery delegate, General Whitfield,
was elected. When the news came that Congress had set March 30,
1855, as the date for the election of the all-important Territorial legislature, Jo Shelby was at Waverly, and he rode over at once to see
Claiborne Jackson.

Over the mint juleps they discussed plans for March 30. Jackson
estimated that about a thousand voters would be needed for the First
District, headquarters of which were at Lawrence, the abolitionist
capital and the target for all the Southern wrath. Jo Shelby was sure
he could recruit about fifty men among his friends and neighbors.
A call for the rest would go out in the Missouri counties of Ray,
Howard, Carroll, Boone, Lafayette, Macon, Clay, Jackson, Saline,
and Cass. Their expenses would be paid out of the Blue Lodge treasury and those who could not come would be asked to contribute
provisions, wagons, and other equipment. The volunteers were to be
paid a dollar a day and whiskey furnished.

Violence was not contemplated, Jackson pointed out, unless it
should be necessary to secure the Missourians their "right" to vote.
Nor was the right of Free State men to vote to be interfered with;
the election must have the color of legality, even though the proslavery men would thrust aside the lawful judges at the muzzle of
the revolver, would "vote" illegally, certify to the accuracy and legality of the poll books, and pack them up and carry them away. If
either Jackson or Shelby foresaw what the consequences of such a
policy would be, they did not care; but it is likely that they believed,
as the proslavery press had been saying, that the Free State settlers,

if discouraged sufficiently at the polls, would give up the colonization of Kansas and go elsewhere. Both Shelby and Jackson undoubtedly were in agreement with the sentiments expressed a few weeks
before by General Stringfellow at a meeting at St. Joseph, where
Stringfellow had delivered himself of this remarkable diatribe:

"I tell you to mark every scoundrel among you that is the least
tainted with free-soilism, or abolitionism, and exterminate him. Neither
give nor take quarter from the damned rascals. I propose to mark
them in this house, and on the present occasion, so you may crush
them out. To those having qualms of conscience, as to violating laws,
state or national, the time has come when such impositions must be
disregarded, as your lives and your property are in danger, and I
advise you one and all to enter into every election district in Kansas,
in defiance of Reeder and his myrmidons [A. H. Reeder was the
governor appointed by President Pierce] and vote at the point of
the bowie knife and the revolver. Neither give nor take quarter, as
our cause demands it. It is enough that the slaveholding interest wills
it, from which there is no appeal. What right has Governor Reeder
to rule Missourians in Kansas? His proclamation and prescribed oath
must be disregarded; it is to your interest to do so. Mind that slavery
is established where it is not prohibited." [5]

Truly, as Eli Thayer says in *The Kansas Crusade*, slavery was a
greater curse to the white man than to the Negro, for it made of the
slaveholders tyrants "who had no correct idea of themselves or anybody else." [6]

How well Stringfellow's admonition was heeded, the bloody annals
record. Kansas was to bleed at every vein, and Americans were to
commit atrocities on their fellow countrymen which make incredible
reading today; but on March 29, 1854, the day before the election,
it all started off gaily enough, with the Missourians in a boisterous
holiday mood as they assembled at the state line with their wagons,
their horses, their flags, their tents, their fiddles, their whiskey jugs,
and their bowie knives sticking out of their boot tops into their jeans.
Captain Claiborne Jackson was in command, and riding with him at
the head of the expedition, on the horse which Billy Hunter had
saddled for him, was Jo Shelby. He was traveling light, but somewhere about him there was tucked away a brace of the ornamented
pistols he was fond of.

The self-enfranchised voters buckarooed their way noisily across the border and pitched camp late that afternoon in a ravine six miles from Lawrence. On their first bivouac the border ruffians had proof that the Free State settlers were neither paupers nor yellowbellies, and if they had been given to reflection they might have realized that there was even some doubt as to whether one Southerner would be enough to whip ten Yankees.

Several Free State men, unarmed, came boldly out to meet them. Among them were Samuel N. Wood, an Ohioan who was to play a prominent part in the Free State movement, and N. B. Blanton, an election judge. Wood seems to have been impelled to the scene solely by curiosity and a stubborn Yankee determination not to be intimidated; Blanton was there on what he conceived to be his duty, and he informed the Missourians that if they attempted to vote he would demand from them an oath as to their place of residence.

When Blanton made his speech, according to the testimony which Wood gave later before a congressional committee, the border ruffians first "attempted to bribe him and then threatened him with hanging, in order to induce him to dispense with that oath." One Blue Lodge worthy announced that he intended to vote eight times without reloading, and the ninth time with a bowie knife. In consequence of their threats, Blanton did not appear at the polls next morning and another judge had to be selected in his place.

Sam Wood's imperturbability in the face of the crowd, many of whom had been having a pull at the jug, and some of his sarcastic comments, enchanted Shelby. He always had a weakness for brave men. He went up to Wood and engaged him in conversation, and as a result Wood invited Shelby home to dinner, an invitation which was accepted. It was the same everywhere with Shelby: people were frequently against what he was doing, but they were never against Jo Shelby.

A discussion of the pros and cons of the Missourians' "right" to vote took place at the dinner table. Shelby advanced all of the arguments of the proslavery men: that if the Missourians were "foreigners," so were the Boston Aid Emigrants; that they had as much right to "settle" here as anybody else; that by so doing they would lose their right to vote in Missouri for twelve months; and that it was no worse for Missourians to overwhelm the polls with proslavery votes than for the abolitionists to seek to impose the will of New England on what, after all, was Southern territory. Shelby added, however, that he himself would not vote if he had to swear he was a resident of Kansas, as his residence was in Waverly. He also told Wood that there were 10,000 Missourians in the territory, ready to vote, although the figure was, to say the least, exaggerated.[7]

The discussion was amiable, though the host's replies are not on record, and Shelby formed a friendship with Wood which survived the Civil War. After a good supper Shelby mounted his horse and rode back to the camp by the ravine, where matters of policy were under discussion.

Since it was obvious that there were going to be more voters at Lawrence than needed, Jackson and Colonel Sam Young made speeches calling for volunteers to go to near-by districts. Shelby elected to remain at Lawrence, where the chief excitement promised to be, but between 100 and 150 of the others volunteered and set off next day for Tecumseh, Hickory Point, Bloomington, Switzer's Creek, and other places. At Switzer's Creek, where the poll books listed but 53 voters, it being a remote hamlet seventy-five miles from the Missouri line, 607 votes were cast the next day.

Someone in camp raised the question as to whether there would be enough "tickets"—ballot forms—to go around. Since a shortage of this item would defeat the purpose for which they had come, a committee was formed which rode into Lawrence and routed out the editor of the Lawrence *Free State* and compelled him to print an extra 300 blanks. All business now having been attended to, the jugs went round again and the fiddles were tuned up. The sound of revelry echoed afar; one settler in the neighborhood testified at the congressional investigation that the Missourians could be heard "hallooing and keeping up a noise all night." [8]

In the morning, Missourians in groups of a hundred "marched with music to the polls." [9] Those who were not carrying drums, fiddles, or flags fired their guns. They had white ribbons in their buttonholes to distinguish them from the settlers, a precaution which seems hardly to have been necessary.

The polling place was the Lawrence postoffice, a three-room building which served not only as postoffice but as living quarters for William Lykins, the deputy postmaster. Lykins was a Missourian, the son of a doctor in Kansas City, and a Southern sympathizer. For a week he had permitted one room of the postoffice to be used as a storage space for bacon, flour, cornmeal, and other provisions, for use of such Missourians as might need them. Lykins, however, was not one of the election judges, and the voting was somewhat delayed when N. B. Blanton failed to show up. Blanton was soon replaced, however, with a more courageous election official, one Robert Cummins, and the voting began.

The first Missourian to present himself was a man named Page, and Cummins challenged him, demanding proof of his residence. Before Page could protest, Colonel Sam Young, a burly, impressive Missouri planter with a boisterous sense of humor, stepped up to the counter and said that he would settle the matter.

Deferentially, he stated that he wished to vote. The election judge asked him if he were a resident of Kansas, and informed him that he would have to take the oath prescribed by Governor Reeder. Young replied that he would not take the oath and that if he intended to make Kansas his future home that was his own damned business.

The election official looked doubtful, but after some consideration, said, "Well, if you're a resident that's all I'll ask."

The Colonel then went to a window, which was open, and shouted to the crowd outside:

"It's all right, boys! Everybody vote!" [10]

From then on, the polls were so crowded that those who had voted could not leave by the same door through which they had entered; to speed the balloting they were hoisted through a rear window to rejoin their companions. Many of them exchanged coats and came back to vote again. Later a passageway through the crowd was effected and two lines formed instead of one. Colonel Young asked the election judges to permit the old men to vote first as they were tired from traveling and anxious to get back to camp.

No concerted attempt was made to keep the Free State men from voting, although the presence of the ruffians outside the polls undoubtedly kept some of them away. A few known abolitionists were pointed out by Southern sympathizers, and several of them were made victims of Missouri horseplay. The editor of the Lawrence *Tribune*, writing about it years later, says that Shelby took part in this roughhousing.

"Shelby," he wrote, "[had] remained at Lawrence, and though then a young man, was recognized as leader. We were then boarding with Colonel Sam Wood, and he brought Shelby home with him to dinner, and thus we dined with the to-be Great Raider of the Rebellion. During the day, Cyrus Bond was pointed out as an abolition fighting man, and was assaulted and shot at and driven over the river bank, making a jump of about thirty feet almost perpendicular. It was said that Shelby fired the shots at Bond, but this we do not know, though we saw the shots fired and saw Bond, a very fat man, running like a quarter horse and wheezing like an old locomotive. . . . [11]

As Bond was being put to rout, four or five Missourians saw Charles Stearns, a vehement abolitionist and a correspondent for the New York *Tribune*, writing in a notebook. They made a lunge for Stearns and seized him. He was a man of slight build, weighing only 125 pounds, and no match for the border ruffians. He was a member of William Lloyd Garrison's fanatic antislavery party, which had denounced the Constitution as a "covenant with death and a league with hell" and demanded that New England secede from the Union, and he was well known to many Missourians present.

When Stearns was seized, Colonel Sam Young's sense of fair play was outraged, and he strode into the fray with arms swinging. A witness later testified that Young "took him [Stearns] up in his arms and asked if they intended to injure such a little man as that, balancing him in his arms at the same time." Then, the witness added, "Colonel Young took Mr. Stearns away, off the ground." [12]

Samuel Wood, Shelby's host of the night before, was also present. He had a greater interest in the election than anyone present, being a candidate for the Territorial legislature. As Stearns was rescued, Wood turned to George Thompson, a Missouri bully who had threatened him the night before at the camp by the ravine, and said, "Is it my turn now?" Thompson merely mumbled something about intending no harm to Wood if the latter "had not meant to insult them last night."

Wood did not reply, apparently feeling that to deny having "insulted" Thompson would concede to him a gentlemanly status which he did not possess. After Thompson backed down, Wood got in line to vote, although the crush was such, he testified later, that he did not get an opportunity to vote until afternoon, "towards night, when I voted."

The Free State men, appalled at the situation in Lawrence, made a last-ditch effort to get some "ringers" to the polls too,[13] even Indians, but the attempt was not successful. However, some outsiders were brought in. As Wood awaited his turn to vote, he says, he saw a contingent of 60 or 75 men approaching, under the command of a "General" Pomeroy who was an agent of the Emigrant Aid Society. This group had not been in town at nine o'clock that morning.[14] As Wood saw them, he called out significantly, "There are some arrivals as well as Missouri arrivals." There were not enough, however, to elect him to the legislature.

Another observer, Lyman Allen, a Free Stater who had just come up from Kansas City on the steamer *Sam Cloon* that morning, was also a witness to the fact that no attempt was made to restrain Free State men from voting. About four o'clock, Allen said, the ground began to be cleared somewhat "and the old men began to leave and they began to decamp. Some of the boys had got considerably intoxicated and [we] could have kept a guard about here during the night. About half of those persons left before midnight, I think, and early in the morning, and the rest drove off in the direction from which they came. There were several persons in the crowd when I tried to vote —not very rugged persons—who became faint and were taken away. It was very laborious getting up to the polls."

Jo Shelby was among the first to leave, and he rode off to Waverly in the company of his neighbors. He was in high spirits and reported to his brother and sister-in-law that there would be no trouble in holding the line for slavery in Kansas, as the Free State men would not fight. In this he could not have been more mistaken.

Though the Lawrence affair had passed off with no more casualties than a Saturday night "shivaree," there were repercussions throughout Kansas and the nation. The Northern press clamored for the suppression of the border ruffians, and the New York *Times* thundered that "it is madness to suppose that any community of American citizens will submit to such tyranny as this." [15] But the South was jubilant. The Charleston *Mercury*, the spokesman of the Slave Power in South Carolina, declared that "the safety of the institution of slavery in South Carolina is dependent upon its establishment in Kansas," [16] and rejoiced that "Kansas is safe! Fanaticism has met its master and been made to crouch." [17]

But far more important than the furor in the press was the effect of the election fraud upon the Free State settlers. They saw now that their existence and homes were at stake, and they prepared to fight. The St. Louis *Intelligencer* threw down the challenge: "It has been the common opinion of thoughtless persons and thickheaded bullies of the West that the Northern and Eastern men will not fight. Never was a greater mistake. The sons of New England and the Middle States do not like to fight. They would rather work, plough, build towns, railroads, make money and raise families, than fight. But fight they will, if need be. . . . The Free State men in Kansas will fight before they will be disfranchised and trampled on. Mark the word." [18]

Among the Free State men who would fight was a bearded, agate-eyed old patriarch named John Brown. He was already in Kansas, at Osawatomie, with his five sons, and now he set to work oiling his guns and writing letters to the newspapers. He was to end on the gallows in Virginia, but his work in Kansas was to go marching on, through four bloody years of Civil War. Others, less fanatic but equally determined, banded themselves together all over the state into the "Free State Volunteers," under the command of Dr. Charles Robinson, and the Southern press was soon screaming about the shipment from New England of Sharpe's rifles and other arms to the abolitionists in Kansas.

Into the Territory also came evil men like Quantrill, Anderson, and Todd, the bloodthirsty guerrillas who fought on neither side, but simply for loot and from the lust to kill. The Border War soon developed into a blood bath the like of which had not been seen before in the history of the Republic, not even in the days of the Indian massacres—one which the United States Army itself seemed powerless to prevent.

From 1855 to 1857, Kansas was laid waste. When Governor John W. Geary journeyed to the Territory to take his post he found "desolation and ruin on every hand; homes and firesides deserted; the smoke of burning dwellings darkening the atmosphere; women and children wandering over the prairies and among the woodlands or seeking refuge and protection even among the Indian bands." He traveled upon highways "infested with numerous predatory bands" through towns "fortified and garrisoned by armies of conflicting partisans, each excited almost to frenzy and determined upon mutual extermination. Such, without exaggeration, was the condition of the Territory at the period of my arrival." [19]

The first violence touched off by the election of March 30, 1855, came in Missouri itself. For daring to condemn the people of Missouri for going to Kansas to vote, the *Luminary*, a weekly published at

Parkville, was destroyed and the type and presses thrown into the Missouri River. The mob which carried out the destruction of the newspaper office held a mass meeting afterward and adopted a resolution declaring that "if we find G. S. Parks or W. J. Patterson [the proprietors of the paper] in this town after three weeks, or any subsequent time, we will throw them into the Missouri River, and if they go to Kansas to reside, we pledge our honor as men to follow and hang them wherever we can take them." [20]

Jo Shelby did not remain idle in Waverly as other, and grimmer, forays into Kansas were made. The next great invasion occurred at Franklin, Kansas, four miles from Lawrence, in October, 1855. Fifteen hundred Missourians gathered for the avowed purpose of crossing into Kansas and wiping Lawrence off the map. Shelby probably was in this group. The abolitionist capital was saved for the time being by a "peace treaty" engineered by Governor Wilson Shannon between the opposing forces, but on the way home the mob plundered the homes of Free State settlers, and one man, Thomas W. Barber, was shot down in cold blood by George W. Clarke, one of the Southern mob and a former Indian agent in Kansas. The killing of Barber roused the Free Staters to a war of retaliation; they began raiding across the border into Missouri and from then on both sides of the line became a battleground.

That was in October; in December, the beautiful new sawmill which Shelby and Howard Gratz had built at Berlin, Missouri, was destroyed by fire, and the evidence pointed to the work of an incendiary.[21] The roving Free State bands had marked Shelby as one of their chief enemies, and they would stop at nothing. The loss from the fire was $9,000, a sizable fortune; and to make matters worse, the sawmill was not insured. Shelby's rage knew no bounds. From that day on he declared relentless war on Kansas.

In May, 1856, occurred the sack of Lawrence, led by border ruffians under the personal command of General Atchison. The excuse, which the Missourians had long wanted, was that two abolitionist newspapers, the *Herald of Freedom* and the *Kansas Free State*, had been declared a nuisance by a Federal Grand Jury (packed with Missourians) and that they were going to abate them. The newspaper offices and the town's leading hotel, a fine 75-room structure with new and expensive furnishings,[22] were wrecked and the entire population driven from their homes. Stores and dwellings were looted and burned, including the house of Dr. Robinson, and altogether property was stolen or destroyed to the amount of $150,000.

In a savage, exultant speech before the looting began, Atchison roared at his men: "Boys, this day I am a Kickapoo Ranger, by God! This day we have entered Lawrence, 'Southern rights' inscribed on our banners, and not one damned abolitionist has dared to fire a gun. No, by God, not one! This, boys, is the happiest day of my whole life. We have entered the damned city, and tonight the abolitionists will learn a Southern lesson that they will remember to the day of their death. And now, boys, we will go in . . . and test the strength of that Free State Hotel, and learn the Emigrant Aid Society that Kansas shall be ours. Boys, ladies should be, and I trust will be, respected by all gentlemen; but by God, when a woman takes on herself the garb of a soldier by carrying a Sharpe's rifle, then she is no longer a woman, and by God, treat her for what you find her, and trample her underfoot as you would a snake. By God, come on, boys! Now do your duties to yourselves and your Southern friends. Your duty I know you will do; and if a man or woman dares to stand before you, blow them to hell with a chunk of cold lead." [23]

The sack of Lawrence marked the real turning point in the Border Wars, as Governor Robinson points out in his history of Kansas, although John Brown and his atrocities were to come after; for the Lawrence outrage was a boomerang. The North was so thoroughly aroused that even President Pierce, who had condoned every act of the Southerners in Kansas, was forced to do something. He appointed a new governor, John W. Geary, to replace the indecisive Wilson Shannon, and although Geary failed in his efforts to pacify Kansas altogether, there was never again to be another large-scale "war." As Governor Robinson says, "Never again was the Governor's militia or the marshal's posse called upon, and United States soldiers [would be] perfectly harmless in their attempt to foist upon the people the territorial usurpation." [24]

Unaware that the verdict of history had been rendered, as is often true of the leading participants, the Missouri leaders were planning another large-scale invasion. Twenty-eight hundred Missourians, the largest force of border ruffians ever to assemble, set up a camp in the late summer of 1856 at the junction of the Kaw and Wakarusa rivers. This was known as the Clarke-Reid-Atchison Expedition, and was under the immediate command of General John W. Reid, a member of the Missouri legislature. The names of the other members of the triumvirate, of course, require no identification.

On September 14 Governor Geary decided that he would visit the Southern encampment and put a stop to the warlike preparations. Accordingly he walked boldly into a council of the Missouri leaders. He had Federal troops behind him in Lawrence; and he ordered that the proslavery men be disbanded and dispersed. There was a lengthy parley, and speeches were made by the Missourians, including Jo Shelby,[25] but the Missourians were licked and they knew it; they would not fight the United States Army—not yet. Governor Geary had the meeting in his pocket; and he chided General Atchison by reminding him that the last time he had seen him, Atchison was presiding officer of the Senate.[26] The Clarke-Reid-Atchison Expedition was a fizzle, and Jo Shelby went home to Waverly.

In his last years Shelby was not proud of his part in the Border Wars. A few weeks before his death, he told William Elsey Connelley, the Kansas historian, as they were discussing the sack of Lawrence, "I was in Kansas at the head of an armed force about that time. I went there to kill Free State men. I did kill them. I am now ashamed of myself for having done so, but then times were different from what they are now, and that is what I went there for. We Missourians all went there for that purpose if it should be found necessary to carry out our designs. I had no business there. No Missourian had any business there with arms in his hands. The policy that sent us there was damnable and the trouble we started on the border bore fruit for ten years. I ought to have been shot there and John Brown was the only man who knew it and would have done it. I say John Brown was right. He did in his country what I would have done in mine in like circumstances. Those were the days when slavery was in the balance and the violence engendered made men irresponsible. I now see I was so myself." [27]

As Historian Connelley says, "These were brave words from one of the bravest and truest soldiers that ever shouldered a musket in America. Only a brave man, and a great man, can bring himself to make such a confession."

The key to the behavior of such men as Jo Shelby, David Atchison, and Claiborne Jackson is to be found in an observation made by Thomas H. Gladstone, a correspondent for the London *Times*, who visited Kansas in 1856. In a dispatch to his paper Gladstone said:

"Having once been taught that robbery and outrage, if committed in the service of the South, were to be regarded as deeds of loyalty and obedience, these ministers of a self-styled 'law and order' were slow to unlearn a doctrine so acceptable." [28] Indeed they were; and though there is nowhere in all the long record a single instance in which Jo Shelby ever did a mean or unchivalrous thing, it was undoubtedly true, as he himself said, that the violence engendered by Southern passions made him irresponsible.

We have his own word that Free State men died at his hands, but they had guns in their hands when they did so, and it was his life or theirs; by the time of the Lawrence raid Missourians and Kansans were shooting one another on sight, and the man who went on an armed expedition into Kansas that year, as Shelby did, knew that he was going into a civil war. The American Civil War began in Kansas, and not, as many people think, at Fort Sumter; and Jo Shelby was a soldier in that war from the beginning.

For whatever may have been on his conscience, he made his confession, and his penance, like a man; and he did his best, after Appomattox, to undo the harm that he had done. He was a man of savage temper, and it was not always under control. One who understood him as well as loved him, Judge John F. Philips of Kansas City, a Union veteran, summed up Shelby's character best when he said, in a funeral oration over Shelby's body at Kansas City in 1897:

"He was not what might be termed a round man, uniform and regular in his mental and moral composition. On the contrary, he was angular to acuteness. It was the sharp angles, the abrupt curvatures in his character that created the constant surprises in his career and lent to his life its singular attractiveness and picturesqueness. There were no dead planes, no monotonous levels in his journey through life, and it ran along rugged mountains, cataracts and varying scenery, much of it exciting, and much of it beautiful." [29]

5. *Steamboat Wedding*

H OWARD GRATZ, in 1856, had had enough. The Missouri River
Valley plantations had become the target of retaliatory raids by
the Kansas jayhawkers, and he and Shelby were marked men. The
burning of the sawmill in December of the previous year had been the
last straw. He chose to return to the civilized atmosphere of Lexington
to become editor of the *Kentucky Gazette,* the paper with which his
name was long associated, and Jo Shelby was left with the sole management of the Waverly Steam Rope Factory. The courthouse records
show that Shelby continued to own only a half interest in the business,
and there is no record that he ever had another partner in Waverly; so
the conclusion may be drawn that the firm of Gratz and Shelby was
not dissolved. Howard Gratz simply stepped down from active
participation in the business to assume the more congenial role of a
Kentucky editor,[1] and Shelby was alone at the helm in Missouri.

He was to prosper mightily for a least three more years, even though
the *Gratz Papers* indicate that the business of Gratz and Shelby had
suffered. This remarkable family history, an extremely rare item, states
that Howard Gratz "might have succeeded as a manufacturer of
hemp and in other notable business undertakings (planned probably
on suggestion from Benjamin Gratz) if the Border Wars with Kansas
and the Civil War had not disorganized Missouri business as completely as business was disorganized by Cresap's war when, in 1774,
B. and M. Gratz were ready to take their places as permanent founders
of Illinois."[2]

Howard Gratz did succeed as a manufacturer of hemp. It was Jo
Shelby's participation in the Border Wars which created a chaotic
condition in the affairs of Gratz and Shelby, and it was the headlong
course which Jo pursued which brought the business to the auction
block in February, 1860, a full seventeen months before he rode off to
his first battle of the war as a captain in the Missouri State Guards.

In 1856, after his return from the sack of Lawrence, the Lexington
(Missouri) *American Citizen* carried this item on June 17: "Upon the
return of Capt. Jos. O. Shelby's company from Kansas Territory,
having been driven out by troops of the United States, notwithstanding
our intentions avowed upon all occasions, of forming a peaceful settle-

ment, and organized alone for the purpose of mutual protection, a meeting being held . . . a committee [was appointed] to draft resolutions expressive of the sentiments of the said meeting. Whereupon the following resolutions were reported and unanimously adopted:

"Resolved, that Capt. Shelby has merited our highest admiration for the courage, coolness and dignity of his deportment under the trying circumstances in which we were placed, and for his kind, careful and impartial conduct towards all under his command, he has won for himself our warmest gratitude and esteem.

"Resolved, that as a testimonial thereof, that as a company, we present him a fine Sharpe's rifle.

"Resolved, that still being desirous of forming a settlement in Kansas Territory, we appoint Capt. Jos. O. Shelby and Jno. S. Percival Esq., to visit Gov. Shannon, and ascertain under what circumstances we will be permitted to make permanent settlement therein.

"Resolved, that all papers friendly to equal rights in the said Territory, be requested to publish the foregoing resolutions."

While Jo Shelby was waging an unequal struggle with the United States government in Kansas, Frank Blair was preparing in St. Louis to make a successful campaign for Congress in the fall. The events of the year 1856 bring the characteristics of the three cousins from Kentucky sharply into focus: the peace-loving Howard Gratz was retiring to an editorial sanctum in Kentucky from which he would emerge only to attend scholarly dinners or make speeches to women's groups;[3] Jo Shelby was being presented with a Sharpe's rifle by admiring border ruffians; and Frank Blair was running for Congress on a platform calling for the gradual abolition of slavery.

From now on Jo Shelby would have enough to occupy any man's time even without his activities in the Blue Lodge. There was the management of the thousand-acre farm, which he still owned with Howard Gratz; there was the lucrative hemp business; there were the steamboats; and there were the continual lawsuits over the shipment of merchandise which seemed to be the inevitable concomitant of the baling business. And he was in love. Betty Shelby was sixteen, in 1857, and a beauty. Soon she was surrounded with beaux, and soon the smitten Jo was submerged in a torment of jealousy which almost suffocated him. The William Shelbys may have thought their daughter rather young to marry at barely seventeen, but Jo's impetuosity could not tolerate the thought of waiting—some other man might get her.

Like many an old bachelor, when he fell, he fell hard. As for the William Shelbys, he simply charmed them down where they stood; no great feat for the twenty-seven-year-old Jo, who had been their favorite for years. The William Shelbys now had a house in town, just east of Jo's house on Mount Rucker, in addition to their farm six miles out in the country. From his porch the jealous Jo could see Betty's admirers coming and going, and it was too much. The wedding date was set for July 22, 1858, at the William Shelby's home in Waverly.

From the first there was never anybody for Betsy but Jo. Although like all the belles of the great plantations around Waverly and Blackburn she had her share of suitors, she was not a coquette, and she did nothing to fan the flames of Jo's jealousy. On the contrary, knowing its explosive qualities, she would go to any lengths not to arouse it. On one occasion she was wearing a ring given her by an admirer—an inexpensive trinket, perhaps a birthday gift—when she saw Jo approaching down by the wharf. In a panic she threw the ring into the Missouri River, a symbol of final decision.[4]

Great plans were made for the wedding. Shelby's steamboat, the *A. B. Chambers*, commandeered as a private yacht for this occasion, would take the entire wedding party on a honeymoon trip to St. Louis. It was entirely in character for Jo Shelby that he did not mind a large entourage of companions on his honeymoon. Nothing suited him better, in fact, no matter what a bride might think. There was a great deal of commotion around the Waverly Steam Rope Company as Shelby penned orders for the finest of everything for the trip, and he kept Billy Hunter running.

Assisting Shelby in his wedding plans was one of his boon hunting and fishing companions, a young Virginian by the name of John Newman Edwards, who had just come out from Front Royal in the Shenandoah to edit the Lexington (Missouri) *Expositor*, a weekly newspaper owned by Colonel Oliver Anderson, Howard Gratz's father-in-law, and one of the most influential papers in the Missouri River Valley.

Edwards was a mild-mannered man whose startling opinions and flamboyant newspaper prose were to earn him the sobriquet of "the Horace Greeley of the West," after his return from the war and his junket to Mexico with Shelby. Under his editorship the *Expositor* was one of the most colorfully written newspapers in Missouri, a land of colorful editors. Old-timers in Lexington still recall hearing from their parents of the flaming social history with which John Newman Edwards filled the columns of the *Expositor*, and particularly the vivid account he wrote of Jo and Betty Shelby's wedding party embarking for St. Louis on their private steamboat, in the cool of the evening, with lights ablaze in the salon, music floating out over the river to serenade the sleepy birds in the cottonwoods on the bank, and the laughter of the young people gayer than any music ever made by Zeiler's Band.[5]

Unfortunately the story he wrote is lost forever. When the Kansas Redlegs (so called from their red morocco leggings) raided Waverly and Lexington in 1862, they burned the *Expositor* building and dumped its files and presses into the Missouri River, for the editor of the *Expositor* had been loud, denunciatory, and pointedly insulting whenever he mentioned Kansas or Kansans in his columns. If the Redlegs had been able to find the editor in, when they called in 1862, they would have thrown him into the Missouri along with his presses or hanged him to the nearest tree; but at that time he was riding with Shelby far away. John Newman Edwards did not fight the war with his pen.

Though the *Expositor* files have long since vanished, and its type fonts lie pied at the bottom of the Missouri, it is possible to piece together most of the details of Shelby's wedding. The story has been passed down to succeeding generations by those who remembered it. Indeed, the town never forgot it.[6]

The marriage ceremony was performed by the Reverend B. M. Hobson, of the Lexington Presbyterian Church, on July 22,[7] before a crowd of wedding guests, among whom were the elite of the Missouri River Valley.[8] Aldridge Corder, a leading merchant and later a banker of the town, was best man. He was Shelby's age, still a bachelor and one of Shelby's closest friends in Missouri; together they had been two elusive beaux of the countryside. Among the guests, we may be sure, were the members of the family from Lexington, Kentucky, including Shelby's mother (who had made a trip to Waverly the year before to meet Betty); Gratz Brown and Frank Blair from St. Louis; such Missouri notables as David Atchison and Claiborne Jackson; young Tom Crittenden, who had just moved from Kentucky to Missouri;[9] and others whose names, if they were recorded, would be equally well known. Miss Elizabeth Corder, daughter of Aldridge

Corder, still living today at Marshall, Missouri, recalls hearing that her father and all the other young men present were reduced to a state of abjection by the stunning beauty of Betsy's bridesmaids, and especially one whose name was Pauline. The name of the beauteous Pauline, alas, has been forgotten, as well as whether she caught the bride's bouquet. But quite evidently she did not need it. There was also the usual contingent in the background, as at any Southern wedding, of Negro servants "dressed to kill," and at least one solemn darky who saw an era ended when Betty said "I do." That would be Billy Hunter, who from now on would have charge of a family of white folks.

It would have been inconceivable of course that Shelby and Edwards would have forgotten the red velvet carpet leading from the front porch of the William Shelby home, which was only a few feet from the dock, and they did not. In a letter to the author dated February 9, 1953, Mrs. Louise Davis Brown of Waverly recalls hearing from older members of the family that "the path leading to the river was carpeted in red velvet. At the bend of the river a brilliantly lighted boat gay with music and the luxuries of Southern hospitality awaited the arrival of the wedding party and close friends, the guests of Gen. Shelby for an excursion to St. Louis."

At the slow speed of a Missouri River steamboat the trip to St. Louis required the better part of a week, so that the wedding trip of Betty and Jo Shelby was one of the longest "river parties" in the history of that historic stream. At St. Louis the newlyweds and their friends spent several days seeing the sights,[10] and Betty and Jo visited members of the family. Surfeited with champagne and steamboat fare, the party may have made the return trip by train.

It would be pleasant to record that the steamboat wedding trip was the beginning of an uninterrupted idyl of married life, but the grim fact is that the next two years were downhill years for the Waverly Steam Rope Company. Apparently 1858 was a good year, for in an exuberant moment Jo Shelby caused to be inscribed a silver pitcher which he presented "To Col. David O. Henton, from Jos. O. Shelby, for the best crop of hemp delivered at St. Thomas in 1858,"[11] but the fiery Jo had a multitude of enemies as well as friends and as a lone business man he was not a success. Without the mature judgment and restraining hand of Howard Gratz, he over-extended himself, and the lavish scale on which he lived soon depleted his capital.

Details of Shelby's business transactions during these two years are largely missing, but it is known that he was involved in ventures of some kind with Frank Blair, who also came to financial grief on a big scale, according to the Blair Papers in the Library of Congress.[12] In 1860 a newspaper account says that Frank Blair was in Lexington to enter satisfaction of a mortgage made by him to Gratz and Shelby, and that he left town hastily, for at the time the citizens of Lexington were "much incensed" with him and if they had known he was in town would have handled him roughly.[13] "Gen. Blair," says the account, "returned to his boat by the way he came [evidently he avoided the main thoroughfare] and not until his boat was gone was it generally known that he was in Lexington."

Whatever the cause, or combination of causes, by February, 1860, the crash had come. The Lafayette County records show that John P. Bowman (Sheriff) as trustee sold Shelby's half-interest in the Waverly Steam Rope Factory, for $4,425.00 to Camillas Barnett, E. S. Fishback, and Thomas Shelby.[14] The sale did not satisfy all of Shelby's indebtedness, for the records also show that in May of the same year Camillas Barnett was suing Henry H. Gratz and Joseph O. Shelby for $3,000. The disposition in this suit does not appear.

Thus the critical winter before the war, that of 1860-61, found Jo Shelby in what were, for him, straitened circumstances. As a landowner he could keep up some semblance of the lordly life of a planter, but he was through with the hemp business forever. As a matter of fact, the war killed the hemp business in both Kentucky and Missouri so effectively that it was never revived as a money crop in either state. Jo Shelby was now a gentleman farmer; nothing more. He and Betsy had one child, Orville, born in August, 1859.

The state of Shelby's personal fortunes, of course, was overshadowed by the threat of war which was now hanging over the whole country. Missouri had been at war since 1855, but it was not until the election of 1860 that the crisis came in the other Southern states. Shelby had long since made up his mind that he would soon be fighting in Southern uniform, and during the long winter he watched events from Waverly. In May, 1861, he received a telegram from Frank Blair asking him to come to St. Louis and "talk" about the situation. He knew what that meant. Blair was going to offer him a Federal commission. It was a preposterous idea, but he decided to go to St. Louis anyway, as he had some other business to attend to. Over in Lexington, Kentucky, his friend John Morgan had just written him asking him if he knew a gun dealer who could supply 100,000 musket caps for Morgan's rifles, to be used against the United States Army if it should attempt to overrun Kentucky. Shelby knew a gun dealer in St. Louis. He would take the next boat to St. Louis, to see if the dealer had 100,000 musket caps.

6. *Missouri and the Union*

ONLY ONE MAN in Missouri in the higher councils of either political party had a full understanding of the course that events were bound to take, and that man was Shelby's cousin, Frank Blair.

Again a member of Congress following the election of 1860, Blair had a direct line into the White House and enjoyed the confidence and friendship of Abraham Lincoln. His brother Montgomery was postmaster general in Lincoln's cabinet and Lincoln had fixed on Frank Blair as the one man who could secure Missouri to the Union, and as the one man who would not hesitate to use any means whatever to do it. Lincoln soon gave him unofficial powers greater than those enjoyed by the Federal commander in St. Louis, General Harney, including the power to remove the General; and until Captain Nathaniel Lyon appeared on the scene, Blair was dictator of the Union party in Missouri and the personification of the Union cause in the state.

Blair's early contacts with Lincoln left him in no doubt that Lincoln meant to maintain the Union by force of arms if necessary. Blair, the Southern aristocrat, knew that this meant war and nothing else. Many in Missouri would later come reluctantly to that conclusion; but because Frank Blair understood it from the first he was prepared to act, when the time came, while others were still debating legal definitions. His accurate estimate of the situation in Missouri enabled him to plot and carry out a master strategy which outwitted the Secessionists and the compromisers from the beginning.

Blair was an unconditional Union man himself, although, true to his Kentucky blood, he viewed the freeing of the slaves as a calamity, albeit a necessary one. He proposed to meet the calamity by shipping them all to Central America as soon as they were freed.[1]

Blair knew that although an overwhelming majority of his fellow Missourians were loyal to the Union, an appalling number of them could be swayed in that loyalty. They were "conditional Union" men. The conditional Unionists fell into two categories. First, there were the rich slaveholders of the Missouri River Valley, most of whom wanted to remain in the Union and keep their slaves. (Many of them agreed privately with old Sam Houston down in Texas that Secession would be a stupendous failure and would result in the subjugation of the South.)[2] They would, however, join the Confederacy overnight, when they found that slavery was threatened, unless they were separated physically from the opportunity to do so.

Second, there were the independent farmers and the "poor whites" of the southeastern counties who were too far down in the economic scale to own many slaves, but whose forebears had come from Kentucky, North Carolina, or Tennessee. If called upon to fight against their blood kindred of the South, they would refuse, and if pushed too far they would take up arms for the South. That was the hair-trigger situation in two sections of the state; as for the western counties, they were lost beyond redemption. The inhabitants of that romantic region, where the passions of the Border Wars had not subsided, were fiercely Secessionist, not because they had any quarrel with the Union but simply because they hated Yankees and would welcome the opportunity to kill them. Only in St. Louis, with its large "foreign" population of Germans, Irish, French, and Canadians, could absolute, unconditional loyalty to the Union be counted on.[3]

Jo Shelby did not know it, but on the day he arrived in St. Louis to buy musket caps for John Morgan, the stage was set for a *coup d'état*, European style, in which Frank Blair and the Unionists would put the city of St. Louis in their pocket and thereby secure control of the Missouri River and hence of the state. The first blood of the Civil War in Missouri was to be shed at Camp Jackson, where Governor Claiborne Jackson had concentrated 700 of his state militia in what was ostensibly a routine encampment for training, but actually was the first step in the mobilization of the Secessionist forces in the state. By a coincidence, Shelby was to be present at the seizure of Camp Jackson by the Unionists, and forced to stand by while "foreign" troops took prisoner the sons of the best families of St. Louis. If he had not already been a convinced Secessionist, the sights he saw at

Camp Jackson that day would have turned him finally and completely against the Union.

In the armed camp which St. Louis had become, Shelby did not find it difficult to buy 100,000 musket caps, especially from a gun dealer of Southern sympathies. But the size of the consignment was something of a problem, for arms were contraband, but it was solved by placing the shiny new caps in red clay flower pots, which were then covered with earth and topped with roses, dahlias, and lilacs.[4] The caps were delivered safely to Morgan a few days later in Lexington, perhaps the largest floral tribute ever received by a live Confederate general.

As Jo Shelby walked the streets of St. Louis, he could not fail to note the warlike preparations, nor the fact that most of the soldiers under arms were Germans, members of the Black Republican Home Guards. He was scandalized and alarmed; it did not seem possible that Governor Claiborne Jackson, who had been in office for five months, should have permitted this organization to exist.

As a matter of fact, Governor Jackson and his dominantly pro-Southern legislature had played into the hands of Frank Blair by a fatal policy of delay. Instead of simply authorizing a convention to vote on secession, as other states had done, the Missouri legislature, at Governor Jackson's request, had authorized an election for a convention which would consider Missouri's relation to the Union and then submit the issue to the people in a general election. The bill calling for the election of delegates to the convention contained a proviso that "no act, ordinance or resolution of said convention shall be deemed valid to change or dissolve the political relations of this state to the Government of the United States or to any other state until a qualified majority of voters of this state voting upon the question shall have ratified the same."[5] To show their confidence that Missouri would secede in a general election, the legislators appended a resolution declaring that "so abhorrent is the doctrine of coercion that any such attempt would result in the people of Missouri rallying to the side of their Southern brethren in their last extremity"[6]

This was a mistake of the first magnitude and reflected Jackson's complete misconception of the popular state of mind in Missouri. Most Missourians did not want war and they agreed with the outgoing Governor Robert Stewart, Jackson's predecessor, that the state's position in the crisis should be one of "high neutrality." When the convention met, it failed to call an election and adopted instead the position that "there was no adequate cause to impel Missouri to dissolve her connections with the Federal Union but on the contrary she will labor for an adjustment of existing troubles as will gain the peace, as well as the rights and equality of all the states." [7]

All this had taken months, and during those months Frank Blair had been equally busy, but not in weighing legal procedure or trying to influence sentiment with speeches. He had been working night and day to create a personal military organization, composed of the Germans of St. Louis, known as the "Turners" or Home Guards. The Home Guards had been drilling nightly all winter, under the stern eye of Prussian drillmasters, in breweries, foundries, and *turnverein* halls in which sawdust had been spread thick to deaden the sound of marching feet. The first company of Home Guards thus to assemble had elected Blair captain, for he was the idol of the German population of St. Louis and it had been largely through the German vote that he had been elected to Congress. He was now colonel of the Home Guard organization, and when he spoke it would move as one man.

Blair's haughty, aristocratic bearing, plus his emancipationist political philosophy, made him the natural leader of these people, and, in fact, of all the so-called "foreign" element of St. Louis. Many of them, especially the Germans, were refugees from tyranny in Europe, and they had brought with them to America the philosophy of the liberal revolution which swept the Continent in 1848. They had no love for slavery or slaveholders. They feared the competition of slave labor as much as they hated the arrogant slaveholders, and their feelings were reciprocated heartily by the Missourians of Southern birth, who detested all outsiders as "foreigners."

From the standpoint of the Southern Missourians, the Germans, though a minority (the Irish far outnumbered them in St. Louis) were easily the most obnoxious of the foreigners. Not only were they Black Republicans; they rubbed the natives the wrong way on a score of other counts. Their harsh rendering of the English language, their beer-drinking habits, their free-and-easy attitude toward the Sabbath (St. Louis enjoyed a Continental Sunday while the rest of Missouri listened to sermons on hellfire and damnation), their heel-clicking reverence for authority, and, above all, their Teutonic industry, earned for them, outside of St. Louis, the appellation of "the damned Dutch" or "the lop-eared Dutch." And when the blue merino flag of civil war was raised in Missouri, the Stars and Stripes came to be known, to the Southern troops, as "the Dutch flag."

Finding himself in such uncongenial surroundings on this bright May morning (it was May 10, 1861) it was natural that Jo Shelby, while waiting for his musket caps to be packed, should seek an atmosphere in which he would feel more at home. The Missouri State Guards were in encampment at Lindell's Grove, just outside the city, under the command of General D. M. Frost, and thither he drove to look up some of his friends among the militia and admire the spotless military order of Camp Jackson, as the encampment was called.

The militiamen had been at Camp Jackson since May third, the date which the legislature had set for their annual training period. At least that was the pretense; the real reason was that Fort Sumter had fallen in April and President Lincoln had made a requisition upon Missouri for four regiments with which to coerce the Southern States. A furious Claiborne Jackson had penned a reply to Lincoln in which he declared that "the requisition is in my judgment illegal, unconstitutional and revolutionary in its object, and cannot be complied with. Not one man will the state of Missouri furnish for such an unholy crusade." [8] The Missouri State Guards had then been summoned to Camp Jackson.

General Frost, the New York born commander of the Missouri State Guards, had made elaborate preparations to avoid any appearance of assembling an offensive force, although the Confederate government had already sent siege guns into the city at Governor Jackson's request. The site of the encampment was selected deliberately, or so it seemed, for its exposed position; it was surrounded on all sides by hills and was vulnerable either to bombardment or to cavalry attack. Frost was at great pains to make it appear that he neither feared an attack nor contemplated one.

Furthermore, the camp was open to the public at all times, and the only flags in sight were those of the State of Missouri and the United States. Officers and men had taken the usual oath to uphold the Constitution, and as further evidence of his peaceful intentions, General Frost had offered previously, in writing, the services of his militia to protect, if necessary, U. S. Government property—meaning the arsenal, with its 60,000 rifles, 1,500,000 ball cartridges, 90,000 pounds of powder, and several pieces of artillery.

Despite the mighty impression of innocence which Frost sought to create, Frank Blair and Captain Nathaniel Lyon—a regular army officer who had been sent in from Fort Riley, Kansas, with eighty regulars to guard the arsenal—believed that Jackson had summoned the militia for the purpose of seizing the arsenal, and they made plans accordingly. Lyon put on a black bombazine dress belonging to Frank Blair's mother, and with a heavy veil to conceal his red beard, rode through Camp Jackson in a carriage. No one suspected that he was not a bona fide old lady, and he noted, as his red beard bristled, that the streets in the camp bore such names as "Beauregard" and "Davis." He returned posthaste to Colonel Blair and reported that there was not a doubt that Camp Jackson was a hotbed of rebellion. Furthermore, word came in about this time that the cannon and powder for the state encampment had arrived from New Orleans on the steamer *J. C. Swan*, disguised as marble and ale.

Lyon, who was by now a colonel, through the influence of Blair at the White House, and soon would be a brigadier general, proposed to move on Camp Jackson at once, and Blair agreed. As a result of his ceaseless activities, Federal troops had been pouring into St. Louis daily, and the Union forces now stood at 7,000, outnumbering the Missouri State Guards ten to one.

General Frost learned of the plans of Lyon and Blair and wrote to Lyon asking if the information were true and if so by what authority the United States Army planned to attack the Missouri militia. He also mentioned the arms which had come in aboard the *J. C. Swan*. He said that he knew nothing of their origin and that he would turn them over to the Federal troops if they would come and get them. Frost's conciliatory attitude failed. Lyon by now had determined upon the seizure of the arsenal himself (in all this he was flouting the authority of General Harney, the top Federal commander in St. Louis, who was no party to the plan and would have scotched it if he could). Lyon also refused to receive the letter Frost had written.[9]

Seven thousand troops, including regiments from Iowa, Kansas, and Illinois, as well as Frank Blair's "Dutch," converged on Camp Jackson, and Lyon demanded an unconditional surrender. Outnumbered as he was, there was nothing for Frost to do but obey. The entire militia were made prisoners of war and marched off to jail, through crowded city streets.

A lady of pro-Southern sentiment wrote in her diary: "Think of it! The German rabble, composed of soldiers of the lower element of the city, recruited from the saloons and dives ... taking as prisoner the sons and husbands of the leading families of St. Louis!" [10]

While the militia were marched out as prisoners, a furious mob of Secessionists gathered. Stones were hurled at the blue-coated troops. Someone fired a pistol. Whether by order of Lyon or not, the Union troops answered with rifle volleys fired directly into the crowd. By the time Lyon issued a cease-fire, twenty-six men lay dead, and one woman had a babe killed in her arms. A twenty-eighth casualty was the Union captain whose men had fired the first volley. He died of his wounds the next day.

The massacre dispersed the mob, but bands of Secessionists roamed the streets of St. Louis until nightfall, looking for trouble. They did not find it, for Blair and Lyon kept their men under cover. Secessionist speakers delivered fiery orations before the Planter's House and in front of street-corner saloons, hurling invective at the "Dutch" and demanding a rope for Blair and Lyon. The saloons, restaurants, and other public places closed their doors hastily as the Southern element worked off its spleen.

Things were quiet again the next day, and the militiamen who had been taken prisoner at Camp Jackson were freed on their parole not to bear arms against the United States. Most of them turned up later in the rebel army under General Bowen on the other side of the Mississippi; the parole was regarded as given under duress and was violated with alacrity when the bluebloods were given an opportunity for revenge.

Among the spectators at Camp Jackson, besides Jo Shelby, had been a heavy-set, bearded fellow who was engaged currently in clerking in his father's harness shop at Galena, Illinois. His sympathies were not with the militia, although he wrote later that he did not understand why they did not seize the arsenal. His name was Ulysses Simpson Grant.[11] Not far away was another St. Louisan with whom Grant was to become better acquainted later on, a fellow in a plug hat who looked always as if he would soon be needing a shave: William Tecumseh Sherman, president of the Fifth Street Railroad.

When Shelby saw Frank Blair, in all probability he denounced him. He would have nothing to do with anyone, family or not, who would use powder and shot on Southern men and women. The voluminous Blair Papers in the Library of Congress make no reference at all to this conversation between these two remarkable cousins; Blair did history a disservice when he did not set down the exact words of Jo Shelby on this occasion. But from other sources we know that Blair sought to quiet him and spoke eloquently of the duty to keep Missouri in the Union; and he ended, as Shelby had suspected he would, by trying to persuade Shelby to accept a commission in the Federal army. Shelby replied that he had fought the damned abolitionists in Kansas and would fight them again, on Missouri soil or anywhere else, and that his border veterans were already at Independence for the purpose of protecting the town from the enemy.

Oddly enough, Shelby was refusing a Federal commission from the son of the man who had just offered Robert E. Lee command of the Federal armies;[12] Frank Blair, Sr., was still very much alive and busy running errands in Washington for Abraham Lincoln, as Frank, Jr., was running them in Missouri. But actually Shelby was refusing much more than a commission. Frank Blair, in effect, was showing him from a mountain top all the kingdoms of the world. As a Federal officer under Blair and Lyon, at this stage of affairs, there was no promotion or preferment to which Jo Shelby could not have looked forward with confidence. In all probability, he could have had, before he was thirty-two, the rank of colonel or brigadier general which was withheld from him in such a niggardly manner by his superior officers in the Confederate army. He could have retained his property at Waverly and perhaps regained his heavy financial losses. But he tossed it all aside as contemptuously as if it had been an unsmokable two-cent cigar, and took the steamboat back to Waverly to fight for a country which could not furnish him a uniform to wear, a gun to shoot, or a horse to ride. He would not see Frank Blair again until after the war, although he would be in frequent correspondence with him on matters of importance, both to their family and to the nation.[13]

At Jefferson City, when news of the Camp Jackson affair was announced to the legislature, pandemonium broke out. The legislators were convoked in special session to debate the passage of Governor Jackson's Militia Bill, which would not only call every able-bodied Missourian into the service of the state but give dictatorial powers to the Governor. George Graham Vest, a friend of Shelby's whose name is remembered as the author of the classic "Tribute to the Dog," leaped onto a chair and waved a dispatch before the assembly, shout-

ing apoplectically, "Frank Blair, Captain Lyon, and the Dutch have
seized Camp Jackson!"

The legislators, most of whom were Secessionists, paused only long
enough to pass the Militia Bill and vote $10,000 for an alliance with
the border Indians. Then they bolted from the assembly hall in search
of weapons. McElroy in his *Struggle for Missouri* says that "muskets,
shotguns, rifles, pistols and pikes were brought out, cleaned up, bullets
molded and cartridges made, and the Governor ordered members of
the staff to seize a locomotive and press on as far as possible to St.
Louis and reconnoitre the advance of the enemy and if necessary
destroy the bridges over the Gasconade and Osage rivers to obstruct
the march." [14]

The locomotive screamed out of Jefferson City with legislators
clinging to its sides. The expedition burned part of a bridge over the
Osage, but, no enemy being in sight, returned to Jefferson City and
resumed its sessions. In the next few days, measures were passed ap-
propriating two million dollars to defend Missouri against the Union,
and the legislators gritted their teeth as they recalled that they could
not pass an ordinance of secession, having delegated that power to a
convention, which would not meet again until December.

Governor Jackson did the next best thing. He used his emergency
powers under the Militia Bill to order all members of the Missouri
State Guards into service, and he commissioned Sterling Price its
major general. Price, a former governor and veteran of the Mexican
War, was one of the most popular men in Missouri. He accepted the
assignment, although he had always been a Union man,[15] and went
at once to Lexington to begin recruiting. His acceptance of Governor
Jackson's commission undoubtedly did much to sway conditional
Union men to enlist in the Missouri State Guards.

General Harney, the Federal commander of the Department of
the West, who had never been in accord with the direct policies of
Blair and Lyon, nevertheless was forced to take notice of the warlike preparations of Governor Jackson. He issued a proclamation in
which he termed the recent action of the legislature "an indirect ordinance of secession" and warned everyone that he "intended to maintain the authority of the Constitution of the United States within
the scope of his command."

He was not anxious, however, for an open conflict with Sterling
Price and he asked Price to come to St. Louis for a conference. Price

came, and Harney reminded him that President Lincoln had issued a proclamation calling for the dispersal of all bands hostile to the United States within the borders of Missouri. He added that the Missouri State Guards now came under that heading. Price assured Harney that his activities as a major general of militia would be confined to protecting the lives and property of the citizens of Missouri. Satisfied, Harney reported his agreement to the War Department.[16]

At first Frank Blair expressed himself as "in hopes that we can get along with it [the Price-Harney agreement] and think that Harney will insist on its execution to the fullest extent, in which case it will be satisfactory,"[17] but several days later he changed his mind, and on May 30 he dismissed Harney from command, as he had authority from Abraham Lincoln to do.[18]

As a result of the St. Louis coup, Lincoln appointed Lyon a brigadier general. Blair's commission in the same rank would come later. The two men now had St. Louis, and they had the arsenal. Soon they would control the entire Missouri River Valley and two thirds of the state. Although the rebels were to win victories, they would never again be in undisputed control of any substantial part of Missouri soil; and historians are agreed that chief credit for this outcome can be assigned to Frank Blair and Nathaniel Lyon. The two men had never met until the fortunes of war threw them together in St. Louis, but no two men were ever better suited by temperament to fight together and work together, unless it were Jo Shelby and John Newman Edwards.

Governor Jackson of course regarded Blair and Lyon as out-and-out rebels against the state authority, and he would have dealt with them summarily if he had had the power to do so. But since the heavy battalions were on the side of Blair and Lyon, he allowed himself to be persuaded to make one last effort for peace.

Through an intermediary a meeting was arranged at the Planter's House in St. Louis. Lyon opened the discussion by remarking that he would leave the conduct of the meeting to Blair, since he enjoyed the confidence of Washington to a higher degree than any other man present; then Lyon proceeded to take over the meeting himself. He became so vehement that Blair virtually was silenced. Lyon would not listen to Governor Jackson, who suggested that the troops on both sides be disbanded; and he listened to Sterling Price only impatiently as the old Roman defended his course.

Thomas L. Snead, Price's aide, who was present at the meeting, says in his *Fight For Missouri* that the conference obviously was useless from the start. "It was to no purpose," he wrote, "that they all sought, or pretended to seek, the basis of a new agreement for maintaining the peace in Missouri. If they really sought to find one, they did not. Finally, when the conference had lasted for four or five hours, Lyon closed it as he had opened it.

" 'Rather,' he said, 'than concede to the State of Missouri for one instant the right to dictate to my Government in any matter, however unimportant, I would (rising as he said this and pointing to everyone in the room) see you, and you, and you, and every man, woman and child in the state of Missouri dead and buried!' Then, turning to the Governor, he said, 'This means war. In an hour one of my officers will call and conduct you out of my lines.' And then, without another word, without an inclination of the head, without another look, he turned upon his heel and strode out of the room, rattling his spurs and clanking his sabre, while we, whom he left, and who had known each other for years, bade farewell to each other courteously, and kindly, and separated, Blair and Conant [19] to fight for the Union, we for the land of our birth." [20]

Jackson and General Price returned at once to Jefferson City, and the executive machinery ground once more as Jackson penned another proclamation calling for 50,000 militia "for the purpose of repelling invasion and for the protection of the lives, liberty and property of the citizens of this state." The proclamation adjured all Missourians to "obey all Constitutional requirements of the Federal Government," but advised them that "your first allegiance is due your own state, and you are under no obligation whatsoever to obey the unconstitutional edicts of the military despotism which has enthroned itself at Washington or to submit to the infamous and degrading sway of its minions in this state."

By this time such a proclamation was little more than sound and fury. The solid Union men, Blair and Lyon, were in the saddle, with all the armies of the United States at their back. Of the 50,000 rebel volunteers called for, only 5,000 were to respond—and they over a period of six months.

It is too late now, Governor Jackson.

PART TWO

The Campaign of the Missouri State Guards

◆●◆

7. *Boonville and Carthage*

BLAIR'S right-hand man, Brigadier General Nathaniel Lyon, had declared war on Governor Jackson's state government of Missouri,[1] and he telegraphed the War Department for 5,000 additional stands of arms and authority to enlist more troops. The Secretary of War replied that the arms would be furnished and granted Lyon's request for permission to increase his forces. Lyon at once set in motion all the troops he could spare from St. Louis for an offensive against the Missouri State Guards. His object was three-fold: to cut off the retreat of Jackson, Price, and the others who had retired to Jefferson City to organize an army of militia; to occupy all of the Missouri River Valley; and to prevent Confederate armies in Arkansas from entering the state and effecting a junction with the Missouri militia.

Arkansas had become a Confederate state on May 6, and the Richmond government had directed General Ben McCulloch, the old Texas ranger, who commanded three regiments in the Indian Territory, to give Sterling Price all the support he could *without invading Missouri*.[2] As long as Missouri was still a Southern state which had not seceded from the Union, the non-aggression policy of the Confederate States was dead set against an invasion of Missouri or any other Union territory. Nathaniel Lyon did not know of McCulloch's orders, but it would have made no difference if he had. Sooner or later the Confederates would invade. If he could prevent them from making a junction with the "barefoot militia," and either scatter the

Missouri state troops or drive them into the remote regions of the southwest, the war against the Union would be over, as far as Missouri was concerned.

The indispensable first condition for the execution of Lyon's plan was to occupy Jefferson City, and this he was prepared to do immediately, and in full force. When word reached Governor Jackson that Lyon intended to march on the state capital, he realized that he could not defend the city with the 400 or 500 militia stationed there under the command of Colonel John S. Marmaduke, a West Pointer. (General Price had been taken suddenly and severely ill.)[3] Marmaduke's men were poorly armed, many of them only with derringers, family fowling pieces, squirrel rifles, old flintlocks, or long knives made of files which had been beaten into shape by blacksmiths. Marmaduke had for artillery only two six-pounders and he strongly advised Jackson to abandon any thought of making a stand in the vicinity of Jefferson City.

Jackson, however, was determined not to let the whole state fall into Lyon's hands by default, as St. Louis had done. He disregarded Marmaduke's protests and ordered him to Boonville on the Missouri River, with instructions to defend it, promising meanwhile that he would order other state troops under General M. M. Parsons at Tipton to his aid. Parsons had 700 or 800 men, but before he could join Marmaduke, Lyon had occupied Jefferson City and swiftly dispatched 1,700 men by steamboat to Boonville. There he debarked at once and began to beat the woods for the enemy. He had not advanced two miles before he found them. The contest was sharp and brief. Two men were killed and nine wounded, on either side; the Federals captured sixty prisoners and Marmaduke's two six-pounders; and the rest of Marmaduke's men fled. Most of them followed Governor Jackson to the southwest, where a junction of all Missouri forces eventually took place, but Lyon had achieved, at least temporarily, one of his two objectives: he had thrown the state forces back into the southwest or "poor white" section of Missouri.

This trifling engagement at Boonville has an historical importance out of all proportion to the numbers involved. As Governor Jackson had known that it would, defeat in this section of the state opened the Missouri River to the Federals all the way from St. Louis to Lexington. Price was in Lexington, but he could not stay there; the river at his door was a broad military highway over which Lyon could move 10,000 men by steamboat without the slightest interference.

News of the defeat reached Price the day after his arrival at Lexington, and realizing that he had no time to equip and organize a force of State Guards, he broke camp and marched toward the Arkansas border with 1,700 volunteers who had come in from the river counties. Overnight he evolved a new plan for the defense of Missouri. First, he would pick a location in southwestern Missouri at which volunteers from the four corners of the state could rendezvous, and there organize his army; second, he would go posthaste to General McCulloch and appeal for the immediate aid of Confederate troops. With 10,000 or 15,000 men he would fight his way back to St. Louis, via Lexington and the Missouri River Valley.

For the rendezvous of the state troops he picked Lamar, in Barton County, and it was to Lamar that Governor Jackson and his militia were soon marching, joined by thousands of others en route.

If Lyon had been in a position to follow up his victory after Boonville, he might have caught up with Jackson, Parsons, and the rest. But Lyon was suffering from a condition which frequently afflicts the winners of too sudden, too easy victories. He was disorganized by the headlong rush of events which had placed him in undisputed mastery of the situation. Caution was indicated, although Lyon was not a cautious man. If he followed the enemy at once, he would endanger communications with his rear, in a country full of Southern sympathizers; to secure these communications (with St. Louis via Jefferson City and the Missouri River) he would have to leave a substantial portion of his force behind him to keep the lines open, and when he caught up with the enemy, he might find him concentrated in strong force, probably augmented by a Confederate army from Arkansas. He was also being plagued by lack of transportation and by continued heavy rains. As a stopgap, he ordered Captain Samuel D. Sturgis and his Kansas Dragoons, over in Jackson County, to pursue Governor Jackson, and added, "I will follow with all the speed I can." [4] He also ordered Colonels Sigel, Salomon, and Benjamin Gratz Brown toward Springfield with their regiments.

Jo Shelby missed the first battle of the war in Missouri at Boonville, although his State Guards cavalry company had been organized for some weeks. That company, composed of forty-three veterans of the border forays, was known as the Lafayette County Cavalry (pronounced La-*fay*-ette in Missouri) and it was mounted and equipped at Shelby's expense. But in May, when the Camp Jackson affair occurred, Betty Shelby was pregnant with her second baby. So fragile and delicate she was that it seemed hardly possible that she had already been a mother at nineteen, and an anxious Jo was guarding her every footstep.[5] For the time being, the cavalry company and the war in Missouri could wait.

In June Betsy Shelby gave birth to a fine, healthy boy baby, whom they named Joseph Boswell Shelby for the good physician of Lexington. As soon as Shelby had assured himself that all was well with both of them, he rode off with Billy Hunter to join the Lafayette County Cavalry at Independence. Dick Collins and the others had preceded him, for there had been a rumor that Sturgis was about to attack the town with his Kansas Dragoons.

The anticipated attack on Independence failed to materialize, because Sturgis had been ordered south. At Independence Shelby found his own marching orders from Major General Sterling Price, and the Lafayette County Cavalry trotted off toward Lamar. It was the first of many a hundred such jaunts in the saddle for Shelby and his men.

At Lamar Shelby was attached to the Second Division of the Missouri State Guards under the command of Brigadier General James S. Rains. Two other militia units also marched in at Lamar, those of John B. Clark and William Y. Slack, to join the veterans of Boonville under General Parsons and Governor Claiborne Jackson. In the absence of Price, who was at McCulloch's camp, Jackson as chief executive of the state assumed command of the new army.

At the moment, the Federal commander nearest to Jackson was Sturgis. By a series of forced marches Jackson managed to elude Sturgis and slip across the Osage, building rafts to do so, without the loss of a horse or a man. To have outwitted the detested Kansans raised the spirits of Jackson's men considerably, and they marched in fine fettle, ready for a fight, especially since they expected to be joined soon by Confederate troops.

United at Lamar, the Patriot Army of Missouri, as it was called, numbered 3,600 men, 500 of whom, however, were totally without weapons. R. S. Bevier in his *History of the First and Second Missouri Confederate Brigades* says that the Patriot Army was "a heterogeneous mixture of all human compounds, and represented every condition of Western life. There were the old and the young, the rich and the poor, the high and the low, the grave and the gay, the planter and laborer, the farmer and clerk, the hunter and boatman, the merchant and woodsman. At least five hundred of these were entirely unarmed. Many had only the common rifle and shotgun. None were provided with cartridges or canteens (as a result of which they were suffering badly from thirst when they went into the battle of Carthage). They had eight pieces of cannon, but no shells, and very few solid shot or rounds of grape and canister. Rude and almost incredible devices were made to supply these wants: trace chains, iron rods, hard pebbles and smooth stones were substituted for shot; and the evidence of the effect of such rough missiles was to be given in the next encounter with the enemy." [6] One of their eight cannon, a brass relic of the Mexican War known as "Old Sacramento," was drawn by a team of oxen for want of horses.

At nightfall on the Fourth of July, about fifteen miles from Carthage, the Missourians made camp, and Governor Jackson and his commanders, knowing that the enemy could not be far off, went into a conference over their maps which lasted until one o'clock in the morning. At that ghostly hour Rains, under whom Shelby was serving, was ordered to awaken his men at daybreak and lead the march of the troops in the direction of Carthage, where Sigel was expected. Parsons was to lead the extreme left, with Slack and Clark in the center and on the right. Thus the Missouri Patriot Army moved in the shape of a phalanx rather than a column.

When the march began, in the clear dawn of a summer day, Shelby was sent ahead to scout the road, and about seven o'clock, after the army had advanced five miles, he caught sight of blue troopers ahead —some of Franz Sigel's "Dutch." Sigel was later to become a famous corps commander for the Union, and a statue would be raised to him in New York, but on this July day he had not yet learned the important lesson which every Federal general sooner or later had to learn, and which Shelby was to teach him at Carthage: namely, that the rebel cavalry, even when they looked like unsoldierly backwoodsmen, were slippery fellows and not to be trusted.

Sigel's main camp was three miles in the rear of the timbered slope on which Shelby could now see the uniforms of the Federals as thick as blueberries in summer. The slope led down to a stream which flowed in a miniature canyon between the two ridges of the plain. To the right, and on the near side of the creek—known as Dry Fork Creek—the timber had been cleared, and a waving cornfield had taken its place.

As soon as his scouts reported the enemy, Jackson halted to draw up his line of battle on a high plateau on the north side of the creek, on which his artillery would command the approaches. Here at Carthage the normal position of contending Civil War forces was reversed, for the Missouri state militia was headed south, in the direction of Arkansas and McCulloch, while Sigel had advanced through Carthage and was facing north.

Sigel's men could see Shelby as well as he could see them, and in no time Sigel's spyglass was sweeping Governor Jackson's battalions, which resembled a worm fence as they struggled into line. Sigel says in his report, "After crossing Dry Fork Creek six miles beyond Carthage, and advancing three miles farther, we found the enemy in line of battle on an elevated ground, gradually rising from the creek, and about one and a half miles distant. Their first line was formed in three regiments, deployed in line, and with proper intervals between them. Two regiments forming the wings consisted of cavalry, the center of infantry, cavalry and two pieces of artillery. The other pieces were posted on the right and one on the left wing. The whole force within our sight must have numbered 3,500 men, with a strong reserve in the rear." [7] The strong reserve in the rear of course was the 500 unarmed volunteers who were waiting to pick up the muskets of the wounded and slain.

While Jackson's commanders were forming their line, Rains went forward to reconnoitre. At a distance of a quarter of a mile from the plateau, he says in his report, he "perceived that the enemy were descending a slope towards a creek skirted on both sides with timber." Whereupon, he says, "I sent orders to Captain Shelby, who was in the advance, to halt and detain the whole command out of view, hoping the enemy would cross the creek when I could oblige them to take a position in the bottom, while I drew up my force on the heights commanding it. My expectations were realized, and after the enemy had crossed the creek I ordered Captain Shelby forward to check their advance." [8]

Thus Jo Shelby received his baptism of fire in the Civil War at half past seven o'clock of a humid summer morning on the fifth of July,

1861, at the hands of the "hired Hessians" of Sigel's artillery. We do not know the name of the sergeant who is supposed to have shot down Jeb Stuart at Yellow Tavern, but we know the name of the captain who missed his opportunity to shoot down Jo Shelby at Carthage as he and his Lafayette County neighbors galloped recklessly in a feint against Sigel's guns that morning. He was Captain Christian Essig, commanding a three-gun battery in support of the Third U. S. Infantry Regiment, Missouri Volunteers, and he is mentioned only this once in all the hundred and twenty-eight volumes of the Official Records of the War of the Rebellion.

When he saw the rebel horsemen, Essig's guns opened up furiously and briefly, throwing spherical case shot in their direction which hit nobody; but Shelby's sortie had the immediate effect of diverting the Federal fire while the Southerners unlimbered their batteries on the hill.

Shelby having accomplished his mission on the left—the Southern left, of course—Rains ordered him back to the main line, and the movement, Rains says in his report, "conducted in the face of both armies, was executed with the precision of the parade ground." [9] It was the kind of bold and heroic gesture that Shelby loved, and he made the most of it.

Rains had called Shelby back, however, only to give him another assignment on the right flank, "to reconnoitre the timber and examine for a crossing." For this task more men were required, and Rains now gave him a cavalry force three times greater than his rank entitled him to [10] and sent him thundering off in the direction of a cornfield to the right. The roar of the guns on both sides rang in Shelby's ears as he rode.

Sigel, meanwhile, had thrown his line forward, at the same time firing on the Missouri State Guards with all seven of his field pieces; but the State Guards' artillery, from its advantageous position on the plateau, swept, with a murderous mixture of grape, canister, scrap iron, and rocks, the slope on which Sigel's skirmishers advanced. Parson's guns, on the left, got into action first, but the greatest damage was done by Captain Hiram Bledsoe and "Old Sacramento" in the center. Bledsoe, with this museum piece, under the direction of Colonel Richard H. Weightman, "opened a steady and well directed fire into the densest of the enemy's masses, forcing them to take refuge in the depression of prairie and finally to retire some 200 yards." [11]

With the enemy falling back, Weightman's brigade now surged forward toward Dry Fork Creek—artillery, oxen, riflemen, camp followers, and all. The vanguard reached a point 400 yards from Sigel's troops on the near side of the creek (he had held a force in reserve on the other side to protect his wagons), waited for the artillery to line up, and then attacked. At close quarters the Missourians' lack of professional combat weapons told on them heavily, and twice they were driven back, "amidst," says Sigel, "the triumphant shouts of the United States volunteers."

Shelby's cavalry, however, had snatched the victory at Carthage from Sigel's grasp. Running the gauntlet of Federal guns on his right, Shelby had drawn such a heavy fire that their commander, a Captain Wilkins, had exhausted all of his amunition in a vain effort to halt him; with no case shot singing in his ears, Shelby and his 150 riflemen had plunged through the cornfield, kicked over a fence rail which separated it from uncultivated land in the bottom, and breached an opening big enough for all of Rains's cavalry to pour through. Sigel now had rebel horsemen on his flanks and in his rear, between his guns and his ammunition train, and he was encircled by a numerically larger force. Through the cornfield and across the creek he could see Rains and his entire brigade streaming, and far to his own right, he could see other rebel horsemen advancing on the opposite flank. There seemed no end to them. Sigel no longer cared what his advance was doing. He gave the order to retreat everywhere, and he admits in his official report that he did so to avert irretrievable disaster. "To advance without the assistance of the artillery seemed to me a movement which could easily turn into a *déroute*," he says. "No time could be lost. One part of our troops on the extreme right and left were already engaged with the mounted troops. ... The moral effect of the enemy's regiments behind our lines, *although the real danger was not great,* could not be denied. To lose our whole baggage was another consideration of importance. It was, therefore, with great mortification that I ordered one part of the troops behind Dry Fork Creek. ... Meanwhile the two large bodies of cavalry had completely surrounded us and had formed into line against our rear."

Fighting now for an escape route rather than victory, Sigel's troops fell back from Dry Fork Creek as fast as they could in the direction of Carthage. As long as they were moving in the right direction, the Missourians permitted them to do so, and Sigel's force gained the heights crowning the north side of Carthage, before Spring River, without molestation. At Carthage, Sigel says, "our rear guard took possession of the town," which is an euphemism for retreating into the town; but he soon found that he could not stop and rest in front of Carthage.

"The enemy," he says, "taking advantage of their cavalry, forded Spring River at different points, spread through the woods, and partly dismounted, harassed our troops from all sides." This was one of Shelby's favorite stratagems during the war, dismounting light cavalry and using them as dragoons whenever he thought they could serve better on foot.

Fearing that the encircling movement of the rebels might cut off his communications with Springfield, Sigel made no attempt to fight at Carthage, but ordered the retreat to continue to Sarcoxie, from which he had set out two days before—a distance, in all, of twenty-five miles. Shelby and the cavalry followed him two and a half miles on the Sarcoxie road, and then desisted, as night came on, well content. Raw, inexperienced amateurs of war, they had met the enemy, a highly trained, superbly equipped enemy, in force equal to their own, and they had chased him twenty-five miles between daylight and dusk. Enough work for one day, surely, and enough glory.

To Brigadier General James S. Rains must go the credit for being the first officer in the war to realize that Jo Shelby, although he never had an hour's military instruction in his life, was a born cavalry commander, who could use the whiplash of the mounted arm to confuse, rout, and defeat a well-armed body of trained professional soldiers whose numerical strength was greater than his own. There were 1,500 cavalry in the Missouri Patriot Army, commanded by officers who outranked Shelby; yet Rains picked Captain Shelby from them all. In doing so he was undoubtedly acting on the advice of Governor Jackson, who well knew what manner of man Jo Shelby was.

As a cavalry action, Carthage ranks with some of the important engagements of the war. It was a decisive engagement in that it permitted Price and McCulloch to join forces and go on to victory at Wilson's Creek, which, in turn, enabled Price to stay in Missouri for another full year. Thus Carthage, like Boonville, had a significance out of proportion to the number of troops engaged. There were only forty-four killed on the Southern side and thirteen on the Federal;

it was not much more than a skirmish on a grand scale, but brilliantly conceived and executed for all that. It was a baptism of fire for Jo Shelby as a cavalry commander, and he acquitted himself as brilliantly on his first day of battle as he would on his last. Shelby's genius was not of the kind that needs maturity to ripen. It was born full blown on the field of Carthage.

Eventually, when the facts of Carthage became known, and the subsequent facts of Wilson's Creek, Sigel suffered much humiliation at the hands of his superiors in the Department of the West;[12] but for the immediate present, he was commended for "brilliant service" by Lyon, who accepted at face value Sigel's report that he had escaped from a trap set for him by a vastly superior force and had conducted a masterly retreat.[13]

8. Wilson's Creek: The Face of War

THE DAY AFTER their first battle at Carthage, the dusty ranks of the Missouri State Guards were drawn up on the prairie outside the town to receive a party of welcome visitors: General Sterling Price, "Old Pap" to his Missourians; Generals Ben McCulloch and N. B. Pearce of Arkansas,[1] with their gaily dressed staffs; 3,000 cavalry of the Confederate States Provisional Army, smartly attired in handsome new gray uniforms, and 1,200 Arkansas militia. The troops of Mc-Culloch and Pearce, every whit as military and as well armed as the Federal troops under Lyon and Sigel at Springfield, marched under a flag never seen before on a Missouri battlefield, the Stars and Bars of the new Southern Confederacy.

As Price, McCulloch, Pearce, and Governor Jackson rode down the ranks in review, the Missourians cheered mightily. Thomas L. Snead, Price's aide-de-camp and acting adjutant general of the Missouri State Guards, wrote in his *Fight for Missouri*, "We were all young then, and full of hope, and we looked with delighted eyes on the first Confederate soldiers that we had ever seen, the men all dressed in sober gray, and their officers resplendent with gilded buttons, and golden braid and stars of gold. To look like these gallant soldiers, to be of them, to fight beside them for their homes and our own, was the one desire of all Missourians who, on that summer day, stood on one of their own verdant prairies, gazing southward." [2]

The Confederate troops were in high spirits, too. The day before, outside of Neosho, within the sound of the guns at Carthage, McCulloch's Arkansas Rangers under Colonel Churchill and Major McIntosh had fallen on a rifle company of U. S. Missouri Volunteers, under the command of a Captain Conrad, and had captured 137 prisoners, 150 stands of arms, and seven wagons laden with supplies.

The Confederates were splendidly armed and equipped, but Price's Patriot Army of Missouri was in an even worse condition than it had been when it started out. General McCulloch, in fact, was appalled at the thought of facing the trained troops of Lyon and Sigel with such a mob, and he made no bones about it to Sterling Price. He was also in favor of sending home those who did not have arms, because they were simply extra mouths to feed in a country where there was nothing to forage except green corn. Volunteers, too, were streaming in from all directions, as news of the rebel victory at Carthage spread, and these but added to the problem, since most of them brought with them nothing but their enthusiasm.

Price told McCulloch that if he could have a few days to gather supplies and set up an armory and forge for manufacturing ammunition, he believed that adequate weapons could be placed in the hands of the men. McCulloch assented and let the Missourians have 615 fine new rifles, although Price could have used three times as many. Then Price marched away to Cowskin Prairie, a bivouac he had selected for its proximity to the lead mines at Granby. The Confederate States Provisional troops quartered themselves at Maysville, where their uniforms were admired by the young girls even more extravagantly than they had been by the Missouri troops.

Price's task at Cowskin Prairie was made the more difficult by the fact that he had no military stores of any kind and no money with which to procure them, even if they had been procurable. He sent quartermaster officers to Little Rock and Fort Smith, the nearest Confederate supply centers, but these officers, traveling as far as Memphis in their search for supplies, did not get back until after the Battle of Wilson's Creek had been fought.

Nevertheless, Price was fortunate in having as ordnance officer Major Thomas H. Price (apparently no relation to him) who was suited admirably for the job. Major Price was surrounded by men who had been handling rifles and shotguns since boyhood and who were adept at improvising ammunition. Lead, thanks to the near-by mines, was plentiful. There was also an abundant supply of powder, the one commodity which Governor Jackson had been able to acquire in quantity, and in the forests on the edge of Cowskin Prairie stood tall trees whose wood could be used to make buckshot and bullet molds. Of such homely materials were fashioned the rifle balls which won the Battle of Wilson's Creek. The arsenal hummed with activity day and night. When it was too dark to see, says an officer of Guibor's battery, "a bayonet made a good candlestick, and at night the men went to work making cartridges, strapping shots to the sabots, and filling the bags from a barrel of powder placed at some distance from the candle.... We soon learned the trick and at the close range at which our next battle was fought, our home-made ammunition proved as effective as the best." [3] Major Price's artillery ammunition was molded on the pattern of round shot taken from Sigel's captured wagons.

By the end of July the effective strength of the State Guards had tripled, with volunteers flocking to Cowskin Prairie, and when the Patriot Army was ready to take the field again, Price had 5,000 men under arms and 2,000 camp followers ready to rush into battle and pick up the muskets of the fallen. Morale continued high, too, for now the word flew about that other Confederate armies besides McCulloch's would soon be on the march into Missouri. Governor Jackson had gone to Memphis on July 12 to persuade General Leonidas Polk, who had authority over Confederate troops west of the river, to send an "Army of Liberation" into the state. Polk needed no persuasion that Missouri was the key to control of the Mississippi Valley and the whole vast region of the Confederate Southwest. In this he displayed a vision lacking completely in the commanders who succeeded him. He did not offer niggardly help. He ordered General Pillow to take 6,000 men from various divisions of the Western District of Tennessee and move into Missouri by way of New Madrid; there he would be reinforced by Arkansas troops under General Jeff Thompson, bringing the expedition to a calculated force of 11,000 men. These men would march at once to Pocahontas, Arkansas, where General Hardee, he of "Hardee's Tactics," would meet them with another 7,000 Provisional Army troops. This Army of Liberation would then sweep through the whole of Missouri and recapture St. Louis. It was a magnificent plan—on paper.

The plan died aborning. Pillow did actually occupy New Madrid, but Hardee just plainly refused to move. He insisted that his men were "badly organized, badly equipped, and wanting in discipline and instruction. One of my batteries has no harness and no horses, and not one of the regiments has transportation enough for active field service." [4] This description would have applied to any Confederate army in the field at any time, but Hardee announced that he would not move "with less than 5,000 men, well appointed, with a full complement of artillery." As Adjutant General Snead says sourly, Hardee "had not yet emancipated himself from the tyranny of axioms which did not apply in the circumstances wherein he was called to act." [5] Yet the Arkansas government was at this very moment—the first week in August—pressing troops on Hardee for the Army of Liberation, which he refused on the ground that he did not have the authority to accept state troops into the Confederate army! The offer was for seven regiments, [6] which would have given him the 5,000 he said he needed. Thompson had 1,400 men, which were never ordered to join McCulloch, and Pillow simply sat idle in New Madrid. [7]

None of this was foreseen at Cowskin Prairie, however, and Price was jubilant over the Army of Liberation. He issued a boastful proclamation announcing that he would not only retake Missouri, but invade Illinois as well; and the anvils rang with a new fury at Cowskin Prairie.

This form of activity had no appeal for Captain Shelby. He was never content to remain in camp for even a day, and now he persuaded Sterling Price that he should be sent on a recruiting mission to the Missouri River Valley, and to Lafayette County in particular. A state convention had met on July 22 at Jefferson City and had set up a Union government of Missouri, with Hamilton R. Gamble as governor. That government would wield the power of the state, insofar as it could, against the South. The time was ripe, Shelby argued, to give to the cut-off Southern sympathizers in the Missouri River Valley an opportunity to flock to the Banner of the Bars, now that the issue of civil war was clearly drawn.

Price gave his assent despite the fact that Shelby's proposed jaunt had all the aspects of a suicide mission. His little company of Lafayette

County Cavalry, now brought up to full strength of 100 men, would have to by-pass the Federal army at Springfield—5,000 strong, at least —penetrate 120 miles into the Federal rear, in order to reach the Missouri River Valley, and recruit for the rebels in a countryside in which the Union Home Guards, with their beer steins and their *lieder*, were present in force at every crossroads village and tavern. He would be six counties north of Price's army, with the enemy between, and four or five days' march in the rear of Sigel and Lyon. Furthermore, Lafayette County, whither he was going, was a garrison center of Federal troops in the area: Lieutenant Colonel White, at Lexington, alone had a force several times the size of Shelby's. Nevertheless, in late July Shelby rode off from Cowskin Prairie with his company and galloped home to Waverly through the Federal lines as nonchalantly as if there were not a blue coat in all Missouri. It was the first of the raids deep into enemy territory which were to make him famous.

As a recruiting mission, Shelby's first dash into Lafayette County was not a success. Major Edwards, in his history of the Confederate campaigns in the West, says, "There was but little rest to the soldiers and small opportunity for recruiting." But he did see Betty Shelby, and having a hundred well armed men with him, he was able to keep the country in "a turmoil and a commotion." By the time he reached Waverly, his hundred horsemen had been magnified in rumor, says Edwards, to two thousand, three thousand men. The cottonwoods at St. Thomas's Wharf at Waverly also got credit for masking "vast and wonderful batteries," overlooking the Missouri, and at least one vicious-looking siege gun could be seen poking its nose along the top of the brush like a water moccasin lying in a creek bed.

This was a wooden gun, painted black,[8] but it was formidable enough in appearance to halt a Missouri River steamboat, the *Sunshine*, sailing along as gaily and brightly as her name. The *Sunshine* was the first of steamboats which Shelby captured during the war,[9] and he had the pleasure of confiscating a hundred army wagons and fifteen hundred sacks of flour destined for the Federals at Leavenworth, Kansas. The wagons had to be abandoned, but there was plenty of free flour in Waverly that afternoon—for white and colored—and when the day's work was done Shelby tied his horse to his own hitching post and had supper with his family.

The terror had not yet struck in Waverly. The Kansas Redlegs, the cutthroats and bushwhackers from over the border would come later, and they would burn Shelby's mansion, his ropewalk, and other property suspected of being his—eventually; but just now, with summer golden on the river and over the peaceful prairie, neither Jo nor Betty was seriously alarmed over the fact that he had to be away from home with the army for a while. He would even take Billy Hunter with him; there were a lot of other stalwart and loyal Shelby Negroes on the place, and Waverly and Lafayette County were true blue to the Southern cause. In a matter of weeks, the Army of Liberation would reoccupy the Missouri River Valley. The war, in fact, seemed about over, back east in Virginia; the entire Union army had been demolished in front of Washington at Manassas Junction and it remained only for the Southern armies to occupy the Lincoln capital and enforce the independence of the Southern Confederacy. Missouri would soon be another star in the new flag, and real peace would come to the Missouri River Valley, for the first time since the settlement of Kansas.

For another week after the capture of the *Sunshine*, Shelby galloped about Lafayette County, making recruiting speeches and exasperating Lieutenant Colonel White. On August 5 Governor Jackson issued a manifesto declaring Missouri an independent Republic. By August 8 Shelby and his men were back with Brigadier General Rains's division of Price's army, marching with the advance toward Springfield in the neighborhood of Wilson's Creek. It is hilly country, scrub-timbered, with cleared patches for corn and a postoffice in the little town of Ozark. Here one of the bloodiest engagements of the war was to be fought—almost as bloody as Bull Run.[10] Many who have heard of the Bloody Lane at Antietam have never heard of Bloody Hill at Wilson's Creek—but it was saturated with the blood of twenty-five hundred Americans before the sun went down. Rains's men bore the brunt of it, and Shelby's Lafayette Cavalry, dismounted at the last and fighting savagely in the brush, wrote their names in the record with all the rest.

They had been living the life of holiday soldiers with little real experience of combat. At Carthage the Yankees had run, as the Southerners had confidently predicted they would, scattered by the gallant mounts of the chivalry. In Lafayette County the amateur cavalry gentlemen had amused themselves by confounding the slow-witted Dutch with wooden cannon and clouds of dust; it was campaigning after their own hearts, and the lordly young planters of Shelby's company had enjoyed it thoroughly. At Wilson's Creek they had a rude awakening to reality. At Wilson's Creek, for the first time, they saw the face of war—close up, in all its hideousness. Wilson's Creek was the Bull Run of the West, and its analogy to the first great battle in Virginia is remarkable.

In both cases the battle was the first conflict on a vast scale in its particular theatre of war; in both cases the Southern troops were panicked into flight in the opening phases of the battle; in both cases they rallied to smash the enemy and hurl him back into the tight ring of defenses of his capital; and in both cases they were so exhausted by the victory that they could not follow it up. In Virginia the Confederates lost the opportunity to march on Washington after Bull Run and perhaps end the war by dictating peace terms from the capital; in Missouri they failed to pursue the defeated enemy after Wilson's Creek and retake the Missouri River Valley, which would have brought Missouri into the orbit of the Confederacy, gained control of the vital upper Mississippi, and perhaps saved the heartland of the South from invasion.

Both Bull Run and Wilson's Creek demonstrated the fatal military weakness of the new Southern nation: its inability to make its victories count.

Before sunrise on the morning of August 10, 1861—the day was coming on bright and clear despite the rain of the night before—three young children were riding horses out to pasture near their home on Wilson's Creek, near Ozark, when a mounted stranger rode up to them rapidly and shouted, "Children, get out of here! They'll be fighting like hell in ten minutes." [11] The three children, a little girl of six named Lavonia Ray, and her two older brothers, whose father was postmaster of Ozark, raced back to their homes and told their parents what the man on horseback had said.

Mrs. Ray rounded up all the children on the place, both white and black, and herded them with the grownups into the cellar, but she could not persuade her husband to retreat. He was sitting on the front porch, holding the baby.

"Roxanna, don't be alarmed," he said. "Some fellows told the children that story to frighten them." Mrs. Ray did not argue, but rescued the baby from his lap and joined the rest of the family in the cellar. Hardly had Postmaster Ray finished speaking when he saw a black line moving in the distance, and he recognized it as an army of marching men. Still Postmaster Ray remained where he was. He had a front seat at the Battle of Wilson's Creek, and he did not intend to give it up.

The column of marching men was the vanguard of Brigadier General Nathaniel Lyon's army from Springfield, up early in the morning to take the Confederates by surprise at Wilson's Creek. In the forefront of the line were the First Missouri Volunteers, St. Louis troops, in which Captain Cary Gratz was commander of Company E, Second Infantry, Steele's Battalion.[12]

As Captain Gratz marched with Lyon down the Cassville Road at the head of his men, Captain Jo Shelby was pulling on his boots outside his tent in the camp of General Rains, which was situated in a rocky hollow in the forks of Wilson's Creek and Skaggs's Branch. Somewhere about was Billy Hunter, roasting green corn and frying fresh-killed beef for breakfast. The militiamen of the Second Division, Missouri State Guards, those that were not still asleep, were washing in the branch or preparing their own morning meal, unaware that there was an enemy closer than Springfield. Near by, the twelve hundred horses of Rains's "huckleberry cavalry" chuffed and snorted and shook their heads. There was not half a mile's distance between Captain Cary Gratz and Captain Jo Shelby when Lyon struck at Wilson's Creek. It is possible that Shelby saw the face of his stepbrother and cousin amid the smoke that rolled across the field that morning, without recognizing it. Whether he did or not will never be known; but undoubtedly he saw it afterward on the battlefield, stilled in death.[13]

The Ray children had far more notice of the beginning of the Battle of Wilson's Creek that the Missourians and Confederates under Price and McCulloch, according to bitter complaints which McCulloch made later in an official report.[14] For reasons which he was not able to discover, McCulloch says, Rains, though in the advance and charged with the duty of reconnaissance, withdrew his pickets about nine o'clock the night before, so that he was without intelligence as to the movements of the enemy on the Springfield road ahead of him until the blue uniforms were actually in sight the next morning.

McCulloch had intended to march on Springfield the night before and attack at daybreak, but he canceled the order at nine o'clock when a light rain began to fall. Most of the men were carrying their cartridges in cotton bags, and McCulloch could not risk their being ruined by damp weather on the march. He gave orders for the men to remain in their tents at Wilson's Creek on the night of the tenth and keep their powder dry. It was his plan to march early next day, if the weather cleared, and attack Springfield at once, in broad daylight.[15]

When the troops heard this, the Missourians became so jubilant that they staged a celebration around their campfires, Missouri style, with fiddles, jugs, songs, and dancing. To Shelby and his young dandies, just back from Lafayette County, it was reminiscent of the old days on the Kansas border. The militiamen were in high spirits because now they would have a chance to show the Louisiana, Texas, and Arkansas troops what they would do to Lyon, Sigel, and the Dutch. For days now they had been smarting under the jibes of their allies at their unmilitary appearance. Even though they did not fall in to the notes of a bugle, at company formation, merely answering a hail from their officers, whom they frequently addressed as "Jedge," and even though they had no regulation uniforms or Maynard rifles, like the troops from the bayou country, they had been fired by the stories of Bull Run, where undisciplined troops had made the Yankees scamper, and they proposed to do the same thing in the morning.

At Springfield Nathaniel Lyon had been as worried about his own inferior numerical strength and his supply situation as McCulloch was over the inexperience, want of equipment, and mule-headedness of his Missouri allies. Lyon knew that Price and McCulloch outnumbered him two to one; he had never heard of Captain Shelby, of course, but he knew that Sigel had been belted dizzy at Carthage by these same forces in front of him, in spite of Sigel's superiority in troops, guns, and ammunition; and he fully expected McCulloch to be reinforced by Hardee and Pillow, at any time, thus tipping the scales against him with a vengeance. He wrote to Frémont: "He [the enemy] has taken a strong position, and is recruiting his supply of horses, mules, and provisions by forays into the surrounding country, his large force of mounted men enabling him to do this without any annoyance from me. I find my position extremely embarrassing and at present am unable to determine whether I shall be able to maintain my ground or be forced to retire."[16]

But Lyon was one of the ablest soldiers ever to wear an American uniform, and one of the most fearless. In the circumstances, he had determined to fight, on the theory that an offense was the best defense; just as McCulloch was deciding to fight for much the same reason.

Thus, with trepidation, both Federal and Confederate commanders approached the battle of Wilson's Creek.

Having decided to attack, Lyon had summoned Sigel and told him of his decision.[17] The movement outlined was to be an encircling one. The Federal forces would be divided into two columns. Lyon himself with 4,200 men and ten pieces of artillery, would attack on the Confederate left, at Gibson's Mill, below which General Rains and the advance guard of the Southern army were known to be encamped. Sigel, with 1,250 men, would move to the east, sweep around the main Confederate encampment, and attack on the right and in the rear. It would be a risky venture, and would depend upon the element of surprise for success. But if all went well, they would squeeze Price and McCulloch like an accordion.

Lyon left Springfield the next afternoon at five o'clock, Sigel at half past six. Marching slowly, and averaging no more than a mile an hour, Lyon arrived at one o'clock in the morning within sight of the guard fires of Rains's outposts at Gibson's Mill. Waiting for daybreak, his troops slept on their arms on the wet ground.

Sigel, meanwhile, carried out his part of the advance according to plan. His column reached the eastern flank of the Southern encampment at daybreak, just as some of McBride's Missourians were going down to the creek for water. He captured forty prisoners, but did it so quietly that he did not disturb the rest of the camp,[18] and in plain sight of the militia tents he planted four pieces of artillery on a hill, just north of the point where the Fayetteville Road crosses Wilson's Creek. He had turned the Confederate right as completely as Lyon had turned the Confederate left. It was now long past daybreak, and until the first shots were fired neither Price nor McCulloch, who was at Price's headquarters in the center, had any cause to suspect that Lyon had even left Springfield.[19]

At the other end of the pincers movement, the redbearded Lyon, on the iron-gray horse which had been a familiar sight in the streets of Springfield, rode through the thickets on the other side of a ridge from Rains's camp, making his dispositions. This was the ridge of Bloody Hill, and he ordered Captain James Totten, his battery commander, to place his guns atop the ridge, to cover the advance of the infantry. Dubois's battery he held in the rear, to cover a possible flank attack by McCulloch's and Hebert's Confederates, who were on the other side of the creek. The outposts at Gibson's Mill, half a mile behind Lyon, had already been driven in; but the sound of the shots had not aroused Rains's camp. In these hills and ravines, sound did not travel far.

But first, as a shield against McCulloch, Lyon sent the First U. S. Infantry, regular troops under Captain Plummer, across the creek, along with a battalion of German Home Guards. He instructed Plummer to prevent, at all costs, the Confederates on the other side of the creek—Hebert's Louisianans, together with some Texas and Arkansas troops—from recrossing the creek and coming to the aid of Rains. Lyon had Rains in a pocket, and he hoped to keep him there.

For the direct assault on Rains's camp he picked the First Missouri Volunteers (holding back two companies, including that of Cary Gratz, to support Dubois) and the First Kansas. The First Kansas today would suffer a heavier loss than any other regiment in the Civil War in a single engagement, with the exception of the First Maine and the Eighth New York Artillery at Cold Harbor—losing 284 men of 600. The Second Kansas Lyon also held in reserve, along with the First Iowa, state militia wearing resplendent gray uniforms which were to cause a great deal of misunderstanding during the battle. The assault troops were to pick their way through the scrub oak thicket, down the slope of the hill leading to Rains's camp, and on either side of a deep ravine.

Lyon gave the signal, the hands of the farm lads from Missouri and Kansas tightened on their rifles, and they plunged silently into the brush, slipping and sliding on the rocky shale of the hillside as they went. Over their heads and across the ravine which separated them, Totten sent a shell screaming, followed by several more in quick succession. That burst of artillery was the opening gun of the Battle of Wilson's Creek.

The pandemonium in Rains's camp as the shells whistled in is described by Colonel James A. Pritchard, who led the first rally of Rains's men, in these words: "We were surprised and aroused from our tents by a discharge of grape and cannon ball from the enemy's batteries, planted on the hills around us. Our situation was in the forks and upon both sides of two creeks with high points all around us. In fact, if the enemy had picked the ground for us, they could not have suited themselves better. We were almost completely surrounded before we knew it ... while we were yet sleeping." [20]

Although they were caught out of reach of their weapons, Pritchard was able to assemble part of his battalion (which contradicts his statement that all were sleeping) and he had the honor of attempting the first counterattack at Bloody Hill. It was a gallant but feeble effort; the panic in Rains's camp was complete. Colonel Snead, coming up with Price's forces as soon as the alarm had been given, says, "Looking up, we could see a great crowd on horseback, some armed, others unarmed, mixed in with wagons and teams and led horses, all in dreadful confusion, scampering over the hill and rushing down toward us—a panic-stricken drove. In another instant, we saw the flash and heard the report of Totten's guns ... not more than one thousand yards away, throwing shot into the flying crowd. And then, in quick response, came the sound of Sigel's guns, as they opened upon Churchill, Greer, Major and Brown (in McBride's sector) and drove them in confusion out of the valley in which they were encamped and into the thick woods that fringed the banks of Skaggs' Branch and covered the hills that rose on either side of that little stream." [21]

It was the last time Sigel's guns were heard that day.

Price, McCulloch, and the rest were fast moving their forces into battle, despite the rout in Rains's camp. McCulloch hurried to his own troops east of the creek (Wilson's Creek runs north and south) and there he found himself in the most unpleasant situation in which a commander can find himself: he had the enemy both in his front and in his rear, Plummer on the north and Sigel on the south. He was completely in the dark as to how the situation with Sigel was developing; but seeing McBride's men fleeing to the rear, he feared the worst.

The truly remarkable speed with which Price whipped his Missourians into line at Wilson's Creek undoubtedly saved the day at Bloody Hill. Private Joseph A. Mudd, of Company B of the Jackson Guards, of Clark's Division, says that "it could not have been more than twenty minutes after Totten's first cannon shot that we were moving at quick step into the line of battle. . . . The infantry of Rains was first on the field, and occupied the right of the Missouri forces. Considering our want of drill and real discipline, we got to the firing line in good shape and certainly lost not a minute in getting there. Some considerable time after the firing began McBride's men came up and completed our line on the left." [22]

When McBride's men fell into line, Clark's men laughed at their outlandish appearance. Even by the elastic standards of the Patriot Army of Missouri they were a tattérdemalion crew; but Private Mudd's own commander, General Clark, was wearing a civilian black slouch hat and overcoat over his uniform, and General Price himself, sitting his horse like a statue and watching the battle, presented an astonishing spectacle. He was wearing a linen duster and a high-crowned wool hat over his major general's uniform of gray jacket and striped, light blue pants.

There has never been, perhaps, a battle which looked exactly like the Battle of Wilson's Creek.

Price and Rains, once their men were in line, determined upon a double strategy: since their men would do their best work at short range, with the shotguns and single loaders, they would wait for the Federal infantry attack, throw it back if possible, and turn the enemy's flank on their left, with 800 of the cavalry. Captain Jo Shelby had ridden up now, along with the rest, and with as many of his Lafayette County Cavalry as he could find. Rains gave the horsemen their orders. As soon as the enemy's infantry opened fire, they were to attack on the left and in the rear of Totten, dashing up the crest of the hill to do so.

The Federal attack came soon enough, and with it began the fighting for Bloody Hill. Colonel Snead says it was so quiet along the line that "in a few minutes the word Forward! was plainly heard, and was quickly followed by the tramp of men, and by the crackling of the brush through which they were coming. When Lyon's Missourians and their allies had come within easy reach of Price's Missourians, out of the ranks of the latter there rang upon the air the sharp click of a thousand rifles, the report of a thousand shotguns, and the roar of Guibor's guns; the battle of Wilson's Creek had begun in earnest." [23]

As the shotguns roared, the cavalry made a futile dash against Bloody Hill. In his report Captain Totten describes the debacle: "The enemy tried to overwhelm us by an attack of some 800 cavalry, which had, unobserved, formed below the crests of the hills to our right and rear. Fortunately, some of our infantry companies and a few pieces of artillery from my battery were in a position to meet this demonstration, and drove off their cavalry with ease. This was the only demonstration made by their cavalry, and it was so *effete* and ineffectual as to deserve only the appellation of child's play. Their cavalry is utterly worthless on the battlefield." [24] It was, on such a battlefield as this.

The Battle of Wilson's Creek, fought as it was throughout, in a hilly jungle with shotguns, bayonets, bowie knives, horse pistols, squirrel rifles, derringers, and the like, was one of the great infantry battles of all time. In a war in which the cavalry mostly got the glory, Wilson's Creek stands as an imperishable memorial to the valor of the footsoldier. Let the cavalry dismount now, and go forward with the shotguns and the rifles, the homemade bayonets, into the brush. No room here for gallant sorties executed with the precision of the parade ground. The Missouri hemp grower, the Arkansas traveler, the Louisiana swamp trotter, and the "huckleberry cavalry" alike must win their spurs on foot today.

Jo Shelby, whose gallant horse had struggled forward with the rest, was learning his trade in a rough, sure school. At Carthage he had seen what cavalry could be made to do, and at Wilson's Creek he saw what it could not be made to do. He was also learning that a farmer on horseback is not a cavalryman, and that having cavalry without artillery is like having fingers without thumbs. From the day that he stepped into a cavalry command, he was never without his artillery, or far from it.

The repulse of the cavalry at Bloody Hill passed almost unnoticed. Drifting clouds of smoke added to the concealment of the participants, and the August sun scarcely penetrated the gloom. The line writhed back and forth like a wounded snake. The rebel yell was not heard at Wilson's Creek; both sides went about their work in deadly silence. "The lines would approach again and again within fifty yards of each other, and then, after delivering a deadly fire, each would fall back a few paces to re-form and reload only to advance again, and again, in this strange battle of the woods. Peculiar in all its aspects, strange in all its surroundings, unique in every way, the most remarkable was the deep silence which now and then rested upon the smoking field— fell upon it, and rested there undisturbed for many minutes, while the two armies, unseen of each other, lay but a few yards apart, gathering strength to grapple again in the death struggle for Missouri." [25] Buckshot is fearful at close range, and a cannon ball, when it makes a direct hit, can cut a man in two. Homemade bullets sometimes flatten out harmlessly, even against a Dutchman's shirt, but a jagged bayonet makes a terrible wound, and the jack oaks in the underbrush are red as sumac with the blood of boys from Iowa and Kansas, from the

Missouri River Valley and the Ozarks. There are shrieks from the dying, and the moans of the wounded, but those who are whole fight on, careful to make no sound. Survival is at stake today. On both sides men hunt one another like deer, and fall upon one another like dogs on a grounded possum. It is anybody's battle so far.

It is now mid-morning, and still no word from Sigel. Lyon, who is everywhere in the fight, feels a sting on the side of his face; he has been struck by flying canister, and blood streams down his cheeks. But he scorns the brandy which Totten offers him, and orders him to take his battery forward to the support of the First Missouri Volunteers, who are faltering. The First Missouri has sweated today, and there is no fault to find with them, but they must hold.

The rebels have seen the First Missouri's sign of weakness too, and somebody hoists a Secession flag, perhaps with the idea of leading a charge; but a man on horseback has a better idea. Somewhere he has got a Federal flag, and he holds it aloft as his comrades renew their butchery upon the First Missouri. For a moment, Totten is deceived (Sigel's troops are expected from that direction), but only for a moment. At the same moment Captain Cary Gratz has spotted the rebel carrying the Stars and Stripes, and a red choler of indignation rises in his handsome face. Benjamin Gratz's son breaks through the line, pistol in hand, rushes up to the enemy, and shoots down the Missourian who is carrying the flag. Before he can rescue it, he himself has fallen, caught in a crossfire of bullets. Five of them enter his body and he is dead on the instant.[26]

Something bad has happened to Sigel, Lyon knows. It is now two or three hours since his guns have been heard. That brisk cannonading a few minutes ago was McCulloch, on the other side of the creek, fighting like a demon.

Where is Sigel! It is not longer a question, but an oath.

As a matter of fact, Sigel has been routed by McCulloch and is out of the battle. He has been guilty, once again, of the incredibly bad judgment which he displayed at Carthage. A European, he knows no more of how to fight Missourians than Braddock knew of fighting Indians; but even that does not excuse him, because he has done nothing since he broke up McBride's camp at daybreak; and he has allowed McCulloch to capture his artillery and put his men to flight without firing a round of ammunition. Through his failure to support Lyon, and with his *dummkopf* conclusions, he has lost the Battle of Wilson's Creek.

The fantastic sequence of events was this: when Sigel scattered McBride, he simply sat down and waited for Lyon to drive the Southerners into his arms.[27] This gave McCulloch a chance to smash Plummer's Home Guards, unmolested, on his side of the creek, although Sigel's guns were in his rear and Sigel could have blown him into the water at any time. The enemy in front of him routed, McCulloch turned his attention to Sigel. But Sigel's Teutons, seeing the Confederate uniforms, mistook them for the First Iowa, and waved a Federal flag in welcome. As they did so, McCulloch opened on them with two batteries. "It is impossible for me," Sigel says, "to describe the consternation and frightful confusion caused by this unfortunate event."

The artillerymen could not be brought forward to serve their pieces; a galling infantry fire poured into them, and every one of their artillery horses was killed. They fled in panic, "followed and attacked incessantly by large bodies of Texas and Arkansas cavalry." Every one of Sigel's guns was captured, and all of his stores. The rout was complete, and none of his troops were seen on the battlefield again that day. McCulloch wheeled about and marched to join Price.

Back at Bloody Hill the wounded Lyon dashed once more on his iron-gray horse to the support of a faltering regiment. It was the First Iowa this time, which had already caused so much trouble today. As Lyon galloped toward the enemy, a bullet struck him squarely in the breast and just beside the heart. Like Jeb Stuart at Yellow Tavern, he toppled from his horse into the arms of an orderly, but unlike Stuart he was dead when he fell. The enemy's wave swept over them, and the orderly fled. The Southerners had not realized the identity of the pocket-sized redhead on the gray horse; his body was identified afterward only by papers in his pockets.

With Sigel out of it, Lyon dead, and all of the Missouri and Confederate forces massed against Sturgis, who had succeeded Lyon, there could be but one outcome. About half past midday, after the fight had raged for more than seven hours, Sturgis gave the order for a general retreat, so that the sun went down with victory for the Southerners on the battlefield of Wilson's Creek. They did not call it by that name. They called it the Battle of Oak Hills, just as Bull Run, in the South, was known as First Manassas.

Postmaster Ray, still sitting on his porch, was impressed into service by the Confederates to help guard prisoners, when the last of the enemy had vanished. As soon as the body of Lyon was identified, it was taken to the Ray home, where the family had emerged from the cellar. There it was placed upon a bed and covered with a counterpane.

General Rains, his surgeon, Dr. Melchior, and other high-ranking officers came into the room for a look at the dead Federal commander. Rains lifted the counterpane from the white face, so pale against the red beard. As he did so, Mrs. Roxanna Ray burst into sobs.

General Rains's nerves were battle-taut, tingling with the exhilaration of victory, and perhaps with something else, for he liked his dram and the day had been a trying one. As he dropped the counterpane, he turned to his officers and said, in a tone of astonishment,

"She weeps because the roaring Lyon is dead!" [28]

9.   *A Star Added, a State Lost*

So FAR ALL the fighting had been in favor of the Southerners. Sterling Price knew that nothing succeeds like success, and although he could not persuade McCulloch to join him,[1] he determined to occupy the Missouri River Valley and raise the 50,000 men that Governor Jackson had called for. As he moved his wagon trains, loaded with Federal rifles and Sigel's captured artillery, into Springfield, he ordered Captain Shelby back to the Missouri River with instructions to "recruit, and annoy the enemy in every possible manner, and keep alive the spirit of resistance by constant and unceasing efforts." [2]

Glad to be back in the saddle, Shelby and his men rode off to Lafayette County again, while McCulloch's Confederates, their brand-new uniforms grimy and bloodstained, moved out toward the Cherokee Nation to defend the territory of a few red men who knew nothing about the white man's war except that they disliked all white men impartially.

After a hundred and twenty miles of hard riding, Shelby and his men fought victorious skirmishes with the Home Guards at Dover, six miles from Lexington, at Tabo Creek and at Salt Fork, in a series of whirlwind assaults which brought Federal Lieutenant Colonel White riding out again from Lexington in a belated attempt to assemble a single force with which to waylay him. But better men than Colonel White were to try that with Shelby, and Major Edwards says, "Baffling all operations inaugurated for his destruction, Captain Shelby thus early gave assurances of those wonderful attributes of genius, intrepidity and activity which were so eminently displayed during a later period of the struggle. Constantly in the saddle, attacking at strange and sudden hours, now cutting off the pickets and again capturing unwary foragers, his movements defied calculation and engendered the greatest fear and hatred, for then the virtues of a manly foe were scarcely appreciated."[3] Shelby was being called everything from a brigand to a guerrilla by Union officers and sympathizers, though he was at some pains to let Colonel White know differently.[4]

When his activities of the day in harassing the Federals had not carried him too far afield, Shelby slept in his own bed at Waverly and visited his neighbors freely while carrying on his recruiting activities. Waverly, the redhot rebel town, was getting ready to honor General Price with banners hung from the windows of the newspaper office[5] and the front porches of the citizens' homes.

Price, after a few weeks of drilling, recruiting, and furloughing his veterans at Springfield, moved on Lexington. The town by now was garrisoned by a force of Chicago Irish under Colonel James A. Mulligan, known inevitably as the Irish Brigade, and two regiments of Illinois and Missouri volunteers. Mulligan's total force numbered 2,780 men, and he stood very little chance alone against Price, who had 4,500. There were 50,000 Federal soldiers in the Department of the West at the time, and a week should have been enough to gather an army at Lexington, via steamboat to its wharves, which would have annihilated Price; but in the confusion created by John Charles Frémont's conduct of his affairs in St. Louis, it was not done.

Enforcements for Price, on the other hand, were arriving from every direction, some of them scattering enemy forces en route. Shelby was already at Lexington when his superior, General Rains, arrived and occupied a position east and northeast of the town. With him was Hiram Bledsoe, promoted since Carthage to the rank of colonel, and Old Sacramento, now known as "the ogs gannon" ever since a blue-coated Dutch artillerist at Wilson's Creek, seeking the range of Bledsoe's masked battery in the underbrush, had shouted, "Vare iss der man mit der ogs gannon?" In addition, Bledsoe's battery now had several pieces of captured Federal field pieces with ammunition to fit.

Mulligan, wondering why he had been deserted, sent out two couriers in an effort to break through to the Federal commander at Sedalia—he bore the unlikely name of Colonel Jeff C. Davis—but Shelby's scouts picked them up, and from them learned something of conditions inside Mulligan's lines. Mulligan intended to fight, and he expected to be reinforced, but if he were not, he would be forced to surrender when he ran out of food and water.

After five days of preparation, during which he occupied the fairgrounds of Lexington, Price was ready. Mulligan had also been busy, constructing around the Masonic College in Lexington "a redan of great strength, with embrasures, parapets and a banquette for barbette guns." Just inside the Federal entrenchments, near the wharf, stood the residence of Colonel Oliver Anderson, Howard Gratz's father-in-law. A hospital flag waved above the familiar red brick house. Down at the dock was a Federal gunboat.

On all sides of the town was Price's Missouri army. Its appearance had not improved during its stay at Springfield. Typical of its bushrangers was the Ozarkian described by a newspaper correspondent as wearing a bright green silk shirt—a shining target on any battlefield —and having bowie knives in his boots. But if the Southerners' appearance had not improved, their weapons had. From Wilson's Creek on, the U. S. Army was their quartermaster department. At Lexington they were ready to hurl Frémont's ammunition back at him, or rather at his neglected aide, Colonel Mulligan.

On Wednesday morning, September 18, 1861, Price ordered an assault of artillery and infantry on all quarters of the town. As his men fought their way into the streets from the fairgrounds, shots were fired at them from the direction of the Anderson house, over which the hospital flag still waved. They charged, and took possession of the mansion, but were driven out again in a few minutes. All Lexington shook with the roar and thunder of the guns, and the first day's fighting ended in a stalemate.

Mulligan's Irish fought bravely that day, and again on the following day when the attack was renewed. It went on for three days, the Federals ringed in what soon became a little inferno within the walls of their fortifications. An unidentified newspaper writer who witnessed the siege says: "So accurate was the aim of the [Southern] sharpshooters that a man, a head or a cap shown for a single instant above the works was sure to be saluted with fifty balls that never went many inches from the mark." [6]

Receiving news that General Sturgis had disembarked troops from the Hannibal & St. Joseph Railway at Utica, forty miles away, for the relief of Lexington, Price transported 2,000 men to the north side of the Missouri River to intercept him, using the lone Federal gunboat which had been tied up at the dock, and which his men had captured on the first day of the siege. With Price's men on both sides of the river, Lexington was now encircled like a pioneer's wagon in an Indian attack. As Major Edwards says, "No brilliant fighting was necessary, and none, therefore, was attempted."

Mulligan's situation was desperate. His men were nearly out of food and water, and the hospital, with its wounded and dying, had become a house of horrors. In their assault on the Anderson house, during which they had held it briefly, Price's men had captured Mulligan's only surgeon, and attempts to get him back, through an exchange, had proved futile. As a result, badly wounded men died for lack of surgical attention. Mulligan said in a newspaper interview later, "It was terrible ... to see those brave fellows mangled and wounded, without skilfull hands to bind their ghastly wounds. Captain Moriarty of the Irish Brigade, who had been in civil life a physician, was ordered to lay aside his sword and go into the hospital. He went, and through all the siege worked among the wounded with no instrument other than a razor. The suffering in the hospital was horrible—the wounded and mangled men dying for thirst, frenziedly wrestling for the water in which the bleeding stumps of mangled limbs had been washed, and drinking it with horrible avidity." [7]

A hospital nurse volunteered to go with a bucket to the spring on which the Federals' water supply depended. This meant running the gauntlet of the rebel fire, but Mulligan, knowing that the sight of a girl would make a silent appeal to the chivalry of the Missourians, let her go. Not a shot was fired at her. The rebels waved their hats and cheered the nameless heroine. [8] When she was safely back, they resumed their methodical, murderous fire. [9]

On the third day, Price hit upon a device for ending the siege without further heavy loss of life. There were a large number of hemp bales lying on the wharf, some of them no doubt from the ropewalk of Colonel Oliver Anderson, and on the morning of September 20, Price ordered them to be thoroughly soaked in the muddy waters of the river, to prevent their catching fire, and rolled them up the hill to the plain surrounding Mulligan's fortifications. He then order a direct assault upon the town.

State Guardsmen with hooks rolled the bales forward, while the riflemen in the rear advanced under their protection. Mulligan's Celts, red-eyed, dry-throated, but still defiant, gazed in amazement as they saw in front of them, on the morning of the 20th, an undulating, advancing wall of hemp bales, looking for all the world like a Missouri River wharf being shaken by an earthquake. First came the startled fire of the riflemen inside their parapets, ineffective against the hemp bales; then the crackling of the Southerners' small arms as they advanced safely within close range; and quickly Price's men swarmed over the parapets, driving in the Federals with the bayonet, and breaching a gap in the fortifications for their comrades in the rear to pour through.

The battering-down siege of Lexington thus resolved itself again into street fighting for the town, but this time the weakened defenders, greatly outnumbered, could not halt their foe. Major Becker of Mulligan's command—he was not an Irishman but one of the St. Louis Dutch—ran up a white flag, without asking permission of Mulligan, and this momentarily halted the firing. General Price, who was in the line, sent over a note to Mulligan under a flag of truce, asking, "Why has the firing ceased?" The reply came back, "General, I hardly know, unless you have surrendered." [10]

Although he ordered the white flag hauled down and the firing resumed, the jaunty Mulligan was whistling in the dark. His men ran out of cartridges shortly afterward, and at three o'clock in the afternoon, as a sudden silence fell upon the Federal lines, Mulligan surrendered. But he was not able to surrender his beautiful new sword, a recent gift, when he met General Price. One of his men had stolen it for a souvenir. [11]

Price was again master in Lexington, but again he could not stay there. He invited Colonel Mulligan, who would not accept parole, to drive with him about Lexington in his carriage; the Lexington

Brass Band played "Dixie," and "Listen to the Mockingbird," two brand-new songs; but it was soon evident that although Missouri's heart might be with the South, her interests, in the Missouri River Valley at least, were still involved with those of the North. As soon as it became known that the Union garrison of 2,600 men had surrendered, there was a rush of the chivalry to volunteer; but they were conditional volunteers, just as they had been conditional Union men. "They were with us," says Colonel J. F. Snyder, one of Price's surgeons, "but first they must return home to arrange their business affairs, and set their house in order." [12] There was also such a rush of chronic office seekers that Price set extra guards over the stairway leading to his headquarters, which were over a photography shop, to keep them out. [13]

As McCulloch had pointed out, occupation of the Missouri River Valley meant a supply line hundreds of miles long for the Secession forces and the certainty of attack by Federal forces several times the size of their own. Pope was in Price's rear, reportedly with 10,000 troops; Sigel at Sedalia was said to have 10,000; General David Hunter at Versailles, another 10,000; and Generals Sturgis and Lane in Kansas each a third of that number.

Price's activities in the invasion corridor leading from the Ozarks to Lexington and the Missouri River Valley had served to arouse Lincoln to the necessity of concentrating an overwhelming force against the rebels. If Jefferson Davis and his government had no plans for Missouri, the lean, gaunt man in the White House had. The campaign which Blair and Lyon had begun so splendidly had bogged down under the showy and incompetent Frémont, and Lincoln ordered him to repair the delay at once. [14]

Acknowledging the realities of the situation, Price gave the order to fall back upon Springfield. Shelby's company, as usual, was in the van of the cavalry which escorted the 8,000 men and their wagon trains southward, through country swarming with Federals. At the Osage River Price halted long enough to build flatboats to cross the river, and then moved into Neosho.

There the legislature had assembled in response to Governor Jackson's call—one hundred per cent Secessionist of course—to ratify his declaration of August 5 and put an Ordinance of Secession on the books. On October 28, after Price had passed through, the legislature passed the ordinance and set in motion the machinery for applying for statehood in the Southern Confederacy. This must wait on the action of the Confederate Congress; hence E. C. Cabell and Colonel Thomas Snead were dispatched to Richmond to conclude an interim alliance with the Confederate government. This they did, with all the formalities of treaty-making, and thus between October 28 and November 28, when the Confederate Congress acted, Missouri was a military ally of the Southern Confederacy and the only sovereign nation (except the Indian nations) ever to become one.

Whether the rump session at Neosho had any authority to act is beside the point. The importance of the Neosho legislature's action was that it added to the armed forces of the Confederacy 40,000 men who fought on both sides of the Mississippi until 1865.

By the time that Price reached Springfield, Frémont's columns were so close on his heels that he continued on into the country—into the neighborhood of Pineville and Cassville, whence the Patriot Army had started out for Wilson's Creek last August. There was indecisive fighting on the battlefield of Wilson's Creek itself, and Frémont's troops finally entered Springfield in a manner concerning which there are conflicting accounts.[15] But a letter from Lincoln caught up with him, and he was relieved of command. Lincoln was thoroughly disgusted with this general who never fought a battle,[16] and in his place appointed General David Hunter, who never fought one either.

It had been Price's intention to lure Frémont, whose measure he believed he had taken, back into the Ozarks and there fight in the bushwhacker style in which the Missourians excelled. Hunter, however, had no intention of allowing Price to pick either the time or the place of a fight; furthermore, on assuming command, he found his army in such a state of demoralization that he determined to fall back on Rolla once more and reorganize. The cause of this demoralization lay deep in the office politics with which Frémont had conducted his department, and which does not concern us here, but the Germans were mutinous over the dismissal of Frémont,[17] and the Germans formed a majority of Hunter's army. Added to that, winter was coming on, in bleak, hostile country, and Hunter had no stomach for any of it. Back he went to Rolla, where Generals Curtis and Sigel would take over in the spring. An indication of the power of the Germans in the Union army was that, no matter what he did, nobody could get rid of Sigel.

Thus the military seesaw in Missouri teetered back and forth, and at the end of the year 1861 the situation was exactly where it had been at midsummer, except that the Southern forces, instead of being a few miles south of Springfield, were now in occupation of it. Price moved his campsite to near-by Osceola for a month. He now had a new task, that of separating the sheep from the goats in his army: those who were willing to be mustered into the Confederate service, now that Missouri was a Confederate state, and those who were going home when their terms of enlistment expired.

It is a tribute to the popularity of Price and the persuasive power of his recruiting officers, such as Jo Shelby, that most of the Missourians enlisted under the banner of the C.S.A., although grumblingly. They would have preferred to fight under the blue merino flag and the Two Bears of Missouri, and they were suspicious of service outside the state. They also felt that they had been misjudged and treated coldly by the Confederacy, chiefly in the person of McCulloch. Barefoot and in rags, as they saw it, they had won victory after victory only to see the fruits of those victories lost through failure of Confederate cooperation; but now that "Old Pap" Price told them to enlist, they did so, although some of them remarked pointedly that they were not going to serve under anybody else except Old Pap.

As soon as he settled down at Osceola, Price sent Shelby again to the Missouri River Valley. That grueling hundred-and-twenty-mile ride into the heart of enemy country was becoming as familiar to his company as the parson's path to church on Sunday morning. These were no pleasure jaunts. As Major Joseph Mills Hanson, the cavalry authority, says in the *United States Cavalry Journal*, "In the intervals between battles Shelby and his company returned three times to Lafayette County in the hope of recruiting a regiment....Few men were gathered, but every one of these expeditions to the Missouri River was a nightmare of danger and exertion which none but the hardiest could endure. For days and nights the raiders marched, almost without rest, hunted on every side by hostile columns; snatching a few brief moments with kindred and friends when the home country was reached, and fighting there to wrest from the enemy the arms, equipment and ammunition to replenish exhausted stocks and supply recruits. Then by similar nerve-straining marches they made their way back over rough and obscure roads, beset by foes still more thoroughly aroused, to arrive in Arkansas on their last ounce of strength." [18]

Back in the Waverly countryside, Shelby returned to the enjoyable occupation of persecuting the Federals in their garrisons, although as one chronicler says of his activities throughout this period, including the battle of Lexington, "a great deal of powder...was wasted with no effect other than the effect of keeping the excitement at fever heat on both sides." [19] Not until he donned the uniform of a Confederate colonel and assumed command of his own regiment and brigade, did Shelby emerge as a figure of consequence in the War in the West.

Recruits multiplied through the winter of 1861-62, that grim season when the North, aroused at last to the fact that a large-scale war was inevitable, made ready to attack the South in earnest. Shelby remained secure at Waverly during the months when the Missouri is practically un-navigable, but by February he was again headed south on the exhausting march he had made six times, and with him, this time, rode Betsy and the two little boys, in a Confederate army ambulance.[20]

Through roads rutted with winter, filled with snow, and bitter with the cold of the western mountains, Shelby pushed his little company. Others, such as Jake Stonestreet, his boyhood friend from Kentucky, also had brought their families along, jostled in Confederate army ambulances.[21] For the tenderly reared Betty it must have been an ordeal, with two small children and no small apprehension for the future. She was leaving behind her every worldly possession, a fine home, a magnificent farm, a life of ease, forever. Ahead lay the rough life of a rebel army camp, and at the end of the road, perhaps the widowhood of the battlefield. It was an exile into hardships such as not even her pioneer Shelby ancestors had faced; and it was made doubly bitter by her husband's estrangement from his family in Kentucky.

But like many Southern women of delicate, flower-like beauty, Betty Shelby had the stamina of a plainswoman and the iron will of the Shelbys in her tiny person. It was not for nothing that the blood of the Vikings flowed in her veins.[22] Where her husband was, there would she be. From the day she wore his ring, she followed him always, and her faith in him was indestructible. Nevertheless, as the ambulance creaked and jolted along the road in the gray, icy, formless world which enveloped her in the foothills of the Ozarks, that faith must have received a severe testing. When the babies cried and the rations were inedible, when the wind whistled through the flapping canvas of the ambulance, the bright hearth at Waverly must have seemed a dim dream of heaven, and the Missouri on a summer's day as distant as the river Jordan.

Billy Hunter was there, too,[23] riding with upturned collar in the cold and keeping a watchful eye on the ambulance, when he was not riding at his master's side. When the boys whimpered too much, he could comfort the younger one or shame the older out of his tears, and he waited on his master and mistress hand and foot; but for the staunch black boy this was a comedown, too. No more a warm bed in clean quarters in the rear of a mansion house; no more starched shirts to lay out, no boots to shine, no fine horses to curry; poor food, poor country, and poor white trash for company. But like the boss's lady, where the boss was, there was Billy Hunter also. He followed his master through most of the war, and when the years had bowed him down, he led his master's horse to a soldier's grave in Kansas City. Like all those whom Jo Shelby bound to himself with hoops of steel, the bond slave followed him to the end, long after he was no longer bond, but free.

They reached Price at Springfield, and the greetings must have been warm. Shelby had done yeoman work in Lafayette County; Price had recommended him for a colonelcy. But there were more urgent matters afoot. Abraham Lincoln had placed Major General H. W. Halleck, a tough and irritable old warhorse, in command of the Department of the West, and General George B. McClellan, before going east to assume command of the Army of the Potomac, had sent peremptory orders into every corner of the Northwest for regiments to take Missouri.[24] Three columns of a formidable army under General Curtis, who had replaced the timorous Hunter, were on the way to Springfield, which was an untenable military position, and the sun of March would soon dry up the roads. Price would fall back upon Cross Hollows, Arkansas, and there join McCulloch. Scouts had already brought in news of Curtis. This Federal commander, approaching from Bolivar, had 8,000 men, 51 pieces of artillery, and a wagon train big enough for an army four times as large.[25] That army was expected soon to join him as the regiments poured in from Minnesota, Wisconsin, Illinois, Indiana, Iowa, Kansas, and even a few renegades from Arkansas.

The First Missouri Confederate Brigade, which literally fought itself out of existence before the end of the war, on both sides of the Mississippi, was given the task of covering Price's retreat. It was known that General James H. Lane headed one of Curtis's columns, and was aiming to prevent Price's movement to Arkansas. This was the hated Jim Lane, the Kansas Redleg, jayhawker chieftain, and veteran of the Border Wars. At Dug Springs, just off the old battle-field of Wilson's Creek, his cavalry became obtrusive and Shelby and the rest of Rains's mounted riflemen struck them with fury, so that their horses bolted away as if they had been lashed with a cat-o'-nine-tails. At Crane Creek a general engagement seemed imminent, for Lane's forced march had brought up the main body of his troops.

Price's skirmishers were able to delay the enemy at nightfall, so that Price had a full day to reach Cassville, where he would have a clear escape route into Arkansas. An icy sleet pelted him all day long, and the wind, which never stopped as it blew from the mountains into the foothills, was biting cold; but on the night of February 15, he crossed Flat Creek for the last time—he had crossed and re-crossed it seventeen times in one day in his tortuous twistings to avoid Lane—and fell back upon Cassville.

There was still a little skirmishing left in Lane's system, but once again the wily Pap had escaped, and Lane's skirmishers knew it; so perhaps their hearts were not much in it. But they tried a few shots at Sugar Creek, received a withering response from the First Missouri Confederates, and retired in confusion.

On the 17th Captain Shelby led Rains's advance into McCulloch's camp at Cross Hollows. The clothing of the Missouri Confederates was frozen stiff as so many boards; the hands that gripped their muskets were blue, and there was not a crust of bread in the entire army of 8,000. Yet Price's achievement had been remarkable. With no government to direct him, no superior to whom to report, no weapons except those which he provided for himself, and no commissary to send him supplies, he had maintained a Missouri army intact for six months, with no help, and delivered it to the Southern Confederacy single-handed. And although his men were out of food when they reached Cross Hollows, it was no beggarly army of camp followers that he joined to McCulloch's regiments. He had 8,000 bayonet guns, one for each man, 50 pieces of artillery, 400 tents, and a wagon train full of useful equipment from the prodigal stores of the Federals.

For the Shelby children McCulloch's camp was a wonderland of strange sights. It was not unlike a county fair on a grand scale, with flags, drums, music, Indians, soldiers, and horses. The Indians were soldiers, too, of Colonel Stand Watie's Choctaw regiment, but no one would have known it from the clothes they were wearing. Although General Albert Pike had ordered 13,000 new uniforms for the Confederacy's Indian allies, and some of them had already arrived, not a single Indian was to receive one. Shortly after Price's army arrived, the former Missouri Patriot Army was clad in splendid new Confederate uniforms, while the Indians, for whom they had been ordered, were still wearing blankets, moccasins, odd shirts and pants, and hats with a feather sticking out of them. General Pike, who had been at the greatest pains to obtain regulation uniforms for his Cherokees, realizing their psychological value in cementing the alliance between the Indian Nation and the Confederacy, was fighting mad over this amiable brigandage; he complained loudly to Adjutant General Cooper in Richmond, but by the time Richmond officialdom got around to reviewing the charges, Price's men were across the Mississippi, fighting at Corinth, wearing Pike's uniforms.[26] There was no doubt about the need of uniforms for Price's men, and the Missourians were all agreed that there was no use wasting good new ones on ignorant savages.

The fortunes of war had brought Price and McCulloch together again as co-equal commanders, but the hostility between the two was now so deep that there was no hope of their acting in concert. Price realized this as soon as he talked with McCulloch at Cross Hollows; he remained one day in McCulloch's camp and then moved a little south to establish his own, at Cove Creek, where some cabins could be had and others could be built.

From Cove Creek Price wrote to Major General Earl Van Dorn, the commander of the entire Trans-Mississippi Department of the Confederacy, and laid the case before him. He had stepped down once before for McCulloch, but he would not do so again, and rather than ask preferment for himself he suggested that General Van Dorn assume personal command of the two armies, with a view to retaking Missouri from the Federals. It was on this rock, of course, that he and McCulloch had always split. McCulloch did not believe it could be done.

Van Dorn, who knew something of the Price-McCulloch feud and of course was aware of the disasters which it had already caused, thought Price's suggestion a good one, and he came up from Pocahontas, Arkansas, to weld the two armies into one and attack the enemy. This he did, on March 6, at Pea Ridge, or Elkhorn Tavern. But the plague of incompetent commanders in the Confederate Department of the Trans-Mississippi had begun. Van Dorn was the first. With the splendid army now at his command,[27] he whipped Curtis so thoroughly that he was sitting in Curtis's headquarters at Elkhorn Tavern the next night; but with the psychopathic fear which afflicted every man who ever commanded in his department, except Magruder, he ordered his troops to retreat from a field on which they had been victorious.

The Battle of Pea Ridge was fought along lines similar to those of Wilson's Creek, with the positions reversed. The main body of the Federals was divided into three separate camps. Curtis was comfortably ensconced around Elkhorn Tavern, where he set up his headquarters; Sigel was at Fayetteville, not far from the scene of his debacle at Wilson's Creek. Van Dorn's original idea was to drive a wedge between Sigel and Curtis, but Sigel was too fast for him. He had already occupied a strong position at Bentonville when he was attacked, and his infantry and artillery drove off a thrust by the Confederate cavalry under McIntosh. By nightfall the Federal forces were joined at Elkhorn Tavern.[28]

There was a rough country road, eight miles long, leading to the Federal rear, and Price, after making an abortive attack similar to McIntosh's, decided to march by darkness into the rear of the enemy. Curtis had blockaded the road, and apparently was not worried about it; but when the sun had been up a few hours he realized that Old Pap and the veterans of Bloody Hill were in his rear, on the only road leading northward. Although the forces of Curtis and Sigel outnumbered the Southern troops, they were nevertheless menaced on all sides by the smaller force, precisely as the Confederates had been at Wilson's Creek.

With forty or more pieces of artillery, and an army flushed with recent victory, Price was able first to lay down a barrage which lasted for hours, and then drive his Missourians in a smashing charge into the enemy's center—Curtis's. Curtis's men gave way, his flanking movements were mowed down, and the triumphant, yelling Missourians drove in everything in sight for two and a half miles. Rains and Shelby were in this swarming mass as it careened across cornfields and into heavy timber; Shelby fought on horseback when he could and dismounted his men, as at Wilson's Creek, when he could not. Rains singled him out for special mention once again at Pea Ridge. In his report, he said, "Captain Shelby acted with his well drilled company during the day with Colonel Gates, on the extreme left, where he was much exposed and did efficient service. In the evening his men were dismounted and served under Lieutenant Colonel Bowman in the gallant charge across the field." [29]

The gallant charge across the field had won the battle in Curtis's sector; but disaster had overtaken the Confederate and Indian regiments under McCulloch. McCulloch was dead, and the confusion resulting from his death had lost the battle for the Southerners, in spite of all that Price and his Missourians had done. McCulloch, like Price, had delivered a smashing attack on Sigel, dislodged him from his position, and captured three guns; but in the elation of victory he had ridden too far ahead of his own lines to reconnoitre. During the battle he had doubled in the role of general and sharpshooter, a Maynard rifle slung over his shoulder. Now one of the enemy's sharpshooters sighted him. One clean shot through the breast snuffed out his life, and he toppled from his horse as Lyon had done at Wilson's Creek. The victory that had been within the Confederates' grasp slipped away with the reins that fell from the dead hands of McCulloch. General Albert Pike, his second in command, was unequal to the task of rallying the men and continuing the fight, as the sun went down, and his Indians proved worthless. They were good at scalping dead men, but the white man's style of fighting did not appeal to them. The dead McCulloch's command was in such a state of demoralization that Van Dorn did not know what to do at first; but when it was pointed out to him that Sigel was now between him and one of his ammunition trains at Bentonville, he became panicky and ordered the whole army to retreat from the field. The Missourians at first did not realize the nature of the movement they were being ordered to make; they had just defeated the enemy and they thought they were being ordered to support McCulloch. Colonel John C. Moore says, "When they found the battle was ended and lost, they were in the savagest of moods and almost mutinous in their criticism of their commanders." General Rains says the same thing in different words: "The movement was reluctantly obeyed by the whole of my command, as the enemy were then in sight and almost within reach. On arriving at the old field and reporting to Major General Van Dorn I was ordered by him to march on the road towards Huntsville. For the first time I realized the fact—the fight was over; the victory within our grasp was lost." [30]

Confederate historians maintain that Curtis was considering surrender when Price and McCulloch surrounded him at Pea Ridge; it is impossible to say, but his first report, written just before he was attacked, on the sixth of March, shows that he was jumpy and nervous. He had received intelligence that "20,000 to 30,000 fighting men" were converging on him, and he was separated from Sigel. "He [Sigel] was to march at 2 this morning ... he must be nearby." The weather was very cold, and it was snowing, but "We will give them the best show we can." [31]

In the race for the most inept commanders, the Federals in Missouri were not far behind the Confederates; but the Confederates would soon so outclass them in this league that there would be no comparison. Van Dorn's was a fair sample of Confederate generalship in the Department of the Trans-Mississippi from the beginning. But it is merciful to ring down the curtain on the scene at Pea Ridge. The Confederates retreated, through the blood-stained snow, into the Boston Mountains of Arkansas, to Van Buren. There would be raids into Missouri territory by Shelby, Marmaduke, and Price, raids that, in Shelby's case at least, would be feats of superhuman endurance, but never again would Missouri soil form a base for Confederate operations, throughout the war. A star had been added to the Confederate flag, but a state had been lost.

PART THREE

Shelby the Raider

◆●◆

10. *A Colonel of the Cavalry*

MISSOURI was gone, and the Confederacy, for all practical purposes, was now an island, or rather a great subcontinent bounded by the Atlantic and the Mississippi, the Potomac and the Gulf. As the snows melted in the Boston Mountains at Van Buren, Price was ordered with his 5,000 Confederates—all those who were willing to go—across the Mississippi to meet a new threat, that of the triumphant Grant marching down the Mississippi Valley into the heartland of the Confederacy, after Shiloh. At Shiloh there had been a blood-letting like that of Wilson's Creek. Albert S. Johnston had been killed, and the Napoleonic Beauregard had fallen back into the vicinity of Corinth and needed help.

At Van Buren Jo Shelby and Betsy made plans. He must go with the army, though it was disheartening to think that the Lafayette County Cavalry would be dismounted now and reduced to the status of footsoldiers. Price made a spirited address to his troops urging them to follow him across the Mississippi. "I go," he said, "but to make a pathway to your homes." [1] There was little alternative for Shelby. The only fighting now was on the other side of the river, and he agreed to take his company to Corinth, but with the proviso that they be allowed to return to Missouri whenever they saw fit. [2] Already plans were forming in his mind for the rescue of Missouri. He had had eight months of service under every kind of condition in the state, and he knew what must be done. In the vast distances of the Trans-Mississippi, cavalry must accomplish whatever was to be accomplished; but now his duty plainly was with the footsoldiers. Major Edwards says, "The cavalry were all dismounted, and Captain

Shelby giving up his horses with alacrity, commenced the same day the infantry drill, and when the hour of embarkation came, led his company to a man upon the boat." [3] He probably did not give up his horses with alacrity, but he did give them up.

Service east of the Mississippi meant an indefinite separation from his family. Betsy and the children would go back to Lafayette County, to the farm of their good friend Mrs. Rebecca Redd, whose four sons were in the army. The Redd farm was near Dover, and Shelby would fight his way back to it, but for the rest of the war he never saw his family more than fleetingly. The letters which he wrote his beloved Betsy, if any of them survive, are not available. The whole world has read the letters which the gallant Stuart wrote his wife, almost daily, from the Army of Northern Virginia; but only Betsy ever read what Jo Shelby wrote from Memphis, "where the pleasant golden days passed like a dream," from the swamps upon the Tuscumbia River around Corinth, "filled with enormous reptiles, which fattened and grew upon the deadly miasma arising from ten thousand dank lagoons and stagnant bayous." [4] We do not even know whether he accompanied her back to the friendly western country near Dover, but probably he did, for he was entitled to a furlough. At the Redd farm they were welcomed by Mrs. Redd, "the matronly mother in Israel" and friend of the Gratzes. Betsy and the children had found a safe haven until their departure for Kentucky in September, 1863.

East of the Mississippi Shelby saw little service except when his Lafayette County neighbors spied some of General John Pope's people and banged away at them. The fever struck Beauregard's army and he retreated from Corinth into the healthful woods around Tupelo, Mississippi. It must have been a fretful task for Shelby, who was never willing to spend a day in camp, to be assigned to guard a bridge across the Tuscumbia River in a yellow fever bottom. He bided his time impatiently. His commission as a captain in the Missouri State Guards expired on June 10, 1862, and his commission as a Confederate colonel was lying on a desk in the War Department at Richmond; but there was a string attached. He must march a thousand miles back into Missouri to recruit his own command, or he would have none. That, however, was precisely what Shelby wanted: to return to Missouri and recruit. He knew where there were 10,000 lean, hard fellows in the bush of central Missouri, and it was infinitely his preference to be given the opportunity which the Richmond government was now giving him. That he should have had a colonelcy a year earlier there is not the slightest doubt; but it was one of the failings of "Old Pap" Price from the beginning that he regarded Shelby as a "boy," just as it was one of the failings of Jefferson Davis that he could not see the military competence of commanders who were not West Point graduates. Davis would give the Missourians commissions, but not until they showed up at the head of regiments and brigades already formed. It was with the greatest reluctance that he had just been persuaded to give Price a commission as major general.[5]

With the stars of a Confederate colonel not upon his collar but in front of his eyes, Shelby bade farewell to the eastern theatre of the war as soon as he received his authority from the War Department to return to Missouri and recruit a regiment. When he left, there were 5,000 Missourians of the First and Second Missouri Confederate Brigades at Tupelo. They fought on every battlefield south of Virginia and east of the Mississippi, and there were only 800 of them when they surrendered at Fort Blakely on April 9, 1865—the day of Appomattox. As General Dabney H. Maury said of them after the Battle of Corinth, "it is no disparagement to any troops of the Southern Confederacy ... [to say] that the Missouri troops of the Army of the West were not surpassed by any troops in the world." [6]

Shelby and his men began their careers as raiders seated on the hard cushions of the railway "cars" leaving Tupelo. The little wood-burning engine of the train hauled them as far as Meridian, Mississippi. From there, in the midst of country infested by the enemy, they must find their own way across the river. Edwards says, "The march to the Mississippi River was rapid and fatiguing. Fort Pillow, Memphis, and every town except Vicksburg and Port Hudson were in possession of the enemy, and the gauntlet had to be run by innumerable bodies of cavalry and a gigantic fleet of gunboats." [7]

They reached the river exactly opposite Helena, a Federal bastion of the Mississippi north of Vicksburg on the west side of the river. Helena was the home of General Tom Hindman, who had succeeded Van Dorn as commander-in-chief of the Confederate forces of the Trans-Mississippi, a tough, able soldier. But they could not call on General Hindman. The town was occupied by the Federals. They had converted the sleepy river port into a wicked-looking fortress of sharpened staves, and abattis of wooden spikes as sharp as bayonets, with artillery emplacements everywhere.

As Shelby's men approached the river they moved as noiselessly as Indian warriors on the trail—as noiselessly as the Cherokees and Choctaws whose fine gray uniforms they had been wearing ever since Pea Ridge. When they reached the river they saw the trademark of the Federal occupation of the Mississippi, two grim-looking ironclads, one lying at Helena wharf and another a half mile upriver. Shelby and his men camped in a grove of cypress trees, hung with Spanish moss, which afforded a natural cover. As long as the gunboats were there, crossing the river was out of the question.

At sunset they were treated to a brilliant and heartening spectacle. As the waters turned to reddish gold, the gunboat at the wharf slid from its mooring and floated silently downriver. The sun faded, the waters turned a deeper, dancing blue, and the gunboat half a mile away sent up two brilliant rockets, fired a gun to leeward, and glided toward them. The lookout was not twenty rods away from the camp in the cypress grove as the gunboat nosed toward the shore, sending out a sheet of ripples across the placid surface of the Mississippi. The lookout saw nothing suspicious, and the gunboat moved on, out of sight.

Not knowing what the situation might be on the Arkansas shore, Shelby would not risk a crossing, but called for six volunteers to take a skiff across, reconnoitre the opposite bank, enter the town if possible, and report back before daylight. Stalwart and bronzed, the men shed their jackets with the telltale buttons and in a few moments, says Edwards, "their oar blades threw up diamond sparks in the moonlight, and their swift bark gradually grew dimmer and less distinct."

It was an enchanted night, filled with moonlight, and the yellow lagoons glistened through the darkness of the cypress trees. Owls hooted hungrily, and the notes of the whippoorwills came faintly. No one slept. The Missourians were going home. "Home," says the biographer of these wanderers, "and a thousand sweet, familiar fancies filled every heart. The night was delicious, and the gigantic cottonwoods threw far out upon the river great shadows that lay so quiet and still it seemed a sin to vex the silence with a whispered word." [8] But the Missourians were not of the sort given to reverie, and they were in the mood for song. As always in such a situation, they called on Jake Connor.

Jake Connor was to Shelby and his men what Sweeny and his banjo were to Stuart and the cavalry corps of the Army of Northern Virginia. There is one in every army. "The inimitable Irish delineator," as Jake Connor was called, "the chief of all serenading parties," was moved to poignant melancholy by the scene around him, and he obliged, in a clear, pleasing tenor, with a half dozen verses of "The Fallen Dragoon," which begins,

> Riflemen, shoot me a fancy shot,
>   Straight at the heart of yon prowling vidette;
> Ring me a ball on the glittering spot
>   That shines on his breast like an amulet.[9]

The fallen dragoon in the song is the brother of the man who gave the order; perhaps Jo Shelby was thinking of the Gratzes as Jake's keening lament rang clear above the dark waters of the Mississippi.

Before dawn the volunteers were back with news—and a flatboat. The town was not heavily guarded, except within the fortifications; the coast was clear, and this was friendly country. Under cover of the false dawn, the Missourians shoved off across the river on the flatboat, and Shelby marched them to a plantation where pretty girls served them breakfast, under the very noses of the Federal garrison of Helena.

That breakfast would be long remembered by the bronzed boys when their hair had turned grayer than the splendid uniforms they were wearing. Along with the ham, the biscuits, the fried fish, and scrambled eggs the color of a five-dollar gold piece, there were goblets of champagne instead of coffee,[10] served by Arkansas beauties who themselves looked good enough to eat.

Champagne as a breakfast beverage probably had never been served before in Helena, and Shelby's company of *voyageurs* that morning, who were to form the hard core of the Iron Brigade, could see that the war was going to have its compensations. Men would go insane under the hardships which Shelby imposed on them, and they would know the agony of wounds, disease, and hunger, but Jake Stonestreet may have been thinking of that breakfast at Helena when he told a reporter for the Kansas City *Star*, many years later, "No man could ride with Shelby for four years and be worth his salt at anything afterward. I did it and I know." [11]

Shelby's destination was Fort Smith, the nerve center and quartermaster depot of the Confederate Army in Arkansas. The road thither
lay in bayou country and along roads strongly guarded by Federal
cavalry, even in the interior, but at Fort Smith they could get horses.
The next six days were spent in marching toward Clarendon, the
first way station, and hot, heavy marching it was. The swamp country
of eastern Arkansas was a fit habitation only for alligators and snakes,
and in July its native population was increased by some billions of
insect pests.

Shelby's Missourians had been accustomed to dashing about the
country in comfortable deshabille, on cooperative mounts; their only
experience as footsoldiers had been in battle. Now they found out
what the life of the infantry is really like most of the time: nine-
tenths sore feet. But their impatience to find mounts did not cause
any of them to complain. If they had to slip through fence rails and
across bayou trails to avoid the Federals, their route brought them to
some interesting back doors. In Confederate country, their smart appearance brought them a cordial welcome from people who would
have set their dogs on the homespun soldiers of the Missouri State
Guards, for as Major Edwards says, "The appearance of a soldier is
the best passport through any country, and better meals and better
treatment have been received by men whose guns were polished or
whose gray jackets were tidy and clean, than if they held a paper
endorsed by Adjutant General Cooper." [12]

Shelby was also a spit-and-polish officer, when he could enforce
such a regime, and now that he was in command of his own men, his
influence was beginning to be felt in a way it had never been as a
militia officer. From the first he saw that his men were well mounted,
well armed, and well uniformed, and even under Old Pap they had
been recognized as the most efficient separate organization in the
army. From now on he would insist on the most soldierly behavior;
even on the march to Mexico his men would find themselves spending
the siesta hour in afternoon drill. For a man who was not a West
Pointer, Shelby had a surprising love for "the precision of the parade
ground."

As he marched toward Clarendon, he was a smart-looking officer
himself. He was wearing a black felt hat over the chestnut hair, its
front brim pinned back, cavalry style, with a gold buckle; the collar
of his uniform was solid gold with the bars of a captain, and buttoned

tight. It gleamed beneath the russet beard he was wearing these days, a luxuriant affair which was not triangular like Jeb Stuart's, but apronlike, wavy and curled at the ends. His mustachios were not fierce, but their tendril-like tips seemed ambitious of extending eventually to the point where they could be tied behind his ears. It was a young man's beard, a bushy beauty; and Jo Shelby was a young man, thirty-one years old now and tough as the hickory wood he recommended to his troopers as a gridiron for broiling meat.[13]

Near Clarendon the Lafayette County Cavalry rested its feet at the plantation of a Colonel and Mrs. Lightfoot, below De Vall's Bluff on the White River. Here again a table for company had been set. Heliotrope and roses smothered the dining room in scent, the table gleamed with linen and smoked with good food. Mrs. Lightfoot informed Shelby that she had made a Confederate battle flag of handstitched silk, and that she wished to present it to his company. The gallant Shelby glowed with pleasure. Luncheon eaten, he drew up his men on the lawn, and they stood at attention as the good Southern lady made her little speech and laid the flag in Shelby's arms. Shelby received it with all the appropriate amenities; he was touched. Thereafter, it was his flag. He carried it in battle.

Colonel Lightfoot had some heartening news for Shelby. Their marching days were over. In one of the many bayous near by was a little river steamer, attractively named the *Charm*, whose captain plied the White River without regard for either Federals or Confederates, on business of his own. Captain Shelby might make a deal with him to take them past the Confederate works and into the camp on the river at De Vall's Bluff. Captain Shelby did, and within three hours his company of a hundred rifles had its first experience of bayou navigation, which, as Admiral David Porter said, is like "skimming along summer seas under the shade of stalwart oaks." The stream, though crooked, was deep, and soon the *Charm* was scudding rapidly through trees whose boughs overhead almost interlaced. Captain Shelby questioned the skipper of the *Charm* concerning the river fortifications which both the Federals and Confederates were reported to have placed along the river; the captain assured him that Colonel Nelson with some of McCulloch's old Texans were at De Vall's Bluff and that he was well known to them.

Colonel Nelson, however, did not know that he was receiving visitors, and when darkness fell all river craft looked pretty much alike to him. Shelby's men, stretched out on deck in the summer night, were aroused by the familiar round of the long roll, on shore, as they approached De Vall's Bluff, and in the clear night ahead they could see an earthwork among the pines, mounted with three guns. Long lines of infantry were moving on the crest of the hill behind the fort, and two field batteries were being rolled up. Just as every match was raised for destruction, and two thousand rifles turned on the innocent little *Charm*, her furnace doors flew open, light poured along her deck, and the rebel captain on the shore saw that she was not a gunboat.

The captain—his name was Dunnington, if that is important—yelled to his men to hold their fire, and reported to Colonel Nelson. The colonel was only half convinced; it might be a Yankee trick. Apparently the skipper of the *Charm* was not as well known as he had said he was. Colonel Nelson sent a guard on board and no communication with anyone was permitted until morning, when everything was straightened out. What the captain of the *Charm* had in mind will never be known, although the curiosity of Shelby and his men was re-aroused some weeks later when it was heard that he had been spying for both sides, and had been hanged at Little Rock for treason to the Confederacy.[14]

Colonel Nelson informed Captain Shelby that he was expecting an attack by the Federals momentarily. They had a great fleet of gunboats in the river, having free ingress from the Mississippi at Helena, and Shelby volunteered to remain and help him meet it. At the end of a week, however, no enemy had attacked, and Shelby told Colonel Nelson that he felt it was time for him to proceed. Nelson told Shelby he could not think of allowing him to do so because of "the state of affairs on the river," and a somewhat edgily polite argument ensued. The matter was referred by courier to General Hindman at Little Rock. Hindman sent back a message of congratulation to Shelby, complimenting him on his courage, but ordering him to remain where he was.

This Shelby had no intention of doing, and he left Nelson's camp at once, alone, to retrace his steps to General Beauregard's headquarters in Mississippi. Beauregard was the ranking officer west of the Mississippi and Shelby informed him that he had a commission to raise a regiment in Missouri, that he intended to do it, and that neither the whole Confederate army nor the Federal army could stop him. He had had enough of the insane vacillation which had already lost Missouri to the Southern cause, at least temporarily, and to Missouri he was going. If Richmond didn't like it, Richmond could keep its commission.

Further fireworks were headed off by the news, received at Beauregard's headquarters, that De Vall's Bluff had been evacuated and the army had fallen back to the Little Rock area. There was nothing to prevent Captain Shelby from proceeding to carry out his assignment. His impetuosity having gained him nothing this time, except an opportunity to expatiate on his plans to Beauregard, Shelby rode back over the road he had just come and rejoined his command at Van Buren.

Here he was pleased to find his old commander, General Rains, wearing a new brigadier's uniform. There would be no more delay. Rains was sending Colonel Vard Cockrell into Missouri to recruit, and Shelby could join him as soon as his men were equipped properly. The recruiting business was picking up, for with the abandonment of the state to the Federals and guerrillas, one as bad as the other,[15] thousands who had hesitated before were now more than ready to "go South." Hindman's recruiting camps would give them the opportunity. These camps would also draw into central and southern Missouri large bodies of Federal cavalry intent on breaking them up. These were the forces which Shelby would scatter and terrorize on his innumerable raids between 1862 and 1864, although the Federals always outnumbered him and the disparity in arms and equipment was often ludicrous. No army in Europe had any finer weapons than the United States Army in the Civil War, or better mounts; their clothing was the best procurable and of their food Admiral David Porter of the Union said that "our commissary department was the best in the world, and the waste of provisions would have supplied a European army."[16]

Shelby did not have a wide range of choice as he looked over the quartermaster stores in the camp of Colonel Cockrell on the Frog Bayou, just below Van Buren. The colonel was delighted to see him and told him that he could make his selection of the meagre stock; but what he got for his men was not much. "Horses and mules of every size, variety and condition were picked up," Edwards says, "saddles, sheep-skins, and blankets were all used for seats; and bark bridles and ropes completed the heterogeneous equipments. Yet the

men had their Mississippi rifles and one hundred forty rounds of ammunition each, and they knew they were going to their own country
to rend from the spoiler whatever of costly accoutrements were
needed." [17]

Before they set out Shelby made a speech to his men in which he
said that he wanted no man who had not enlisted for the duration.
His men would swear to fight for the South until she was free—for
twenty years if necessary—or step down now. None did. The company was then mustered into the Confederate service, "and the ab-
surdly mounted soldiers rode away northward." [18] Although Shelby
may have resembled a young Quijote with a hundred Sancho Panzas,
it would have been a mistake to laugh. What did he need? Just one
hundred new guns and one hundred respectable horses. He would
requisition that number from the Federals in a single battle. Nobody
in the world of officialdom ever gave Shelby anything, and as Major
Hanson points out, "In a country of great distances and such primitive conditions as existed in the Trans-Mississippi region of that day,
campaigning was always rigorous and a commander of Shelby's ex-
haustless resource and driving power was of incalculable value. . . .
There was always plenty of food in the southwestern states for those
who knew how to get it, and Shelby did. His Iron Brigade and his
later division fought the war on pork, corn and beef, plenty of each,
while he also managed, either by requisitions or captures from the
enemy, to keep his men fairly well clothed and very well mounted
and armed." [19]

It took five days to traverse the Boston Mountains, but once in
Missouri the southwestern communities vied with Cane Hill, "which
opened it hospitable granaries and her rebel daughters vied with each
other in helping the tired, hungry soldiers." At Newtonia—scene of
bloody fighting later but a sleepy, peaceful little town now—he fought
a skirmish with Federal pickets, whose commander, Major Hubbard
of the First Missouri, did not seem to have much stomach for a fight,
feeling safe in his superiority of numbers. Even when three of his
men were killed in an exchange of shots, he did not pursue the bushwhackers, as he assumed them to be, and Shelby and his men crossed
first into Bates and then into Johnson County. Both counties looked
as if they had been burnt to the ground by a prairie fire. Here the
Brothers' War, or at least the Neighbors' War, had been carried to
its insane, inevitable conclusion. Wrath piling upon wrath, vengeance

topping vengeance, had reduced the country to a desolate ruin. For years after the war this region would be known as the Burnt District.[20]

As Shelby's column rode past the blackened chimneys which reared their lonely shafts from the charred rubble, a rumor reached him that Colonel John T. Coffee, Hindman's recruiting officer in southern Missouri, was hard pressed on the Osage River. He countermarched rapidly across Johnson County, reached Coffee's command, but found him safe enough. Coffee had outridden a large Federal force. After resting, the combined columns marched north again. At Grand River, Coffee turned west to Independence and Lone Jack, and an impatient Shelby spurred his horsemen toward Lafayette County. Scouts brought back the news that a regiment of infantry was encamped on his old real estate development at Berlin, or Dover;[21] but this force did not lie between him and the Redd Farm.

A metamorphosis had taken place in the appearance of Shelby's cavalry during the long ride up from the Boston Mountains, so that he was not ashamed of his company in front of Betsy. Edwards says that "the rich prairies had furnished their best six year olds for these heavy riders," and he had acquired—Edwards does not say where—"as fine McClellan saddles and bridles as ever gleamed upon the Potomac, or went down in the battle's van before Jeb Stewart's [sic] reckless raiders."[22] Since he had not fought a major engagement since leaving the Boston Mountains, Shelby may have obtained these from Coffee, who had been in Missouri for several weeks ahead of him. And if some of his men's outfits were now partly Federal government issue, that made no difference. Autumn was coming on in another month and the jackets bought by the Richmond government for the use of the Indians in Arkansas in June would be scant protection against the freezing weather to come.

The Federals at Dover obligingly moved out, and Shelby moved in. A perusal of the records in Missouri at the time discloses that the Union commanders did not wear themselves out galloping after bushwhackers, and Shelby moved about freely. He was by no means traveling incognito. But this time he did not find it necessary to dash about Lafayette County to find recruits. He set up his headquarters at Waverly, and from every section of the surrounding country troops poured in for enlistment. Governor Gamble, the Union Governor, had assisted him by ordering every able-bodied man in Missouri into the Federal militia. That meant that Southern sympathizers would have to fight against their kinsmen of the South. "They resolved that if they must take part in the war, they would choose upon which side they were to fight." [23] These were grim young men whom Shelby took into service of the Confederate States and ideal recruits. They were the enlisted men of whom a recruiting sergeant dreams: fit, intelligent, and mad as hell at the enemy instead of at a government seeking to draft them.

At Waverly Shelby issued his famous proclamation (obviously not written by him), the "Document That Brought the Boys Out of the Brush in Missouri." The proclamation read:

"Freemen of Missouri: You stand face to face with one of those terrible issues which comes but once in a lifetime. Hamilton R. Gamble [Union Governor of Missouri], false to his birthright, his country and his God, in obedience to orders from Washington, has resolved to draft you into service and force you to fight against blood, kindred, home, friends, neighbors, brothers. Will you do it? Can you turn your back on this your country in this her dark hour of peril and grief and see the mad waves of anarchy and despotism sweep away all vestiges of family ties, sacred firesides, and everything that makes life worth living?

"Missouri, her young brow dark with silent agony, appeals to you by all her ruined hearthstones, all her murdered sons, all her insulted daughters, all the bloody past—heavy with the victims of hired Hessians and pitiless jayhawkers—to rise now, fly to arms, gird on the sword, to swell the grand, eternal chorus,

> " 'Wave Missouri, all thy banners wave
> And charge with all thy chivalry.'

"Through the providence of an Almighty and all-seeing God, I have reached here to alleviate in some measure your great distress. I am duly commissioned by the Confederate Government to recruit a cavalry regiment for the war and to make all arrangements necessary in connection with my government as one of its officials. Too long you have bowed your heads in quiet submission. Too long you have remained silently watching the red wing of revolution sweeping over your state. Too long have you waited for something to turn up, for the war to cease, for foreign intervention. Those who would be free must strike the first blow. We missed you at Carthage, we missed you at Springfield, we missed you at Elkhorn, when death's gathering gloom was spreading its dark wings, and the blood of your blood and flesh of your flesh went down on the sod, their backs to the field, their feet to the foe. We missed you in Mississippi after Shiloh's bloody sunset embers had faded from the Southern sky and other regiments and other generals rushing on again for another carnival of death. But come now! Come in twos, fours, tens, twenties. Come in squads, in companies and singly, bring horses if you have them, guns, swords, pistols, blankets, but above all bring the firm unalterable purpose in your hearts that come what may you will light again your patriotism at the altar of your bleeding country, and swear in the broad, grand sunlight of your prairies, Missouri must and shall be free!

"Delay is death, ruin dire and dreadful. By all you hold dear in life, by wife, by mother, by smiling babe, by your hopes of heaven, help us now to drive back the invader! Our banner is on the breeze, our feet are on our native soil. Close up, comrades! Close up, Missourians! Land is ahead; day is breaking. One more effort, one long pull, one strong pull, one pull altogether, and the day is ours. Already I hear your response. Already I see the gathering in. Soon, very soon, will come our battle cry:

"'Now gallants, for your lady's sake,
Upon them with the lance!'

"One great aim with me will be to give quietude and repose to the neighborhood around my headquarters. To do so, all Negroes and suspicious persons caught after sunset within my lines will be dealt with in the severest manner.

"Union men too old for service in the ranks, who make their age a pretext for spying and newsbearing, must cease all communications with the Federal commanders or suffer the just punishment of an outraged and violated country."

This proclamation is undoubtedly the work of John N. Edwards, the fiery editor of the *Expositor*. Soon after he became Shelby's adjutant, about the time of the Battle of Lone Jack, Edwards took over the onerous (to Shelby) job of writing Shelby's battle reports, and the result is still somewhat startling. From the fall of 1862, when Edwards became his amanuensis, the usually dull pages of the Official Records, when they relate to Shelby, are ablaze with rhetoric and enlivened with quotations from the romantic poets. Edwards was a devotee of the Sir Walter Scott school of literature, and to him every Missouri swale and hill crest was a Field of the Cloth of Gold, and "every loping, gray-clad farmer boy a knight in armor." [24]

Edwards himself was one of the most modest and lovable of men, a student, a poet, and a gallant soldier. (He had more horses shot from under him than any other man in Shelby's brigade.) He had a round, childlike face, with a high forehead, a drooping mustache, and innocent blue eyes that forever beheld a world of wonders. As a writer Major Edwards was a Bombastes Furioso in an age when floridity of style and extravagance of expression were considered the hallmarks of good writing. He could scarcely think, much less write, except in hyperbole; nevertheless he was touched with the divine fire. There was a streak of genius which showed, hard and fine, in the trashiest of his outpourings, so that his pictures come alive. To read his works, which sometimes requires patience, is to have the rewarding experience of coming suddenly upon a masterpiece among the garish colors of the circus posters. Chivalry was his religion and Beauty his passion (of flowers he said that they were the noblest work of God, saving only Woman), and for Shelby he had an attachment that amounted to idolatry. The two were inseparable in battle or barroom, and although they disagreed after the war on the important issues of Reconstruction, they remained closer than brothers to the end of their days. At Waverly Shelby learned that Edwards was fond of writing proclamations and battle reports, which Shelby was not. By common consent, Edwards henceforth wrote all the reports—a fact which must be borne in mind in reading the Official Records. [25]

Shelby enlisted one thousand men in four days at Waverly, [26] enough for ten cavalry companies, and he had well earned a commission as colonel. But he had marched a thousand miles from Mississippi to do it, and as Major Hanson says in *The Cavalry Journal*, "Thus a man who on his merits ought to have had his colonelcy a year earlier finally got it by finding every man for his regiment." [27]

Shelby had no time to ponder over the merit system of promotion, however, for Colonel Vard Cockrell had really engaged the enemy this time, at the Battle of Lone Jack, over in Jackson County, and although he had driven the Federals from the town, it was the old story of a Confederate force's not being able to hold the victory it had gained, and the Federals were gathering a preponderantly large force to run the recruiters out. Just as Price had irritated Lincoln into swift action at Lexington, so Cockrell stirred up a hornet's nest at Lone

Jack. Edwards says, "The bloody battle of Lone Jack startled the confident Federals like an earthquake, for their choice regiments lay in gory heaps among the burnt and smouldering timbers of the town and as one man they rushed after Cockrell with shouts and cries of vengeance."[28]

For once Major Edwards was not overstating the case. The Battle of Lone Jack had been a battle to the death. The Federals, taken by surprise at four o'clock in the morning, thought they were surrounded by Quantrill and his men, whose war cry was extermination, and they fought like trapped animals. The Confederates, many of them, were fighting in sight of their burned and ruined homes. They gave no quarter, and when they fought their way into the town and found the hotel filled with Federal sharpshooters, they did not attack, but set fire to the hotel and roasted the entire garrison alive.

Purposeful men in overwhelming numbers would now be in pursuit of Cockrell and Shelby and their new recruits. They must get their men back to Arkansas. Cockrell moved first, and he did not need to bid Shelby to follow. As at Carthage, he rose to the occasion with an intensity that showed his men what it meant to ride under Shelby. Major Edwards has given an unequaled description of the ordeal to which he now subjected his cavalry.

"While the pursuit was fiercest, Captain Shelby gathered up his raw recruits and followed after Cockrell, on a parallel and lower line, with speed as great and anxiety as heavy. The cohesive power of danger is probably stronger than any other, and in all that long line of undisciplined horsemen—fresh from the balmy breezes and downy beds—not one faltered, not one missed answer in the constant roll calls. Rest and refuge were almost gained. Crazy and blinded from eight days and nights of uninterrupted marching, the command staggered into camp on the little stream of Coon Creek, in Jasper County, to snatch a few hours sleep before nightfall and before the march was resumed, for Captain Shelby had wisely determined to leave nothing to chance that might be accomplished by energy. To those unacquainted with the effects produced by loss of sleep, the sensations would be novel and almost incredible. About the third night an indescribable feeling settles down upon the brain. Every sound is distinct and painfully acute. The air seems filled with exquisite music; cities and towns rise up on every hand, crowned with spires and radiant with ten thousand beacons. Long lines of armed men are on every side, while the sound of bugles and harsh words of command are incessantly repeated. Often, upon almost boundless prairies, destitute of tree or bush, the tormented dozer turns suddenly from some fancied oak, or mechanically lowers his head to avoid the sweeping and pendent branches. Beyond the third night stolid stupor generally prevails, and an almost total insensibility to pain. Soldiers in Shelby's division have been known to go incurably mad [29] and not a few cases of hopeless idiocy have resulted from his terrible raids. On the march men have dropped from the saddle unawakened by the fall, while on more than a dozen occasions his rear guard has pricked the lagging sleepers with sabres until the blood spouted, without changing a muscle on their blotched, bloated faces." [30]

There was to be no rest at once for the men who survived the march. At Coon Creek, near the old battlefield of Carthage, Shelby's men were attacked by a detachment of the Sixth Kansas Cavalry while they slept. Awakened by the shots and shouts of the enemy, they struggled to their feet as some of them had done at Wilson's Creek and fought Indian style from behind trees until Shelby could rally them. For five minutes the conflict raged evenly. Then the Kansans seemed to have spent themselves, and they retired, hovering in the neighborhood for quite a while, awaiting their chance to make a flank attack. When they did, they were met by a rear guard of Shelby's men under a Lieutenant Blackwell, the men swimming the creek to defend their camp, and the enemy cavalry finally was driven off, after having harassed the sleepy Confederates for three hours. This was "the Battle of Coon Creek." The Federals lost eleven men, Shelby none; but some of his valuable horses were disabled and had to be destroyed. Thus when he reached a point of safety, Elm Spring, for another halt, a number of his men were again on foot.

Many accounts, including Edwards', say that Shelby received his commission and his command of the Iron Brigade at Newtonia, or just north of Newtonia. This is an error. Shelby himself sets forth the circumstances in correspondence with General John S. Marmaduke dated October 27, 1862.[31] Speaking of the encounter at Coon Creek, Shelby says: "After three hours fighting, we succeeded in driving them back. We then continued our march south into Arkansas unmolested, but during the whole march we traveled night and day. After we had reached a point of safety, we halted and shod a portion of our horses, but soon received an order from General Rains to report, which we did, at Elm Spring. We were then ordered to McKissick Springs. During that time we had no transportation except a few two-horse wagons that we had purchased after entering the state. At McKissick Springs we were ordered to report to General Hindman, at Pineville. On our arrival at that place, we found that the general had not reached there, and we were then ordered some fifteen miles north of there, at a point on Elkhorn Creek, where Colonel Hays and Colonel Coffee were encamped. That was on or about the 9th of September, and at said encampment we were met by General Hindman, who caused the three regiments, consisting of Hays' and Coffee's and the undersigned, to be thrown together, which constitutes this brigade, and command of same being given me by the general himself. We were then ordered to Camp Kearny, 6 miles south of Newtonia."

He signed that report JO. O. SHELBY, Colonel, Commanding Cavalry Brigade.

At Camp Kearny, something else new was added. The gold buckle which Shelby wore on his black felt hat was no longer used merely to pin back the slouch brim. Its clasp now anchored firmly a great, curling plume of midnight hue to match the hat. Shelby's Black Plume was soon as familiar to the Missouri troops as the gay ostrich plume of Stuart was to the Virginia troops; and if he modeled his headgear after the great Virginian he had every right to do so, for Shelby was the Stuart of the West.

11. *The Iron Brigade: First Newtonia*

IN THE AUTUMN OF 1862, the Federals in Missouri badly needed another Nathaniel Lyon. General Henry Wagner Halleck, for all his asperity and soldier-like noises, could not make up his mind what to do, as general-in-chief of the armies of the west. "Old Brains," as he was proud to be known,[1] never deigned to lead an army in the field. In the final analysis, he left the problem in 1862 to his field commanders, with the result that each divided his forces, or remained where he was, in pursuance of his own theories of the war.

The new battleground of the Trans-Mississippi Department of the Confederate States[2] resembled an isosceles triangle. The lower left-hand tip was the Indian Territory west of the Confederate head-quarters at Fort Smith, where the rebels had an arsenal and machinery for making munitions—and a stranglehold on the state of Arkansas. The right-hand tip was Helena on the Mississippi River, an important port now held by Curtis and his victorious army of Pea Ridge. The base of the triangle was an imaginary line extending past Little Rock on the west to Helena on the east. The apex of the triangle was the St. Louis–Jefferson City area of northeast Missouri.

General John S. Phelps was Union military governor of Arkansas, a somewhat honorary post, and he argued, with good reason, that all of the Confederates were now in Arkansas, or about to be, and that they were in a better position than ever to dart with the rapidity of a snake's tongue in the direction of the Missouri River Valley, unless blocked by an overpowering army. He did not see any point in keeping an army idle at Helena and he repeatedly urged an all-out attack on Arkansas.

General Curtis, on the other hand, did not wish to abandon Helena. He was willing to spare some troops—in fact, he had sent General Steele to Pilot Knob to secure southern Missouri while General Scho-field advanced on Arkansas in the southwest—but he wanted to remain in Helena in sufficient force to secure the town. Helena lies on the Mississippi River just above Vicksburg. For the Confederates to capture such an important troop transfer base would mean that they could send perhaps 30,000 or 40,000 troops to the aid of the Con-federate eastern armies at any time, just as Price had crossed with his 5,000 to Corinth. Curtis regarded the threat to Helena as much more real, being closer, than a threat to either Jefferson City or St. Louis; and for Phelps's opinion he had no regard at all. "Phelps has his heart set on Little Rock, which at this time seems to be only an encum-brance," Curtis wrote to Halleck on October 2, 1862.[3]

General Schofield was the man about whom the controversy really centered, for it was he who was at Springfield; it was he who would be reinforced, or not, for a march on Little Rock; and if he did not make such a march ultimately, or in fact do something, a revitalized Confederate army would surge back into the scrub oak country around Springfield for the third time.

Schofield had 10,000 men, a wholly inadequate number for an Arkansas campaign. But Schofield was in need of reinforcements only because he insisted on leaving heavy garrisons behind him everywhere he went—at places such as Springfield and Rolla, which were in no danger. In common with the other Federal commanders in Missouri he was jittery about the interior of the state and felt that it was much too rebellious to be left ungarrisoned. The necessity of operating like an army of occupation hampered the Federals in Missouri from the first.

Halleck ordered Curtis to cooperate with Schofield, but when Curtis took the suggestion at face value and dispatched General Steele to Pilot Knob, Halleck was alarmed. His order evidently had been on a par with that given McCulloch by the Richmond government when it had ordered him to "support" Price without invading Missouri. "I fear," Halleck telegraphed Curtis, "that you will regret dividing his army [Governor Phelps's Arkansas army] and that the part left at Helena will be useless or lost. Unless you find it absolutely necessary to withdraw General Steele he ought to operate from Helena. The moment Cincinnati and Louisville are relieved I can give you more troops from Illinois and Ohio." But Halleck, the general-in-chief, gave Curtis no orders to follow in the dilemma. "You know your own condition better than I do," he said, "and must decide about this. At so great a distance I can only advise." [4]

Curtis was not perturbed; he was due for promotion soon and would be leaving anyway. He simply wired back, "I had to divide the Helena force to do anything," which was certainly a correct statement. However, he soon found that he was displeasing Schofield as well as Phelps, besides alarming Halleck. Schofield wrote Halleck, "I had no thought of asking for a part of General Steele's force simply to assist me in holding Pilot Knob and Rolla, but to place him in condition to move immediately and effectively on Little Rock if he was not already prepared to do so." [5] General Curtis retorted, in this indirect exchange, "General Schofield has most of the forces in the Southwest and daily asks for more." [6] The situation was somewhat eased, the last week in September, by the arrival of General Blunt from Kansas with his brigade to report to General Schofield. With Blunt's brigade, he had 6,500 men for duty, besides those he had left behind as garrisons, and two inactive regiments, which he says were "without organization or equipment."

Thus it will be seen that the entire effective force of the Federal armies facing the Confederates in Arkansas was now only 9,500 men, counting Curtis's 3,000 at Helena. The time was ripe for another march to the Mississippi to cut Federal control of the river by seizing Helena. A Nathaniel Lyon would have done it for the Union; a Jo Shelby would have done it for the Confederacy if he had had the requisite wreath and stars on his collar.

No authorization of the Richmond government would have been required, for Richmond had learned its lesson in the Price-McCulloch fiasco; the discretionary powers of the commander in the Trans-Mississippi Department were now being broadened to such an extent in the fall of 1862 that it would be only a few months until Jefferson Davis would say that the commander west of the Mississippi "has the power to execute the laws, and that is all I have." [7] The great distance between the Confederate capital and the vast empire of the Trans-Mississippi, of course, made such an arrangement the only practical one.

But at this crucial moment in the history of the new nation, the Trans-Mississippi was no longer under the control of an able and energetic commander-in-chief. General Tom Hindman had been demoted for enforcing the conscript law too ruthlessly,[8] and in his place had been named General Theophilus H. Holmes, who had assumed command on July 16, 1862. The order of the Adjutant General's office, appointing him, indicates the latitude which he enjoyed. The order read: "Major General Holmes is assigned to the command of the Trans-Mississippi Department. He will repair without delay to Little Rock, Ark., and establish his headquarters at such place as in his judgment the interests of the service demand."

Holmes was deaf and superannuated; the suspicion was strong that he had been let go in the eastern armies for his blunders at Malvern Hill,[9] where he had had an important assignment.[10] But he was a friend of Jefferson Davis,[11] and one of those "men of military education and experience in war" whom Davis esteemed so highly.[12] At Malvern Hill the battle had been under way for some time before Holmes remarked, "I believe I heard the sound of firing," [13] and he was no better equipped to deal with the complex problems of the Trans-Mississippi Department than he had been to command a division at Malvern Hill.

"Old Granny Holmes," the troops called him, and although it was obvious even to him that Helena should be the objective of the next campaign, he did not march on Helena for twelve months. That he could have marched to the Mississippi at any time is demonstrated by the fact that he did march to the Mississippi, when it was too late; and was able to do so when his own military situation had deteriorated. He attacked Helena on the day that Vicksburg fell; yet the Official Records show that on September 28, 1862, while Shelby was still in the vicinity of Newtonia, Holmes had in his department an army which outnumbered the Federals in Missouri nearly three to one.[14] Furthermore, that Davis expected big things of his fifty-seven-year-old protégé is indicated by the fact that the new Secretary of War, George W. Randolph, promised him that "unless prevented by unforeseen contingencies, one fourth of all the arms purchased and manufactured will be forwarded to you with suitable supplies of ammunition."[15]

Thus the ineptitude of the Federal commanders of the Department of the West was of little benefit to the Confederacy; the Richmond government could always go Washington one better in sending out to the Trans-Mississippi Department officers who were resolutely unqualified to command. As Major Hanson says, "To the authorities both at Washington and Richmond, the vast region west of the Mississippi was a sort of precursor of Blois in the A.E.F., a salvage yard into which officers might be shunted who could not be used anywhere else.[16] Throughout the war its destinies were guided mainly by local favorite sons and 'lame ducks' from the main theatre of operations who had either failed or passed out of favor, though still too prominent as personages to be summarily dismissed. Jo Shelby, riding and fighting endlessly, was too busy to curry favor in such quarters, while many greybeards among his superiors looked upon his youth with distrust."[17]

Shelby was not to get along with Holmes, for self-evident reasons, but right now, in the last week of September, 1862, his attention was occupied elsewhere. He was still at Camp Kearny, six miles south of Newtonia, Missouri, trying to scrounge enough equipment for 3,000 men and place his brigade on a war footing. In the next five days followed two swift, savage engagements at Newtonia which are of no importance historically except that at Newtonia Shelby's brigade fought as a unit for the first time.

For many of his men, however, it was not the first fighting they had done since they had joined the brigade. As always in this prairie type of warfare, the main battle at Newtonia had been preceded by a series of clashes. In one of these, shortly after the brigade reached Camp

Kearny, Colonel Upton Hays had been killed. He was a popular officer and his death cast a gloom over the camp. On September 14, Shelby heard that a gang of bushwhackers, composed of Pin Indians and runaway Negroes, was encamped in the timber near Carthage. This band was reported to have killed and scalped inhabitants of the neighborhood. Shelby summoned Captain Ben Elliott with Company I, of his own regiment, and gave orders to show the desperadoes no mercy. Elliott surprised them in their camp, and "everywhere amid the heavy brushwood a silent scene of killing was enacted, none praying for mercy, well knowing that their own previous atrocities had forfeited it, and often, with the stoical hardihood of their race, uncovering their breasts to the unerring revolvers." In the camp a dozen scalps were discovered, and one, a woman's, "was particularly noticed. The long, soft hair had still its silken gloss, though tangled all amid the curls were clotted drops of blood." [18]

On the 23rd Shelby also sent Major David Shanks with five companies of his regiment into Granby to drive out a force of 500 Federals who were occupying the town and supervising the working of the lead mines. The lead mines at Granby, it will be remembered, were those which had furnished Price at Cowskin Prairie with the bullets his men had used at Wilson's Creek. The Federals were surprised and retreated in disorder, leaving a quantity of lead which they had accumulated. Shelby's men loaded it into wagons and sent it back into camp.

These were but forays, however, and Shelby's biographer says that up to now the men had been "lying in front of Newtonia in the warm September sunshine ... delightfully pleasant, and the cavalry drill, which was new to the soldiers, went merrily on." [19]

On September 29 Brigadier General Salomon, the nearest Federal commander, who had been with Sigel at Carthage, sent a scouting party of 150 men under a Colonel Lynde to see what move the Confederates might be making to occupy Granby on a permanent basis. They found no Confederates at Granby, but they made contact with some of Shelby's men, killed two pickets, and captured a prisoner. That touched off the battle of Newtonia.

On the morning of the 30th Salomon moved against the town, which the Confederates now occupied, "with five thousand as pretty Dutch as ever bolted a bologna or swallowed the foaming lager," [20] plus the Sixth Kansas Cavalry and some Indian troops.

The Confederates had a numerically superior force, but one which was superior in no other way. Three or four thousand of them were Cherokees, Choctaws, and half-breeds from the Indian Nations; for the rest, there was only Shelby's brigade, 2,300 strong,[21] and 200 Texans under the command of a Colonel Hawpe.

Colonel Douglas Cooper, who commanded the Indians, ranked Shelby by virtue of seniority, and he assumed command of the entire force at Newtonia. Cooper ordered Shelby to remain in the rear of the town until it should be known whether or not Newtonia could be held; he ordered Hawpe's Texans into the town, perhaps remembering the Alamo, and he planted his artillery ahead of the town. Among the guns was probably Old Sacramento, although the reports do not say so; but at any rate Colonel Hiram Bledsoe was in command.

Salomon attacked at once, and with Teutonic efficiency. He had two six-gun batteries, and he dueled Bledsoe and the Confederate gunners until their ammunition gave out. Poor Bledsoe was left by Cooper standing beside his empty guns on the bare prairie while Salomon sent some of his German troops—the Ninth Wisconsin—in a wide, circling movement to flank Newtonia. These skirmishers poured such an enfilading fire into the Texans that they were forced to withdraw. At this juncture Cooper called on Shelby to send a regiment to the rescue. He sent Lieutenant Colonel Gordon, whose sabres began to ride down the Wisconsin footsoldiers with such avidity that Salomon ordered the entire Ninth Wisconsin back out of town and onto a ridge, where they could mass for a stand. This was a mistake; Gordon's men rode straight ahead, and despite their emptying saddles, put the Ninth Wisconsin to flight. At their heels now were all of Cooper's yelling Indians, ready to murder prisoners and take scalps unless prevented by the white troops.

Salomon's European army training stood him in better stead at Newtonia than Sigel's had at Carthage. Although his forces had been thrown into confusion as the cavalry and Indians swarmed through them, he managed to pull his entire force together, in retreat, and rally at the timber line which skirts the prairie just outside Newtonia. Here he massed his regiments in a phalanx, with batteries at the ends; and Colonel Cooper drew off his Confederates to prepare for an all-out attack.

This took perhaps an hour or two; but when he and Shelby were ready, they threw everything they had into the assault, head-on, which was Shelby's style of fighting, and at Newtonia for the first time the men of the brigade saw his black plume streaming in battle.

Salomon's line could not withstand the murderous weight of that assault; Salomon had lost heavily in the fighting for the town; and now his entire line gave way. There was no question of falling back to re-form it; the line was smashed and splintered by the yelling Indians and the no less demoniac white horsemen from Missouri and Texas. Shelby and his regiments drove Salomon's army furiously for twelve miles, just as he had driven Sigel for twenty-five at Carthage.

Long after midnight the Confederates and their Indian allies were sorting out the guns, blankets, and provisions which the Federals had left behind with their wagons. They had not been able to turn their attention to the plunder until a late hour. The burial parties had kept them too busy. Of the enemy alone, a thousand dead had been counted.

Scanning the Official Records at this point makes it obvious that if Shelby had written his own battle reports throughout the war, they would have added up to a very slim volume indeed. Of the battle of Newtonia he wrote: "On the 30th, we fought General Salomon at Newtonia, defeating him very badly." [22] That is all.

The morning of October 4 found Shelby's flag, the one Mrs. Light-foot had given him, floating from the top of the tallest building in Newtonia. It also found General Schofield's army, about ten thousand strong, on the march. When scouts brought in the news, Colonel Cooper decided not to risk a battle. He sent Shelby northward to engage Schofield's advance and delay it as much as possible; and he began packing.

Shelby fought and fell back; fought and fell back. It was to become an old story with him: covering the retreat of a Confederate army. The man who should have been given ten thousand cavalry and ordered to occupy St. Louis—*which he could have done, with a sufficient force, at any time in the next two years*—was engaged in protecting the skins of a few worthless Indian troops who even now were going nowhere but home. When Shelby fell back into the vicinity of Camp Kearny again, he found that the army he was protecting was a phantom.

General Rains, who was in chief command in this area, although he was not present at Newtonia, ordered the white troops back to Little Rock; and as for the Indians under Cooper, they had taken the nearest short cut back to the Indian Nations.

Schofield was not pursuing, either, and Shelby found himself alone with his brigade on the green and peaceful prairie—with nothing to eat for the next five days. In a letter to General John S. Marmaduke, Shelby said, "We were then ordered back to Mudtown [by General Rains] which retreat required about five days. Said time the command being without any breadstuff, and as for salt, we had been without that ever since we left the Missouri River." [23]

The Confederate soldier was salt-hungry throughout the war. It was bad enough to be without food; to be without salt was worse.

12. The Iron Brigade: Camp at Cross Hollows

S HELBY'S REPORT to Marmaduke, in which he dismissed the battle at Newtonia in a single line, was contained in fuller form in a long letter, dated October 27, 1862. It was one of the few reports Shelby ever wrote himself and shows that he had a concise and literate, but colorless style, with a tendency to use such adjectives as "said" for shorthand effect. There was no nonsense about it. The letter was written to Marmaduke because he was now Shelby's superior in a drastic shake-up of command.

Only the exigencies of the situation and the absence of his adjutant could have commanded such concentration on Shelby's part. His brigade was in a bad way. He does not complain of their weapons (he had supplied these himself out of his own stockpile, captured from the Federals), but one fifth of his men were sick, all of them were in rags, he did not have enough wagons for transportation, his horses were unshod and half of them were disabled.

Pointing out that when he arrived "my men were well mounted, being on as good horses as the country could afford," Shelby says: "During all that time [since August 18, when he ended his nightmare march at Elm Spring] we were some forty miles in advance of General Rains, and were required to scout all of the country in his front from Cassville west to Scott's Mill, 18 miles west, which required, on an average from 700 to 1,000 men daily. We were joined, about the 27th of September, by Colonel Cooper, who assumed command. On the 30th, we fought General Salomon at Newtonia, defeating him badly.

On the 3d of October they [the enemy] were heavily reinforced by their forces from Springfield, and then moved on us in such force as to drive us from Newtonia. We were then ordered back to Mudtown, which retreat required about five days. Said time the command being without any breadstuff, and as for salt, we have been without that ever since we left the Missouri River, as none has ever been issued to us.

"From Mudtown we were ordered to Black's Mill; from there to Huntsville, and thence to the Camp Ground Meeting House, north of this; from thence here, 4 miles east of Maguire's, on Richland Creek.

"In the engagements above mentioned, we have had a good many horses killed and wounded, and we have had frequently to do thirty to forty hours without forage. Our horses have been under the saddle ever since General Hindman organized the brigade. Our men, from being so poorly clad, and owing to the excessive duties they have been compelled to perform, are rapidly becoming unfit for service. Our brigade reports now some 500 sick. We have a great many men without a blanket, overcoat, shoes or socks. There are not more (as regimental report shows) than one half our horses fit for duty. We have had no iron or time to shoe our horses. Our horses are beginning to die pretty fast, owing to the heavy labor they have been compelled to do. As for transportation, we were furnished some five wagons by the division quartermaster; all the balance on hand we have collected ourselves. We have never drawn any clothing, shoes, salt, or anything else. All we have in the way of transportation is one wagon to the company, and they mostly two horse wagons. We have but a few cooking utensils, which we likewise have purchased with private means. We have a great many horses unserviceable for the want of shoeing. The strength of our brigade when first organized was 2,319, all of which were reported for duty until within the last few days. Since this cold spell of weather set in, our reports show but 1,068 men for duty. The increase of sickness in Jeans' and Gordon's regiments is 100 per day."

It is characteristic of Shelby that he merely states the case to Marmaduke without complaint and without suggestion. He also does not mention the fact that despite the condition of the brigade, there had been almost daily skirmishes since Newtonia. From the 17th to the 28th the weather had been sufficiently moderate for the Federals to keep thrusting at the outer fringe of Confederate territory in useless cavalry raids. On the 22nd, they appeared in some force at Huntsville,[1] and Shelby took to the saddle with his thousand effectives and chased them through the town in a snowstorm. On the 28th, a larger force of Federals under General Herron menaced the hospital which Hindman had built at Fayetteville, but after an hour's skirmishing other Confederate cavalry, under Colonel Jesse L. Cravens, drove them back.[2] By this time Hindman's entire force, consisting of 2,500 white infantry, 3,600 white cavalry, and 3,000 Indians, was pretty well established behind the barrier of the mountains around Cross Hollows and Van Buren, and it was at Cross Hollows that Shelby sat down to write his letter to Marmaduke setting forth his necessities.

A review of the circumstances leading up to the appointment of Marmaduke to the command of the Confederate cavalry has to begin on April 16, 1862, when the Confederate Congress passed its first Conscription Act. General Beauregard, by virtue of his rank, was the commander of the Trans-Mississippi District, as it was still called, and he sent General Hindman, an Arkansan, into the district to raise an army. There was considerable discontent in Arkansas, because the inhabitants felt that the transfer of Confederate troops east of the Mississippi River, after Pea Ridge, meant that they had been abandoned by the Richmond government. Their resentment was heightened by the fact that Arkansas had ranked high on the list of Southern states in supplying troops to the Confederate army, since May of '61. Governor Rector issued a proclamation intimating that if the south-western states were to be abandoned, they would "seek their own safety," [3] that is, withdraw their troops to their own borders for defense. Hindman was to straighten out the matter by assuming charge of conscription in Arkansas and raising an army to secure the state.

Hindman was not only a first-class soldier but a good administrator, and he moved into the control of affairs in the Trans-Mississippi with all the vigor of a Jo Shelby. He commandeered arms and ammunition, medicine, all sorts of supplies, and a million dollars in Confederate money at Helena, Memphis, and Napoleon.[4] He also sequestered two steamboats and brought them up the Arkansas River for use in transporting troops and supplies from Little Rock. He burned thousands of bales of cotton to keep them out of the hands of the enemy, allowing families to retain ten pounds each for their personal use,[5] and he informed Governor Rector that if Arkansas did not continue to supply troops to the regiments already raised,[6] he, Hindman, would gather them with his conscription officers. Desertion, as already noted, he shot from the army with firing squads, and he gave authority "to various persons to raise companies and regiments and operate as guerrillas." [7] Among these was Quantrill, and it may be that Quantrill's nod from Tom Hindman was all the Confederate commission Quantrill ever had.[8] Hindman also realized the importance of supplies to an army. At Arkadelphia and elsewhere, "military posts were established. . . . Measures were adopted for manufacturing many important articles for army use. . . . Machinery was made for manufacturing percussion caps and small arms. . . . Lead mines were opened and worked; a chemical laboratory was established and successfully operated . . . in the manufacture of calomel, castor oil, spirits of nitre, various tinctures of iron and other valuable medicines." [9] In the field, he constructed river fortifications with the utmost energy and drove Curtis from the west bank of the White River in a swamp-and-bayou campaign with which a Shelby narrative is not concerned except that De Vall's Bluff, where his company joined the Confederates of Colonel Nelson, was part of Hindman's chain of defenses.

In short, Hindman understood the magnitude of the struggle. He also understood the importance to the Confederacy of the resources of the Trans-Mississippi, with its broad prairies, its endless supply of food, its cattle and its horses, its ocean ports on the Gulf of Mexico, and its border with Old Mexico through which the goods of Europe could flow into the South for the sustenance of its armies and its people. To preserve this great reservoir of national strength, he was planning to clear the Federals out of Missouri with an expedition of 30,000 to 35,000 men, as soon as he could collect them from all over the four states of his district. At Little Rock he beat the drum of preparedness for this expedition so loudly that on September 18 General Schofield was deceived into believing that it was already taking place.[10] He also completely fooled General Schofield as to the number of his troops. Schofield said he was reliably informed that Hindman had 30,000 men [11] although, as we have seen, the number was actually around 10,000 in Shelby's area, 3,000 of them Indians.

This useful officer, who had been about to weld his economy and his army together and create a Third Front for the Confederacy—an idea which the Richmond government did not endorse until 1864 when it was too late—was removed from supreme command in the summer of 1862, as mentioned earlier, when "the good old granny limped over from Richmond, possessory orders in his pocket, and a lieutenant general's stars upon his collar" [12]—General Theophilus H. Holmes.

General Holmes, being deaf, probably did not hear all of the complaints addressed to him—though he heard one against Shelby—but he knew enough of the situation to know that the inhabitants of the state were roiled at the Confederate government, and he set about soothing them. His policy was to protect Arkansas, keep the peace, and send as many men as he could east to General Pemberton, who was hard pressed on the other side of the Mississippi. He vetoed Hindman's plan for operations against Missouri and ordered him to report to Little Rock. This was soon seen to be a mistake, however, and Hindman was ordered back to take charge of the army in northwestern Arkansas, but with strict orders not to use it for aggression.

In McCulloch's old post as field commander, Hindman used the opportunity to get rid of deadwood in his command and also to settle old scores. Like McCulloch, he had an aversion to Brigadier General James S. Rains, and as his superior he soon forced Rains's resignation.[13] Colonel Coffee, who with Shelby and Upton Hays had organized the brigade, was also dismissed summarily. In the reshuffle, General John S. Marmaduke was appointed cavalry commander.

Marmaduke was a man who spoke Jo Shelby's language. Like Shelby he was a Southern aristocrat from the Missouri River Valley, born in Saline County, of Virginia-descended parents who had both wealth and social position. His father had been governor of the state. Marmaduke had served in Albert Sidney Johnston's Utah expedition. After commanding the Missouri troops at Boonville, he had resigned to follow Johnston in the Confederate service across the river, and had fought at Shiloh. Hindman knew him for a good soldier, and after Corinth he asked the Confederate government to send him Marmaduke to command the western cavalry. When he arrived to take command on October 22, 1862, he found his division about 7,000 strong, including Shelby's Missouri Brigade, and he also found that Schofield was preparing to attack him with his newly organized Army of the Frontier. This was to be six weeks later, on November 28, when Jo Shelby was to demonstrate for the first time that he deserves to rank among the cavalry immortals.

During those six weeks, however, Shelby's brigade at Cross Hol-

lows "came as near not doing anything as any time during its existence," says Historian John C. Moore, who was a member of it.[14]
Colonel Moore undoubtedly is speaking in the military sense, for in
their necessitous condition Shelby's men were busy foraging for anything in the way of supplies they could lay their hands on. They
were also getting acquainted with their colonel, which they had not
had time to do before, on the march from Waverly or in the series
of bloody skirmishes which had followed one after another since Elm
Spring.

He was a hard man to know. The angularity of his character was
never so pronounced as when he was made restless by the inanition
of camp life. "The square, massive lower face, hidden by its thick
brown beard"—says his biographer—"was sometimes hard and pitiless,
and sometimes softened by genial smiles breaking over his features and
melting away all anger suddenly. Extremes met in his disposition,
and conflicting natures warred within his breast. He was all hilarity,
or all dignity and discipline. Lenient today, the men sported with his
mood; tomorrow his orders were harsh as sullen drums, and his men
trembled and obeyed. In the languor of camp life he might be list-
less and contemplative, or nervous, energetic and rapacious for air
and exercise as a Comanche brave. He would discuss by the hour
politics, war, famine, crops, and field sports with the good old citizen
farmers crowding around his quarters, when a change would come
over his desires rapidly and the auditors were dismissed by a wave
of the hand as he galloped off to where his troops were drilling and
maneuvering."

Around his own campfire, however, when the day's hard work was
done, his social qualities would stand out best, says Edwards. "Acces-
sible, kind, and bluff, and free spoken, he sympathized with the troubles of his soldiers, made their cause his own, and promised them that
all differences would be smoothed away and adjusted." His officers
soon learned that he would not tolerate the jealousies and rivalries
arising out of ambition and vanity; and if the brigade was not free
of them, at least they were hidden from Old Jo. For self-seeking
officers he had nothing but contempt, and he wore his colonel's stars
for a solid year after he assumed command of a brigade, in much the
same manner that Lieutenant General Jackson wore a forage cap and
private's blouse: they would do for the business at hand. Gold lace
was pretty in drawing rooms, but it fooled nobody on the battlefield.

For his men, however, he demanded the best the country could afford, and some of them found to their dismay that when they had cached away something special on their own, Old Jo, if he could find it, regarded it as community property of the brigade. "I remember," Major Stonestreet told a reporter after the war, "that once I had not owned an extra shirt for a long time. I captured some calico from a Yankee settler, and Confederate women made me half a dozen beauties. I put them in my tent and resolved that I would never have another grayback on me as long as I lived. I was called away for a couple of days and when I got back my shirts were gone. Shelby had given them to a lot of young dudes who hung about the tent as staff officers because they considered themselves too good to go into the line. I was hot, but it didn't do any good. 'There is plenty more where that came from, Jake,' was all I could get out of him." [15] Major Stonestreet's indignation may be judged from the fact that he referred to his brother officers as dudes. There were all sorts in the army of the Trans-Mississippi, but it is not likely that any of Shelby's staff officers fell into that class.

On November 5 Shelby's brigade was joined by a band of 150 gimlet-eyed foragers who could have given any of his Missouri farm boys cards and spades in the business of looting settlers in remote spots—and killing them afterward. They were guerrillas under command of a Lieutenant William H. Gregg, and their company was beginning to be well known by the name of Quantrill's Band, for their captain, William Clarke Quantrill. Captain Quantrill, who had been operating under the loosely granted authority of General Hindman, had gone to Richmond to see if he could persuade the Secretary of War to give him a commission under the Partisan Ranger Act. Thus he was not present when his bushwhackers were assigned to Shelby's Missouri Cavalry Brigade, on the 5th, but some of his most fair-haired boys were. Among them were Dick Yager, Cole Younger, and two Missouri brothers, Frank and Jesse James, who were to make a name in the world for themselves after the war.

The boys were tired when they arrived at Shelby's camp in Arkansas. They had ridden a long way, by the old Fort Scott and Fort Gibson Road, and they had paused for an exhausting two-hour fight with Federals at the town of Lamar, in Barton County. When they had not been able to take Lamar from the Federals, they had set fire to it. [16]

13. *The Iron Brigade: Cane Hill*

SHELBY'S EXPLOIT at Cane Hill first marked him as a Confederate cavalry commander who, as Governor Fletcher said, was one of the most dangerous men the Federals had to deal with during the war. At Cane Hill Marmaduke's two brigades of cavalry—two thirds of Hindman's mounted forces—would have been routed and most of them captured if Colonel Shelby had not hit upon the idea, at the peak of the emergency, that a force of thirty companies, attacking in all directions, can cover a retreat much better than a single brigade which is badly outnumbered.

Because Cane Hill is scarcely a pinpoint on the battle maps of the Civil War, Shelby's brilliant improvisation has been passed over and forgotten except by students of the cavalry and by Missouri historians, such as Moore and Edwards, who wrote in gasping admiration but with no meticulous regard for the historical facts which form the background of heroic deeds. The facts of the Battle of Cane Hill, however, are indisputable. The disgruntled report of the Federal commander, General James G. Blunt, whom Shelby whipsawed as his men rushed forward to claim the victory they had won, is evidence that Shelby is entitled to all the encomiums and eulogies heaped upon him by the Missouri historians. And if they scramble some of the collateral facts in so doing, it must be remembered that they were there; and that the man in the Civil War equivalent of a foxhole, or riding a terrified horse in a cavalry melee, was not in the best position to describe an entire battlefield accurately.

The expedition to Cane Hill was Hindman's idea. Relegated to active command in the field, he gave General Holmes no peace until he had gained permission to enter Missouri and attempt to clear the border of the enemy. He knew that General Blunt, with his Kansans, was somewhere around Fayetteville, and he knew that another Federal general, a new one, Francis J. Herron, was in the vicinity of Yellville, where he was menacing a Confederate arsenal and saltpetre works. Blunt was reported to have 8,000 men and actually had 5,000; Herron was in command of the First Iowa, Tenth Illinois, and Second Wisconsin regiments, all crack troops, in addition to Missouri and Arkansas Union troops. Hindman was alarmed by their presence and determined to get them out.

Holmes knew that Hindman was bent upon a Missouri campaign, but the Richmond government was importuning him for Arkansas troops to reinforce the Confederate armies east of the Mississippi. In fairness to General Holmes it must be said that he did not have enough troops to reinforce Vicksburg and reconquer Missouri too; but he was not planning to do either. He simply played off one demand against the other; when Richmond wanted troops east of the Mississippi, he spoke of the need in Arkansas and Missouri; when Hindman wanted troops he complained that the Richmond government was always after him for soldiers. Nevertheless, he yielded to Hindman to this extent: Hindman could use his troops of the northwestern Arkansas forces to drive the enemy from the Arkansas River Valley, if possible, and end the threat of invasion; but after that he must return with his forces to Little Rock.

Hindman agreed, and sent off Marmaduke with two brigades of cavalry through the Boston Mountains on November 17, 1862, for the purpose of drawing off Blunt and preventing him from making a junction with Herron. Blunt was even closer than Hindman thought. He was fifteen miles south of Maysville, at a place called Lindsey's Prairie. Infiltration of Arkansas by Federal troops was going ahead without interruption, and Hindman was fully justified in his apprehension that an attack on Van Buren and Little Rock was in the making.

Shelby's brigade moved at the head of Marmaduke's columns through Van Buren on the night of the 17th, camped for a few hours, and then swung into the saddles again—"on and on over the rugged road, the swollen and rocky streams, through the eternal solitude of the Boston Mountains, whose gigantic peaks, pine-crowned and majestic, rose up into the cold, gray clouds, winter on their hoary heads, but not upon their feet; and down again to the lovely valley of Cane Hill, nestled in among the great blue hills as cosily as a domestic housewife." [1]

They arrived at Cane Hill, four days ahead of the battle, by the Telegraph Road....

That term has a familiar ring in Confederate history, and a clatter of terrible urgency ... blue troopers in the moonlight on the Telegraph Road in Virginia, as Sheridan rides for Richmond . . . with Yellow Tavern and a dying Stuart at the end, in '64. . . . But on the Telegraph Road to Cane Hill, there had been no sergeant in dusty blue to empty his pistol at the rebel colonel on the horse . . . the one in the plumed hat, as he breathed the frosty air of the mountains. The Telegraph Road through the Boston Mountains, for Shelby, was a beginning, as the Telegraph Road in Virginia, for Stuart, was the end.

There had been Federals in the neighborhood a few days before, under the command of Lieutenant Colonel Lewis R. Jewell of the Sixth Kansas—mark the name, for he figures in a curious way in the Battle of Cane Hill—but except for a few scouts whom Colonel Jewell had left in his rear, the Federals had trotted on back across the mountain to General Blunt. As a result of the report made by Jewell to Blunt, the latter sent word to General Schofield that if given a small reinforcement he could take both Van Buren and Fort Smith—provided Schofield sent General Frederick Steele to occupy the attention of Holmes so that he could not reinforce Hindman. It will be seen that Hindman and Blunt both had the same plan, a leaf straight out of the pages of Caesar and Napoleon . . . divide and conquer.

The second day at Cane Hill, Shelby sent out scouting parties. One of them sabred a party of Pin Indians while they were sleeping, and another made contact with the scouts Jewell had left behind, but came off badly in the encounter.[2]

On the third day of camp the soldiers were pleasantly awakened. "Even before the most industrious soldier would have risen in all probability from his frosty blankets," says Edwards, "a young and beautiful girl, Miss Susan McClellan, a fair rebel living four miles to the west of Cane Hill, came tripping into camp, bareheaded and *en déshabille,* to inform Colonel Shelby that six hundred Federal cavalry, from the direction of Fort Smith, had just passed her father's house to surprise him. The roses on her cheeks deepened beneath the admiring gaze of her auditors, but her fine eyes never quailed, nor did her patriotic earnestness waver. Giving her a guard of honor, ten stalwart cavaliers, Colonel Shelby said to her that the enemy's movements were known, and that his men were concealed behind a large fence bordering a level cornfield through which the Federals must advance. . . . Sure enough, Miss McClellan had not preceded their arrival more than thirty minutes, and her preparations to see the fight had scarcely been completed before the Federals entered the cornfield in fine style and advanced in line of battle upon the crouching Confederates."

The fight which Miss McClellan tidied up to enjoy now ensued, but there are two versions as to how it ended—Federal and Confederate. Major Edwards says that three thousand muskets poured hot shot into the enemy from behind the snaky fence, and that "the well dressed line melted away like snow in a thaw, and shivering to the pitiless shock every living man turned and fled in one rushing, frenzied mass ... the yelling Confederates following on foot until distanced in the race."

General Blunt makes a one-line report of this affair: "A detachment sent from my command attacked a large reconnoitering party of the enemy and scattered them." This sounds like a report of the affair of the day before, when Major Edwards says that a small scouting party was driven in; but it is not, for it is a report of activities on November 25, the third day in camp, and the day on which Major Edwards insists that a victory was won for the edification of "the fair rebel" who had entered the camp *en déshabille*. Edwards says that afterward they cheered Miss McClellan, Marmaduke thanked Shelby for his "watchfulness," and made known the fact that "the ladies of Little Rock had presented him with two beautiful banners to be given to the company and regiment which most distinguished themselves in the next battle." It was a great day, the twenty-fifth of November, the first on which the homespun knights actually had a Guinevere present, and Major Edwards made the most of it.

Blunt was in no mood for either jousting or jesting. He had his eye on Van Buren, and his spies had informed him of Marmaduke's advance and disposition of his forces, which were just south of Cane Hill. Blunt had no great opinion of the enemy in front of him. "Shall strike him at daylight, unless he runs," [3] he wrote to Schofield, and late in the evening of November 26 began his march to Cane Hill.

Cane Hill is at the beginning of the Boston Mountain chain, and Blunt arrived there two days later, having covered a distance of thirty miles. Tersely he describes the beginning of the battle:

"I marched at 5 A.M. on the 28th, leaving the (main) road and making a detour to the left, by a blind track; struck one that was obscure and unfrequented and entered Cane Hill directly from the north. As I had anticipated, they had no pickets on this road, and I met no resistance until within half a mile of their camp."

The Confederates were expecting Blunt; he could not have moved 5,000 men, 30 guns, cavalry and wagons across the prairie and a mountain just a few miles distant without their knowing it, but they were not expecting him to make a detour, and if his infantry had not unexpectedly lagged behind his cavalry, he would have caught them napping.

Shelby's report says, "Having had due notice (eighteen hours previous) by the general commanding that the enemy were advancing, we endeavored to be on the alert, but I must confess (though it may reflect somewhat upon myself) that the enemy, by skilfull management, fell upon me sooner than I desired, considering that a portion of our division was encamped some distance in my rear and I had but little time to give them the notice required; yet I had sufficient time to place my men in their proper positions and await the coming of the hated foe." [4]

The style is not Shelby's; plainly Captain Edwards has rejoined him and taken over the duty of writing reports. The report says that "we had expected [the enemy] to advance either on the Cincinnati or Fayetteville Road, our position covering both." Shelby had only two guns with which to cover the two approaches. (There were only six in Marmaduke's entire command.) Two little six-pounders, turned in opposite directions, awaiting the coming of 5,000 men and 30 pieces of artillery. And only 2,000 men in the rear to meet the hurricane of fire which 5,000 men and 30 pieces of artillery can loose. (Carroll's brigade had only 389 out of 1,700 present; the rest were Shelby's [5] but he had only about two thirds of his normal muster roll of 2,500.)

Blunt, however, was one of the Federal commanders who always believed the reports of Confederate strength which Hindman's spies brought him, and as he marched through the town of Cane Hill, on a cloudy November morning, he believed that Marmaduke had 8,000 men, probably with artillery to match. He would not have marched through Cane Hill at all if he had known that the 200 Kansas cavalry trotting in his rear, hauling two light mountain howitzers and four heavy guns under a Captain Rabb, were his only effective force at the moment. The other 4,800 of his men were still struggling over a mountain road seven miles in his rear, but Blunt says that "Of this I was not apprised until my advance was engaged." [6]

With the enemy in sight, Shelby trained both guns on the Fayetteville road, into which Blunt and his cavalry escort had channeled, and hurled a few shells in their direction. At the same time Marmaduke's videttes, lurking in the brush in a gorge between two hills, opened fire on the blue-capped horsemen of the Third Kansas. Sabres swinging, the Kansans rode into the defile, and the videttes, whom Blunt had mistaken for "the grand guard"[7] of the enemy, fell back. By this time the Federal gunners had set up their six guns and were blasting away at Shelby's position on the summit of the hill. The sound of cannon brought Marmaduke apace from the main camp, but knowing the strength of the enemy—and not knowing that that strength was divided—he adopted an immediate policy of watchful waiting. For the next hour Shelby's gunners exchanged broadsides with the Federals, who strangely made no move, and Marmaduke formed two lines of defense on the ridges in back of him.

When he halted just south of Cane Hill, Blunt was in the position of a stagecoach driver, hurtling along a mountain road, who looks around at a turn to discover that his perch and two wheels is all that is left of his vehicle. He was at the head of an army, but it was nowhere in sight, and the enemy was in front of him. He sent a staff officer—Major V. P. Van Antwerp—at a gallop to see where his laggard columns were, with orders to "bring them on the double-quick" for a flanking movement to dislodge the rebel gunners on the hill "and perhaps capture their artillery."[8] Van Antwerp took a long time, for he had to ride a great distance—this was the delay which puzzled Marmaduke—and when he returned he had only four companies of the Eleventh Kansas and a four-gun battery. The others, he reported, "were too far in the rear and the men much too fatigued by the march to reach me in time."[9]

With ten guns, however, Blunt could sweep the field, and with six companies at hand he decided to risk battle despite what he believed to be the superiority of the enemy's forces. Sending four companies ahead under Major Van Antwerp, to attack, and retaining the two companies of the Third Kansas in reserve, he ordered the reinforced batteries to begin a work of destruction on the ridge which sheltered Marmaduke's main line and Shelby's guns.

Thus, after a false start or two, began the engagement at Cane Hill, Blunt, the well-named soldier, dismisses the opening clash with one line in his report. Van Antwerp, he says, "after the artillery had been very destructive to the enemy, compelled them to abandon their position." [10] Major Edwards, who was a participant as well as an eyewitness of the battle, says the same thing in different words:

"In sooth, it was a glorious sight. A strong northwest wind tore down the yellow leaves in great gusts of broken pinions, and flared the rival flags in broad defiance above the rival armies. Every movement of Blunt could be plainly seen in the valley below, and his long lines came gleaming on

> " 'Ere the life-blood warm and wet
> Had dimmed a glistening bayonet.'

"Collins opened first and shot a great gap in the leading regiment while the stars and stripes went down dimmed in the battle's van. A hundred eager hands grasped the fallen banner, but a fresh discharge scattered the regiment like chaff to the shelter of the woods beyond. There went up a fierce yell from the Confederates, and their skirmishers ran swarming down the hill to engage at closer range. Battery after battery rolled up to the front and poured a terrible fire upon Shelby's devoted brigade, waiting for the onset—a fire rarely if ever surpassed for terrible accuracy and precision. Ahead of all [the Federal guns] plied their bloody trade, and shredded life and limb away like stubble in the lava tide.... When Blunt threw forward a large force of infantry for the assault . . . three times they came to the death grapple and three times Shelby's lone brigade hurled them back in confusion. Suddenly, two heavy [Federal] columns broke away to the right and left, and General Marmaduke knew further resistance would be useless. The bugles sounded retreat, and Shelby moved off in magnificent style, bringing with him his dead and wounded." [11]

It will be seen that to Edwards, the incurable adventurer and romanticist, any battle was a "glorious" sight, whether it was being won or lost; but Shelby had no time for heroics and from the moment he had seen Blunt's overwhelming forces advancing up the valley turnpike at nine o'clock that morning, he had realized that General Marmaduke was in a trap. As Edwards says—this time without exaggeration—Shelby's outstanding trait was "an almost infallible divination of the enemy's designs and a rare analysis which enabled him, step by step, to fathom movements and unravel demonstrations as if he held the printed programme in his hand." [12]

The outstanding factor in the present situation was that, in the rugged country to their rear, retreat would be difficult. By the same token, so would pursuit. In an intuitive flash, Shelby had the answer. To make retreat easy, it would be necessary to make pursuit difficult. A lone brigade against five brigades would stand no chance in covering such a retreat. But a brigade is thirty companies. Suppose you placed thirty companies at distances an eighth of a mile apart along the route...properly concealed...that would be thirty firing positions. The positions could not be held, of course, but that would not be necessary. The company next the enemy would only have to fire at point-blank range, break rapidly into column, gallop immediately behind the other twenty-nine still formed, and take position again for the same maneuver. Thus, advancing forces would meet continually a solid, deadly tempest of lead driving into their very faces, and the companies delivering their fire in rotation would have ample time to reload carefully and select the most excellent positions.

It is one thing to dream up such academic solutions while seated in a comfortable chair at the War College or before a fire with brother officers in a club. It is another to improvise such a plan and put it into execution with the enemy swirling about you and one of your two guns suddenly smashed by the direct hit of an enemy shell, which was what was happening now...but Shelby did it. He not only saved Marmaduke's command at Cane Hill, he evolved on the spur of the moment a plan which he used to bloody perfection over and over again when he was on his great raids into Missouri.

Somehow, in all that confusion, he got word to his regimental commanders, Gordon, Jeans, and Thompson, and to Elliott's and Quantrill's scouts (still commanded by Gregg), as to what they must do. And somehow, in that six weeks at Cross Hollows, he had built an organization which could receive such orders, under such circumstances, and carry them out.

Shelby's brigade—it would earn the title of Iron Brigade—was alone in the fight now. Colonel Carroll's Arkansans had cut and run in the very first breath of the hurricane, "and thundered away to Van Buren, carrying tidings of defeat and disaster." [13] Collins and Bledsoe were staring at their disabled gun, so badly smashed that it could not be moved by horses. But they and their cannoneers did more than stare. They gathered up the entire gun carriage, "crippled but triumphant," [14] and staggered under its weight down the incline of the ridge. It was not the first time that day—the fight lasted all day, thanks to Shelby, until the last man got clean away on the other side of the mountain—that the men of the brigade took the place of the horses of the artillery when the horses could no longer move the guns. From ridge to ridge, Colonel Carroll observes, they bore their guns, "unwilling to leave any trophy in the hands of their country's enemy." [15] His admiration is all the more touching in view of the fact that his own men had fled somewhere back of the landscape.

Marmaduke fell back first to his reserve line on the second ridge, then to another, then to still another, and finally to a large mound or pillar, completely nude of vegetation, at the base of the Boston Mountains, where he was able to plant his artillery firmly and gather all of Shelby's men about him for a breathing space. He had been able to accomplish this because Blunt's progress had been painfully slow. There was nothing in the copybooks about what to do when the enemy retreats by means of a series of offensives, and the slow-witted Blunt apparently never realized exactly the nature of the operation Shelby was conducting.

"I felt assured," he said, "that they had resolved on a desperate resistance, and made my arrangements accordingly; but after getting my force across a deep and rugged ravine, and deploying them in position, ready to advance upon their long and well formed line, I discovered, to my disappointment, that they had again retired, and were in full retreat to the mountains." This happened four times in three miles, according to his own statement.[16]

After three miles of retreating, Shelby style (*"Let the enemy's advance pass before firing!"*)[17] the men, the horses, and the artillery of the brigade were firmly ensconced on their pinnacle, and Shelby's gunners were able again to direct their fire at the enemy's infantry. Apparently the ease with which they had escaped to a formidable position now made both Marmaduke and Shelby reluctant to proceed at once with the retreat. Men and horses would welcome a rest; but morale was high. In fact, the brigade was jubilant as Shelby's men gazed down at the blue-gray haze of the valley below. They had a steeplejack's view of the Federals, and their situation was pleasing. Just then the sun, which had been behind the November clouds all day, burst through with a fiery, winter-glazed radiance which almost reached the tips of the Boston Mountains in the southwestern sky.

A wild shout went up at the happy omen, and Shelby, pointing to the blazing sky with his plume, said, "It is the sun of Austerlitz!"

Recently he was becoming acquainted with military history under the tutelage of Edwards. But it was not the sun of Austerlitz for Marmaduke; the swarming Federals in the valley still outnumbered him five to two.

Blunt reconnoitred the ground in front of Marmaduke's new position and decided that the terrain was not suitable for an artillery bombardment;[18] and he had had enough of flank attacks. He ordered his men to take the hill by storm.

This they did, and not all the picaresque prose of the Southern historians can conceal the fact that the men of the Second Kansas, the Eleventh Kansas, and the Third Cherokee Indian Regiment made a charge at sunset that day as brave as any in American history. Blunt says his Kansans were bloodthirstily eager to come to grips with the Missourians, and he was doubtless right, for there was bad blood between them to start, and at Cane Hill Shelby had been thwarting and tormenting them all day.

"The resistance of the rebels was stubborn and determined," Blunt says in his report. "The storm of lead and iron hail that came down the side of the mountain, both from their small arms and their artillery, was terrific; yet most of it went over our heads without doing us much damage. The regiments named, with a wild shout, rushed up the steep declivity, contesting every inch of ground, and steadily pushing the enemy before them, until the crest was reached, when the rebels fled again in wild disorder." [19]

The rebels retreated, but not in wild disorder, for Shelby again covered the retreat in precisely the same manner as from Cane Hill, down three miles of winding mountain road, toward the valley in which Van Buren stands. Blunt paused on the mountain top long enough to bring up the rest of his artillery, then sent his Indians (whom Edwards says he had "stimulated with drink") and the Eleventh Kansas after the Confederates, but once again he was confronted with the mystery of an enemy who was supposed to be running, but actually was fighting. "About every half mile," he says, "the enemy made a stand [thus contradicting his own description of "wild disorder"] and as often the howitzers of the Eleventh Kansas and Third Indian would put them to flight, leaving more or less of their dead and wounded behind them. Thus the fight continued for three miles."

Three times during the three-mile retreat, Shelby's horse was shot

and killed beneath him—a horse for every mile. All three were sorrels
—one of them cut down by eleven bullets at once—and during the
rest of the war Shelby would ride only a sorrel, believing that he
bore a charmed life as long as he rode one. A pistol ball carried away
his black plume, his uniform was soaked with the blood of the horses,
and the blood of one of his officers spurted into his face as the enemy's
shrapnel swept them—but he remained with the rear company until
the last of Marmaduke's regiments had streamed to the base of the
mountain in the oncoming dark.

At the intersection of the Cove Creek road with the Fayetteville
road, leading to Van Buren, Shelby again brought his guns into position. (One of the two wrecked guns had been patched up sufficiently
to go into action again, so that he now had five.) With darkness
upon them, he expected Blunt to try one last charge before giving
up the pursuit.

His surmise was correct. Blunt hurled the three companies of the
Sixth Kansas under Lieutenant Colonel Jewell straight into the rear
of the Confederates, with sabres and carbines, for a distance of half
a mile; his men were again deceived into thinking that everything
on two feet ahead of them was running. The order of the day was
passed to Shelby's gunners once more: *"Let the enemy's advance pass
before firing!"*

Blunt admits that he was ambushed. "As soon as the party we were
pursuing had passed through the defile," he says, "they opened upon
us a most destructive fire, which, for the moment, caused my men
to recoil and give back, in spite of my own efforts and those of the
officers to rally them; whereas, if they had, after receiving the enemy's
fire, passed on 200 or 300 yards, we could have secured, in a moment
more, what we so much coveted—the enemy's artillery."

Jewell went down, mortally wounded, and Shelby ordered a charge.
"Emboldened by their success in defending the defile and checking
our advance," says Blunt, "they raised a wild yell and advanced toward us. . . . I succeeded in rallying the companies of the Sixth Kansas, who had suffered severely, and formed them across the valley."

The stand made here was necessary for salvation, as Major Edwards says. His own horse had been killed, and Edwards' eyewitness
description of the savage scene on the wild mountain side, as dark
came down swiftly, is one of his best: "Blunt's troops took no prisoners, and had broken through the rear by one long bloody, tenacious

charge. The narrow road, rough and filled with huge stones, was crowded by a rushing, thundering, panic stricken mass, riding for life, as imagined, down a huge hill and over a deep stream at the bottom. It was a fearful moment. The ground shook and sounded as if undergoing some terrible convulsion. Sabres were whirling, pistols cracking incessantly, the peculiar Indian yell—a wailing, mournful sound, loud above all—and thus the human avalanche rushed down. It was swallowing up Shelby's lines as it came. He could erect no barrier strong enough to check it. In a moment then he ordered his regiment to open its ranks for the tide to sweep through, which it did with the rush of a hurricane, knocking men right and left over precipices and into deep pools. Hall Shindler, attached to the staff of Colonel Shelby, while bravely attempting to bring some order out of the confusion, was literally ridden over, and finally knocked by a blundering horse down a steep place into the water below." [20]

Shelby's horse was shot from under him for the fourth time that day, and as he rolled away from its kicking, shrilly neighing form, he heard the thunder of the guns die down. Night and a flag of truce had ended the battle, and only the terrible sounds of the wounded men and the mangled horses, mingled with the noise of the rushing stream, were heard. Shelby got to his feet, called to Edwards in the dark, and the two of them fumbled for the bridles of a pair of riderless mounts. General Marmaduke was somewhere back there, at the head of the line. Shelby's presence of mind, and the devotion of some of his officers, had saved the cavalry brigade of the Army of Northwestern Arkansas that day.

What happened next has been made the subject of much historical embroidery. A number of Southern historians [21] say that Blunt sent over the flag of truce, asking a suspension of hostilities to gather up the wounded and bury the dead, and asking for the body of Colonel Jewell. A highly imaginary conversation is recorded in which Blunt is supposed to have told Marmaduke and Shelby, "Your men fought like devils.... Two hundred and fifty of my best men fallen, and more heroic young officers than I can hope to get again." Shelby is quoted as having asked, "How many men did you fight us with today?" and Blunt is quoted as having replied, "I am ashamed to tell you, but more than you had to meet me."

In all probability, Shelby asked some such question, and got no answer from Blunt as to his strength; the rest is purest moonshine.

In the first place, Colonel Jewell was not dead. He was wounded, although mortally. (He died later in the Federal camp.) Secondly, Blunt did not send over an officer with a flag of truce. Marmaduke sent one to him. That was the lull in the firing when Shelby's horse was killed. Having seen Marmaduke's officer galloping up with a white flag, Blunt directed that "not a gun should be fired until I give the word." [22] He granted the truce, he says, "out of consideration for Colonel Jewell and others who had fallen upon the ground they then occupied, and whom I feared they might brutally murder ...convinced though I was at the time that it [the flag of truce] was a cowardly trick, resorted to to enable them to make good their retreat and save their guns." [23]

So far from admitting 250 casualties, Blunt reports that he had four men killed and thirty-six wounded, four of them mortally and "since dead." As for the calibre of the troops opposing them, remembering the flight of the Arkansas troops, he said later, "I am prepared to meet and with my little army whip 25,000 of such chivalry." [24] And he added that "an officer who came inside our lines [under the flag of truce] that night acknowledged that they were badly whipped and worse chased."

Such conflicting reports are the rule rather than the exception in the official accounts given by participants in the war west of the Mississippi, and they are not unknown in other theatres. General Blunt was a most sarcastic man,[25] and as a result of the Battle of Cane Hill the District of Western Arkansas was added to his command. But the plain fact is that, thanks to Jo Shelby and his adaptation of Indian warfare to the cavalry, Blunt had been unable between 9 A.M. and sunset to capture an enemy whom he outnumbered five to two and who was never more than a few yards away at any time.

14. *The Iron Brigade: Prairie Grove*

THE BATTLE OF CANE HILL had been a feeling-out fight. Marmaduke, halted with his division at Dripping Springs at the foot of the mountain down which he had been driven, sent a courier to Hindman for orders. Hindman sent back word for Marmaduke to stay where he was; he himself would be coming up with 9,000 men additional and twenty-two guns to strike Blunt at Cane Hill. Hindman knew that his force vastly outnumbered that of Blunt, and although his equipment was in poor condition and his rations meagre, he had Holmes's permission to fight [1] and nothing on earth could have kept him from marching on Cane Hill.

Blunt had retired into Newburg, one of several little towns in the vicinity of Cane Hill which, though it appears to be in a valley, is actually one of the low-lying ridges north of the Boston Mountain chain. There he was separated from Hindman by some forty miles of rugged and sterile mountain range, through which the roads, if they could be called that, were excessively bad. At his own back, however, there was an excellent road, the main highway running north to Fayetteville and Springfield, along which General Herron could march to his reinforcement at the drop of a telegraphic dispatch.

Blunt was in much the better spot, militarily speaking, of the two, and the morale of his men, Pin Indians and all, was high. They had made the enemy run, in their first invasion of Arkansas; they had seen their superior artillery scatter great bodies of rebel horsemen whose rags fluttered like pennons in the hot hurricane. Confident and cocky, as they swilled down great quantities of the peach and apple brandy for which Washington County is famous, they were ready to enjoy another such uneven contest any day.

General Blunt, however, still believed that Hindman had 25,000 or 30,000 men [2] (Hindman had a positive genius for mystifying the enemy as to his strength), and on December 3, when spies brought him word that Hindman was on the move, he telegraphed General Herron, in something like alarm, suggesting an immediate consolidation of forces.

Herron was not as close by as he had been; he had fallen back from the Huntsville-Yellville neighborhood to the peace and quiet of Springfield, and was camped on the old battlefield of Wilson's Creek, but he responded immediately to Blunt's call. He telegraphed the same day: "Will move both divisions entire at noon today and will make good time to your position.... The distance is so great it may be necessary for you to fall back a short distance, but I will do my best to make that unnecessary." [3]

Hindman's plan of campaign was perfectly shaped and adapted to the country in which he would wage it. This whole area between Van

Buren and Fayetteville, a distance of fifty or sixty-five miles depending on the route traveled, is crisscrossed with country roads as thick as blood vessels. There are four principal roads leading through the mountains, but Hindman was concerned with only one: the Cove Creek Road, which branches off the Telegraph Road nineteen miles above Van Buren, and strikes for Fayetteville through defiles, valleys, and eventually over prairies. This Cove Creek Road, however, has a little offshoot of a road at a place called Morrow's, which runs directly into Cane Hill—and the distance is only seven miles. That was Hindman's route: Telegraph Road, Cove Creek Road, turn off at Morrow's, march seven miles to Cane Hill. And while he did so, the plan was to send Marmaduke and Shelby straight ahead on Cove Creek Road until they came to another back trail—the Maysville branch—where they would gallop to the left and rear of Blunt and attack him on the flank.

If this plan is objected to on the ground that it leaves General Herron out of the picture, the objection is valid. Hindman had asked Holmes to take care of Herron by using some of the troops at Little Rock to make a feint in his direction and thus distract his attention while the main force of the expedition surrounded Blunt. Holmes had agreed to do this, Edwards says,[4] but he did not do it. Perhaps because Herron seemed to be retreating toward Springfield, or perhaps because he feared an attack on Little Rock from the direction of Helena—where no danger threatened—the General-in-chief of the Trans-Mississippi Department simply drew his troops about him like an old man drawing on an overcoat against the cold, and did nothing.

On the morning of December 3, then, as Blunt became duly informed, Hindman assembled his troops at Van Buren and marched up the Telegraph Road to join Marmaduke. There was never any doubt about Hindman's plan, as the author of *Confederate Military History* at this point seems to think.[5] Blunt was Hindman's quarry; Herron did not enter into his calculations at all. The only thing that was in Hindman's mind as he joined Marmaduke was this: Blunt could use these back-country roads too. While he was turning off the Telegraph Road, marching north and turning right to Cane Hill, what was to prevent Blunt from slipping across the mountain by the same road along which he had driven Marmaduke and Shelby three days before? To permit Blunt on that road would be to put him on

the road to Van Buren and Little Rock. Hindman could easily out-
smart himself here.

To seal off this route, and to confuse Blunt as to his real plans,
Hindman now sent Colonel J. C. Monroe with the Arkansas Brigade
(they were back again, minus Colonel Carroll) on foot up the boulder-
strewn road over which Shelby had fought, with instructions to fire
on Blunt's pickets from the crest of the mountain and kick up enough
commotion to make Blunt believe that they constituted the advance
guard of the main force.

Shelby's brigade (now designated the Fourth Missouri Cavalry)
was reserved for the real work of drawing the enemy into a battle
in which he could be whipped. It must be done quickly, for Hindman had barely enough ammunition for one battle "and not sufficient subsistence and forage for seven days at half rations." [6] These
meagre supplies had been accumulated with extreme difficulty. The
Arkansas countryside was exhausted, and even if supplies had been
available, the river at Van Buren was so low that they could not
have been transported by water. In Hindman's own words, "These
facts made it certain that I must soon retire the greater part of my force
toward Little Rock, hence it seemed important . . . that Blunt be driven
from his position." Hindman was relying on his superiority of numbers to encompass Blunt. With 11,000 men, he outnumbered the
Kansan better than two to one.

As Monroe's Arkansas riflemen—dismounted—moved cautiously
along either side of the road against the mountain which loomed
ahead of them at Dripping Springs,[7] the rest of Hindman's army
moved in a northerly direction on the Cove Creek Road. It was a
typical mountain creek road, difficult of passage for poorly shod
horses, wagons with wheels loosened by much jolting, and frayed
harness which frequently snapped as the caissons strained and struggled over the outcroppings of rock—but Hindman pushed his command eight miles the first day. Although this was good progress,
considering the obstacles, he was, on the fifth of December, only
half the distance to Morrow's crossroads—a full day behind schedule
in a movement in which time was vital.

On the fifth, while the infantry was making its eight-mile march,
Shelby's scouts, ranging ahead, encountered a peacefully trotting company of bluecaps of the First Kansas, with a captain in the lead. "After

a sharp little fight," says Shelby's report, "my advance ... drove him back in great confusion." [8]

That brush, of course, advertised their position to Blunt: as soon as the men of the First Kansas reported back to Cane Hill, the Federal general sent a "much larger scout" over the mountain to look into matters on the Cove Creek Road. Under fire from Shelby's men, they retreated, having seen enough: Shelby had unlimbered his batteries and dismounted the entire First Regiment of his command in case they should try a charge. Major Edwards' disappointment that they did not do so is keen in his report: "During this engagement," he says, "the First Regiment, Lieutenant Colonel B. F. Gordon, and the Third, Colonel G. W. Thompson, [were] dismounted and formed as support to Bledsoe's battery, now in position, with lighted portfires and eager gunners, keen for the fray that grew fainter and fainter as Colonel Jeans' [cavalry] pushed them hard and heavily, until the grand old mountains gave no murmur back, and all was silent, cold, and still."

As the Federals escaped in the direction of Cane Hill, Hindman suggested to Shelby that he send Major Ben Elliott by another mountain trail to try to head them off, and interrupt Blunt's flow of information: Elliott departed on this assignment at nightfall with a battalion of scouts, "but owing to the darkness of the night, the rugged and impassable road, and the ignorance of the guide," Elliott, that trained V. M. I. graduate, got lost in the mountains, and "the expedition failed in its essential points." [9]

Long before the winter dawn of the sixth, Shelby had every man in his brigade awakened, armed, and in the saddle for a pell-mell dash to Morrow's crossroads, to take possession of the approaches to the road which leads direct to Cane Hill. At Morrow's, they found the neighborhood swarming with Federals. Shelby attacked, for he knew that Hindman was in motion behind him, and should be almost within hailing distance. Shelby was a cavalryman, but he knew when to dismount. The time was now. He waved his men from the saddle with his plumed hat, and every man who had a gun capable of firing at even shotgun range advanced on the wooded mountain. Blunt's pickets, too, knew that this was it. They stood and fought, when they could, but they were up against hill fighters, these bluecoated boys from the plains of Kansas, and Shelby's men smashed them three times as they attempted to form a line below the crest of the ridge.

Shelby's report says that the three companies which he had ordered into the advance "drove in the enemy's pickets with great rapidity and execution, although he made three different stands and fought me three times." The men, he says, "were this morning keen for a fight, and went furiously up the steep and rugged mountain at the double quick for miles."

Actually it was five miles, five miles of fighting through treacherous gullies and over rock slabs which would have slowed down the hardiest infantry that tried to cross them on the double-quick; but Shelby's men were mountain goats, in addition to being "half alligator and half horse." When they finally gained the heights and saw no more enemy in sight, they were staggering from exhaustion, and the reaction from battle tension. Their legs buckled, and they threw themselves panting on the ground, careless of where their weapons fell.

The infantry was not far behind, and when Hindman rode up, he saw that Shelby and his men had fought themselves into the state of collapse from which soldiers cannot be aroused, unless they are relieved; he ordered them back to camp. The infantry—these were Parsons' brigade—was directed to hold the ground which Shelby had gained. Colonel Monroe, who had carried out his assignment on the mountaintop the previous day and had rejoined Parsons, was ordered forward with skirmishers of the Arkansas brigade. For the rest of the day, Monroe harried the enemy on the downward slopes, "charging a superior force of the enemy's cavalry with great boldness and vigor, breaking his ranks, and only ceasing to pursue when recalled." [10]

Shelby's men were permitted "some little sleep," but not until they had cooked three days' rations and made preparations to move northward again: they must bivouac tonight on the Maysville Road, along which Hindman would push one prong of his two-pronged attack in the morning. The attack by the Maysville Road, with Marmaduke and Shelby leading the way, was to be the important one. They would describe a wide circle, crossing the Fayetteville and Cane Hill Road as they did so, assail Blunt on his left and in his rear, dislodge him from Cane Hill, and drive him into the waiting arms of Parsons —the old man of the mountain, who would blast him as he fell back into the already bloodstained ridges.

It was a good plan, though it was to miscarry. In fact, if it had not been for Herron, Blunt on the morning of the seventh would have faced a choice of being destroyed or leaving the country altogether—providing he could find an escape route across the plains. General Schofield, the supreme Federal commander in the West, saw it all later when he exclaimed angrily that Blunt and Herron were bunglers who had been outwitted "in detail," [11] thus unintentionally conferring a compliment on Hindman, who had thought of everything.

Shelby's men, however, on this Saturday afternoon—the sixth was a Saturday—were thinking of nothing but food and sleep, and they rolled into their blankets as soon as they had eaten their rations in the camp on the Maysville Branch. No jugs and fiddles this Saturday, or dances before the campfire, as on the warm and starry field at Wilson's Creek. "After encamping," Shelby reports, "I doubled my guards, threw out infantry skirmishers in every direction, under the charge of trusty officers, and lay down with the conscious satisfaction that neither Federal, Kansas jayhawker nor Pin Indian could surprise us, and if they came they would meet with a bloody and hospitable welcome, for I had ordered my entire brigade upon the slightest alarm to form rapidly as infantry and sleep upon loaded arms."

On the night of the sixth, Hindman held a last-minute conference with his infantry division commanders, General Francis A. Shoup (like Marmaduke a West Pointer), G. S. Shaver, M. M. Parsons, J. F. Fagan, and D. M. Frost, who had commanded the militia at Camp Jackson. While the plan for the next day was being worked out in detail, a courier from Shelby brought news that Federal forces, presumably Herron's—were encamped to the west and north, a few miles up the Fayetteville Road. Shelby had not made the mistake that Rains made at Wilson's Creek. His scouts knew the whereabouts of all the varmints in the countryside, including Herron's. The presence of Herron was very bad news; Hindman's whole plan was predicated on the supposition that the Fayetteville Road would be enemy-free; but it was too late to change, and he gave his final orders. Shelby was to find Herron in the morning and attack him. The whole army would follow, rout him if possible, and countermarch to fight Blunt. It was a large order, but Hindman was a fighter, and as he explains in his report, "to withdraw without fighting at all would discourage my own troops and so embolden the enemy as to insure his following me up. His sudden concentration of troops justified the opinion that a movement against me was intended in any event." [12]

At three o'clock in the morning, Hindman was up and about, and so were the troops, but his artillery and wagon trains were hardly in shape to move at all, much less advance into battle. It took a full hour to set everything right that had gone wrong at the last moment, and in his report he says, "The command was not set in motion until nearly four o'clock, and then the route proved so excessively bad, and the detentions so frequent from the breaking of artillery harness and debility of the battery animals that the infantry failed to march above two miles an hour." [13] For the animals dying of starvation there was no forage; for the men there were half a day's rations left. In such condition, and worse, the troops of the Southern Confederacy fought for four years. For the sublime insanity of their sacrifice, their war is remembered, when all the other foolish wars are forgotten.

Shelby's brigade moved much faster. His horses were in better shape—he kept them fed no matter how shrill the cries from the plundered commissaries or the requisitioned settlers. At three o'clock his men, refreshed from their long sleep, rolled out of their blankets, munched their rations, and rode off, a little stiff-legged, in the direction of the Telegraph Road from Fayetteville. There, a little before sunrise, they made contact with the enemy, a company of the Seventh U. S. Missouri Cavalry Volunteers, followed at a short distance by renegade Arkansas cavalry of the First U. S. Arkansas.

Jo Shelby, out of the mountains, with room to turn the cavalry, could wield it like a whip, and the crash of the carbines against the blue troopers was like a flash fire on the Telegraph Road.

The Federals, sleepy-eyed with cold, were startled awake by the explosion, and for some these few instants of wakefulness were the last. First Lieutenant Lafayette Bunner's men—they belonged to Company M—were piled up like a railroad wreck. The next instant, Shelby's borderers, slouch-hatted, Federal-overcoated, and scraggly-bearded (not many of them were old enough to own a set of whiskers), were riding into their fellow Missourians with sabres swinging, like farmhands cutting brush.

Lieutenant Bunner was a very young lieutenant, and he tried to make a brave show in his report: he says he engaged the enemy, but that is not true.[14] Those of his men not unhorsed, taken prisoner, or dead, took headlong flight to the rear, Bunner among them. A captain tried to stop him, but could not; the commanding officer of the advance, Major James M. Hubbard, impatiently ordered the stricken company to take cover behind the main column, and he himself fell away into a wheatfield to receive the shock of the enemy's headlong charge.

Said General Hindman, in brief but unstinted praise, Shelby, "making his dispositions rapidly and with excellent judgment, attacked them front and flank, routed them completely, killed and wounded many, captured over 200, with the train of a regiment, and pursued the fugitives five miles in the direction of Fayetteville in the line of battle formed by Herron's infantry. My infantry was yet in the rear, moving as rapidly as possible." [15] But Hindman's report covers the ground too quickly. This was a day of events in the life of Colonel Shelby—events which transcended in importance any effects of his cavalry operations on the success or failure of an obscure battle in a forgotten campaign.

The three companies which always formed his advance were commanded by Major David Shanks, one of the iron officers of the Iron Brigade, and in their rear were three more of the First Regiment under the command of Lieutenant Colonel Charles A. Gilkey. Finding Herron's men formed in a battle line, Shanks ordered a charge, led by Jeans, Ben Elliott and the guerrillas of Quantrill's company under the command of Lieutenant Gregg. The enemy broke and fled precipitately at the first impact, scattering into the woods which lined the road. The six companies of the advance plunged after them with grim determination, for prisoners meant overcoats, boots, and weapons. As always, the United States Army was Shelby's quartermaster corps.

Shelby went up and down the line, spurring it on, but the headlong plunge carried him into danger. The boys of the forward company, bent on the chase, had disappeared as if the earth had swallowed them up. Shelby found himself riding amid a teeming rabble of the enemy, with only half a dozen men around him, and, right in front, a whole regiment of Federal cavalry, under the same Major Hubbard who had sought vainly to form a line in the wheatfield.

Shelby looked about him with a fierce and exasperated glare. Where the devil were Shanks and Elliott? He had a thousand men a moment ago. Now he had only two light guns and half a dozen members of his staff. Gordon's men were dismounted, out of sight in his rear in the dry bed of a creek, where he had left them to cover the Fayette-ville Road, and Shanks and his guerrillas were off chasing Federals like rabbits through the woods. Even his two guns were useless; they could not be unlimbered, and Hubbard's men had ridden them down and were sabring the gunners. Hubbard had a hundred men between him and the artillery. The Federal major recognized Shelby by his plume, and advanced upon him, brandishing an exultant pistol.

"You are surrounded and overpowered, sir," Hubbard said. "Sur-render your men immediately, sir!"

Shelby's gunners, gashed and bleeding, tried desperately to empty their pistols at the careering horsemen, but it was all over with them in a moment.

"Surrender, sir, do you hear!" shouted Hubbard. "Surrender, or I fire! You are surrounded."

This was true, but not for long. Shanks had heard the sound of firing, and had sent his cavalry thundering along Telegraph Road to the rescue. His shaggy borderers, hundreds of them, were between Hubbard and Herron, and now rode head-on for Hubbard with sabres uplifted. They were close enough for Shelby to recognize the faces of individuals in the van. One of them was a lean, craggy Mis-souri boy from Clay County, riding with reckless disregard of his own safety. He was Alexander Franklin James, better known in American folk history as Frank James, brother of Jesse; and Shelby would never forget the sight of his face as he rode with the rescue party that day on the Fayetteville Road.

Shelby smiled with pleasure, and he was a courtly sight as he swept the plumed hat from his chestnut hair, white teeth sparkling in the chestnut beard, and turned to Major Hubbard.

"You are mistaken, Major," he said. "It is you who are my prisoner. Look around you." And he halted the advancing column with a wave of the plume.

Hubbard did not need the admonition. He restored the pistol to its holster, and tugged at his sword belt. Contemporary accounts quote him as saying, "I am caught, nicely caught." He loosened the buckle of his belt. "Here is my sword. I only ask quarter for my men." This with a look in the direction of the guerrillas, whose reputation was well known.

"Take back your sword, Major," said Shelby. "It was never stained, as I have learned, with the blood of the helpless around Newtonia. I always respect an honorable foe." [16]

They really talked like that, in those days.

Hindman was now on the Fayetteville Road with 10,000 men. One thousand had been left with his wagons at Hogeye, just south of the highway. Shelby fell back, with his prisoners and his plunder, for he deemed it "not only imprudent but highly dangerous" to pursue the enemy farther.[17] On any other occasion Hindman's heart would have been gladdened by the sight of the substantial fruits of victory which Shelby's men were dragging with them—12 standards, 32 wagons, 400 to 500 stands of arms, 200 prisoners, "besides quantities of clothing, commissary stores, quartermaster's supplies, negroes, horses, mules, and every variety and description of articles a corrupt Government can furnish to hired freebooters and cutthroats and thieves." [18] But the "hired freebooters" were on Hindman's flanks, and he had to make a decision quickly.

In his own account of his movements of the morning, Hindman says, "I remained with Parsons' brigade, hoping to get some intelligence from the enemy at Newburg. Receiving none, at 11 A.M. I went forward about two miles and overtook the marching column. It was painful to observe the exhaustion of the men. They had marched about fifteen miles. The rations of all had been insufficient for thirty days. Many, overcome with fatigue, had been left by the roadside. Brigadier General Shoup met me and stated that Marmaduke had fallen back before the enemy's infantry . . . and that therefore he had put his men in a position to resist attack." [19]

This was at Prairie Grove, from which the bloody battle of the day takes its name. Shoup has been criticized for turning his face to Herron, at Prairie Grove, instead of forming one main body with Frost, for the purpose of making a concentrated attack on either Herron or Blunt; but at the time Hindman approved his action, whatever he may have thought of it long afterward.

The truth is that at this juncture there was no decision which Hindman could make that would have changed the course of events. Herron was speeding south on the Fayetteville Road, recovered from the shock of his surprise; and over toward Cane Hill dense columns of smoke at Rhea's Mill indicated that Blunt was moving north, destroying his depots as he went, to unite with Herron. Hindman was astraddle the road between them, his men facing in two directions, Shoup, with Marmaduke and Shelby, looking north, Frost, with Monroe and the rest of the infantry, looking south. At Prairie Grove Shoup had occupied the only possible position in the vicinity; Hindman says so. "I found," he says, "the position taken by General Shoup an exceedingly strong one." [20] If he had had sufficient ammunition, he could have held it.

The smoke indicating Blunt's activity decided Hindman on his course. "The interval of time in which I might have attacked Herron was past," he says. "Circumstances did not permit me to avail myself of it for the manifest reason that at the favorable moment the rear of my column could not be where the head was. Evidently the combined forces of Herron and Blunt would speedily attack me. I made such arrangements as seemed best to meet that contingency." [21]

The line of battle determined upon was in the shape of a horseshoe, conforming to the shape of the hill with the church on the summit. Around the spire of that peaceful country church, within a few hours, were enacted scenes of horror seldom equaled on a battlefield on the American continent, and not even exceeded by the most revolting of the suppressed details of the Death March of Bataan. That men lost their minds on the battlefields of Missouri is not to be wondered at; that the survivors were ever sane and well-balanced again is a greater cause for wonder, and may even be doubted.

Shoup's division and Shelby's brigade of Marmaduke's division constituted the front line in the periphery of battle at Prairie Grove. Shelby's dragoons were dismounted once more, filling the center and right opposite the line taken by Herron upon the far side of Crawford's Prairie, on a bluff that rose up steeply behind a stream flowing toward the Illinois River. Frost's division, to which had been added the brigade of Texans, the veterans of Newtonia, and Clark's Missouri Regiment, commanded by Brigadier General Roane, was held in reserve to await the coming of Blunt. MacDonald's regiment of Missouri cavalry—Colonel Emmett MacDonald, who vowed never to cut his hair until the Confederacy was established—was held in readiness to meet any attack upon the flanks.

At noon sharp, the Federals opened up with artillery; the Confederate gunners answered with a roar, but Hindman gave quick orders to stop the firing. There must be no waste of ammunition in pointless artillery duels. Marmaduke and Shelby awaited the infantry attack. An hour later, at one o'clock exactly, it came—wave after wave of the bluecoats, supported by a tremendous artillery fire. They were permitted to come within sixty yards of the Confederate lines, where, says Hindman's report, "making gallantly past one of our batteries, and having it a moment in its possession, Fagan's Arkansas brigade, part of McRae's brigade, and the Missourians under Shelby delivered a terrific fire from their shotguns, rifles, and muskets, and charged the enemy furiously." [22]

Hawthorne's regiment of Arkansas troops recaptured the battery, and under the onslaught of the countercharge, the Federals retired to the prairie. Once again Herron threw a charge against Shoup's position, and once again was repulsed.

On the other side of the hill at Prairie Grove, Blunt was coming up. To the front and left of Shoup he formed a line of battle two thousand yards long, and began advancing to the thick undergrowth on that flank. Hindman threw Frost in that direction, although his men were somewhat impeded by the undergrowth, and once again a Federal assault failed. Says Hindman, "One of Marmaduke's regiments (Shelby's) shared the honor of this brilliant achievement. The enemy now brought up his artillery, many pieces of which were rifled, and endeavored to shake our troops by playing upon the entire line for nearly an hour. Then he attacked with all his infantry, at the same time threatening the extreme left with a heavy cavalry force and attempting to turn the right. MacDonald's Missouri cavalry defeated him in the last maneuver. Lane's Texas cavalry and Roane's brigade deterred him from seriously assailing the left, and Shoup's division, Shelby's brigade, of Marmaduke's division, and Parsons's and Shaver's brigades of Frost's division, gloriously repulsed him in his desperate attacks upon their lines. He again fled beyond the prairie, leaving his dead and his wounded, and the colors of several of his regiments, in our hands, besides a number (275) of prisoners. Some of these were ascertained to be of Totten's division, which had arrived upon the field, still further increasing the disparity of our forces."

As Blunt fell back, his men stumbled through a live chamber of horrors in the peach and apple orchard which masked his artillery line of thirty guns. Let Major Edwards describe it. "In this orchard were five gigantic ricks of straw, dry and combustible almost as gunpowder. Hither some two hundred wounded Federals had crawled, to burrow in the warm covering and find shelter against the bitter cold. Shells from their own lines fired the frail protection, and before any effort could be made at rescue their heart-rending cries told all the dreadful agony of the conflagration. The sight was sickening and appalling. Two hundred human bodies lay half consumed in one vast sepulchre, and in every position of mutilated and horrible contortion, while a large drove of hogs, attracted doubtless by the scent of roasting flesh, came greedily from the apple trees and gorged themselves upon the unholy banquet. Intestines, heads, arms, feet, and even hearts were dragged over the ground and devoured at leisure." [23]

It was worse at Prairie Grove than it had been on any other battlefield for the Missourians. Writing in 1867 Major Edwards said, "Few of Shelby's soldiers will forget the horrors of their night bivouac on the gory field at Prairie Grove. Around them in every direction lay the dead and dying, the full glare of a cold battle moon shining white upon the upturned faces, and the chilling wind singing freezing dirges among the naked and melancholy trees. Soon upon the night air rose great heart-sobs wrung from strong men in their agony, while the white hoar frost hardened the fever drops into ice that oozed from clammy brows. Death stalked in silently among the sufferers and plied his busy sickle.... The night waned, the trees shivered, and the cold, hard sky was rough with spirit wings fleeing away from the blood and dust of the trampled earth. Through all the long, long watches, the burial parties from both armies flitted over the field with lights that gleamed like phantoms, and mingled friendly in a common work of mercy. Daylight came slowly and solemnly, yet the dead were not buried, and many wounded were dying slowly and lingeringly in the dark and lonesome places. Fires were strictly forbidden all along the lines and sleep was necessarily an utter impossibility. During the night the rumbling of laden wagons and the clatter of horses' feet on the frozen ground could plainly be heard in the direction of Fayetteville, and scouts brought constant word that Blunt was being reinforced." [24]

Their own wagons were on the move too, though no sound came from the turning wheels, muffled in blankets as they rolled west and south to the Boston Mountains.

Thus ended the Battle of Prairie Grove, almost upon the altar of a quiet country church. Do not look for it in the ordinary history textbook; it is not there. An unimportant battle, in which only a few hundred died.

This time Blunt sent the flag of truce, and the two commanders, Blunt and Hindman, met. Case-hardened soldiers though they were, both were sobered by the ghastly sufferings inflicted in the campaign, and agreement was reached whereby "certain terms for conducting the war in the future" were to be observed, "to mitigate, if possible, some of its unnecessary rigors," and to encourage speedy exchanges. It was stipulated that hospitals and hospital stores were not to be captured, and that better facilities for communication between opposing commanders should be set up. This conference was conducted with the greatest courtesy on both sides, and some of the terms agreed upon were lived up to, although Blunt later accused Hindman of using this cartel arrangement as an opportunity for espionage.

From a military standpoint, the battle was certainly a draw; but Hindman's men had scarcely twenty rounds of ammunition apiece at the end, and their food had long since been eaten; their battery animals had dropped from exhaustion, and some of the Arkansas troops—two hundred of them—had deserted to the enemy. Hindman could not stay where he was, nor could he fight another day. He "determined to retire, and gave the necessary orders for that purpose."

The sad, gaunt army of northwestern Arkansas retired toward Little Rock by three routes, Shelby and Marmaduke by way of Dripping Springs, the way they had come. At Dripping Springs another horror was piled onto the horror which the men had suffered. Hindman, enraged at the desertion of the Arkansas troops, sent over to Shelby a deserter, named Phelps, for execution. "In sight of the whole brigade," says Edwards, "drawn up in hollow square, the doomed man came out to death, a curious, wondering expression on his face, as if he did not understand the solemn preparations. The firing party tied a white handkerchief over his eyes, and the poor criminal knelt a few moments in silent prayer, the cold breezes blowing his straggling locks about a brow very pale and rigid. It ended at last, and his freed spirit went shrieking down the wind to the ocean of eternity." [25]

Weary, barefoot, starving, Hindman's army struggled on back into the Arkansas River Valley. Marmaduke went into winter quarters at Lewisburg, on the north side, and Shelby's brigade rested. They would not break camp again until the last day of the old year. Blunt and Herron, unopposed, started south on December 27 in a forced march and drove Hindman, who had only 4,000 men, from Van Buren, chiefly by artillery bombardment. Six steamers at the dock were lost (two of them burned by the retreating Hindman), and Blunt destroyed all of the food stores in Van Buren which he could not use, amounting to 13,500 bushels of corn, among others. Having dealt this disheartening blow to the hungry Confederates, the Federal commanders withdrew across the Missouri line to their own comfortable headquarters at Springfield.

Thus ended the year 1862, on a note of savage despair and frustration for the Confederacy in the west. General Joseph E. Johnston, commanding on the east side of the river, had written to General Holmes asking about the possibility of reinforcements in his sector. Holmes replied unconcernedly, "My information from Helena is to the effect that a heavy force of the enemy has passed down the Mississippi on transports, doubtless for the demonstration [sic] upon Vicksburg. Thus it seems certain that any force I can send now from here would not be able to reach Vicksburg." [26]

It was not necessary, of course, for him to reach Vicksburg; he could have sent Hindman or Shelby to Helena with 10,000 men and rooted out Curtis, who had not half that number. Those transports he had mentioned would be streaming past Helena down the Mississippi to Vicksburg for the next nine months because of Holmes's failure to deal with Helena. But he resolutely refused to do anything, even make a recommendation to the Richmond government; the most that he would do would be to ask General Hindman what he thought about the possibility of taking Helena and seizing control of the navigation of the Mississippi. [27] In the same breath, however, he was declaring, "I have written to the Secretary [of War] that I shall be satisfied if I can hold Arkansas and the Indian country." And he was gratified to think that he was in no danger. "I have made every inquiry possible," he told Hindman, "and do not believe that we are in any danger of an invasion from Helena."

But what Hindman thought made no difference now. As a result of Prairie Grove, Hindman was to be blamed for Holmes's failures; he was to be sent east of the Mississippi to an obscure post, and the only other man in the Department of the Trans-Mississippi capable of command at this critical juncture, Jo Shelby, was only a colonel. He commanded a brigade and his responsibilities were those of a general, but they were not to make him a brigadier until he demonstrated that he could march to the gates of Jefferson City, on his Great Raid—and even then they would not give him the men to seize Missouri's capital.

The Trans-Mississippi was an empire as big as all Europe, and potentially as rich. But the Confederate government, entrusting its control to such men as Theophilus H. Holmes, was trying to win without it.

15. *The Iron Brigade: Marmaduke and Shelby*

ON THE DAY that Blunt burned the stores at Van Buren, Hindman determined to try to accomplish in Missouri by means of a raid what he had not been able to accomplish in a campaign. He ordered Marmaduke and Shelby, reinforced by Monroe and MacDonald, to strike at the Federal line of communication between Springfield and Rolla, the terminus of the St. Louis railway line which was the jugular vein of the Federals in Missouri. He meant to remove the threat to Arkansas by destroying the enemy's base at Springfield, and open again that 120-mile route to the Missouri River Valley along which Shelby had so often galloped, and on which Price with his Patriot Army had marched from Wilson's Creek.

It was the first of two raids by Marmaduke and Shelby into Missouri; the second was attempted in the spring of 1863, to the vicinity of Cape Girardeau, six weeks before Holmes finally made up his mind that an attack on Helena was possible. The first expedition, set in motion on New Year's Eve, may be rated a success, so far as the accomplishment of its lesser objective is concerned: it drew the Federals away from Arkansas, but how much of an accomplishment that was is open to question, for as Thomas points out in his *Arkansas in War and Reconstruction* Blunt and Herron could not subsist their army at Van Buren.[1] By the same token, neither could the Confederates. The second thrust, generally known as the Cape Girardeau expedition, represented a useless expenditure of effort, and weakened the Confederates at a time when they should have been mustering every ounce of strength for their drive to the Mississippi at Helena in July.

Both expeditions were marked with the endless incidents of a Shelby raid: the dreadful marches, the bloody hand-to-hand fighting, the banter with the country girls, the ruthless punishment, by firing squad or simple massacre, of Union bushwhackers and guerrillas, and the gala pursuit of prisoners when a scattered enemy was no longer in position to fight. In winter, the overcoat-bearing Federal was esteemed especially for his pelt, and Shelby permitted his men to take hundreds of prisoners in fights where only hundreds were involved. There was no feeding problem, for prisoners were "paroled" instantly, foodless and sometimes pantsless as well, and left to see how they could make out on the charity of their Union sympathizer friends. The brigade ate well, too; there is talk of sweet sorghum molasses served by handsome country girls, with great rashers of ham and eggs for breakfast, and savory steaks broiled over hickory sticks at night—except on the occasions when they were starving. It was either a feast or a famine for Shelby's men.

After Newtonia, Cane Hill, and Prairie Grove the brigade was beginning to take on an identity. Shelby had men now who were willing to follow him anywhere, into anything. This was partly due to the solicitude which he showed for them, but only partly. The basic reason for their devotion was that they had become inordinately proud of Old Jo, and were becoming proud to be known as Shelby's Men. That pride, which was the thing called *esprit de corps*, was composed of many ingredients. First of all, as the Arkansas private said, Jo Shelby *looked like somebody*. He looked like Jeb Stuart, with the plume, and in an army whose standards were none too high, his command was no unworthy miniature of the Cavalry Corps of the Army of Northern Virginia.[2] Furthermore, he *was* somebody, as you'd find out quick enough if you got gay with him. He was also smarter than the entire high command of the enemy in the Department of the West; and as for fighting—well, they had seen him fight, on the plains and in the mountains. He fought like the man who invented fighting, and the men of the Missouri Cavalry Brigade looked on him as the perfect commanding officer: colorful and dashing, but with a recklessness so shrewd that it amounted almost to caution. This combination made an irresistible appeal to the Missouri character, for it was the quality they most admired. From trusting and respecting Old Jo, they had come to idolize him, by the end of 1863, and they knew that as soon as the higher-ups got smart and made him a general, he was going to lead the entire army back to the Promised Land of Missouri, and that when the roll was called up yonder they'd be there.

With such thoughts in their minds, though hardly articulated, and their stomachs comfortably full, Shelby's men rode off from Lewisburg on the morning of December 31, 1862. Their destination was Yellville, where they would be joined by other cavalry under Mac-Donald and Monroe, but they moved in a westerly direction, through the mountains, on account of the scarcity of forage. En route to Yellville, Shelby surprised a band of about a hundred jayhawkers ("tories and deserters") killed a large number, and captured twenty-seven.[3] "The vigor with which his troops attacked and pursued those scoundrels," says Marmaduke, "terrified them, and broke up, for the time at least, the lawless bands in this part of the mountains."

The settlers in this territory, even those engaged in peaceful pursuits, were one hundred per cent Unionist, and foraging could therefore be carried out with the greater enthusiasm; but Shelby insisted, as always, on paying for supplies requisitioned, especially if they consisted of stock which the farmer would have to replace.

Major Jake Stonestreet recalls that on this march they came to one especially well-stocked farm. "We had captured some supplies," he says, "and every man of us had on a new federal overcoat. The planter was a Union man and welcomed us joyfully. 'There's my hogs,' he said, 'and there's my sheep and here's my mule lot. Boys, help yourselves.'

"Then Shelby undeceived him. His people had been killing ours whenever they could catch them, and he made ready for death. Shelby, however, paid him in good money for everything we consumed and hired him as a guide through the mountains, afterward giving him a safe conduct back home. A year afterward, that fellow rode nearly a hundred miles to shake Shelby's hand."

Shelby and MacDonald reached Yellville simultaneously, on the fourth of January, and on the sixth MacDonald stormed an isolated Federal outpost on Beaver Creek, scattering the garrison of 300 and taking 20 prisoners. Here MacDonald made a bonfire of the enemy's supplies: Marmaduke's orders were to carry nothing that could not be transported easily on a forced march.

Shelby, with Elliott's scouts in his van, did the same thing at Ozark, which had a slightly larger Federal garrison. By now General E. B. Brown, at Springfield, was alerted. Indeed, the entire Department of the West was alarmed. The Federals had thought that Marmaduke's cavalry was wintering on the Arkansas River in a state of demoralization and defeat. Now they were reliably reported to be moving on the Federal bastion of the southwest with 5,000 picked men and two pieces of rifled field artillery drawn by ten horses each, and moving fifty miles a day. General Brown had only 2,000 men—2,099, to be exact—and though he had four guns, two of them were small brass cannon and the other two, old twelve pounders, more fit for the ornamentation of a city park than for the defense of a town. The Federals had not only denuded western Missouri of forage, they had denuded it of defenses, and General Curtis, who had succeeded Schofield at St. Louis, conceived Brown to be in a desperate situation. Actually he was not, for Marmaduke had only 2,300 men, Brown was sheltered behind heavy fortifications at Springfield, and even though his guns were not first-rate, they outnumbered Marmaduke's two to one.

Nevertheless Curtis was almost in tears when he heard of Marmaduke's march. He telegraphed Brown: "You and your troops are heroes. I hope God will spare you strength for tomorrow. I expect a desperate effort early in the morning. All the troops, especially the cavalry, should be ready. Herron started with two divisions eastward from Fayetteville on the 6th. He will soon be behind or near the foe. Don't weary in well doing. The eyes of the country are on you. Your general feels for you deeply. God grant you success." [4]

If anyone needed sympathy under these circumstances, it would seem to be Marmaduke. He was in the midst of a situation which could easily shape up into another Prairie Grove, operating far from his home base, with no supplies, and soon to be confronted with two large bodies of the enemy, each the equal of his own, converging to meet him. But the fact that they were actually on Missouri soil, and equal to the enemy in front of them, was enough for Shelby's men: it was more advantage than they usually had, and when they struck Springfield, they struck it with fury. They were dismounted at Springfield, as were MacDonald's men, and fought as infantry; a cavalry charge against the rifle pits and fortifications would have been suicide. Under cover of artillery fire, MacDonald led the attack.

All day long, until darkness put an end to the fight, Marmaduke's

2,300 fought the enemy in a house-to-house battle for Springfield, amid the crash of falling and burning timbers as the Federals set fire to their stores. Their attack had been swift; Brown says in his report that Marmaduke "moved right up and commenced the fight by cannonading the town" before dismounting his infantry and moving to the attack across the prairie.

Brown was a brave soldier as well as a good one, and he won the respect of the Confederate troops that day. Edwards says that "he did what no other Federal brigadier general ever did in front of Shelby's brigade ... rode its entire length under a severe fire, clad in bold regimentals, elegantly mounted and ahead of all so that the fire might be concentrated on him. It was reckless bravado, and General Brown gained by one bold dash the admiration and respect of Shelby's soldiers. They fought him often and often after Springfield, and had the fortunes of war placed him in their hands I am positively certain that he would have been paroled and sent to his own lines with marks of soldierly esteem." [5]

As Brown appeared in front of their lines, Shelby's men held their fire momentarily, and someone yelled, "Don't shoot that man! Let him go!" The cry, "Let him go!" was echoed all along the ranks, but unfortunately their admiration for Brown's heroism was not shared by a rebel sympathizer in Springfield. Brown's adjutant says that the General "was treacherously shot from a secesh residence while leading a charge of his bodyguard when the day seemed to be lost." [6] He attempted to remount his horse, but could not, and was carried from the field.

At this point, when pressure on the Federals seemed greatest, "Shelby, seizing the opportune moment ... rushed to the terrible charge at the doublequick, driving before him the frightened foe, who fled, abandoning all stores, stockade, fort, and a piece of artillery." The gun, a field piece captured in the town's graveyard, was added to Collins' battery. One of their own officers admits that Shelby's attack had been so fierce as to throw them into "a panic-stricken rout." [7]

At five o'clock of that winter day, Marmaduke had a tenuous grip on the gutted town—the Federals had not fallen back one step without applying the torch—but Springfield was still swarming with Federals, and they were heavily barricaded behind whatever cover they had not abandoned—houses, stockades, and fences. They had not given up yet.

Marmaduke decided to withdraw his men for the night, out of the town and onto the prairie. As soon as he did so, he received word that reinforcements for Brown were on the way to Springfield. That was enough for Marmaduke. His first objective had been accomplished. Springfield was a wreck, the great Federal depot destroyed. Rather than risk his next objective, which was to cut the Rolla communication line, he decided to move off in the direction of Hartville, where he expected to be joined by a Confederate force coming up from Pocahontas, Arkansas, under Colonel J. C. Porter. Porter's brigade, numbering 825 men, was a reinforcement reluctantly wrung from General Holmes, and represented all he was willing to contribute out of his whole department to bolster Marmaduke in his operations in the interior of Missouri.

Federal garrisons at Sand Spring and Marshfield fled at the Confederate approach, leaving only their burning stores as beacons on the march to Hartville. At Marshfield Marmaduke was met by Porter, who also brought news that fresh Federal troops, 2,500 of them, had moved into Hartville. Marmaduke determined to give battle at once. He hurried on, Shelby's brigade leading the advance.

At Hartville the pattern of Springfield was virtually repeated, except that it was a triumphant victory for the Confederates. After three hours, the enemy, under Brigadier General Fitz Henry Warren, retreated, leaving Marmaduke in possession of the town. But Marmaduke sustained a sore loss: Colonel Emmett MacDonald was killed. Major Edwards was also captured, though later exchanged. Federal General Warren in his report lays claim to having escaped from Hartville "without the loss of a musket or cartridge box," but actually, says Marmaduke, "his men retreated rapidly and in disorder, leaving the dead and wounded, many arms, ammunition and clothing on the field and in my possession."

Marmaduke's troops were now in no position to go farther. They had no baggage whatsoever, and they were attempting to live off the country, an impossible feat. Two hundred of his horses, succumbing to the rigors of winter, had been left to die by the roadside; his men were thinly clad, many without shoes, and the stores they had hoped to capture had been burned. Furthermore, there were two large Federal armies in the neighborhood, with reinforcements arriving hourly. Marmaduke "deemed it best not to put myself in battle between two forces" and marched for Batesville, Arkansas, as rapidly as the condition of his command would permit. At Batesville he would await the coming of spring, for another foray into Missouri.

Marmaduke is justified in saying, as he does, that "the object of the expedition was fully accomplished, and more." He had marched 300 miles "on miserable, unshod horses," forced the enemy to gut its supply depot for the entire southwest, at Springfield, destroyed all of the militia stores as far as Hartville, and thrown a scare into the enemy as far away as St. Louis.

The march to Batesville was one of intense suffering, and by the time Shelby's men reached the White River Valley, they were so desperate for food that they no longer cared whether the settlers were loyal Confederates or not—if there was any food left on the farms of this desolated region, they took it, despite Shelby's stern orders against looting. Major Jake Stonestreet, who rode at Shelby's side on that nightmare march, recalled years later an incident in which Shelby himself was involved.

"On that raid," said Stonestreet, "we were half-starving, and Shelby and I rode down to the White River to water our horses. A detachment of the troops was doing the same thing just below us. Among them was Dick Gentry [who later went to Mexico with Shelby]. He was a gallant private and a good fellow. Slung across his saddle was a sack, carefully tied and bleeding at one end. Shelby demanded what he had got there.

" 'Been having my clothes washed,' said Gentry.

" 'You'd better get back to camp,' said Shelby, 'or your clothes will bleed to death.'

"Gentry was lodged in the guardhouse at Shelby's order. That night a quarter of fresh pork found its way to Shelby's headquarters. Shelby looked at it and said, 'I haven't an idea where this comes from, but go round to the guardhouse, orderly, and tell 'em to turn Gentry loose. No use keeping a man shut up all his life for a little laundry.' "

The arrival at Batesville, in the deep freeze of late January, was not auspicious. The supply train which had been ordered from Lewisburg to meet them was marooned by snowstorms in the mountains which had flooded creeks and banked the snow high upon the winding roads. Shelby's men were forced to bivouac in the open, destitute of tents, cooking utensils, and even a change of clothing; but the good citizens of Batesville came to their rescue, and they had food. Shelby's biographer says that the townspeople welcomed them as their own, "lavish of their food and raiment." The sick were taken into their houses, "nursed, cured, and sent back comfortably clad." The old brigade, he says, "even kept the memory of these generous people green, and struck many a gallant blow for them upon dark and bloody fields."

Best of all, of course, were the pretty girls. In Batesville were charmers as beautiful as any in all Arkansas, which is to say as in all the world. Those of Shelby's soldiers who were not sick were soon lovesick. His camp, pitched among giant oaks on the south side of the river, was named Camp Nannie Wilson "in honor of one of Batesville's most lovely daughters," and as soon as the huts and barracks had been built, the men found a gay social life in the town, for the next two months.

"Balls, promenades, flirting, coqueting and matchmaking followed in rapid succession," says Major Edwards. "The young, dashing officers put away all battle visions, and lived as if life were one long gala-day of vows, and sighs, and tresses of hair.... 'Twere long to tell what troths were plighted, and what dainty, jeweled hands rested lovingly in great brown ones down by the garden gates, as twilight lingered in the lily beds, and the breath of 'low, mysterious roses' came up from the dim *parterres*."

That was when spring was well under way, and it was a spring that would live in the memory of the Iron Brigade forever. Who could forget the sight of beautiful girls watching the cavalry drill—drill which the gallant Shelby turned into "tournaments" [8] for their benefit —or the Great Sham Battle which they staged for the ladies of Batesville?

The Southern cavalrymen were getting the reward for which they chiefly fought, next to food: the adulation of the fair.

After the sham battle Shelby made a great occasion of presenting to his men the two silken banners made by the ladies of Little Rock. Captain Yandell Blackwell's company got one. But the men of Jeans's regiment, in Shelby's opinion, had so covered themselves with glory that he would make no invidious comparisons: he gave the second flag to the entire regiment.

Another attraction of Camp Nannie Wilson was Captain Dick Collins' black bear, a cub recently found by hunters in the Boston Mountains. This lumbering infant, bought by Captain Wave Anderson, Shelby's ordnance officer, and presented to Collins' battery, was "a veritable, good-natured, intelligent bear." [9] It bore the euphonious sobriquet of "Postlethwaite." The men fed, petted, and boxed him; ladies "came from a distance to stroke his black coat and surfeit him on sweetmeats and delicacies." Unchained and thoroughly domesticated, Postlethwaite roamed at will among the regiments, "thrusting his ugly face into saucepans and stew kettles." Minor engagements of the future would find him at his post, amid the spraying shrapnel; in major engagements he was removed to a place of safety with the horses. But he was no hero, Postlethwaite, for he "dodged and shirked like a veritable coward whenever the shells and grapeshot rattled about his gun." Of his subsequent history nothing is known, except that, riding on a caisson to the various Armageddons of Shelby and his men, he was the most traveled bear in Missouri outside of a circus.

As the green lace of April on the trees gave way to deeper foliage, Marmaduke and Shelby were seen more often in earnest conversation, and two electric words ran down the ranks of the brigade, now at its full strength of three thousand:

"*St. Louis!*" [10]

These words would have brought on a convulsion, uttered in the presence of General Theophilus H. Holmes, but Holmes was no longer in command of the Trans-Mississippi Department of the Confederate States. Jefferson Davis had been persuaded to replace him at last, although he did so with reluctance and then only demoted him to command of the District of Arkansas; but the four states of the Department were now governed by Lieutenant General Edmund Kirby Smith, who had made a record pleasing to the Richmond government in Kentucky, and Holmes could no longer interfere with Hindman's "darling project" of invading Missouri. Hindman was gone—transferred at his own request [11]—and Marmaduke and Shelby were the inheritors of his mission.

Kirby Smith, as he was generally known, had been sent to the Trans-Mississippi chiefly because of Holmes's failure to use his Louisiana troops to support Pemberton, hard-pressed on the Vicksburg side of the river,[12] and Smith, with orders to remedy the situation in Louisiana, established his headquarters first at Alexandria and then at Shreveport. He was not a fortunate choice as a commander in the Trans-Mississippi, which needed a Napoleon or a Stonewall Jackson— or a Jo Shelby—but at least he was not suffering from premature senility, as was Holmes, and Marmaduke and Shelby found him easier to get along with.

Marmaduke was cautious in his first dealings with Smith, for the new general-in-chief was an unknown quantity. He feared that Smith might take alarm if he announced that he intended to make a demonstration upon St. Louis, and he used the scarcity of food for his men in Arkansas as justification for another expedition into Missouri. No other explanation will suffice for the curious endorsement which Smith placed upon Marmaduke's report when it was received. As if apologizing for the temerity of the two cavalry leaders in attacking the Federals in Missouri, he wrote: "The expedition under General Marmaduke into Missouri was made more particularly on account of the scarcity of forage in Arkansas, it being deemed probable that he would be able to sustain himself, and thereby relieve Arkansas in great degree of the large amount of forage it was supplying the army in that section." [13] He need not have feared that Jefferson Davis would think Marmaduke had gone on a fool's errand, for in one of Davis's last letters to Holmes he had said, "I look forward ... to the day when, Arkansas secure, you may advance into Missouri and compel the enemy to look to the defense of the Upper Mississippi instead of conquest of the lower portion of its valley." [14]

On April 18, 1863, Marmaduke set out on his second Missouri raid with the most formidable force of cavalry the Confederates had ever assembled on the soil of that state. He had shifted his theatre of operations from the western border of the state; indeed it was his plan to make such a demonstration in central Missouri that all Federal forces would be drawn as by a magnet to the Iron Mountain region, a hundred miles from St. Louis, and "away from Northern Arkansas and extreme Southwest Missouri." [15] The task of drawing them away, by a series of feints, he assigned to Shelby. While this was being done, it was Marmaduke's plan to put himself between Ironton and St. Louis, as a jumping off place for a "demonstration" in the direction of either St. Louis or Jefferson City. If the Federals rose to the bait, it would have the effect of de-garrisoning the state, and would siphon all of their troops into northeastern Missouri, where they had been in the beginning. Under such circumstances, both Marmaduke and Shelby were convinced, a Missouri Confederate army, 50,000 strong, would spring from the freed soil and overrun the state. Shelby and Marmaduke spoke each other's language, and they worked together like forefinger and thumb. There was nothing whatever the matter with Marmaduke's plan, except that he allowed himself to be diverted from it.

The original intention was to strike a crippling blow at Rolla, the nerve center of the Federal supply line in Missouri, but when Marmaduke reached the Eleven Points River with his cavalry and his eight guns, he found that the country had long since been swept clean of forage, and that the hundred-mile march to Rolla would have to be conducted through a wasteland. Much nearer at hand was the opportunity to attack General John McNeil, who was stationed at Bloomfield, with an outpost at Patterson, in Wayne County. Marmaduke estimated that McNeil had 2,000 men. He himself had 5,000 men, not all of them armed; but with this number he estimated that, after capturing the outpost at Patterson, he could surround McNeil. "If successful in capturing McNeil," he says in his report, "I anticipated that my whole command could be well armed and finely mounted for vigorous action."

On the Eleven Points River Marmaduke divided his army into two columns. One, under Shelby, consisting of Shelby's and Burbridge's brigades, would move by a circuitous route to Patterson, throwing out scouts in a northwesterly direction to create the impression of a force marching in that direction. At Patterson he was to join the other column, composed of Carter's and Greene's brigade, who would have marched via Doniphan. Marmaduke would march with Carter's column.

Shelby galloped to within thirty miles of Patterson on the 19th, covering that distance overnight, and sent ahead 450 men under command of Lieutenant Colonel Giddings, with one battery and orders to kidnap the Federal picket line in front of Patterson so that they could not give an alarm. Then he was to advance on the town and take it by surprise. Giddings carried out the first part of his assignment handsomely, scooping up a lieutenant and twenty-four men, about twelve miles from Patterson, at daylight; but he underestimated the distance to the town from that point, and opened up an artillery cannonade at a distance of two miles, to cover his entry. The sound of firing alarmed the Federal commander, Colonel Edwin Smart, a man almost as notorious as McNeil and as anxious to elude capture. Smart lost no time in evacuating Patterson before Giddings' mounted column had covered the distance of two miles, and he set fire to the town as he went. When Marmaduke arrived at Patterson on the 20th, he found Shelby in possession of the burned-out town, and the enemy flown. Smart had retreated to Pilot Knob.

On the 21st, Marmaduke sent Carter east to Bloomfield and Shelby north to Fredericktown, to cut off McNeil's escape route at that point, which was assumed to be in the direction of Ironton. "If he remained in Bloomfield, Carter would whip him," says Marmaduke, "and if he attempted to get to Ironton, Shelby would capture him."

McNeil, had in fact, been ordered to Ironton, as Shelby learned from captured dispatches, but hearing that he was about to be caught in the pincers of two columns of rebel cavalry, he turned west and ran like a hunted animal for the strong fortifications of Cape Girardeau on the Mississippi River.

In exasperation at McNeil's having given him the slip, Marmaduke now threw strategy to the winds and concentrated on the chase of the Palmyra butcher. He ordered Carter's column to Cape Girardeau, but the brigade was hampered by high water, marshes, and bad roads —this is swampy country—and their horses, worn down by heavy marching and lack of forage, were no match for the fleet steeds of McNeil. By the time they came within sight of the heavily fortified river port, McNeil was safe in his headquarters at Cape Girardeau.

Marmaduke now ordered Shelby to join him, preparatory to an attack on Girardeau. Shelby made another of his notable night marches—thirty miles over bad roads—and joined Marmaduke four miles from the bristling guns of the Federal forts which ringed the town. A day's scouting of the vicinity, however, convinced Marmaduke that an assault on the town would result in nothing but heavy Confederate losses. There was an abundance of evidence that the telegraph wires had been busy, and that Cape Girardeau was now being reinforced from every direction, by land and water. Most formidable of the reinforcements was Vandever's force of 3,500 cavalry and artillery, marching toward him on the Jackson and Fredericktown road.

There was nothing to do but retreat, and Marmaduke made the only decision possible. He could not go back the way he had come, however; the only escape route to Arkansas in this God-forsaken swamp lay across the St. Francis River, a bayou stream now out of its banks in flood. To get across he would have to build a bridge for the footsoldiers, swim his horses over, and float his artillery on improvised rafts. Meanwhile the dogs of war were snapping at his heels, in the shape of Vandever's column, and McNeil would soon march out to join him. Marmaduke ordered Shelby to make a "demonstration" on the road leading from Jackson to Cape Girardeau, to distract their attention.

It was beginning to be a familiar story—Shelby's covering the retreat of a Confederate army whose commander had walked into a trap. In a few hours, however, Shelby had so embroiled himself at Cape Girardeau that Marmaduke was afraid a full-scale battle would ensue. "Shelby's demonstration," he says, "amounted almost to an attack."

Actually, it was an attack. Shelby rolled his artillery up to the unsuspecting battlements of the river town, kicked up a mighty cannonade with his twelve-pounders, and hurled Shanks's entire regiment against the First Nebraska Infantry, which came out to meet them. Shanks drove the Nebraskans back upon the stockade; but again the Federals emerged in force, and for a time it seemed that there would be a battle that no one wanted. Marmaduke, seeing Shelby so heavily engaged, could not begin his retreat. "I deemed it necessary," he says, "to bring Carter's column up to his [Shelby's] support. On arriving [I found] that Shelby had driven the enemy's pickets and advanced forces into their works." But "the enemy were admirably posted," and he ordered Shelby from the field on which he seemed disposed to linger.

"My retreat," says Marmaduke, "was orderly and slow. Vandever and McNeil did not seem anxious for a fight. Light rear-guard fighting was of daily occurrence. Shelby's or Carter's brigades were habitually in the rear and always did their duty. On several occasions I offered battle when the advantages in position were greatly in my favor. My object was to give ample time to the bridge party."

The bridge, a flimsy, swinging affair, was erected by Marmaduke's engineers while Shelby brought into play his old game of confusing the enemy by appearing on all sides of him at once, hurling a concentrated fire first from one point and then another, as if his little six-pounders were the signal guns for a thirty-gun barrage; by this razzle-dazzle he so perplexed McNeil's bluecoats that they forgot to use a parallel road across the swamp which would have led them straight to the St. Francis River and the axe-swinging engineers of Marmaduke's "bridge party." Their failure even to cling to the coattails of such a disorganized retreat, into a swamp which should have proved an effective barrier against escape, was going to look bad in McNeil's report, and he knew it. Taking refuge in the excuse that "the nature of the country was such that a strong rear guard could retard a heavy column with ease and almost with impunity," he wrote to his superiors in St. Louis: "I deeply regret that despite the excellent quality of the force in pursuit, and the splendid and effective artillery placed at our disposition, Marmaduke was allowed to make a successful retreat into Arkansas, saving his guns and his baggage, but trust that an examination of the reports made by the various brigade and regimental commanders will exonerate me from blame in the premises."

Colonel Shelby was the last man to cross the bridge on that retreat, and with his sabre he cut adrift the logs on which the dismounted cavalry had escaped.

Once across the St. Francis, they were molested no more by Federals, and once across the St. Francis they understood why. The "road" was a slightly elevated quagmire from which there was no turning off, surrounded by swirling, slushy flood waters of unknown depth, which turned the rank vegetation of the swamp into a fetid vegetable soup. Men and horses sank to their kneecaps in the soughing, tundra-like humus of the "road"; artillery wheels would not turn, and the guns were half carried by the men across one sucking mudhole after another, until their strength gave out. The horses, as always, had given out first; the poor beasts keeled over and were left to die as the march lengthened to an interminable ninety-six hours. This was John Henry country, where the sun don't ever shine; the roof of branches overhead shut out the light by day, and closed in like a coffin lid at night. Cottonmouths and alligators shared their bivouac; men went insane in the midnight watches from hunger, fever, and exhaustion. Somehow, after four days, the division staggered "home" at last, into the streets of Jacksonport. Behind them they had left thirty dead, sixty wounded, and one hundred and twenty missing.[16]

16. *Helena: Disaster in the West*

THE FAILURE of the Confederacy to win the war through a successful defense of its own territory—the only way it could win—has
been ascribed to many chief causes, from the effectiveness of the
Union blockade to the failure of the army's supply system to Longstreet's dilatory tactics at Gettysburg, but the plain truth is that these
were but incidental and unavoidable results of an over-all plan that
was defective from the beginning.

The inability of the Richmond government to realize that the
Mississippi River Valley and the Trans-Mississippi Department of the
Confederate States—not the Atlantic seaboard—constituted the heartland of the Confederacy, doomed the Southern cause from the start.
The conclusion is inescapable that the government never had any
master plan to prevent this vast region from falling into the hands of
the enemy, and as a result of this aimless drifting—the consequences
of which we have already seen in Missouri—the Confederacy was reduced, for all practical purposes, within two years to an area which en-
compassed only Virginia, the Carolinas, and Georgia. The defense
of the west was neglected in favor of a grandiose plan to win sweeping, spectacular victories in the east which would bring the Army of
the Potomac to its knees and secure European recognition and possibly
intervention.

This was folly, both military and diplomatic. There was never a
chance of direct European intervention, and the Confederate armies
in Virginia were never able seriously to menace Washington, although
it is only a hundred miles from Richmond as the crow flies. Yet the
delusion that the war could be won in Virginia was persisted in stub-
bornly for four years. As Major General J. F. C. Fuller, British
military authority, says:

"As the defensive was by force of policy and circumstances thrust
upon the South, Jefferson Davis should have recognized at once that
the strategic frontier of the Confederacy did not coincide with the
political. While the latter ran from the Potomac to the Ohio, and
thence to Columbus on the Mississippi and westwards along the Missouri, the former ran from the Potomac along the Alleghany mountains
to Chattanooga, thence along the Tennessee River to about Savannah,

across to the Mississippi at Fulton, (Arkansas) and from there to Little Rock on the Arkansas River." General Fuller might have added that if the Confederates had controlled Missouri in 1861, this line could have ended not at Little Rock but at St. Louis. General Grant himself said, as we have already noted, that the Confederates could have had St. Louis and all Missouri, if they had acted.

Abraham Lincoln, who was in many respects the military genius that Jefferson Davis imagined himself to be, knew all this better than anyone, even Grant, and in homelier language he said the same thing. Conferring with Admiral David Porter and General McClellan at McClellan's headquarters in Washington, at the beginning of the war, Lincoln pointed to a map of the Mississippi, and exclaimed to Porter:

"What a lot of land these fellows hold, of which Vicksburg is the key! Here is the Red River, which will supply the Confederates with cattle and corn to feed their armies. There are the Arkansas and White Rivers, which can supply cattle and hogs by the thousand. From Vicksburg these supplies can be distributed by rail all over the Confederacy. Then there is that great depot of supplies on the Yazoo. Let us get Vicksburg and all that country is ours. The war can never be brought to a close until that key is in our pocket. I am acquainted with that region and know what I am talking about, and as valuable as New Orleans will be to us, Vicksburg will be more so. We may take all the northern ports of the Confederacy, and they can still defy us from Vicksburg. It means hog and hominy without limit, *fresh troops from all the States of the Far South*, and a cotton country where they can raise the staple without interference." [1]

Abraham Lincoln said it: the Trans-Mississippi Department of the Confederate States had not only the food, but the men and the money (in the form of cotton) that the Confederacy needed to win; the North could not win as long as the South had access to the land of the Arkansas River, the White River, and the Red River; and Vicksburg was the key to that vast and rich empire.

If Vicksburg was the key to Confederate victory, Helena, Arkansas, on the west bank of the Mississippi, was the key to Vicksburg. Just below Memphis and above Vicksburg, possession of Helena at any time in 1862 or early 1863 (when Holmes obdurately refused to act) would have snapped Federal control of the Mississippi River like an over-age rubber band and anchored the Potomac line of the Confederacy upon Little Rock.

Helena hard to invest, perhaps you say, and hard to hold? At no time did General Samuel R. Curtis, or Benjamin M. Prentiss, who succeeded him, have more than 5,000 men at Helena and there were six times as many men on active duty in the Confederate Army of the Trans-Mississippi, including a full brigade stationed at all times in the Indian Territory to protect the Indians against only Holmes knew what.

True, an assault on Helena would have brought the Federals down-river in force, but it would have prevented or at least crippled Grant's movement on Vicksburg and would also have brought about that consummation devoutly to be wished: an opening of a third front for the Confederacy and the consolidation of that line down the Appalachians from Virginia to Arkansas which, as Major General Fuller points out, was indispensable to Confederate victory. With the Federals rushing their armies downstream to retake Helena, they would have had to leave the back door open for an invasion of Missouri. Either way, they were vulnerable unless they were willing to bring an overwhelming army into the area to guard all their flanks. That, at the risk of being repetitious, would have relieved pressure on Lee and Johnston, and on Pemberton at Vicksburg; it would have shifted the entire center of gravity of the war and brought the full strength of the Trans-Mississippi army into the contest at the time it was most needed.

But to turn his department into a battlefield was the last thing on earth that General Holmes wanted.

In June, 1863, however, so many Federal troops had been siphoned out of Missouri to reinforce the Union armies east of the Mississippi that General Holmes felt safe in telegraphing to Kirby Smith at Shreveport: "I believe we can take Helena. Please let me try it." [2]

Smith replied the same day: "Most certainly do it."

On June 16, therefore, Holmes journeyed to Jacksonport to confer with Marmaduke and Shelby and with General Sterling Price, who had been reassigned to Arkansas after a long absence across the river. At Jacksonport, Holmes outlined his plan. Three Confederate divisions, rendezvousing at Clarendon on June 26, would move by divergent roads and attack Helena at daylight on the Fourth of July. Price would attack from the west, Brigadier General James F. Fagan from the south, and the brigades of Marmaduke and Shelby, together with that of General L. M. Walker, from the north. The Confederates outnumbered the Federals nearly two to one, but even so the task of taking the city would be a formidable one, for Helena was literally a ring of concentric defenses, with the Mississippi River, now in full flood, at its back.

General Holmes had a plan of the fortifications of Helena, not a very good one, as it turned out. On the map the town was a perfect square, right on the edge of the Mississippi River.

Looking west on this map, one sees that the river runs straight across the bottom of the page. There are six roads leading into Helena (not counting the Levee Road along the river, which is no more than a city street and is not a point of access for the Confederates). Two of these roads, the Sterling Road on the north, and the Lower Little Rock Road on the south, meet in the town and are physically the same road. Like the Levee Road, they parallel the river, though curving away from it gently at both ends of the town. In fact, the ellipse formed by these two roads—the Sterling Road and the Lower Little Rock Road— sits there very much in the shape of a hat above the square face of the town. The other four roads, all of which enter Helena from a westerly direction, are like feathers sticking out from the hat.

Reading left to right, these roads are: the Upper Little Rock Road; a road running directly from the center of the town which has no name on the map but passes Graveyard Hill, the Upper St. Francis River Road, and the Old St. Francis River Road. Their names indicate their points of origin, and their directions. The first two lead off into central and southern Arkansas, in the direction of Little Rock, the other two toward the Missouri border and the swamps from which the Iron Brigade has but lately emerged.

Across these roads, in the shape of an inverted bowl, the Federals have dug rifle pits which are manned by such troops as the Forty-third Indiana, the Thirty-third Iowa, the Twenty-eighth Wisconsin, and the Thirty-third Missouri. In back of their rifle pits, at a distance of about half a mile, stand four Federal forts, designated by them as A, B, C, and D, or rather as D, C, B, and A; they are lettered from right to left on the map, as if the map had been drawn by a lefthanded man. It makes no difference, because to the Confederates the three avenues of approach are known as Rightor Hill (covered by forts A and B) on the Sterling road, or north side, of Helena; Graveyard Hill, on the road running out from the center of town; and Hindman Hill, on the south, so called because here stands the home of General Tom Hindman. Graveyard Hill and Hindman Hill are guarded by only one fort each, but the construction of the rifle pits and the gun emplacements are such that the Federals can send an enfilading fire in all directions—unless they are attacked on all sides at once, and hence kept too busy to do so.

The success of the attack on Helena depends absolutely on perfect coordination. Every Confederate unit must strike simultaneously at daylight, every rifle pit of the enemy must be carried, every gun silenced, and the defenders driven back into the town upon their main fortification, Fort Curtis. This is a square citadel or redoubt in the center of town, bristling with crossed spikes and manned by no fewer than twenty siege guns, pointing in all directions. Fort Curtis, too, must be taken from all sides at once, or there is no hope of taking it at all.

Seldom has a Confederate army been given a rougher assignment than the assault on Helena.

Holmes's General Orders outline the plan clearly:

"The attack on Helena will be made tomorrow morning (July Fourth) at daylight, and as follows:

"1st. Major General Price, in command of McRae's and Parson's brigades, will proceed by the best route, assume position, assault and take Graveyard Hill at daylight.

"2d. Brigadier General Walker, with his cavalry brigade, will, in like manner, proceed to the Sterling Road, where he will hold himself in position to resist any troops that may approach Rightor Hill; and when that position is captured, he will enter the town and act against the enemy as circumstances may justify.

"3d. Brigadier General Fagan will proceed by the best route, assume position, and take the battery on Hindman Hill at daylight.

"4th. Brigadier General Marmaduke will proceed with his command by the best route, assume position, and take Rightor Hill at daylight."

Mark the day. It is the Fourth of July, 1863—the second most important Fourth in American history, if not *the* most important. For on that day, defeat settled permanently on the banners of the Southern Confederacy, and not all the heart-bursting rides of men like Shelby and Stuart could any longer save the armies and the government. The Fourth of July, 1863: Lee's beaten army is falling back from Gettysburg. The three-day battle for Pennsylvania ended yesterday. Pemberton, at Vicksburg, was ready to quit yesterday, but he has waited until

today, hoping to get better terms for his troops if he surrenders them
on the Fourth of July. And at Helena, three Confederate forces are
converging upon General Prentiss's works for a bloody and useless
attack whose failure will mean the loss of Arkansas in six weeks and
the bottling up of the Trans-Mississippi army for the rest of the war.

The attack is set for daylight; the Federals have been up and at their
posts since 2:30 A.M., waiting for it. There is a good deal of argument
in the official reports as to whether the Confederates started the Battle
of Helena on time. Holmes says that they did not, and blames Price,
chiefly, and Walker, secondarily. Holmes charges that Price lagged
for a full hour after sunrise in his attack on Graveyard Hill, and that as
a result the enemy was able to throw the combined weight of its
artillery and rifle fire at Fagan, when he attacked; Price says that he
made only "a brief halt" to rest his troops before commencing the
attack at daylight, and that his two brigades, under Parsons and McRae,
attacked simultaneously and according to plan. Holmes says that
McRae was derelict in his duty because he did not obey Holmes's
order, given hastily at the last minute, to reinforce Fagan after Fagan
was repulsed; McRae says it would have been madness to attempt it;
Marmaduke admits his attack from the north was "a failure" but
blames General L. M. Walker for not supporting him on his front
and left. Walker says that he did what he was supposed to do; and
the record would seem to bear him out. Marmaduke shot Walker dead
in a duel afterward as a result of their quarrel as to who was at fault
at Helena.

It was a mess, a bloody, unholy mess, but the Confederate soldier
in the ranks, as always, covered himself with glory. For twelve solid
hours in the tanglefoot of the felled logs, the deep ravines, the impassable gullies, the rifle pits, the blazing artillery, the thunder of the
heavy guns from Fort Curtis, and the barricaded streets of Helena
itself, the boys from Missouri, Texas, and Arkansas fought like the
swamp tigers they had become. They were driven back in the end
because the attack was not coordinated and because the Federals could
concentrate their fire always on the Confederate weak points. Nevertheless, since the Confederates outnumbered the enemy 7,646 to 4,129,
with artillery support, their attack should have been overwhelming.

All of the Confederate reports are acrimonious and contradictory.
The best account of what happened to the Federals comes from their
side. General Prentiss says that the attack began on his front and right

at daylight. His front was Graveyard Hill. That was Price. His right was Rightor Hill. That was Marmaduke, Shelby, and Walker. Prentiss thus exonerates Price from the charge that Holmes made—that Price lost the battle through delay. The Federal commander says that Price attacked first, or so nearly first that it was practically simultaneous with the others, and that four hours later, Price was still attacking as furiously as ever. In fact, if we are to believe General Prentiss, and there seems no reason not to, Sterling Price and his Missourians were the heroes of Helena. Prentiss, in writing of Price's division, sounds more like a general praising his own men than an enemy commander describing an attack upon himself. Few generals have had this sort of tribute from an enemy:

"For four hours," Prentiss wrote, "the battle raged furiously, the enemy gaining little, if any advantage. Now however, the attack in front became more furious; the enemy covered every hilltop, swarmed in every ravine, but seemed to be massing his force most particularly against Battery C [at Graveyard Hill]. I now signaled the gunboat *Tyler*, the only one at hand, to open fire in that direction. The enemy, Parsons's and McRae's brigades, nothing daunted by the concentrated fire from Fort Curtis, Batteries, B, C, D, the *Tyler* and all the infantry I could bring to their support, and led, as I since learn, by Lieutenant General Holmes and Major General Price in person, charged upon Battery C. Twice they were repulsed, but the third time, exhibiting a courage and desperation rarely equaled, they succeeded in driving my small force at the point of the bayonet and capturing the battery. Dividing his forces, and sending a part, as a feint, to menace Fort Curtis, the enemy then assaulted Battery D, to reach which they must pass through a deep ravine and encounter a heavy cross fire."

Here Price's advance faltered, under that murderous fire, and getting no support from either flank, was surrounded and made prisoner by troops whom they outnumbered three to one!

The failure on the flanks had been complete—Price's victory in the center was a useless effusion of blood. He and a weeping Lieutenant General Holmes gave the order to retreat at about 10:30 A.M., although it was not until about 3:00 P.M. that the day was seen to be irretrievably lost and all brigades set in motion away from Helena.

What had happened, on the flanks?

Nothing good, from the very start.

Fagan's attack failed and Marmaduke never attacked at all.

The failure of Fagan's attack is soon accounted for. *He had left his artillery behind!* (out of necessity, he says), and his men had practically to crawl on all fours to the Battle of Helena through the barriers which the enemy had set up. He says that "the road was completely filled with felled timber, the largest forest growth intermingling and over-lapping its whole length, while on either side precipitous and impassable ravines were found running up even to the very entrenchments of the enemy. It was utterly impossible to move my artillery or ammunition train along this road. The obstacles were so great, indeed, that I was under the necessity of directing every officer of my command to dismount and proceed on foot—a dire necessity which subsequent events gave occasion seriously to deplore. After crawling through the interstices of the closely jutting limbs and boughs, and climbing over the thickly matted timber for a mile, my line of skirmishers, who had been ordered by me not to fire, came within sight of the enemy. I went to the front, and could plainly see that the enemy was on the alert, and evidently waiting and expecting an attack. Not having been apprised of the obstructions in the road, I had made no arrangements to remove them. The limited time to daylight would not allow even of an attempt to take my artillery along. To conform to orders, it was necessary for me to move with the utmost celerity. Freeing myself of everything except my column of infantry, I pushed along with all the haste in my power. At daylight I reached and attacked the enemy in his works."

Despite his lack of artillery and the exhaustion of his men from having to cover an obstacle course before reaching the scene of action, Fagan carries four lines of Federal rifle pits by assault, and follows up with an attack on Fort Hindman, which is bloodily repulsed. Price has taken Graveyard Hill (also without artillery, for, like Fagan, he has been forced to leave his behind, and for the same reason!), but in the center the Confederate flag is planted squarely on the enemy's fortifications; it is the crucial moment of the battle and despite Fagan's reverses, there may still be time to take Helena—if the Confederate forces on the north have been attacking successfully.

They have not attacked at all. Marmaduke and Walker have taken up positions on either side of Rightor Hill at daylight, but somehow or other, large Federal forces are on every side of them. There are massed batteries and infantry between Walker and the river; the enemy is in Marmaduke's rear at Rightor Hill, also with batteries and infantry, in such force that he is afraid to move forward. Twice he sends a courier to Walker demanding that Walker attack the forces in his (Marmaduke's) rear so that he, Marmaduke, can carry out his assignment of taking Rightor Hill. Walker, after looking over the situation, concludes that if he moves from where he is, Marmaduke will be surrounded on four sides instead of just on three; he also makes it clear in his report that he considers he has done his duty when he protects General Marmaduke's flank by holding his position on the Sterling Road.

Marmaduke wrote angrily: "The attack upon Fort Rightor by my command was a failure. I have every reason to believe that my troops would have carried it had it not been for the force on my left and rear, which occupied that position after daylight, and which could and should have been prevented from taking that position, and after they had gained that position, could have been driven from it by General Walker's brigade, which did not come to the support of my left until 7 A.M.; and during the whole engagement his force was more than half a mile to my left and rear. I could see the force which engaged Walker's brigade, and at no time did it exceed 500. I think 300 a big estimate."

Jo Shelby played a much more active part in the Battle of Helena than Marmaduke's inaction would indicate, but he was severely wounded at Helena and turned in no report on the battle, being under the care of a physician at Batesville for several weeks afterward. His assignment to Marmaduke's command at Helena was another piece of bad luck on the part of the Confederates (the Iron Brigade had been part of Price's division and was detached from it by Holmes at the last moment), for Shelby was the only Confederate commander who was able to bring up his artillery at Helena. Shelby had marched through country fully as rough as that which Fagan and Price had encountered, but they had left their guns behind, *whereas Shelby had his with him*— for once again the men of the Iron Brigade had substituted for the horses when the horses could no longer move the artillery, and soon after daylight were blazing away at everything Federal in sight, including a troopship in the river! Never, on any battlefield of the Civil War, did Shelby leave his artillery behind, and never, on any battlefield, did he ever lose a battery.

Let Marmaduke tell the story of his troubles of the early morning, before Shelby's activities of the next eight hours are traced:

"When three miles from the fort (on Rightor Hill) I dismounted my whole force, except one company under Major Benjamin Elliott. I then moved forward. When within two miles of the fort, I found the road and country thoroughly obstructed, the enemy having chopped down the trees and rendered almost impassable that approach to the fort and the town. The country was exceedingly rough. I was delayed some half hour or more by my guides, who lost their way and reported that they were completely lost and unable to guide me farther, in consequence of which I did not get into position until a little after daylight, but before sunup. The enemy's pickets and skirmishers were encountered some three quarters of a mile from the fort, and driven to within 150 yards of the fort. In this the enemy lost several killed and wounded, and five prisoners. *Shelby's brigade was in the advance,* and so narrow was the road, and so rough and rugged were the hills, that the troops could only march by the flank, and the artillery with great difficulty was brought up piece by piece, and by hand. By the time that the advance had reached within 200 yards of the fort, and those in rear brought up and deployed along the ridges, the enemy had brought to my left and rear a body of infantry and several pieces of artillery which, during the whole day's fight, poured upon me a deadly fire. I now had a heavy force in my front, infantry in rifle pits and artillery in position, which it would have been difficult with my whole force to have carried. In addition, I had the force on my left (of infantry and artillery) thoroughly protected by the levee, which engaged a large part of my force and, on every attempt to advance, enfiladed my line. It was from the sharpshooters and artillery on my left and rear that I suffered my greatest loss, and not until they were dislodged could I have advanced. I twice dispatched to Brigadier General Walker to advance and assist me in dislodging them. It was not done."

The enfilading fire which Marmaduke speaks of was being received in part by Shelby, who was chafing, fretting, and fuming because Marmaduke would not permit him to attack Fort Salomon on Rightor Hill.

Says Major Edwards, in the only account extant of Shelby's participation in the battle:

"In plain view, the Mississippi river lay wrapped in an impenetrable veil of fog, that whirled and twisted in vast formless clouds upon the sleeping town (at daybreak; but Helena was not sleeping) and on the giant trees upon its banks. At sunrise it lifted sufficiently to see glimmering through the gloom the dark sides and the inevitable black, pitchy smoke of an ironclad escorting a large steamer, whose roof and decks were blue with uniforms. Shelby opened directly upon the crowded boat; the ironsides answered immediately and from all the bastioned walls the grim redoubts of Helena there went up on this Independence Day a crash and thunder of artillery more discordant than a war of elements. From the town a splendid six-gun battery ran out and took position in the plain below to silence Collins's guns; the ironclad shelled him all day, and Fort Salomon plied its busy Parrotts almost beyond endurance. Under this heavy and enfilading fire Shelby formed his brigade for the charge . . . [after] waiting impatiently for orders to advance, asked permission to assault Fort Salomon, but was refused. . . . General Prentiss concentrated a fearful fire upon Shelby from artillery and infantry." The Federals had been reinforced following the defeat of the Confederates on the other two sides of the Helena triangle, and it was in this storm of shot and shell that Shelby was wounded. A minie ball struck him at the elbow, coursed through his arm and came out at the wrist. All of Shelby's men agreed that in the excitement of battle Shelby was impervious to pain: Major Jake Stonestreet, who was standing next to him by Collins's battery, says, "I was near him and he did not even draw in his breath." [3]

In addition to being wounded, Shelby has had two horses shot from beneath him at Helena; although faint from loss of blood, he returns to the little inferno of Rightor Hill as soon as the arm is bandaged; he is worried, as always, about his artillery. Price's infantry can be seen retreating through the streets of Helena, past houses "vomiting flames of death," and the great grim citadel playing its siege guns like a hose of fire in every direction; it is pretty obvious now that the attack on Helena has failed, and the messenger from Holmes is not long in coming. At 11 A.M., a little less than eight hours since Shelby's battery was hauled to the foot of the declivity at Rightor Hill, Marmaduke gets the order to retire.

"Volunteers to save the battery!" shouts Shelby, pale against the chestnut beard as he sits his horse weakly. "Fifty volunteers to save the battery, boys! Shelby's Brigade never lost a battery, and with God's help, never will. What do you say, Colonel Gilkey?"

Gilkey and hundreds of others have a good deal to say in the smoke and confusion; and Major Edwards says that Shelby could have had a thousand volunteers; but fifty is enough, and these Colonel Gilkey takes forward into the pit of death at the foot of the hill to cut the dead battery animals from their traces, drag the bullet-rent and riddled wheels by the severed harness from the path of the Federal advance, and flee with the rest. New horses are found for the guns; "everyone worked for dear life and dear honor." When Marmaduke's retreat finally was begun, with the Iron Brigade in the rear, Federal pursuers were not three hundred yards away—"pressing on furiously, infantry, cavalry and artillery, and shouting and killing as they came." Fifteen of Gilkey's men died to save the battery.

General Prentiss was satisfied to save Helena; the pursuit did not extend beyond the fortifications. If you care to read his report all the way through, you will find that after Price's retreat, he was expecting another attack on his left flank, where Fagan had been inactive ever since his first, headlong rush, but Prentiss says that afterward, when he counted the Confederate dead and wounded, he understood why they did not come back to the attack. These pages make painful reading, for at the end of the reports come the official figures of the strength of the Confederate Army of the Trans-Mississippi *after* *Helena:* 31,933 in the District of Arkansas; 23,597 in the District of Western Louisiana; 11,717 in the District of Texas.

Sixty-seven thousand men, and half of them were on furlough or sick leave on July 4, 1863!

This was the army which was never used.

The great storms which rumbled over the dying Confederacy in the summer of 1863 were accompanied by lesser gusts and squalls which blew ill fortune like a disease borne upon air currents into every corner of the decaying mansion which was the "proud imperial South."

The history of Confederate operations in Arkansas in 1863, after Helena, requires no time in the telling. Although there were marches and countermarches, with the wounded Shelby leaving his sick bed to lead a charge on the road to Little Rock, the upshot of it all was that by September 10, General Frederick Steele of the Union army was comfortably settled in General Holmes's old headquarters at Little Rock, Price and Holmes had retreated to Arkadelphia, whither their stores had been transported, and Jo Shelby, his arm still suppurating, was pondering bitterly the news from Missouri.

Quantrill, who seems to have detached himself at will from whatever command he was assigned to, now rode a thousand miles to Lawrence, Kansas, where he sacked and burned the town and murdered sixty unoffending civilians. The Federals, under a General Ewing in that district, issued their famous Order No. 11, which ordered that rebel sympathizers and their families in the whole western Missouri River Valley be dispossessed and driven out of the area. The order included Jackson, Howard, Lafayette, and Johnson counties. The family of Mrs. Rebecca Redd and Jo Shelby's family, who were still staying with the Redds, were included.

Word of this came to Shelby at Batesville. He got in touch with Frank Blair and Benjamin Gratz, no matter how (the records here again are lost), but General Blair made arrangements for Betty and the children to go through the lines to Lexington, Kentucky, and the old home on Mill Street. That great and gallant gentleman, Benjamin Gratz, came to Waverly in person to get them, and he also escorted Mrs. Redd back to Kentucky. On this trip he went out to look at the 1,000-acre farm which Shelby and Howard Gratz had owned, and which Howard now owned by himself, and bought it from his son. (Shelby had thoughtfully deeded his share in the farm to Howard Gratz, so that it was not confiscated in 1861 along with his home on Mount Rucker.)

It was also about this time that Shelby got permission to go on his Great Raid Into Missouri, the longest and most daring raid of the Civil War, which was a war of raids. He would not have got permission from such fellows as Price and Holmes, or even Kirby Smith; but there was a new factor in the situation in the person of Thomas C. Reynolds, the new Confederate governor of Missouri. Claiborne Jackson had died of cancer the previous December; his successor was a man as energetic as himself. When Shelby asked permission to invade Missouri, Reynolds overruled the military and said, "Go." And he added as he shook hands with Shelby—it had to be the left one—"The buff sash of a brigadier awaits the issue."

17. *Shelby's Great Raid*

"Ho Boys! Make a Noise!
The Yankees are afraid!
The river's up, hell's to pay—
Shelby's on a Raid!"
—"Shelby's Mule" [1]

THE OLD MEN dreamed in the sun on the porch of the Confederate Home at Higginsville....

Fifteen hundred miles to the Missouri River and back again.... with 800 men in thirty-four days ... through a state filled with 50,000 of the enemy ... and 600 of them dead in sixteen days, 600 sabred and shot and six-poundered in a dozen fair fights ... and some not so fair. We know because we got their rifles, every one of them ... from the Illinois Yankees and the Black Republicans and the Lop-Eared Dutch ... with 300 wagons to carry them in. Jo Shelby never had so many wagons ... and forty stands of colors. Old Jo said that we destroyed a hundred thousand dollars worth of enemy property ... but that's not counting the million dollars in supplies of the best fed, best equipped army the sun ever shone on ... in the Federal Department of Missouri ... yes sir, boy ... there were 10,000 troops out of the 50,000 in the Department of the West who couldn't catch us ... though they tried ... 10,000 bluecoats who stayed home from Chattanooga because of Shelby's Raid.... You've heard of Shelby's Raid? Jeb Stuart's Ride around McClellan? Hell, brother, Jo Shelby rode around MISSOURI! ...

Fifteen hundred miles to the Missouri River and back again ... with 800 men in thirty-four days ... to the gates of Jefferson City!

What if they had given us 10,000 men? ...

The Civil War was a war of raids, and Shelby's raid into Missouri in September and October was one of the most daring of them all. It was accomplished with fewer men against greater numbers than any other raid of the war, and it may be quite possible to prove that because of Shelby's ceaseless activity on horseback he covered more miles as a Confederate raider than any of the other great Southern cavalry leaders. It was this daring foray into Missouri in 1863, coupled with his smashing defeat of Pleasanton the following year at Newtonia —the last battle fought west of the Mississippi—which caused Pleasonton to say that Shelby was the greatest cavalry leader the South had, bar none—and that from a man who had fought Jeb Stuart for three years.

The compliments were not being passed freely in Shelby's direction on September 22, 1863, however. The older heads were wagging dubiously; it was felt that Shelby was a show-off and a fool, and headed for certain destruction. The only men in high spirits, aside from Shelby and Governor Reynolds, were Shelby's Missourians. With Old Jo in sole command, they did not doubt that they would get where they were going. As Major Edwards says, "Preparations for raids to Missouri were never long in the making, and this one grew as swiftly as a young man's love." [2] The preparations, in fact, had been a little too enthusiastic, as far as General Holmes was concerned, and he summoned Shelby to Arkadelphia for the purpose of giving him a lecture.

Holmes had been in a state of acute depression ever since the failure of the attack on Helena. The old man's heart was broken; during the retreat he had remarked tearfully to Marmaduke that the Army of the Trans-Mississippi was now "an army of prisoners, and self-supporting at that." [3] His terrific disappointment had not caused him to sink into apathy, however; he was more morose and excitable, and harder to get along with, than ever. When Shelby entered his presence, he blurted out, without preliminaries,

"Sir, your men are nothing but a set of thieves, and their thieving must be stopped."

Shelby stiffened. "Sir," he said, "whoever told you that, lies."

"I believe it is true," said Holmes.

"Why?" asked Shelby.

"Because everybody says so."

"Do you believe a thing when everybody says it?" inquired Shelby.

"I certainly do," said Holmes.

"Do you know what everybody says about you?" inquired Shelby.

Holmes fell neatly into the trap. "No, sir, I do not!" he snapped.

"They say that you are a damned old fool," said Shelby, and walked out.

Major Edwards gives a watered-down version of this conversation, but Major Jake Stonestreet, who was present, says it took just about this form; it is also quoted thus in Hollister and Norman's *Five Famous Missourians*.[4] With the backing of his commander-in-chief, Governor Reynolds, and liberated from the tyranny of superior officers whose chief characteristic was timidity, Shelby was in no mood to take further orders from the bunglers under whom he had served since '61.

He knew of course that with 800 men he could not secure a foothold anywhere in Missouri, but on the day that he set out, Rosecrans, driven back from Chickamauga, was vociferously demanding that most of the Federals in Missouri be sent to reinforce him at Chattanooga; it was a critical time for the Confederates east of the Mississippi and the threat of a new Confederate invasion of Missouri would hold a substantial number of Federal troops west of the river. On the other hand, if the Federals were foolish enough to strip the state of troops, believing the Confederates too weak to invade, Jo Shelby could drive to Jefferson City as easily as he had once raided to Waverly, and raise the Stars and Bars above the capital. The consternation which this would cause would produce startling changes in the course of the war; it might even make the Richmond government do something.

The situation in Missouri as Shelby rode north to Caddo Gap on September 22 was one of terror and bedlam which not all the 50,000 troops of Major General Schofield could control. Kansas Redlegs roamed the Missouri River Valley settling old scores from the Border Wars and murdering those suspected of being rebel sympathizers, and their families. Bushwackers on both sides, and many who were in reality on neither side, operated freely throughout the state, looting and killing. The German newspapers protested bitterly that anyone who had "a German face" was in constant danger of having a dagger plunged into his heart. Fraud and corruption in connection with U. S. government supplies were so rife that Schofield had reprimanded General Blunt—a good soldier—for having allowed frauds of monstrous size to be perpetrated under his very nose.[5]

The whole of Missouri was a Donnybrook fair, with civilians murdering one another wholesale, while the officers of the army supposed to protect them robbed the government blind. Shelby was so enraged at the state of affairs in Missouri that he who had made the most sparing use of firing squads now kept them busy day in and day out.

Bands of guerrillas were so numerous that Shelby had been in

Missouri about a week before the Federals realized that a Confederate expedition was among them. In fact, on October 1, 1863, eight days after he had left Arkadelphia, President Lincoln wrote to Schofield: "There is no organized military force in avowed opposition to the General Government now in Missouri, and if any such should re-appear, your duty in regard to it will be too plain to require any special instructions."

Abraham Lincoln was so convinced that the Confederates in the West had been liquidated by the success of the Vicksburg campaign that he was chiding Schofield for his failure to keep order in a state where there was no enemy to fear. Wrote Lincoln in the same missive: "Your immediate duty in regard to Missouri now is to advance the efficiency of [your] establishment, and to use it, so as far is practicable, to compel the excited people there to leave one another alone." [6]

As this was being written in the White House, Shelby and his 800 men were cutting a swath of destruction in the state which would cost the Federal government a million dollars in destroyed supplies. As Colonel John C. Moore said of him after the war, Shelby could do anything with the cavalry, wield it like a whip or drive it like a wedge. He also seemed to have the power of making it invisible when he wished, and the Irishmen in his command, at least, like Jake Connor and Jimmy Grady, would have sworn that he could ride between the raindrops when he wished to keep dry.

All such praise, boiled down, merely means, of course, that Shelby was one of those rare individuals who seem to have no limit to their physical endurance, and he had the good fortune to have native intel-ligence to match his physical strength. That such praise is not too high, under the conditions that existed, is indicated by the crackling telegraphic dispatches which fill up no fewer then *one hundred* pages of the Official Records.[7] From the top commanders of the Depart-ment of the West down to mere lieutenant colonels and majors, no one ever knew where Shelby was until after he had been there, ex-cept at Marshall, Missouri; and at Marshall, where he was surrounded by a vastly superior force, he drove his command through a solid wall of the enemy and escaped, though encumbered by artillery and heav-ily loaded wagons.

First blood of the Great Raid was spilled just north of Caddo Gap in the Arkansas mountains. Shelby had just been joined by Colonel David Hunter with fifty men. Major Ben Elliott, who was always in the vanguard of the Iron Brigade, discovered a camp of Confederate deserters and Union jayhawkers just beyond the gap. They were attacked, and seventy-nine of them killed and thirty-four captured. All but three of the prisoners were condemned to death by a military commission and shot the next morning. The last to die was a notorious Captain McGinnis, leader of the band and a New England Puritan despite his Irish name. He was given time to pray, and he prayed for his enemies.

"Oh God," he began, "bless the Union and all its loyal defenders; bless the poor ignorant rebels who persist in hardening their hearts and stiffening their necks; bless Mrs. McGinnis and her children; bless the Constitution, which has been wrongly interpreted; and eradicate slavery from the earth."

"Come, come, old man," said the captain of the firing squad, "the command has already gone and I will get far behind."

"I am ready, young man," said McGinnis, "and may God have mercy on your soul." He bared his breast and six Confederate riflemen shot him dead. The Confederates believed that his jayhawkers had murdered twenty Southern sympathizers in the neighborhood.

At Roseville was the First Federal Arkansas Infantry, composed of just the kind of fellows the Missourians liked to catch up with—deserters from Hindman's Arkansas army, Union Negro soldiers, and white men who, though Southerners, were Union sympathizers. These latter belonged to Illinois and Missouri regiments. Shelby let Quantrill (now back from Richmond) and Gregg do a little preliminary work on these people, knowing that they would enjoy the assignment.

Taken by surprise, most of the Federals—between 300 and 400—were captured. Those who could be identified as Arkansas deserters were shot instantly. The Negroes were not treated as soldiers. They were stripped of their uniforms, each given a sound thrashing, and ordered back to their masters; they were told if they showed up in the enemy's ranks again, and captured, they would be hanged. The bonafied Union soldiers were treated in gentlemanly fashion, given provisions, paroled, and dismissed.

One of the Union prisoners had been wounded in the initial attack. He was brought within Shelby's lines and placed on a bed of leaves. He was a farmer of the neighborhood, and among those whom Quantrill and Jim Thorp had rounded up were members of his family, two women and three little girls. One of the women was the man's wife, the other his sister. The prisoner seemed to be wounded badly. Shelby did not know quite what to do with him, and the five females had set up such a wailing that Major Edwards says it was "distressing to behold."

Shelby explained to them that he could not linger, but that he would not leave them in distress. He ordered a blanket, overcoat, and some provisions set down for the family; he then asked his boys if they would contribute something in the way of cash. Edwards says that Confederate money—and the Missourians had precious little even of that—was "showered" upon the family—and that even a few greenbacks appeared. Shelby himself contributed several greenbacks, and pressed a purse of coins upon the wife. "What it contained," Edward says, "even he himself could scarcely have told. But be sure the Recorder of his many actions knew, and reckoned it to the uttermost farthing."

Shelby's curious blend of caution and recklessness is nowhere better demonstrated than in the fact that throughout the war, as far as any records show, he never carried anything but United States money upon his person.

Whenever he was called upon to produce money, which was seldom, he could always manage to find a few greenbacks of large denomination in one pocket or another. It was not that he did not trust his government; it was just that some other people did not. When General Lee surrendered at Appomattox, he had two brand-new Confederate twenty dollar bills upon his person. You may see them today in the Confederate Museum at Richmond, together with the handsome uniform in which he surrendered. Lee and Shelby were both dead broke at the end of the war; their vast estates confiscated, but Lee was always among friends, or at least surrounded by a large army; Shelby was always followed, like a criminal, by overwhelming forces of the law, and he felt that it was the better part of wisdom to carry a couple of bucks in his shoe, so to speak.

It was not until October 4, when Shelby had marched 250 miles to Neosho in southwest Missouri that the Federal commanders in the area were fully aware of what the Shelby expedition meant; but even then they misjudged his ultimate destination. On his previous three raids into Missouri, he had headed by one devious route or another for Waverly, and they began concentrating forces of larger or smaller size between Neosho and Waverly—see the endless dispatches in the Official Records. Even Major General Schofield thought that Shelby was merely on a raid into southern Missouri and that he would wheel around and head home for Arkansas in a short time. Nobody thought he was heading for Jefferson City.[8]

Furthermore, the savagery of his destruction and the amount of supplies he had captured made Schofield and the others in the top ranks of the Department of the West believe that Shelby's main object was to gather up as much booty as he could before returning to Arkansas. True, Schofield said, let's get behind him and prevent him from returning to Arkansas, so that he will be trapped in Missouri, but not many Federal commanders wanted to tangle with Shelby unless they were part of an overwhelming force sent against him.

From Roseville, which is in Logan County, Arkansas, the command passed on to Neosho via Huntsville, Mudtown, and Bentonville. At Bentonville Shelby sent a Colonel Horace Brand with a small detachment to recruit in northeast Arkansas and make a demonstration against the Federal railway terminus at Rolla. En route to Neosho, which had been the only capital of the Republic of Missouri when the state was for two months an ally of the Confederacy, Shelby's raiders destroyed mile after mile of telegraph lines. At Bentonville it was discovered that Sigel and the Dutch had been there recently and burned the town. There Shelby was joined by Colonel Coffee and 100 men. Sitting their horses and looking at the charred ruins of Bentonville, neither Shelby's nor Coffee's men needed any exhortation for the work ahead of them.

Neosho proved a prize indeed. It was occupied by a garrison of 400 Federal cavalry, and there were about 500 splendid horses in the command. The garrison was concentrated in a large brick courthouse, which Shelby surrounded and began to blow apart with shells from his Parrott guns. The beleaguered Federals ran up a white flag in short order, and Shelby's men where soon taking inventory of one of the finest Federal supply depots in Missouri. Besides the horses there were 400 Sharpe's rifles, 400 new navy revolvers, and four splendid cavalry overcoats, together with pantaloons, boots, spurs, hats, underclothing, medicines, blankets, socks, and commissary supplies, as well as "now and then some rare demijohns of glorious Bourbons." As the Iron Brigade rode off from Neosho, there was not a gray jacket in sight, except Shelby's. It was a curious sight: bluecoated cavalry trotting along beneath the Confederate flags with the red sumac in their hats which had become the insigne of Shelby's men.

Bower's Mill, the next town on the line of march, was notorious as a rendezvous of thieves, cutthroats, and prostitutes. At Bower's Mill Shelby simply exiled the population and set fire to every house in town at once. There is a Bower's Mill in Missouri today, as respectable a community as any; it should be, for no spot on earth has been more thoroughly purified by fire.

Southwest Missouri was one vast depot of the finest supplies an army could wish for, and Shelby was destroying methodically everything he could not carry safely—at Greenfield, at Stockton, at Humansville, and Warsaw, after leaving Bower's Mill—but it was not his purpose simply to turn Missouri into a desert for the Federals. His destination was Jefferson City, where he meant to strike a swift, savage blow that would jolt the Confederate nation into a realization of the vulnerability of Missouri. To get there fastest, and before the Federals could assemble a large force to intercept him, he had sent out three scouting parties in the direction of Springfield, with orders to cut every wire between there and St. Louis. Nobody knew better then Shelby what would happen to him if the telegraph circuits were left open. Every Yankee in the Department of the West would turn out to meet him. As he approached Cole Camp from Warsaw, in Benton County, he had not heard from the detachment commanders— Lieutenants Williams, Wills, and Captain Lea—but he could feel confident that they had carried out their mission, for he encountered no enemy force of any size.

Cole Camp was a rural, agricultural district which had been turned into an Eden by its industrious German settlers. Shelby sent ahead scouts into Cole Camp. Being clad in blue uniforms, of course, they were welcomed by the inhabitants and entertained hospitably. In fact, those whom Shelby sent ahead found the work much to their liking. In his account Major Edwards says, "Dan Ingram reveled in the delicious cider; Peter Trone made love to innumerable moon-faced girls; Dave Shanks devoured their sauerkraut and patted the matronly fraus under their double chins; Hooper chatted about crops and bologna sausage, swearing his forefathers came from Amsterdam, or Rotterdam; Langhorne traded saddles twenty times and got one at last to suit him; Yandell Blackwell sang "Villikins and His Dinah" over rousing bumpers of sparkling Catawba; Lieutenant Selby Plattenburg begged books, magazines, or newspapers; McCoy talked Irish to the Dutch and Dutch to the Irish; Toney wrote letters to his innumerable sweethearts in Missouri and made every house a postoffice; Gordon went in heavily for cheese and Gentian apples; Judge Shindler [Sam Shindler, for whom Shelby named one of his sons. Ed.] discussed politics and the Emancipation Proclamation; Newt Hart and Ed Stonehill sought news from St. Louis, and inquired about the girls there; Coffee electioneered for Congress and explained his position; Maury Boswell bought wooden shoes to feed his horse in; Elliott stood aloof, a grim Saul among the prophets, listening only for bugle blasts and rattling musketry. Being clad in Federal uniforms, the impositions were easily kept up." [9]

Even after the main body of the rebels rode in, the truth was not at first revealed. Shelby was wearing a blue uniform on this occasion, not wishing to undeceive the Cole Camp population until he had made a survey himself of the situation.

A man described as "a tall, lank, kill-dee sort of fellow" darted out of the brush with a Mississippi rifle in his hand, and greeted Shelby.

"Well, boys, I'm glad to see you sartin," he said. "I heerd Jo Shelby was coming this way and I sorter made up to have a pop at him with this here weapon.

"Ah!" said Shelby. "What command do you belong to?"

"Well—ginral—I suppose you are a ginral from the feather in your hat and your big crowd behind, I don't exactly belong to any regiment but I'm as good a Union man as anybody, and me and the boys just formed a kind of gurilla company for home service, you know, drawing our arms and ammunition from Warsaw."

"Whom do you fight?" asked Shelby. "There are no rebels here, I reckon."

"Bless yer soul," said the good Union man, "plenty of 'em hereabouts and damn bad ones too, but we have been workin' on 'em lately and only day before yesterday we killed old man Beasly, Tom Mays, and two of Price's men just home from the army."

"Did these men make resistance," asked Shelby, "and had they been lying out in the brush?"

"No, not exactly, but they were rebels, you know."

"So are we rebels," said Jo Shelby. He turned to Major Elliott. *"Take this man to the rear and shoot him!"*

It was done, and Shelby's biographer says that the man was so terror-stricken as he was dragged away that he could not speak.

At Florence the raiders beheld a curious sight. Every man, woman, and child had fled from the place. Everything had been left behind. Doors were left open, furniture in place, stores were left stocked. "One peculiarity of the place struck everyone with surprise, and it was the vast quantities of eggs in every house, store, barn and tenement. Hogsheads were filled with them, boxes, barrels, buckets, pans and baskets contained countless thousands, and yet the numbers were only half enumerated." The raiders feasted on hundreds of omelets for supper.

At Tipton, the railway center in Moniteau County, there was a small Federal garrison, which made a token resistance but soon fled before the rebel onslaught. Their flight was so precipitate that they did not even carry their flag with them. Some of Shelby's men, remembering the burned homes and the murdered settlers in the area through which they had passed, tore it down and trampled it in the mud.

They wreaked other destruction at Tipton of a kind more calculated to cripple the enemy. They tore up the Missouri Pacific Railroad track for miles, burned the depot, and set fire to a large number of freight and passenger cars. Before entering Tipton, however, Shelby sent Captains Warner Lewis and Bill Edwards to reconnoitre the town. As they galloped about, a locomotive and one passenger car came hurtling across the prairie from Sedalia, at twenty-five miles an hour, and Captain Lewis undertook to do battle with it. He fired several times at the engineer's cab, but the train merely passed on. When Shelby heard of it, he told Lewis that he could see that he was a new hand at capturing locomotives. The proper way, said Shelby, was either to displace one of the rails slightly (which might be possible with one of the home-made Missouri bayonets formed out of blacksmith files) or else place an obstruction on the track which would cause the locomotive to slow down. Shelby would have been disappointed if he had known that the lone passenger on that train was Lieutenant Colonel Thomas T. Crittenden,[10] the future Governor of Missouri, who had been a guest at Shelby's wedding. Shelby was particularly anxious to cross swords with him because Crittenden was a Kentuckian and Shelby viewed his present affiliations as a disgrace to their native state.

This was October 10, and Shelby had been on the road since September 22. He had stolen or destroyed hundreds of thousands of dollars of enemy property, and terrorized a good part of western

Missouri; and the Federals had not even concentrated a force in his neighborhood. The reason for this seeming paralysis of action may be found in the Official Records. The colonel commanding at Springfield—headquarters of the District of Southwestern Missouri—was a Colonel John Edwards. The frequency with which his name appears in the accounts of Shelby's raid is confusing at first glance because the Confederate John Edwards is also mentioned frequently.

On the morning of October 6, 1863, Union Colonel Edwards sent this dispatch to the Federal commander at Neosho (who was no longer there): "The enemy, if he does not divide, will be 2,000 strong; now at Carthage, and trying to go into Jackson County but will be driven back, and will try to get out again into Arkansas. That we must prevent. Follow up rapidly in his rear and give him battle wherever you can. I will leave today, via Greenfield, with three pieces of artillery and a column. Colonel Campbell is at Cassville, and has Captain Stark's ammunition. I shall order him . . . to go to Newtonia. I will go from Greenfield in the direction of Lamar and hope to form a junction with you." [11]

General Schofield accepted this mistaken diagnosis as gospel and made arrangements accordingly. The telegraph wires were warm—those that had not been cut. Schofield wired General Ewing, of Order No. 11 fame, to "meet and destroy" Shelby in the Jackson County area—which is up near Lexington and far from Shelby's actual route. Ewing replied that he would concentrate all of his men at Butler in Bates County. He might as well have concentrated them in Montana. Schofield then wired Brigadier General Holland at Springfield to "call out all of the militia of your district which you can make available in the pursuit of Shelby. Prevent his escape into Arkansas if possible."

Thus Shelby was afforded quite a head start in his march towards northeastern Missouri. By the time he reached Tipton, however, his whereabouts was known, and the telegraphic dispatches which were circling the wires now reported not only Shelby's daily, but his hourly movements. Brigadier General Totten—the Captain Totten of the Federal batteries at Wilson's Creek—reported to Schofield that Shelby left Cole Camp at exactly twelve noon on October 9.[12] All of Missouri was now swarming with Federals on all sides of Shelby; it did not make much difference which way he went. He was outnumbered ten to one on every side, and now that the Federals knew he was moving on Jefferson City, his chances of a spectacular raid on the capital had gone glimmering.

Shelby now knew that Brown's was not the only large Federal force in the neighborhood which would soon be concentrating its attention on his raiders; northeastern Missouri held tens of thousands of the enemy, and all of these would soon be enclosing him. Nevertheless, his little army (now numbering 1,200) was a colorful sight, with its fine horses, its 300 wagons, and 40 stands of colors. No lumbering draft animals drew these wagons; Shelby had captured so many fine cavalry horses that he could move his wagons at top speed, especially since many of them were empty. Boonville was soon in sight, and a delegation, including the Mayor, came out to greet him and assure him of their Southern loyalties.

Camped outside Boonville, Shelby received word that General E. B. Brown, the Union commander who had been cheered by the Confederates at Springfield for his reckless bravery in the line, was marching in his direction with 4,000 men. Bennett H. Young, author of *Confederate Wizards of the Saddle*, says: "Brown . . . was not afraid of Shelby. In this respect he was better off than some of his associates." [13] Brown knew that the man who bagged Shelby would win a renown in the western armies which would secure him undying fame. Although he was unknown even in the South, Shelby was already a legend among the Federals, who had to fight him.

Brown was so afraid that Shelby would not attack and let himself be captured at Jefferson City that on October 11 he marched to meet him at Boonville, hoping to lure him toward the capital, where he could be engulfed from all sides. Brown's advance had reached the city limits when some shaggy-looking fellows of almost inhuman aspect rose up out of the ground and fought so fiercely that his trained German troops fell back. Brown's bluecoats rallied and fought a skirmish with Hooper's men which lasted, off and on, until ten o'clock that night. In camp, Shelby was busy repairing the axle of his rifled gun, which had been broken, and his biographer says that he was in extreme pain from his wounded arm, which again had begun to suppurate. Nevertheless he was cheered by the news, brought in by Captain Jim Wood and a detachment of 100 picked men, that the new $400,000 bridge over the Lamine River near Boonville had been blown up, burned and destroyed by Wood's men. There had been 40 Federals in a blockhouse at the bridge, and Wood's men had either captured or killed all of them.

From this point, the official report of operations turned in by Shelby on his Great Raid is an account of his escape from the trap which all northeast Missouri had become.[14] "At daylight of the 12th," he says, "my pickets were again driven in and the camp aroused. Forming a line of battle immediately and choosing a good position, I waited an hour for General E. B. Brown, intending to give him battle then, but he not accepting the proffered wager, I moved out slowly on the main Marshall and Boonville Road. I captured in Boonville one iron-fourpounder, which, not having any ammunition of sufficient size, was destroyed, with many stands of arms and colors. After traveling perhaps for two hours uninterruptedly, General Brown again charged my rear furiously, and I saw that he must be checked then and there. At the crossing of the Lamine the banks are rugged and precipitous, so stationing Major G. P. Gordon with his regiment on the western side I had him to dismount and ambush them, leaving two companies on the eastern side to fire and then retreat in apparent confusion. The bait took completely, and the yelling, shouting Federals dashed into the stream and up the farther side of the Confederates in ambush. A hot, close, deadly fire from rifles and revolvers left 50 dead on the spot, many wounded, and the rest routed and demoralized. [Editor's Note: Shelby used this trick in nearly every battle of the war, yet it never failed to deceive the enemy. Its success apparently depended upon the fact that every Federal commander who outnumbered Shelby usually outnumbered him so greatly that he could not believe that Shelby was not in full retreat, and that all a pursuer had to do was to catch up with him.] This modified General Brown's desire for a more vigorous pursuit, but toward night he came on again with a heavy force of cavalry and artillery. Near Jonesborough, at the crossing of the Blackwater, I took up my position and waited for developments. Very soon the enemy made a furious attack. In twenty minutes I silenced their batteries, charged and drove them three miles, then leaving the ground covered with their killed and wounded. After this my rear was left unmolested, and I halted for the night about six miles from Marshall, sending a scout to Arrow Rock, which returned about ten o'clock, reporting all quiet there. On the morning of October 13th, I broke camp early and started for Marshall."

It was at Marshall that Shelby, commanding 1,200 men, was surrounded by 8,000 or more. The Federal commanders must have been jubilant. Whichever way the weary Confederate cavalryman turns his horse, there are six armed men in his path. The old fox is bagged at last; what a triumph to lead Jo Shelby a prisoner to Governor Gamble at Jefferson City!

Since Shelby's official report differs in no particular important instance from that turned in by General Brown, it may be accepted as correct. "When within a mile of the town [Marshall]," the report continues, "my advance sent word that a heavy body of Federals were formed in my front too, too strong to be attacked by them. I immediately galloped to the advance and found, sure enough, General Ewing drawn up with 4,000 Federals, of all arms, ready to receive me. The force in the rear would be on me in an hour, I knew; so I determined, if possible to defeat Ewing before Brown came up. Dismounting Major Shank's regiment, and forming it at the bridge over which we had just crossed, I ordered him to destroy it and hold Brown in check to the last extremity. In the attack upon Ewing, Hooper held the left, Hunter and Coffee the right, the artillery, and battalion, with Gordon in the center, the cavalry all dismounted. Ewing had admirably chosen his position, which was a high ridge, with a deep ravine in his front between his lines and mine. The men were eager for the fight, and when the order was given to advance, went to the Federals right gallantly. For two hours the fight raged evenly along the entire line.... On the left Hooper held his ground against overwhelming numbers, and Gordon and the rest fought manfully. I ordered a charge along the whole line. Hunter and Coffee doubled Ewing's left wing back upon his right, gained the town of Marshall, my artillery sweeping the crowded streets [of pursuers] with fearful slaughter. Just as their rout was inevitable, the roar of artillery in the rear warned me that Brown was hurling his columns upon the heroic and devoted Shanks, and must bear him back. For two mortal hours, Shanks, with his 200 men, held Brown's 4,000 in check, although he brought to bear upon him the weight of his artillery.... In the meantime General Brown, unable to drive Shanks from his position, had crossed the creek above and below him, and was coming up on either flank rapidly. Shanks... fell back a short distance, and formed again. ...Brown soon formed a junction with Ewing, however, and their combined forces, outnumbering us eight to one, looked absolutely fearful. . . . I determined to retreat, knowing it was madness to continue the unequal contest.

"My rifled gun had again become useless. The trail, which was shivered by a cannon shot at Helena, broke off short, and left it unmanageable. I determined to save it, if possible, and had it fixed up, under a hot fire, with poles; but in crossing a deep ravine it hopelessly gave way, in which condition it was well spiked and left.

"Withdrawing my forces by regiments, and forming them as if to charge, got my entire command mounted in splended order, with the ordnance wagons in the center, at the same time keeping up a fire of grape and canister with the remaining piece of my artillery. The enemy's twelve pieces of artillery were playing upon my ranks, but the men withstood their fire without flinching.

"As soon as my command were mounted and straightened out, I saw the Federals were almost entirely around me, and only on the right was there a way open for escape, and this every minute getting narrower and narrower. The undergrowth here was thick and matted, almost impassable for cavalry; besides, directly in my way was a deep ravine, or ditch. This, however, I had bridged two hours before. Now gathering my command well in hand, I dashed at the enemy's left, knowing that this was his weakest point, and besides, if I succeeded in forcing this line before he swung his right around, I could change my front and have the entire force behind me. Hard blows were given and received, the Federals gave way before the momentary shock, and Gordon, Coffee, and the battalion passed safely through, but the head of [David] Hunter's regiment, being entangled in the thick brush, did not keep well closed up, and the Federals, rallying, dashed in between him and the rear of Gordon, thus dividing them. Hunter, seeing it impossible to join me without a great sacrifice, turned squarely to the right, and by a quick gallop placed the whole enemy's force in the rear. *My object was thus far safely attained.*"

It certainly was. Novelist Paul Wellman, a Kansan who is a student of the Shelby legend, wrote in a feature story on October 2, 1938, when he was a member of the staff of the Kansas City *Star:* "The Union volleys rolled up a typhoon of sound. The first horsemen in the charging force went down but the leader's black plume still floated. The raiders plunged squarely into the gray powder cloud ahead of the fire. There was a shock, the rapid tattoo of revolvers, and the glitter of sabres. Then the Confederates were through—miraculously, unbelievably through. How they did it will always remain a mystery but they actually sheered through Ewing's line as if it had been made of cheese instead of men and found themselves free on the other side."

There ought to be equal praise for Hunter—he was not with Shelby at the time, because of the terrain, but he got away too.

Shelby took another chance here. Although he was still menaced by the forces from which he had escaped, he waited for an hour "for the separated forces to come together." Shelby was determined to go to Waverly; there was nothing there for him any more except nostalgia; and it was not on the way back to Arkansas. Nevertheless, he went home. Home, for Jo and Betty Shelby, was never anywhere but the little steamboat town on the Missouri where they had been married. "I continued my retreat to Waverly," says Shelby, "and they (the combined forces of Brown, Ewing) pressed me sorely for eight miles. By forming a two squadron front, and taking advantage of every natural position, I drove the enemy back. [All these "I's" that dot the report, remember, are not Shelby's; they were sprinkled through the report as from a salt shaker by his adjutant.] At Germantown they made a desperate onslaught, but meeting them with promptness and firmness, they fell back in confusion."

The truth here seems to be that Ewing and Brown were merely prodding Shelby's retreat with large bodies of scouts to find which way he was going. It was necessarily a large operation, even for scouts, because Shelby had dozens of routes by which he could travel, all of them equally dangerous.

Herein lies the real demonstration of what a cavalryman Jo Shelby was. It might be argued that he raided 750 miles to Boonville and the neighborhood of Jefferson City safely because the Federals were misinformed as to his movements and were looking for him somewhere else; but that argument now falls on its face, because every one of Major General Schofield's 50,000 troops in Missouri knew exactly where Shelby was: he was in the Missouri River Valley and 750 miles from the nearest Confederate reinforcements. To go home, to Arkansas, he had to run the gauntlet of the entire Federal Army of the West, and they were tough troops—Germans and Kansans mostly.

Yet—Shelby went home just as fast as he had come. What the enemy was doing never bothered Shelby when he knew he had to go somewhere.

Excerpts from his report tell the rest: "At three o'clock in the morning I passed through Waverly, and then turned directly southward. At Hawkins's Mill, finding my wagons troublesome, and having no ammunition except what the men could carry, I sunk them in the Missouri River, where they were safe from capture. The 14th, 15th and 16th were spent in constant travel, halting long enough only for feed and a few hours rest. At Johnson County, 2,000 Federals attacked us; but were repulsed; on the evening of the 16th, I encamped within eight miles of the Osage River, making through from river to river in two days. On the 17th, 18th, and 19th, I traveled hard, fighting once at Carthage; crossed the Springfield road three miles east of Keytesville, all the time followed by a large force, and on the 20th was rejoined on the banks of the Little Osage, in Arkansas, by Hunter, Hooper, and Shanks, with their entire commands in fine spirits."

Hunter, Hooper, and Shanks had had a much rougher time going south than Shelby. They had traveled almost as rapidly as he and encountered more Federals. They had fought and defeated Federals at Florence, Humansville, and Greenfield; at Humansville they had run into an advance of 2,000 of McNeil's men, and while they could not claim a victory, had held it in check until the three columns passed safely through. But McNeil was fast after them, says Shelby, and when the eight large horses carrying their last heavy gun were unable to follow "the devious and zigzag march of the cavalry," and fell out, the harness traces were cut, "the gun was left, after being thoroughly spiked, and the wheels and axles chopped into kindling wood."

Shelby lost only two guns to the enemy during the war, and left them both so thoroughly spiked as to be useless.

"After uniting my command," continues the report, "and seeing the jaded and forlorn condition of my horses, I determined to march by easy stages to the Arkansas River. For three days I was unmolested ...but Colonel William F. Cloud, hearing of my escape from Missouri, came hard after me with 3,000 men. I retired slowly before them, and they as slowly followed, never urgent in their pressure until we arrived at the foot of the Buffalo Mountains. They made a weak charge, easily repulsed. They followed us to Clarksville, where I crossed the Arkansas River."

This was on October 26, and most chroniclers, including those of the Official Records of the War of the Rebellion, choose this date as the end of Shelby's Raid. It took him until November 3 to get to Washington, Arkansas, where he halted finally; and hence in his report says the raid lasted forty-one days. From beginning to end, it did.

Shelby's report, which has never been seriously challenged as to the facts set forth, concludes:

"I have traveled 1,500 miles, and found the people of Missouri, as a mass, true to the South and her institutions, yet needing the strong presence of a Confederate army to make them volunteers. The southern, southwestern, and some of the middle counties of Missouri are completely desolated. In many places for forty miles not a single habitation is to be found, for on the road we met delicate females fleeing southward, driving ox teams, barefooted, ragged, and suffering even for bread."

Here the report ends abruptly, except for some figures given by Shelby. He had a stubborn contempt and a stubborn dislike for stupid superiors, and he never asked anybody for anything, not even in his report to Marmaduke after First Newtonia, and he liked Marmaduke. Edwards wrote this report, no doubt about it; but it must have been one of the few that Shelby ever read because it has a minimum of rhetoric and a multitude of facts. Shelby evidently turned editor for once. This is what he reported:

Number of Federals killed and wounded.   600
Number of Federals captured and paroled.   500
Number of forts captured and destroyed. . 10, at an aggregate cost of $120,000.
Amount of property destroyed, consisting of rails, ties, tanks, cattle-stops, telegraph wires, bridges and piers. . . $800,000
Number of guns captured   600
Number of stands of colors taken   40
Number of revolvers   600
Number of wagons captured and destroyed.   300
Number of horses and mules captured   6,000
Amount of supplies (U. S.) used and destroyed. $1,000,000

Pieces of artillery taken (1)
Number of recruits gained........................   800
Amount of ordnance captured and destroyed (reduced to
cost) $50,000

Wearily, almost sarcastically, Shelby signed the report, which was
addressed to Sterling Price's adjutant thus: "Hoping this report may
prove satisfactory, I remain, major, very respectfully, your obedient
servant."

He had shown them. But he must have felt a strong sense of personal frustration. His arm was bothering him, too, the one that had
been suppurating for weeks. It was clean and healed now, but stiff.
For the rest of his life it was all the fingers of his right hand could
do to perform ordinary tasks like signing his name; he could still manage to fire a revolver, shooting at a peacetime target; but he could
never again wield a cavalry sabre.

On the occasion he mentions in his report that "ammunition was
low" he drove his men one hundred and six miles in eighteen hours.

As Major Edwards rightly says, "Search the annals of the Confederate war for another such feat and the inquirer will surely go un-
rewarded."   ·

18. *The End of the War in the West*

IN THE SPRING OF 1864 occurred the Red River campaign of the
Federals, which, though it added no glory to the Federal arms,
posed the only serious threat to the Confederate Department of the
Trans-Mississippi ever made during the war.

It was the pet project of General Nathaniel P. Banks, who had
gained no fame opposing Stonewall Jackson in the Shenandoah Valley in Virginia, and had been shunted into an obscure post at New
Orleans. There were those who were unkind enough to say that
Banks was more interested in taking over Kirby Smith's cotton empire—a gold mine for speculators—than he was in clearing the west of
rebels. Nevertheless he obtained General Grant's reluctant permission
to ready an expeditionary force against Shreveport in late March,[1]
to be supported by a large force of gunboats under the command of

Admiral Porter. At the same time, Sherman, who was ranking officer in the Tennessee-Arkansas area, was notified to order General Frederick Steele, at Little Rock, to march southward, advancing upon Shreveport from the other direction, and assist Banks.

The threat to the Trans-Mississippi Department was a major one, for Banks had 30,000 men (including 10,000 under the command of A. J. Smith, detached temporarily from Sherman's command) as well as Porter's naval flotilla, while Steele had 15,000 all told, scattered through Arkansas. To match such a force, Smith would have had to assemble every effective under his command in the Army of the Trans-Mississippi, from the four corners of the vast department; an impossible task, and he had no navy.

Price, who had succeeded Holmes in the Arkansas command, hurried to Louisiana with his infantry brigade to meet Banks, leaving Fagan, Marmaduke, and Shelby—his top cavalry commanders—in the Ouachita River country with instructions to prevent Steele from marching south to join Banks.

The combined Confederate cavalry force was less than half that of Steele; but the mission which Price gave his cavalry commanders was accomplished in record time, almost wholly through the dogged determination of Jo Shelby and his Missourians. Although Steele outnumbered his small brigade twelve to one, Shelby fought him almost daily for two weeks, smashed his transportation, reduced him to a state of siege at Camden, and forced him to retreat to Little Rock once more without ever getting closer to the Red River in Louisiana than the Little Missouri in Arkansas. The Camden expedition was one of Shelby's most brilliant cavalry exploits, and the one that has received the least attention.

At Little Rock, General Steele, whom Edwards admired as "a finished and elegant gentlemen," grumbled a little on the short notice he was given to assemble his forces (he got the order on March 27, only three days before Banks started out with his impressive Army-Navy coalition), but wired Sherman, "I am confident of being able to do my share of the work before me." [2] On April 2 he left Little Rock with 12,000 men and a large wagon train, mostly empty, moving on the road to Camden via Arkadelphia and Washington. Shelby was at Princeton, whither he had been ordered the week before to hold the line of the Saline, cover all roads to Camden, "and annoy the enemy in every disagreeable manner his known ingenuity might invent." When Shelby learned that Steele was on the march and would cross the Ouachita River at Arkadelphia, he gave orders for his troops to move that night at moonrise—twelve o'clock precisely by the almanac.

While the troops were cooking five days' rations, a message came from Colonel Colton Greene, one of Price's commanders, informing Shelby that the Confederate Congress had confirmed his appointment as a brigadier general. Just before sunset the soldiers were drawn up on the prairie and their orders read to them. It was their first inkling that their commander had been promoted.

"Soldiers of Shelby's Brigade!" the orders read. "You march in four hours to attack the enemy. He is strong, well equipped, and not deficient in courage, but I intend that you shall ride down his infantry and scatter his battalions by the splendor of your charge. You have just four hours to say your prayers, make your needful preparations, and nerve your hearts for the onset. It will be desperate, because you are brave; bloody, because you are reckless; and because today, I am a brigadier general. I have told you often about our homes, our country, and our glorious cause—today, I simply appeal to your ambition, your fame, your spotless reputation and your eternal renown!"

No more was needed. A shout went up; their hopes were realized. Old Jo was a brigadier. Next day, April 2, they fought with a new pride in themselves and with a savage joy, as they struck the rear of Steele's column on the Arkadelphia Road, killing forty-four and capturing fifteen in a series of sporadic attacks. A veteran of Steele's command is quoted in *Five Famous Missourians* as saying, "Shelby made them attack the rear of Steele's army of 15,000 men (Figures vary. Ed.) only a few thousand of them, yet they charged like they had been the vanguard of an army of thirty thousand. We drove them back, it is true; but they charged again; we drove them back and they charged again; and thus they charged until night put an end to the remarkable contest." [3]

From then until April 21, when he was ordered back to Fagan's command, Shelby gave Steele no rest on the road to Camden. On April 3 he fought the enemy's cavalry rearguard in a blinding spring storm in which snow, hailstones, thunder and lightning mingled, falling back only when Steele ordered two full brigades under General Carr—Shelby had 1,200—and going into bivouac at Prairie d'Anne on the fifth, joining Marmaduke, who had 3,000. Marmaduke had also made a desperate stab at Steele the day before, and had failed to halt him. Steele was in high spirits at having beaten off the largest force of the enemy. He wired Sherman: "Marmaduke, with his whole force, including Shelby . . . are in the Prairie d'Anne but will run as soon as we move." [4]

At Prairie d'Anne the Confederates did not run, but fought a six-hour battle, or skirmish, if you will [5]—as long as they had fought at Wilson's Creek—three hours of which were devoted to a duel between Steele's and Shelby's artillery. At nightfall Marmaduke's army fell back in good order, across "a naked prairie," "smooth as a sea of glass," with Shelby covering the withdrawal. He fought one more engagement with Steele's men—at Poison Spring on the 15th, in which there were heavy casualties on both sides—before Steele finally shook off the Confederates and occupied Camden. At Camden Steele was virtually a prisoner. But he was so relieved to have gained the safety of a fortified town that he wrote jovially, "This is a strong place. The Confederates have fortified it for us." [6] By the same mail he sent word to Halleck that he would move to the Red River as soon as he brought up his supplies from Pine Bluff. In his haste to move from Little Rock, he had carried only a minimum of rations (they were unprocurable anyway in the hostile countryside), but he was not worried, for he had a tremendous wagon train and expected it to be provisioned at Pine Bluff, where there was a Federal commissary and quartermaster depot. Once in Camden he sent most of his wagons, with an escort, to Pine Bluff, under the command of a Colonel Powell Clayton. His scouts had assured him that there were no rebels in that direction.

At Marks' Mill, Fagan and Cabell attacked this procession on one side, while Shelby, who had galloped ten miles over parallel and connecting roads to encircle the train, attacked from the other. The attack was a rout and the surprise was so complete that Shelby lost only one man killed in action. His report says: "I had advanced scarcely a mile in the direction of Marks' Mill when I met the Federal advance coming rapidly in the direction of Mount Elba. I determined to charge them first, last and all the time. . . ." These are Major Edwards' words of course, but there is no doubt that Shelby's borderers fell upon Colonel Clayton's wagon train with an abandon unsurpassed during the war. Here was Steele's whole baggage, the plunder of an army. Colonel Clayton's men, caught in a hurricane of fire and steel on all sides, fought furiously; it took the Confederates three hours to kill or capture two thirds of them before "the sober shades of evening came down upon one of the most final and crushing victories of the war." Again that is the report of Shelby's unconservative adjutant, but it is confirmed by Colonel Clayton's report. The Federal commander offered no excuses, made no attempt to mitigate the disaster. He wrote: "The attack upon our train at Marks' Mill resulted in its entire capture. We have lost 240 wagons, five pieces of artillery, and without doubt the whole escort. The fight was very severe, and lasted about three hours. The escort consisted of Colonel McLean's brigade, and between 300 and 400 cavalry, altogether about 1,500 men; they were crushed by overwhelming numbers of the enemy. A portion of the cavalry and a few mounted officers succeeded in cutting their way through after everything was lost."

Everything was lost so far as reinforcing Banks on the Red River was concerned. As Major Hanson, the U. S. cavalry writer, says, "Not much was ever said about the debacle at Marks' Mill [yet] it was one of the most substantial successes gained by the western Confederates during the war. It forced General Steele to abandon Camden and retreat to Little Rock." [7] Its effects were even more far-reaching than that. If Steele had been able to join Banks, the Red River expedition might not have ended in ignominious failure, as it did,[8] and the Confederate Department of the Trans-Mississippi would have had an abrupt termination in the spring of 1864. Furthermore, the supplies captured at Marks' Mill formed no small part of the supplies which were used by Price and Shelby on Price's invasion of Missouri in the autumn of that year.

Steele's retreat to Little Rock was accomplished in an even more uncomfortable manner than had been his advance to Camden. He was hampered by rain, bad roads, lack of wagons, and incessant attacks by the Confederates—at Princeton, at the Ouachita River, in the Saline Bottoms, and in a skirmish at Whitmore's Mill. His numerical superiority was still so great, however, that there was not the slightest chance of defeating him in an all-out battle, although the attempt was made at Jenkins' Ferry, where four thousand of Steele's men fought a bloody battle to cover his escape. The Confederates suffered 443 casualties, and Steele an uncomputed number,[9] probably as great;

Confederate historians have claimed that he lost nearly a thousand men. Steele got away, but to do so he had to destroy nearly all that was left of his baggage and trains, according to his own statement. Rain had turned the region into rivers of mud before the battle. That the Confederates did not follow Steele into Little Rock is probably attributable to the condition of the roads.

On May 27, 1864, Shelby was appointed Confederate commander north of the Arkansas River and given the assignment of organizing the vast number of Confederate conscripts there into serviceable commands, as well as recruiting for a new campaign in Missouri in the fall. Arkansas was a paradise for deserters and evaders of the Conscription Act, and many of those who professed to be in the Confederate service had turned bushwhacker. Major Edwards describes the situation:

"Ten thousand men within the conscript ages—Texans, Missourians and Arkansans—were scattered along the valley of the White River, three or four to a house, drinking, gambling, smuggling, trading cotton for Memphis whiskey, and swapping sweet potatoes with the Federals for flat tobacco and pocket knives. . . . A sort of freemasonry existed between the quasi-Southerners and Federals. . . . Horses were taken from their plows and negroes from the furrows whenever it suited the convenience or pleased the fancy of these professed Confederates spending their time in rioting while the country bled at every pore."

A proclamation from Shelby sounded like a bugle blast in the White River Valley. Until June 10, he announced, every able-bodied man could ponder what he wanted to do, but after that: "You shall fight for the North or South. I will enlist you in the Confederate army; or I will drive you into the Federal ranks. You shall not remain idle spectators of a drama enacted before your eyes. . . . There is no time to argue. . . . I command you at once to rush to arms. Every officer with recruiting papers will report at once to my headquarters and colonels or generals professing to have regiments or brigades will come immediately to receive instructions for future operations. . . . I do not bully; but I strike. . . . Come up like men, or go to General Steele like men, but whatever you do, remember the tenth of June." In the same document, he promised "to hang all who failed to rally to their country's flag."

"They knew the man, they knew his soldiers," says Edwards, and the countryside was quiet in a week. Throughout the summer, Shelby rode through northern Arkansas, superintending this operation and fighting Federals wherever he found them. One of the best known incidents of his career occurred in June, the capture by cavalry and artillery of the Federal ironclad *Queen City* at Clarendon on the lower White River. The *Queen City* was as formidable an ironclad as any in the fleet; she carried nine guns.

At midnight, Shelby's favorite hour for beginning operations, the light dragoons of the Iron Brigade got quietly off their horses on the river bank while Dick Collins' cannoneers rolled their guns by hand across a bridge muffled with weeds for a distance of a mile, and got them into battery on shore, close to the moonlit superstructure of the *Queen City*.

Major Edwards' report of the capture of the queenly vessel is one of the best examples of the prose with which he startles readers of the staid Official Records of the War of the Rebellion:

"It was a beautiful moonlit night. White fleecy clouds hovered over the sleeping river, over the doomed craft with all her gala lights in bloom, and over the crouching lines of infantry and the yawning cannon. The silence was broken only by the measured tread of the sentinels and the deep striking of the time bell. Just as the white hand of morning put away the sable clouds of night four pieces of artillery sent their terrible messengers crashing through the boat. Then the infantry opened with terrible effect, and in ten minutes the *Queen City* was a helpless wreck upon the water, her captain surrendering unconditionally."

Three other Union gunboats raced to the rescue of the *Queen City* —but she blew up before they could reach her. Battery Commander Collins and his men had run a terrible risk, however, just before the *Queen City's* magazines went skyward. They had rushed aboard and dragged off two 12-pounder boat howitzers. The other Union gunboats, one of them the *Tyler*, which had taken part in the battle at Helena, manning a total of twenty-six guns, began to fire in the direction of Collins' guns. In a final nose-thumbing gesture, Collins stood his ground for a short time and fired a few six-pounders in the direction of the *Tyler*.

If Shelby had been in the habit, as Jeb Stuart was, of writing letters almost daily from the field, they would make an interesting diary indeed for the summer of 1864. He was undoubtedly in high spirits, doing the kind of work he liked, punishing bushwhackers with the firing squad and gallows when crimes had been committed, and driving the less guilty into the army.[10] He was wearing the buff sash and the wreathed three stars of a brigadier at last, although rank never seems to have mattered to him;[11] and he was governing all North Arkansas boldly from his favorite headquarters, at Batesville, where his soldiers had wintered so gloriously in '63 at Camp Nannie Wilson.

General Steele knew what Shelby was doing and begged reinforcements from General Cadwallader Washburn and A. J. Smith at Memphis to stop him. The reinforcements were refused and warfare in Arkansas was reduced to a few minor clashes between mounted men in remote districts, and raids on steamboats, which were almost as common as cows in the bayou country. Nevertheless, prisoners occasionally were captured on both sides, and Steele treated his Confederate prisoners with courtesy and consideration. Shelby developed a warm regard for Steele as a result, and characteristically desired to send him a present. It must be a grand one, naturally, and worthy of the recipient, but Shelby had just such an article. Someone had sent him a magnificent Mexican sombrero, embroidered with flowers and worked with decorations of gold, including gold coins sewed into the brim and a wide gold band. This Shelby put aside, intending to send it to General Steele under the next flag of truce. Unfortunately the sombrero was blown out of Shelby's tent and into a campfire, ruining it beyond the possibility of sending it to anyone as a gift. Shelby swore in exasperation,[12] and in 1867, when Edwards was writing an account of the war, he asked his biographer to set forth the circumstances and ask General Steele, who was still living, to accept the will for the deed.

Two months to the day from the time Shelby assumed the role of military dictator in North Arkansas, he wrote an enthusiastic letter to Price's adjutant, on July 27, saying that he had 5,000 men under his personal command and that he was ready to invade Missouri again as he had done last year, "without its costing the Government a dollar," and predicting that he could raise 10,000 additional men in Missouri to seize the state. He also pointed out that the Federals, with their grand offensive taking place east of the Mississippi, had stripped Missouri of defense forces, which was true. (Even Shelby could not have known, however, how true it was; General Rosecrans, who now commanded the Department of the West, admitted later, after Price's Missouri campaign, that even the militia had been reduced to "skeleton" organizations in St. Louis and other important cities.[13] It was the time to strike, and swiftly, in the Shelby manner —but in full force.

Shelby's letter had hardly reached his superiors before the word came from Kirby Smith, the top commander of the Trans-Mississippi Department and the virtual president of that autonomous region, that the invasion would take place, and that Major General Sterling Price had been appointed to lead it. Smith's official order, dated August 4, gave Price instructions "to make immediate arrangements for a movement into Missouri, with the entire cavalry force of your district."

The promptness with which Kirby Smith acted was not owing to Shelby's insistence—Shelby seldom talked about anything else except an invasion of Missouri—nor to the obvious fact that Missouri was vulnerable, which Shelby had demonstrated so brilliantly on his raid of a year ago.

Smith's decision was the result of pressure from the government at Richmond, now beleaguered as never before and seeking, in its extremity, at last, to make use of its troops west of the Mississippi River. The call from Richmond was, in fact, a Macedonian cry; Jefferson Davis, who had agreed cautiously with Holmes that troops could *not* be sent east of the Mississippi in 1863, when with a little energy it could have been done, was now demanding that Smith send his entire force, when it could not be done. Smith said so bluntly; to attempt it, he informed Davis, would be to invite "another Vicksburg or Port Hudson." [14]

The alternative selected was the invasion of Missouri, which was dictated by political as well as military considerations. The presidential election of 1864 in the United States was approaching. Grant's casualty lists were horrifying the North, and General Lee at Cold Harbor was fighting with the same tenacity of purpose which had driven a Union army from the very same spot, at the gates of Richmond, in 1862—McClellan's army, down the Peninsula and back to the Chesapeake. Sherman in Georgia had not yet convinced the South that he meant business;[15] some optimists, including Jefferson Davis, were comparing his position to that of Napoleon in Russia,[16] and meantime, if Missouri could be recaptured before November, the

voters of the North might repudiate Lincoln at the polls. So at least ran the reasoning in the high councils of the South.

In all this chimerical thinking, the plan to invade Missouri was alone not visionary; the state was open, as Shelby said, and a blow struck in that quarter with all the troops at Kirby Smith's disposal would, if successful, open a third front in the war, relieve the pressure on Lee and Hood—and the Army of the Trans-Mississippi might strike into Illinois or even across Kentucky into Virginia.

Smith, however, bobbled the expedition from the start, and although much blame attaches to Price for the manner in which he conducted his "Great Raid," it is fair to examine the nature of the orders he was given. Smith permitted him to take only the three divisions of Fagan, Marmaduke, and Shelby, and a brigade of Louisiana troops attached to Marmaduke's command. (Shelby was now signing his reports "Brigadier Commanding Division," and he was as fully entitled to the rank of major general as Marmaduke, to whom it had been given; furthermore, he had furnished five of the nine brigades for the expedition, out of his own command and the "camps of instruction" in Arkansas, where his "reformation" program, as he called it, had been converting bushwhackers into soldiers.) Smith's order advised Price that "these skeleton organizations [the three divisions] are best adapted for an expedition in which a large addition to your force is expected. These weak brigades should be filled by the regiments raised in Missouri, and you should scrupulously avoid the organization of any new brigades. . . . Rally the loyal men of Missouri, and remember that our great want is men. . . ." (He had 40,000 or more troops on which to draw if he had been willing to spare the time from administering the Cotton Bureau to bring them in from all over the three other states of his department.)

Nevertheless, Missouri was invaded on September 19, and "Price's Great Raid" cut a swath twenty-five miles wide across the state, from Bloomfield in the southeast, north toward St. Louis, and then westward across to the Kansas line at Westport Landing, before he fell back to Arkansas and the Canadian River country for the last time. Of the more than 400 battles and skirmishes fought in Missouri during the war, sixty-five took place in the campaign of 1864; it is possible here only to record the major developments and Shelby's part in them.

Price assumed command at Camden (Arkansas) on August 29,

which gave the Federals ample notice—twenty-one days—of his plans, and as early as September 3, two weeks and two days before he marched, Federal General Cadwallader Washburn at Memphis "sounded the tocsin" of a new rebel invasion of Missouri.[17]

On September 13 Price and his commanders reached Powhatan, in northeast Arkansas, where they found that the impatient Shelby had already moved part of his division ahead to Pocahontas "on the selected route to Missouri." At Pocahontas next day, a concentration of all forces of the expedition took place. From the 14th to the 19th, Price organized his army and assembled a huge wagon train. Shelby and his lean, swift travelers of the Iron Brigade, stood open-eyed and close-mouthed as they watched the assembly of that baggage train, which Major Edwards says was "as long as the tail of Plantamour's comet."

All of this did not look like preparations for an invasion to Shelby's men, whose lightning mobility was largely due to the fact that they were seldom encumbered with anything heavier than a Yankee over-coat in cold weather. (Most of Shelby's men were wearing Union uniforms now; and many of them were shot by the enemy when they were captured in Missouri in these uniforms.[18])

Sterling Price had not learned a single thing since Wilson's Creek. When he marched on the 19th, he had 12,000 men, of whom only 8,000 were armed, and only 14 pieces of artillery—all he had col-lected in a month and a half. And he had encouraged the army of camp followers to come along, eating their heads off in country which had long since been stripped of forage. He was also taking into Mis-souri almost as many food and draft animals as he was to take out. Shelby, who should have commanded the expedition, and Marmaduke, who had been given the commission which Shelby deserved, both noted with dissatisfaction that the Sterling Price who had sat his horse like a statue in the hail of lead at Wilson's Creek now liked to campaign in an ambulance because of his great girth, and take fre-quent naps. Price was suffering the physical deterioration which goes with obesity, and encased as he was in uncomfortable folds of flesh, he no longer had the bulldog quality which had held Missouri single-handed for a year in 1861-62.

At Fredericktown Price received information that the strength of the enemy at Ironton was only about 1,500 and that General A. J. Smith's force in the vicinity of St. Louis constituted the only major threat in his path. Price ordered Shelby to proceed at once with his division by way of Farmington to a point on the St. Louis and Iron Mountain Railroad and destroy all bridges in the vicinity. This Shelby did, but traveling thirty miles a day, while the speed of the main army was twelve, he was soon so out of touch with his commander-in-chief that Price had suffered a bloody repulse at Pilot Knob, a heavily fortified place which he made a blundering attempt to capture, before a courier caught up with Shelby at Potosi notifying him to rejoin the main force. An indication of the savagery with which the Confederates attacked at Pilot Knob is the fact that out of 94 men lost by Marmaduke in the assault, 14 were officers. Such a high percentage of officers lost, in comparison with men in the ranks, means that the charge was all-out and desperate indeed. General Ewing paid high tribute to the Confederates in his report, especially to General Cabell, who, he says, "led the assault, swept upon the plain in handsome style, yelling and on the double quick." [19]

When Ewing heard that Shelby was on the way, and was told by prisoners that Price had 12,000 men against his 1,100, he evacuated Pilot Knob during the night, blowing up the fort, magazine, and iron foundry as he went, although the forces of A. J. Smith were only twenty-four miles away at Mineral Point and could have reinforced him. Both Ewing and McNeil had good reason to fear a firing squad, or the gallows, for crimes against civilians, if captured.

When Shelby arrived next day from Potosi he found the delighted soldiers of Old Pap, Marmaduke, and the rest picking among the ruins of Pilot Knob, which were glowing like a landscape of hell even in daylight, because an immense pile of charcoal next to the iron works had been fired and was still red hot and luminous. Among the loot, besides food and blankets, were sixteen pieces of artillery; these Price ordered destroyed, although a lieutenant of Shelby's command, Selby Plattenburg, had captured thirty-nine artillery horses, complete with equipment including harness and two caissons, on the Potosi raid and had brought them along.

Price was now within striking distance of both St. Louis and Jefferson City; he chose the latter, although St. Louis was undefended except by a small force of raw militia. Its inhabitants were in a state of panic. They had been "supping on fear and horror" ever since it was learned that Price and the army of bushwhackers was approaching.[20]

Price was relying heavily on the Southern "underground" or Copperhead organization in Missouri, known by various names but chiefly as "The Knights of the Golden Circle," to supply him with information, and he had sent a spy into the St. Louis area, an inexperienced member of Shelby's command who was selected because of his extremely youthful appearance, which would enable him to move without suspicion within the enemy's lines. This spy was filled with misinformation when he returned; he brought word to Price that at St. Louis the Federals could muster a force twice that of his own. Major Edwards says that the spy, whose name was Jim Ward, had remarkable success in obtaining an audience with General Rosecrans himself, and received the information straight from the Federal commander in the West. If so, General Rosecrans must have been delighted at the opportunity to talk with one of Price's agents and give him an earful; Rosecrans had a good counterespionage system himself, when it came to the Knights of the Golden Circle. At any rate, Price abandoned any idea of attacking St. Louis and moved on Jefferson City, where he attacked and defeated the Union defenders on October 7.

Around the events of October 7 and 8 centers all the controversy concerning Price's actions in Missouri. The question is: Could he have occupied Jefferson City on the 8th, after his victory on the 7th, and raised the Confederate flag over the State Capitol of Missouri? The undisputed fact is that he did not make the attempt. His consolidated army had been in front of Jefferson City on the 7th, a large body of Federals had moved out to meet them, and Major General Fagan's division drove them back, after bloody fighting, into the fortifications of the city. Having won the day, the Confederates expected to continue the assault on the next day. Price decided that it would be fruitless. He had received more "information."

In his report he says, "I had received positive information that the enemy were 12,000 strong in the city, and that 3,000 more had arrived by the North Missouri Railroad before I withdrew my troops to the encampment selected, whereupon I gave immediate instructions for General Shelby to send a sufficient force to burn the bridge and destroy the railroad west of Jefferson City in the direction of California, the county seat of Moniteau County." Price added that he hoped to capture a sufficient number of arms at Boonville, Sedalia, Lexington, and Independence to "arm my unarmed men." He also makes the puzzling statement on the same page of his report (p. 631) that he was "acting as instructed in my original orders." [21] (His orders were to move into Kansas "if compelled to leave Missouri.") Nevertheless, at Jefferson City, he desisted from the attack, and moved west. It is not too much to say that if he had killed and captured every Federal on the Kansas border, the outcome of the war would have been affected not one whit.

On the morning of the 8th, as Price moved toward Boonville, Major General Alfred Pleasanton, former cavalry chief of the Army of the Potomac, arrived at Jefferson City to take charge of the Federal forces, which actually numbered 5,000, or not much more than half of Price's strength. Seeing the rebels in retreat, Pleasanton sent 4,100 cavalry under General John B. Sanborn after them.

Price was now bound down that lonesome road, leading from Boonville to somewhere in the southwest, which had been traveled by every hard-fighting Missouri army of the South since Nathaniel Lyon had seized St. Louis in that long-gone spring of 1861. The Missouri Expedition had ended in failure, so far as offensive operations were concerned, but yet to come were some of the bloodiest battles in the War in the West: the actions on the Little Blue on October 21st, the fight at Independence the following day, and the smashing defeats of the Confederates at Westport and the Marais des Cygnes in Kansas, on the 23rd and 25th respectively. Westport has been called, inaccurately, the "Gettysburg of the West," but only because of the large numbers involved. At Gettysburg the course of the war was determined by the outcome; at Westport there was no doubt of the issue, for Rosecrans and Pleasanton had assembled a mighty arm to crush Price from all sides, and had him in a trap. At Marais des Cygnes, the *coup de grâce* was administered; and the sequel to Marais des Cygnes, the second battle of Newtonia, is important because it saved Price's army from capture and wound up Shelby's Civil War career in a blaze of glory. At Second Newtonia, he not only saved the army, he won for the Confederacy the last battle of the war west of the Mississippi.

From Boonville on the 12th Shelby moved in obedience to Price's order. From then until the 22nd, he and his division lived the nightmare existence of the Missouri cavalry in action, retreating, but fighting every few miles of the way. Shelby says his men were tired to the point of exhaustion when they reached Independence two days before the great holocaust of Westport. He had passed through his old home at Waverly, "where the rude hands of war had stripped from the quiet little town much of her wealth and beauty"; many buildings had been destroyed, among which were his factory, his dwelling house and every other habitation supposed to be his;[22] and the fatigue which Shelby was suffering when his men reached the Little Blue, where they fought a skirmish, was intensified, no doubt, by the sight of his burned home and a longing for his family far away in Kentucky. Shelby never suffered melancholy long, however; and fighting was a daily occurrence and an urgent business. As Edwards says, "Danger gathered fast. Rosecrans had assembled a large army and was advancing from Sedalia; additional cavalry forces were coming from Boonville, while Kansas was ablaze and her cruel militia swarming to the front from the far west." The "cruel militia" were commanded by Blunt, old foe of Shelby and Marmaduke, and by Curtis. The Kansans under Blunt fell back before Price's column, attempting to burn a bridge over the Little Blue, but Marmaduke halted this operation and later burned the bridge himself, once he was safely over. At the Little Blue, the Kansas Redlegs were commanded by Colonel Jennison of border-struggle fame—or infamy, depending on how you looked at it; he was soon joined by General Curtis from Kansas City, and the Battle of Independence was fought. Marmaduke sent to Shelby for aid. Fagan's troops actually were nearer to Marmaduke, but Shelby's were mainly Missouri River Valley men who could be counted on to fight the Kansans to the last ditch. They did, and with Marmaduke's and Price's men, drove Curtis out of Independence.

Price was so elated by the victory at Independence, and by Blunt's retreating, pursued on foot by Shelby's dismounted men, that he issued a proclamation announcing that he would dash at the enemy on the morrow and take Sunday dinner at Fort Leavenworth, Kansas. It was one of his failings, never cured in four years of war and disappointments, that he always proclaimed on the eve of battle that he would annihilate the enemy in the forthcoming struggle. What Price did not know was that at this very moment Federal armies were converging on him from all sides; Rosecrans was not a Halleck or a Schofield, and being already under the displeasure of Grant for his bungling at Chickamauga, he had gathered every available man in the west and was about to lead an army of some 20,000.

Except for the victory of Marmaduke and Shelby, Rosecrans would have surrounded Price and annihilated him. Rosecrans says in his report that he never believed that the Confederates could crack General Curtis's line on the Big Blue; hence instead of sending A. J. Smith to Independence, which would have hemmed them in, he allowed him to fan out southward from Lexington in the direction of Chapel Hill. He believed that Price, balked at the Big Blue, would have to turn in that direction. But once the Kansas line was breached, Price went westward, and Rosecrans had to revise his plans. Orders were sent to Smith to change his direction and march westward to Hickman's Mills, but by the time he got there, Price had retreated from Westport. The bird had flown.

Big Blue and Westport were fought the same day—October 25. Actually they were two faces of the same coin. Shelby's division fought at both—at Big Blue from 7:00 A.M. to 1:00 P.M., and at Westport until the Confederates were driven from the field. At Westport Shelby made the acquaintance, for the first time in real battle, of Major General Pleasanton, the only Union cavalry commander who, like Shelby, could march 200 miles a week and fight continuously while doing it.[23]

The trap was sprung on the pleasant Sunday morning of October 23, 1864. There is a high and spacious plain between the Blue and Westport; the great battle was fought on an enchanting prairie landscape. No scrub oaks and gullies, as at Wilson's Creek; no sunken roads and thorny abattis, as at Helena; no rugged mountains, as in Arkansas. Some 30,000 troops could be seen with the sweep of a field glass. It was like a European battlefield, in the Napoleonic style; or like an immense parade ground. Marmaduke caught the first impact of the attack by Pleasanton, on one side; Shelby was soon in a death grapple with Curtis on the other.

Shelby's report gives this account of the participation of his division: "The 23rd of October dawned upon us clear, cold, and full of promise. My division moved squarely against the enemy about 8 o'clock in the direction of Westport, and very soon became fiercely engaged. The enemy had regained all the strong positions taken from them the day before by General Thompson, and it became imperatively necessary to force that flank of the enemy back. Inch by inch and foot by foot they gave way before my steady onset. Regiment met regiment and opposing batteries draped the scene in clouds of dense smoke. While the engagement was at its height Collins burst one of his Parrotts, but fought on with his three guns.... Again were the Federals driven within sight of Westport and here I halted to reform my lines, intending to make direct attack upon the town. About 12 o'clock I sent Jackman's brigade back to the road taken by the train, for it was reported that General Marmaduke had fallen back before the enemy—although he never notified me of the fact and I never saw his couriers which I learned afterward were sent—and thus my whole right flank and rear were exposed. Jackman had scarcely reached the point indicated when he met an order from General Fagan to hasten to his help at a gallop, for the entire prairie in his front was dark with Federals. Jackman dismounted his men in the broad and open plain and formed them in one long, thin line before the huge wave that threatened to engulf them. Collins with one gun hurried forward to help Jackman, and opened up on the advancing enemy.... Fresh lines of Federals forced Jackman to mount his horses, and he fell back after the train, fighting hard. Now, my entire rear was in possession of the enemy, and the news was brought that Thompson was fighting for dear life at Westport. Withdrawing him as soon as possible, and with much difficulty, for he was hard pressed, I fell back as rapidly as I could... the force I had been fighting at Westport coming up just behind, when, reaching the road, the prairie in my rear was covered almost by a long line of troops which at first I had supposed to be our own men. This illusion was soon dispelled, and the two great waves uniting, came down upon one little brigade and Colonel Slayback's regiment. The prospect was dark and desperate. Not a bush or tree was to be seen for weary miles and miles, and no helping army could be seen anywhere. I knew the only salvation was to charge the nearest line, break it if possible, and retreat rapidly."

As at Marshall on his Great Raid, Shelby at Westport accomplished the seemingly impossible feat. With his instinct for picking the weakest point in the enemy's line, he cut his way through. "My command was saved, and we moved off after the army, travelling all night."

Similar disaster had befallen the rest of the army, which Shelby rejoined the next day; and an even greater disaster was to befall Price. Pleasanton caught up with him on the Marais des Cygnes and dealt him such a smashing blow that the Confederates ran, some of them throwing away their arms. They were human, and in the last twenty-four hours they had had all they could stand. Shelby was not present when Pleasanton struck; he was twelve miles away on the prairie. A tearful Price sent him a courier with this despairing message: "Tell General Shelby that he alone can save the army."

Shelby did it. He galloped back and joined Fagan on the prairie stretching away from the river. With sufficient cavalry on hand, Fagan was able to interpose his division between Price's infantry and the enemy, until Price could reform his columns, and march off in the direction of Carthage. What memories for the Missourians along this road! General Pleasanton, who had already seen Sanborn's division "very much shaken" by Shelby at Westport, when he cut his way through, was beginning to appreciate that in Shelby he had a cavalry foe such as he had not seen since he left Virginia.

Marais des Cygnes had been a disaster in another respect—Brigadier Generals Marmaduke and Cabell had been captured. Price had only two brigadiers left—Shelby and Clark. Clark was appointed to command Marmaduke's division, and on the 28th the command reached Newtonia. Shelby had a brush with some Federal cavalry, killed a bushwhacker captain, and chased them off. But it was no more than a gnat sting. He camped on the edge of the prairie and his men lay down to a sleep of exhaustion. The other divisions of the army passed on beyond him and encamped on the prairie. The condition of horses and men made a halt for rest absolutely necessary, and Shelby took up a position in the rear to fend off an attack by pursuers. It was known that the Federals were on Price's trail in large numbers in triumphant hope of destroying his army before he could escape into Arkansas.

The organized pursuit was not long in making its appearance. At three o'clock in the afternoon of the 28th, "while resting comfortably a few miles south of Newtonia," according to Shelby's report, a large force under General Blunt appeared and "drove in our pickets quite briskly, and came charging on with their usual vitality. Dismounting every man of my division, I formed my line of battle just in time to meet the onset. Jackman held the right and protected Collins's two pieces of artillery, which opened with good effect. Thompson and Slayback were on the left, and I sent a good detachment under Major Gordon to watch well my extreme left flank, and then moved steadily forward with a loud and ringing cheer. The men never hesitated from the first, but drove the enemy all the time before them and advanced two miles into the prairie, exposed to a heavy artillery fire from the first, and if *I had had a mounted regiment of my own command I could have charged and taken their splendid battery*."

The contest lasted two hours, before Blunt finally retreated. He did not abandon pursuit, but Shelby once again had covered the retreat of a Confederate army and saved it from destruction.[24] Long before Shelby gave the order to his men to remount, Price and his remnant of an army were far away, in slow and painful progress to the Arkansas border and the Canadian River country.

Such was the battle of Second Newtonia, last battle of the Civil War west of the Mississippi. Jo Shelby won it.

In Price's report of the Missouri expedition, he had this to say of Shelby (and it must be remembered that the two were never particularly fond of each other): "Brig. Gen. Shelby, commanding division, added new luster to his past fame as a brilliant and heroic officer, and without disparagement to the other officers I must be permitted to say that I consider him the best cavalry officer I ever saw."

PART FOUR

Mexico

—◆●◆—

19. *Revolt Against Surrender*

THE RETREAT SOUTH from Newtonia was a famine and a pestilence. Most of the wagon trains had been left behind, with all of the food, and smallpox broke out on the third day after they crossed the Arkansas River. Men died by the wayside in an agony of delirium, but as long as life remained in any of the victims, none was abandoned. There was no shrinking from contagion.[1] Each detachment in detail mounted guard over the wagons bearing their burden of horror, taking their chances with the rest. At last the ghastly expedition limped home into Louisiana and Texas.

For the rest of that winter the Missouri Cavalry Division was stationed at Pittsburg, Texas. While the Army of the Trans-Mississippi stood idle (it was never to fire another shot) a court of inquiry in Shreveport was investigating charges of dereliction of duty against General Price.[2] This struck Shelby as about as useful a procedure as performing an emergency operation on a corpse. Price had procrastinated and napped, literally, during the disgraceful Missouri venture, but it would do no good to cashier him now. Eventually the investigation came to nothing, and it was announced that General Price had gone home for a long visit. It was a visit from which he was never to return.

The winter of 1864-65 must have been truly "a winter of discontent" for Shelby. Even under normal conditions he was the most restless of men. Activity of some sort, preferably on a grand scale, was as necessary to him as breathing. Now, brooding under the pines of Pittsburg, where his men watered their cattle by the lazy streams, he saw that the prediction made by General Holmes to General Marmaduke at Helena had come true at last. The Army of the Trans-Mississippi was an "army of prisoners, and self-supporting at that." The enemy could simply ignore them, and this was the crowning insult of all.

Shelby also knew that the news from the North was taking all the heart out of the army's idle divisions, and that most of the men were simply anxious to have done with the war and go home. He saw the disintegration writ in letters so large and so plain that he decided to take action independent of Kirby Smith and of the Confederate government itself.

Shelby had a high personal regard for the old commander of the Trans-Mississippi Department, but he had no faith in Kirby Smith's enthusiasm for fighting against odds. He became convinced that a change in commanders was the only solution, a change inaugurated by the generals themselves. He knew from experience that he could not hope for the command himself, because of his "youth" and reputation for recklessness. Of those who might be available, and acceptable to the other commanders, Shelby preferred Simon Bolivar Buckner. He determined to lead a *coup* which would oust Smith, place Buckner in command, consolidate the Army of the Trans-Mississippi on the barrier of the Brazos River, and continue the war—preferably in alliance with one of the two regimes in Mexico. It was a bold plan, and a typical Shelby plan.

Shelby reasoned that many Confederates from Lee's and Johnston's armies would join them rather than live under the heel of the Yankee conqueror, and that eventually he and Buckner ought to be able to offer to Maximilian or to Juárez an army of 75,000 or 100,000 veterans,[3] enough to give the Yankee government pause, especially since Mexican forces in an equal or greater number could be joined to the Confederates. The North would be faced with indefinite prolongation of the war, and it was well known in the South that the North was weary unto death of the struggle. The New York papers had been full of it for a year.

A negotiated peace, Shelby believed, would ensue. Then a vast new empire in the Southwest and in Mexico could be opened up for emigrants from the South—all those who refused to live under the oppressor's yoke, and their families. It would be a resurrection of "the proud Imperial South," as Major Edwards called it, on a new and greater frontier. Let the Yankees have their Black Republic; Buckner, Shelby, and their men would create a new and larger Confederacy in the Southwest.

This was the Grand Design.

One may imagine that Major Edwards had a great hand in it, or even that it was substantially his idea. Like Shelby, he thought in heroic terms, and his imagination was always riotous. He was the perfect companion-in-arms for Shelby, who was his ideal of a man and a soldier; and they were complementary in the sense that Edwards could arouse Southern patriotism to fever pitch with his prose as Shelby could with his oratorical eloquence.

By the time the spring flowers had come to full bloom on the prairie, Shelby and Edwards had perfected their plan on paper.

Two events enabled them to carry out the first step—the unseating of Kirby Smith. One was an order from Smith to Shelby to move his division to Fulton, Arkansas, preparatory to a new thrust into that state; the other was the news of Lee's surrender. Shelby was at Fulton when the paralyzing news came. And paralyzing it was. Public morale, which had been at low ebb, collapsed. General Cooper's Choctaws and Comanches, who had been fighting under the Confederate flag, were the first to act. They announced that they were going home to the reservation, and went. Delegations of white citizens visited Shelby and inquired the army's plans. He pistol-drove them out of camp for their trouble.

News of the lenient terms granted to the Army of Northern Virginia also had had a profound effect. Even the officers of the Army of the Trans-Mississippi, who would have embraced Shelby's plan eagerly a year ago, were now disaffected and eager only to get it over with. Furthermore, the army was widely scattered throughout three states, Texas, Louisiana and Arkansas. The difficulty of consolidating and supplying its divisions would have been enormous.

Kirby Smith decided to ask the governors of the three states to assemble for a final meeting at Marshall, Texas, in May, to decide a course of future action. Under the loosely knit Confederacy, governors of states were commanders-in-chief of state forces in the field and had final authority.[4]

The generals of the Trans-Mississippi Department were also summoned to Marshall, and they all came except "Prince John" Magruder, who remained in Galveston, where he watched with savage eyes a Federal fleet, beating in from the Gulf, filled with Negro troops to occupy the Department of Texas. He had already had as many lives as a cat, had Magruder, and he was to have many more, as an imperial land commissioner under Maximilian and as a darling of the lecture platform back in the States, to mention only two.

Magruder remained in Galveston because he had got wind of the palace revolution which was about to take place and he did not want to fall in with any plan advanced by Shelby. There was a submerged jealousy between them which was to come to the surface later in Mexico in an argument over rank. Perhaps they were too much alike to be downright fond of one another.

The Marshall conference convened. Shelby came down from Fulton; Smith from Shreveport; Hawthorne, Buckner, Preston, and Walker from the bayou country, along with a lot of lesser lights. The governors went into an executive session.[5] Shelby invited all of the military to a separate meeting. Kirby Smith, however, did not attend. He knew that the younger generals were ready to depose him, and he remained at the home of a friend in Marshall, awaiting their decision.

Shelby took the floor. "Gentlemen," he said, "the army no longer has any confidence in General Smith. We must concentrate everything we have on the Brazos River at once, and the men must have a leader whom they trust. Fugitives from Lee and Johnston will join us by the thousands, and we shall be able, at the very least, to interpose an army of a hundred thousand men between them and disaster. Mr. Davis is on his way here, and he alone has the right to treat of surrender. Our intercourse with the French is perfect. Count de Polignac[6] is our emissary to Louis Napoleon, and General Preston should go at once to Mexico to learn from Marshal Bazaine whether it is to be peace or war between us. Every step to the Rio Grande must be fought over; we will march into Mexico and reinstate Juárez or espouse the cause of Maximilian. It makes no difference which."

He paused, then added, "Surrender is a word which neither my division nor myself understand."

Shelby's gift for infecting others with his own enthusiasm did not fail him here, as it had not failed him when he persuaded Price and Marmaduke, much against their will, to permit him to strike at the enemy after Helena.

The suggestion that Louis Napoleon would ally himself with a nonexistent Confederacy was madness; yet none of the commanders present pointed it out. They acceded to the plan with enthusiasm.

Shelby grew more eloquent, picturing the flood tide of emigration which would create a new Southern empire in Texas and Mexico; and he climaxed his peroration by nominating Simon Bolivar Buckner to command the new army.

"General Buckner has reputation, he has the confidence of the army, and he is a soldier of fortune like ourselves," said Shelby. "Who but Buckner should command us?"

In the absence of Magruder, Buckner ranked next to Smith, so that the nomination was a logical one. The description of Buckner as a soldier of fortune, however, could not have been more wide of the mark. He was a business man at heart, with a secret ambition to write verse. His record as a commanding general had been, to say the least, an indifferent one. Caution, which is hardly a characteristic of soldiers of fortune, was his fundamental trait, and of all those in the room he was the least likely to succeed as commander of an expedition such as Shelby proposed. Nevertheless, he was so deeply flattered by Shelby's oratory that his judgment was swayed; he accepted the nomination when it was offered to him, although later he was to repudiate it.[7]

It was a stirring scene, as Shelby concluded, and every officer in the room stood up to cheer the new leader. In a splendid new uniform, and with his magnificent physique, Buckner at least looked the part. Major Edwards says that he was as handsome as Murat and that the gold lace on his uniform shone "as if it had been washed by the dew and wiped in sunshine."

Buckner made a gracious speech of acceptance and assured all of those present that he would entertain no proposal of surrender.

Shelby again took the floor.

"Since there is some embarrassment about this, gentlemen," he said, "and since the business must be done boldly, I will ask the honor of presenting this ultimatum to General Smith. We must make haste, for it is some good leagues to the Brazos, and I shall march to the nearest enemy tomorrow and attack him. If I do not overthrow him I shall at least keep him at bay in the movement southward." It was a maneuver at which Shelby had grown expert from constant repetition.

Kirby Smith was waiting for him in the living room of his friend's home. There were tears in his eyes as they rested on Shelby's sinewy frame.

"General Smith," said Shelby, being intentionally cruel to cover his deep embarrassment, "the army has lost confidence in you."

"I know," said Kirby Smith.

"They do not wish to surrender."

"Nor do I," said Smith, wearily. "What would the army have?"

"Your withdrawal as its direct commander," said Shelby, "in favor of General Buckner. Then, concentration of the forces of the Trans-Mississippi upon the Brazos River—and war to the hilt."

A shadow like an eagle's wing passed over Kirby Smith's face. He arose slowly and faced the younger man who was deposing him.

"What is your advice, General Shelby?"

"Instant compliance, sir."

"Very well," said Smith, and walked to a writing desk.

The order was signed, and Edmund Kirby Smith resigned in favor of Simon Bolivar Buckner as commander-in-chief of the Army of the Trans-Mississippi. Smith remained only as chief executive of the civilian government of the Department—a post in which he had kept the paddles of the blockade runners turning for four years.

Shelby rode off under the stars to his division, now camped at Stone Point near Kaufman, Texas. The thoughts that were in his mind were far away on some dusty road leading into the sunlight.

Whatever Buckner intended to do with his new-found rank, he was never to do it. On Smith's return to Shreveport, bewildered and heart-broken, the Old Man found two communications: one from the governors of every State in the Department except Reynolds of Missouri, directing him to give up the struggle; the other from Colonel John Sprague, U. S. A., demanding the surrender of the Army of the Trans-Mississippi to General John Pope.

Smith hemmed and hawed and corresponded with Colonel Sprague. He refused at first to meet the terms demanded by Pope, asserting that they were too harsh, but when Pope modified them, he gave in. He ordered Buckner to surrender, just as if he had not resigned his command in favor of Buckner, and Buckner obeyed. He went down to Shreveport and signed the articles, ending the existence of the Army of the Trans-Mississippi forever.

It was several days before the news reached Shelby. By the same courier came an order from Kirby Smith directing him to march at once to Shreveport with his division, there to lay down his arms and give his parole to General Pope not to bear arms again against the United States. From Shreveport the men of the Missouri Cavalry

Division would take such transportation home as the Federal authorities might think fit to provide.

Shelby was in a towering rage. He did not blame Smith, whom he regarded as a superannuated fool. The full torrent of his wrath was turned on Buckner, who, he now recalled savagely, had surrendered the first army of the Confederacy at Fort Donelson, as well as the last now at Sheveport.

Consigning Buckner to a pit of hell which even the devil would shun, Shelby compared him to Benedict Arnold, the gatekeepers of Troy, and all the turncoats of history. The profanity which he loosed would have been sufficient to take all of the curl out of his beard if the atmosphere had not been heavy with an impending Texas storm.

Shelby did more than give way to verbal explosions, however. Buckner had surrendered, but not the soldiers. They would not have had time to reach Shreveport yet. Very well. A blow struck in that direction might turn the "surrender" into a Donnybrook Fair, and prevent its taking place at all. Shelby gave the order to hitch up his howitzers—but first he sat down and penned a furious proclamation "To the Men of Shelby's Division."

"Soldiers!" he wrote. "You have been betrayed! The generals whom you trusted have refused to lead you. Let us begin the battle again by a Revolution. Lift up the flag that has been cast down and dishonored. Unsheath the sword that it may remain unsullied and victorious! If you desire it, I will lead; if you demand it, I will follow. We are the Army and the Cause. To talk of surrender is to be a traitor. Let us seize the traitors and attack the enemy. Forward, for the South and Liberty!"

There was no printing shop in Stone Point and no paper worthy of a proclamation. Wallpaper was ripped from the wall of a store, over the storekeeper's protests, and the proclamation, when posted, was as gaudy as anything of its kind during the French Revolution. It was done in bold letters of red, black, and blue like those of a circus advertisement. Shelby's brown-faced boys read it slowly, those of them that could read, and scratched their sunbleached hair. For a while there was silence. Then someone gave a shout.

"On to Shreveport!"

The rebel yell went up, and the townspeople of Stone Point shuddered.

At dawn the division was on the march again, in full battle array.

The impedimenta which soldiers gather during months of idleness was left behind, and they traveled stripped for action.

But man proposes, and God disposes. The storm which had been gathering since the day before broke, and a cloudburst came out of the sky which was a gullywasher even for Texas. The deluge swept away all the bridges between Stone Point and Shreveport, and water rose to the saddle girths in streams which had been dry land the day before. The roads disappeared in the torrent along with the bridges, and the Missouri Cavalry Division bivouacked the second night in a shallow lake which had been prairie up to yesterday.

The third day they toiled on through the muddy wreckage of the countryside, their horses straining and the wheels of their artillery barely turning.

Now a new tide was rolling out to meet them, a wave of army stragglers bearing the news that it was all over. The surrender at Shreveport was already taking place, in the public square of the town. Division after division of the Army of the Trans-Mississippi was marching in, stacking arms, giving their paroles, and taking the road that was outward bound. There had not been for them even the mournful glory of an Appomattox, where a cease-fire was needed to silence the guns forever. The Army of the Trans-Mississippi had surrendered—or been surrendered—without firing a shot.

Only one small grain of comfort in the debacle remained for Shelby. From paroled officers he learned that Kirby Smith had not surrendered until it was clear that the governors of the states would no longer permit their divisions to fight, and that he had held out for the very best terms he could get. Thus the Old Man's conscience was clear and his honor bright. Shelby was glad of that, for he admired Kirby Smith. But, unreasonably enough, he still blamed Buckner.

The end had come, but the men of the Missouri Cavalry Division would not march in and surrender with the rest. They turned aside from Shreveport, and at Corsicana, Texas, on a green and undulating plain with the sun shining again on their ragged butternut, they bivouacked together as a Confederate army division for the last time.

There was great argument in the camp that night. For months every man of them had known of Shelby's plan to take refuge in Mexico if the Confederacy should go down; the great question was, to go or not to go. For those with families and sweethearts back home, of course, the matter was already settled.

There is no record anywhere of Shelby's farewell address to his men when they fell in for the last time. One of them, Thomas Westlake, who went to Mexico and wrote a history of the expedition on three scratch pads which may be examined in the Western Historical Manuscripts Collection of the University of Missouri, reports the scene in his laconic fashion: "In the Morning General Shelby Formed his men around him on the open Pearie and made a Speach to them Recounting many of the hardships and Struggels of the Four Years past. He said he was not going to surrender but was going to Mexico and Requested all that would to go with him." [8]

Major Edwards says that Shelby did not make a speech for the history books. He was impatient, as usual, to be on his way. From the evidence, what he did say was, in effect, "Boys, the war is over and you can go home. I for one will not go home. Across the Rio Grande lies Mexico. Who will follow me there?"

Several hundred men stepped forward. Estimates of the exact number vary. Major Edwards says five hundred; Thomas Westlake thinks there were only about a hundred fifty. There is no way of telling, for sure; from now on the size of the expedition would vary, not from day to day but from hour to hour.

A sergeant bore forward the old barred banner of the division and drove its staff into the ground before Shelby, who stood with bared head, tears in his eyes, as the volunteers surged around him. Buckner had been the poet of the outfit, Shelby recalled; the thought occurred to him now that if Buckner had stayed, he would have seen that though the banner's red was faded and torn, its bars of blue still shone with the white stars of hope.

The partings were said that night. They were the partings of comrades in arms, and they have been the same, no doubt, since the Land of Nod; and after the last goodbye, Shelby and His Men—no longer the Missouri Cavalry Division—camped on the prairie over beyond Corsicana.

Tomorrow, they must make their preparations, elect their officers, and gather up their arms; but tonight, in the cool grass, they slept, and their dreams were not of home but of the golden mines of Sinaloa.

20. *From Texas to Mexico*

THE ORGANIZATION formed next day was that of a regiment, with Shelby as colonel.[1] By the time the Rio Grande was crossed, it would be a brigade. In the election of officers Shelby received every vote but his own, so that he was commander-in-chief by acclamation.

When it came to balloting for the lesser ranks, however, not all of his officers fared so well. Never before had soldiers had such a golden opportunity to express a candid opinion of their superiors without fear of retaliation, and never was better use made of it. Unpopular officers were demoted right and left; others were rewarded in outbursts of generosity which added yards of mythical gold lace to the tattered sleeves of their uniforms.

One major found himself a corporal; several lieutenants were newly breveted captains and majors. The election results were announced amid exuberant and raucous laughter. Those who were demoted stepped down sheepishly, without apparent rancor, and Shelby let his rangers enjoy themselves. But any of those who may have regarded the new organization as a military jest were to find that Shelby in his new role would take his responsibilities more seriously than ever, and that he could still, when need arose, jerk the reins of discipline in a manner to make the eyeballs pop.

Officers elected, the brigade set about arming and provisioning itself for the march ahead. This presented no problem. Texas was one vast artillery park of fine French and Austrian cannon run through the blockade to Galveston and Matamoras. These stood idle on the prairie, where their late gunners had left them. Quartermaster and commissary stores were plentiful and there were stands of imported muskets in all the towns. Corsicana was no exception.

Shelby dragged into his camp ten brand-new Napoleon howitzers, 2,000 Enfield rifles, 40,000 rounds of small ammunition, bushels of gun caps, pistols, and cartridges, and 500 dragoon sabres. Each man already had a Sharpe's carbine and 120 rounds of ammunition apiece.

On the road to Waco they found an abandoned wagon train which had been bound from Brownsville to Shreveport. It had been abandoned with all of its provisions intact—salt pork, lard, bacon, rice, dried fruit, molasses, wines, whiskeys, pickles, preserves, jellies, cakes, and tins of sweet English biscuits with which the "gold laced tapeworms" of the Confederate Cotton Bureau had been wont to regale themselves.

Gorged with food, and amid exclamations of profane wonder at the pampered life of the bureaucrat, they took up their march in the direction of Houston, armed as cavalrymen have never been armed before or since.

At Houston there was the largest depot in the state, filled with all kinds of supplies, and into these Shelby meant to have a look, since they were the property of the Confederacy and he and his men had a long and uncertain journey ahead of them. Word reached him as he advanced that the countryside was alive with bandits and cutthroats of every description. The breakup of the Confederate armies had removed the last stabilizing influence in East Texas, and the Federals under General Sheridan had not yet assumed full control. Murder, looting, and raping were the order of the day. It was Bloody Kansas all over again.

Shelby swore that he would protect government property and hang looters wherever he found them, and he lectured his men on the job ahead, which must be performed before crossing into Mexico; but as his brigade speeded up its march, he found that his own men were being mistaken for another band of renegades, and that there was a wholesale evacuation of territory in his path.

It was not until he neared Houston that Shelby was able to demonstrate what his real intentions were. Hearing that bushwhackers had taken over the town, he sent a light cavalry force of 100 men under Captains James Meadow and James Wood into Houston, with orders to seize all the stores and hold them for distribution to ex-soldiers and the needy among the civilian population.

Meadow and Wood reached Houston none too soon. Two thousand army stragglers and ne'er-do-wells were milling about, drinking whiskey and debating the best way to batter down the doors of the government warehouse. All of them were armed with some of the Confederacy's last muskets and cartridges.

As Wood and Meadow drew up at the head of their butternut cavalcade, the ruffians blinked owlishly at them. Despite their youth, Shelby's captains were bearded to the eyes and saddle-colored from the sun, and they had a ferocious appearance.

Wood's voice was the first to be heard. It was like a pistol shot. "Disperse!" he said. "We are Jo Shelby's men."

One of the border ruffians laughed. "The war's over, young feller," he said, waving an empty jug. "Every man for himself and the devil take Tom Hindman [General Hindman was now a commander under Magruder]. Whyn't you give yore parole and get? And Jo Shelby too?"

"My friend," said James Wood, "Jo Shelby is the ranking Confederate general in Texas right now and every shoelace of government property is under his protection. As soon as he gets here, flour, bacon, clothes, and medicines will be distributed to the women folks, and nothing at all to drunks and scalawags. Now git! My men and I have ridden thirty miles and we're hungry, so we'll stop to eat. If any of you are here at supper time, we'll blow you into hell."

One by one the armed loafers began to fall away at the rear. The name and fame of Shelby was known from one end of the border to the other. As the ranks of the renegades began to thin, they fell away by tens and twenties instead of ones and twos, shuffling their feet and squinting at the sun as if they were going no place in particular, but were anxious to get there. Jim Wood grinned like a skunk eating bumblebees, and the sunburned horsemen dismounted to cook supper.

After supper, and some reassuring words spoken to the townspeople of Houston, the column remounted and rode back to Shelby's camp on the prairie.

Similar scenes were enacted at the Texas crossroads communities of Tyler and Waxahachie, and by the time Shelby reached Austin, the state capital, word of his vigilante work had preceded him, and the citizens turned out to give him an ovation.

Governor Murrah welcomed them on behalf of the State of Texas. He was a tall, stooped man with burning eyes in a wasted face, and two spots of crimson on his cheekbones—he was dying of consumption. He had remained to guard the gold and silver of the Confederacy, three hundred thousand dollars worth, in the sub-treasury at Austin. In the end he would ride away to Mexico with Shelby in the Confederate uniform that was to be his shroud.

Shelby camped just beyond Austin on the banks of the Colorado River and a good many of his men drifted back into town for girls and drinks. It was a misty, ominous, cloudy night, full to the brim with darkness and spattered with invisible rain. Though May and

June are the dry season in Texas, the weather had been fractious ever since Shelby had left Corsicana, and tonight gave promise of being another howler.

It was a good night for dirty work—which was not long in coming. A band of guerrillas, under the command of a notorious Captain Rabb, for whom Shelby was on the lookout, rode silently into Austin in the rain-filled dark, intent on looting the three hundred thousand dollars in the sub-treasury, whose presence was itching the palm of every bushwhacker in Texas.

The silent horsemen, two score strong, sped to the State House where the money was kept. Some of Shelby's men, reveling in the town, saw them, bolted to the saddle, and rode for the brigade. When they returned the church bells of Austin were ringing furiously and the home guard was marching out of the armory to the long roll of the drums.

Shelby dashed for the State House, and when his column reached the square, Rabb and his guerrillas had already battered down the doors and were inside, sacking the vault. Every light under the Capitol dome seemed ablaze. Shelby asked no questions. He threw a tight cordon of men around the State House, and sent forty men with Sharpe's carbines to rush the doors while the rest shot out the windows of the building.

Shrill cries of agony went up as the volleys from the carbines crashed into the treasury room where the freebooters were stuffing their clothing with American double eagles, British sovereigns, French hundred-franc pieces, and gold ingots. In their greed to get at the gold they had flung a king's ransom in silver—U. S. and Mexican silver dollars—to the four corners of the room. Now the raiders fell in writhing heaps, blood spattering gold and silver alike, as Shelby's men fired again and again in the narrow confines of the treasury vault.

Not a dollar was lost and not a man escaped. Captain Rabb's bullet-riddled body was buried under those of his men. Only one man reached the exit, a shaggy giant of a plainsman in filthy clothes of tanned goatskin, who staggered out of the gloom, smoke, and horror to fall dead with a ringing sound like that of a moneybag spilled. He had taken off his trousers, tied the bottoms together, and filled them with gold double eagles. No silver dollars for him. Shelby's men dragged him onto the grass of the State House Square and left him there, a reddening bundle of gold-filled rags.

When the wild work was done Shelby posted sentries who walked their posts in blood splashing to their knees, while he conferred with Governor Murrah as to what was to be done. Murrah suggested that since the money was Confederate government property, it might be well to divide it pro rata among the men of Shelby's brigade, none of whom had seen a paymaster for months before the war ended. There was an official precedent for such a distribution: by order of the Confederate government, the last train from Richmond, bearing the gold of the Treasury Department, had distributed the money to soldiers straggling home from Appomattox, all along a route which extended from Richmond to Washington, Georgia.

Shelby, however, refused to touch a penny of the treasure, on the ground that it might cause him and his men to be mistaken for bushwhackers. "I came into the war with clean hands," he said, "and with God's help I will go out of it with clean hands."

He made known his decision to his men on the steps of the Capitol.

"We know what the world would say," he told them. "We shall not take the money." He paused, then squared his shoulders.

"We are the last of our race," he said. "Let us be the best as well."

It was the old magic that touched everything he did. There was no dissent or grumbling among the ragged paupers in front of him—far from it. The entire brigade cheered. Old Jo was right. They couldn't take the money. It was the bond they would give to history. Once again, a thing was right if Jo Shelby did it, and that was all. They reformed their column and rode out through the blustery night to their camp on the Colorado River.

But their night's work was not done. As they approached the camp, they heard the shrill sounds of horses neighing, and a great commotion among the tents and wagons. Another band of bushwhackers was after their horses.

Unlimbering their carbines, they fired into the mass of horses and men—taking care not to hit the horses—and then they dismounted and charged the renegades with bowie knives and sabres. Thirty-nine of the robbers were cut to pieces on the sward, out of about fifty who had been in their number originally. The rest fled, most of them on foot, their own horses having scattered in panic.

The night of slaughter was over at last. A thunderstorm broke, and Shelby decided that at daybreak he would move for San Antonio. The dead he would leave unburied as a warning to others.

His men fell into their bedrolls wearily, heedless of the thunder's roll, the lightning's flash, or the sabred bodies of the Texas horse thieves scattered in grotesque heaps throughout the camp, almost within reach of many a sleeper's arm. There were so many nightmares in the day's work for Shelby's men that sleep always came to them calmly and peacefully.

San Antonio had been a gold rush town and a city of gilded sin since the spring of '61. Far outside the theatre of actual war, it had stood nevertheless midstream in the swirling tide of the blockade, a port of entry not only for supplies and munitions of war, but for the finest luxuries the European markets could afford. In San Antonio anything could be had for a price. While the rest of the South tightened its belt during the four years of the war, King Cotton held high carnival in the city on the San Antonio River.

It was a mardi gras of prosperity which attracted all the least attractive human elements in any war—speculators, profiteers, contractors, gamblers, prostitutes, and fugitives from the draft. With the collapse of the armies and the hauling down of the flag, San Antonio had become the capital of the desperadoes of Texas. As Shelby's column clanked toward the city, "ruffians," as Major Edwards says, "had taken possession of the city and were rioting in royal fashion, sitting in the laps of courtesans and drinking wines brought through the blockade from France."

Seven men had been killed in street fighting, in the twisted thoroughfares which made San Antonio look as if it had been laid out on the pattern of a rattlesnake's nest. Besides the seven murders, a dozen stores had been sacked, renegades had levied a *préstamo* on citizens to pay for their revels, and a commissary train had been burnt.

The Mayor and a committee of citizens rode out twenty miles to Shelby's camp to urge him to hasten into the city and restore order. The brigade was asleep when they reached camp, but when Shelby was informed of the situation, he roused his men from their slumbers and they rode all night into San Antonio.

Patrols were sent through the streets, rounding up the scalawags; guards were stationed at the corners; and Shelby appointed two of the most trusted men of the brigade, D. A. Williams and Alonzo Slayback, as provost marshals for each side of the river. There are no files at all of San Antonio newspapers of this date in the universities and libraries; we have to rely on Major Edwards, who says as usual that men were hanged and shot, without giving details; but we may be sure that Slayback and Williams did their duty, and that for a day or so were exhibited the bodies of looters, so that the rest took warning and left town.

Major Edwards was enchanted with San Antonio, "the antique, half Mexican city where the Spanish death flag wound above the Alamo," and after order had been restored, he wrote in his journal, "Peace came upon the city with the balm of a southeast trade wind and women walked forth as if to a festival. The Plaza transformed itself into a *parterre*. Roses bloomed in the manes of the horses and after Cannae there was Capua."

If San Antonio was the capital of King Cotton, the Menger Hotel was the capital of San Antonio.[2] A cool, inviting oasis in the now stifling heat of early summer, it was (and still is) a rambling, two-story building of stone and stucco with lemon and orange trees in its patio. The host, Otto Menger, whose family had been in the brewing business in St. Louis, served the best of food and wine, combining in his cuisine a hearty German love of good eating with the best of French and Creole recipes. The bar of the Menger was of noble British Honduran mahogany and the range of its whiskeys unexcelled. It was by now the last refuge of rather paunchy patriots who declared in loud voices that the South would fight on, and that the Yankee forces of occupation under General Philip Sheridan would find the Department of Texas too hot to handle.

These gentlemen, in their flapping linen coats and their black string ties, had been in retirement during the riots, but as soon as Shelby restored order, they were back in the bar, as noisy and vocal as ever.

Shelby recognized the type with a faint smile. They were the same stay-at-home Southerners he had met throughout the war, whom he compared to prairie dogs. When the coast is clear and nobody is in sight, Shelby remarked, there is the most infernal barking, chattering, cavorting, and yelling ever witnessed, outside the burrow; but let a strange shadow appear on the horizon and every furious dog among them is popping back into his underground den.

In the Missouri campaign of 1864 these same gentry, most of them members of the Knights of the Golden Circle, as the Copperheads called themselves, had come into his camp with mysterious books, innumerable signs, grips, signals, passwords and incantations, to aid the cause; General Sterling Price, riding about in a buggy because of his great bulk, had placed great reliance on them, though they had never enabled a Confederate soldier to take or hold a foot of ground.

But there were good men at the Menger too—some of the best brains in the country, and some of the stoutest hearts. There was "Prince John" Magruder, no longer aloof now that Galveston had fallen, Governor Reynolds of Missouri, Governor Henry Watkins Allen of Louisiana, General Lyon of Kentucky, Colonel William B. Broadwell, the genius of the Confederate Cotton Bureau under Kirby Smith, Governor Murrah of Texas—whom Magruder had asked to empty the prisons of Texas to swell the expedition—and Edmund Kirby Smith.

The Old Man alighted from an ambulance in front of the Menger, as dusty as any footsoldier. He had traveled incognito all over Texas, fearing the wrath of the soldiers whom he had surrendered. Shelby, taking his ease on an upstairs balcony of the Menger, saw him and recognized him. After the Old Man had entered the hotel, Shelby went downstairs, careful not to be seen, and looked at the name on the register.

Smith had registered as "William Thompson."

Shelby noted the room number, which was that of an outside room on the second story. He went into the street to look up. The blinds were drawn and the curtains down.

Shelby sent for Jake Connor, the lieutenant of artillery who had been the minstrel of the Missouri Cavalry Division. Jake was bandmaster of the brigade.

"Jake," said Shelby, "old men need air and sunlight. They should not commence hibernating in June. Get your band together for a serenade."

"To whom?" inquired Connor.

"Never mind to whom," replied Shelby. "Just get your band together. And as you go, order also that all men not on duty get under arms immediately and parade in front of the balcony."

At sunset the entire brigade was massed in the square in front of the Menger Hotel, to the wonderment of the townspeople, and Jake Connor's band struck up, "Hail to the Chief." There was no sign of a stir behind the blinds of Kirby Smith's room.

"Play 'Dixie,' boys," said Shelby. "If the Old Man were dead, that'd fetch him."

The familiar stirring strains went up, but still there was silence behind the blinds.

"This is downright selfish of him," said Major Edwards.

"Wait!" said Shelby, holding up a hand to halt the music. "Boys, that old man up there is Kirby Smith. Let's give him a cheer."

The cheer rose up in a roar, and the blinds were flung open. Kirby Smith came out onto the balcony, a look of eagerness and wonderment on his face. Since the surrender, he had feared these men more than the Yankees. Now, as they cheered him, tears streamed down his face and he could not speak. But Shelby could, and did.

"General Smith," he said with a magnificent flourish of his hat, "you are the ranking officer of the Trans-Mississippi Department and we are here to report to you. Command, and we obey; lead us and we shall follow. In this public manner, and before all San Antonio, with music and banners, we come to proclaim your arrival in the midst of that little band which knows neither dishonor nor surrender. You were seeking concealment, the night and obscurity of your self-appointed exile, and you have found guards to attend you, and the steadfast light of patriotism to make your pathway plain. We bid you good morning instead of good night, and await, as of old, your further orders."

Smith came down, amid the playing of the band, and the men of the Army of the Trans-Mississippi mobbed him with affection; but he was too old for new adventures, and the greeting was also goodbye.

Shelby had now set up his expatriate headquarters behind the cool shades of the Menger, while his men savored the delights of San Antonio. The streets were safe again, patrolled by Williams and Slayback's guards, and the girls, both Mexican and Texan, walked arm in arm with Shelby's men in the *paseos*, with flowers in their hair and laughter in their eyes. Serenades, led by Jake Connor, went on day and night beneath the balconies of the town, while the Stars and Bars floated hither and thither, borne aloft triumphantly by the wanderers like the Ark of the Covenant. The soldiers had money in their pockets —paid them by the merchants of San Antonio in return for their protection—and they spent it freely. Phil Sheridan was still far away. The days were loud with laughter, and the nights were filled with music.

Shelby let his men frolic through the sunshiny June days, while he plotted his Mexican adventure with the band of exiles at the hotel.

Among his "No Surrender" Confederates Shelby had his eye in particular on John Magruder. Though there was no love lost between them, Shelby was not a man to waste talent, and he knew that Magruder possessed talents of a superlative order.

He had fought with distinction in Virginia, though transferred to the Trans-Mississippi afterward, because General Lee, some said, had found him difficult to work with. He had had a brilliant career in the Army of the Trans-Mississippi, capturing a Federal steamship with only "cotton-clads" at Galveston; and he was a man of immense soldierly bearing, standing six feet, four inches tall, who would have been an impressive figure at any court.

He had been an officer in "the old army" before the war, a hero of the Mexican War, and the darling of New York and Newport society. General Winfield Scott, the wittiest man in the old army, adored him as extravagantly as the youngest society matron. At an elegant dinner at Newport, when someone had inquired of him how much an officer's pay might be, he had turned to his butler and inquired, "James, what is my salary?" That was John Magruder.

He was penniless now. He had given up his commission in the United States Army to join the Confederacy and at fifty-five he could still fight all day and dance all night. After the capture of the *Harriet Lane* [3] by the cotton-clads, he had danced till dawn with blood on his uniform and a bullet wound in his body, though he had been some fifty-nine hours without sleep.

Magruder was in love with all beautiful women and was beloved by them all his life long. He wrote love songs and could sing them in a clear tenor, though in ordinary speech he was somewhat embarrassed by a tendency to lisp. He was loved by his men, too—with a devotion equaled only by Shelby's men for Shelby himself—and it was as inevitable that he should be attracted to the Mexican expedition as a nightfly to the candle.

Realizing that Magruder could charm the birds off the trees, Shelby asked him to go at once to Mexico City. From Monterrey he was to send Magruder ahead of the expedition to talk with the Emperor Maximilian.

Between San Antonio and Eagle Pass the brigade got a preview of the kind of country it would be marching through henceforward—a dreary range, full of mesquite and black chapparal. On the first night of the march from San Antonio, bushwhackers attempted to make off with seven mules from the camp, and in the ensuing melee fourteen men were killed, three of them Shelby's.

The next day two scouts from the rear—James Kirtley and James Rudd—brought in news of a Federal force of 3,000 approaching, under the command of a Colonel Johnson. Shelby penned a note to the Federal commander and sent it into his camp by another of his adjutants, Major Jim Moreland. The note read:

"Colonel: My scouts inform me that you have about three thousand men and that you are looking for me. I have only one thousand men, and yet I should like to make your acquaintance. I will probably march from my present camp about ten miles farther today, halting on the high road between San Antonio and Eagle Pass. Should you desire to pay me a visit, you will find me at home until the day after tomorrow."

Colonel Johnson received Moreland affably and said he would think about it. But next day he wheeled his command northward and trotted away. The war was over and Shelby could go to the devil or Mexico, as far as he was concerned. No doubt Johnson had his orders, too.

At Eagle Pass Shelby set up camp again, and here the flag of the Missouri Cavalry Division was lowered for the last time. In a reverent ceremony it was weighted with stones and sunk into the Rio Grande by Elliott, Slayback, and Gordon. Inside its folds Shelby laid his black plume, which had been his own private Confederate flag. No man felt like making a speech. None was made.

Shelby lined up his howitzers on the river bank in plain view of the garrison of Piedras Negras, on the Mexican side of the river. Then he sent Lieutenant Colonel Frank Gordon in a skiff with a flag of truce and twenty-five armed men to parley with Governor Bieska, civil governor of the State of Coahuila, who was in command of 2,000 Mexican troops in the town.

Biesca was a man of pomp and dash himself, and he rode into the plaza to receive Gordon, surrounded by a glittering staff. A meeting was arranged, and Shelby came over later in the day. There is no record of the conversation which the two men held behind closed doors, but there is no doubt of the case put to Biesca by Shelby. It must have been something like this:

"The war in the United States is over now and Secretary of State Seward has given the French their marching orders, politely but firmly. If they do not withdraw from Mexico, the gates will be open for United

States intervention. There are a million troops under arms in the Grand Army of the Republic, and they are being held in readiness for just such an event. Already General Grant has ordered General Sheridan with 50,000 troops to station themselves in Texas, awaiting a move into Mexico. It will be 1848 all over again, with the United States flag flying once more over Chapultepec. You can forestall this, Governor Biesca, by recruiting the soldiers of the late Southern Confederacy into your armies, by marching at once to Mexico City, and reinstating Benito Juárez as rightful president of the Republic. I have 1,000 men, and the brigade can soon be recruited up to division strength. And not only disbanded Confederates, but discharged Federals, will join you. In this they will have the blessing of General Grant, who commands all things in the United States now and would rather win an undeclared war against the French than a declared one. What is your answer, Governor Biesca?"

Biesca was enthusiastic. The fortunes of the rebels were at a low ebb, with Juárez in hiding in the United States, Porfirio Díaz cut off in the South, and the French, who treated the Mexicans like dogs, riding high in most of the towns and in a large area around the Capital.

Biesca offered Shelby control of the three states of Coahuila, Tamaulipas, and Nuevo León, reserving for himself only civil authority over Coahuila, and suggested that Shelby make Piedras Negras his headquarters until his brigade could be recruited to division strength. With 20,000 men they would attack General Jeanningros at Monterrey and thrust for Mexico City.

Shelby could have asked for nothing better. It was a dream come true, and far more quickly than dreams usually do. He thanked Biesca warmly, explained that the decision must be left up to his men, and promised to return the next day with their answer.

The brigade was assembled, and Shelby outlined Biesca's offer in glowing terms. Before the vote was called for, Shelby made no secret of the fact that he wished to accept the Juaristas' offer.

"Boys," he said, "if you are all of my mind, and will take your chances with me, it is Juárez and the Republic from now on. You know Biesca's offer. What he fails to perform for us we will perform for ourselves, and if his promises turn out to be Mexican ones, there will be scant laughter over any American trapped or slain by treachery. We will cut his gizzard out."

A long debate followed, full of the high-flown oratory in which the Missourians and Texans delighted. Shelby took part in it spiritedly, although it was evident that there was not much doubt about the outcome. In Shelby's secret heart he was of a mind with those who opposed him. The two natures that warred within him constantly—the romantic and the practical—had come to grips in the supreme test, like Jacob wrestling with the angel, and the practical had won out, for Shelby was clear-eyed enough to see that Biesca had offered him exactly what he wanted: unlimited authority and the certainty of victory in the end. It was a glittering prize that had been dangled before a tramp general of an army which no longer existed. But that other side of Shelby's nature, the romantic one which longed for plumes and lances, had given in reluctantly. He was glad that the matter would be settled by others than himself.

In the end every single vote, except Shelby's, was cast for Maximilian. The eloquent Alonzo Slayback, who had recruited for Shelby in the vast and interminable brush of Arkansas, and Ben Elliott, who next to Shelby had been the leader of the Iron Brigade in a hundred battles, spoke for the Empire,[4] and the picture their fancy painted was a Mohammedan's dream of Paradise in Imperial Mexico. Shelby's deep gray eyes were alight; if he was ever to regret, it was not at this moment. His men had won his battle against himself, and his next words showed that he was aware of it.

"If that is your answer," he said, "it is mine too. Henceforth we will fight under Maximilian. Tomorrow at four o'clock in the afternoon we commence the march for Monterrey. Let no man repine. You have chosen the Empire, and perhaps it is as well, but good or bad, your fate shall be my fate and your fortune my fortune."

Biesca merely shrugged when he was informed of the decision. He thought the gringos mad, but it made no difference. His garrison of irregulars could not prevent Shelby from marching on; Shelby's howitzers would blow them into the Rio Grande. Being an Indian, he accepted the situation philosophically. He rolled a cigarette and pointed out to Shelby that since his *peregrinos* would need money, and since Juárez needed cannon, a deal might be made. He proposed to buy Shelby's howitzers and munitions for $16,000 in silver, and $40,000 in worthless Juárez scrip.

This was most generous, and at the moment Shelby and his men needed money more then they needed howitzers. They were no longer in Texas, where everthing had been free. They were in a town of mud huts in a land of strangers. The trail that lay ahead of them, to Monterrey and Mexico City, was no more then a narrow path through a most formidable wilderness of thorny mesquite and ugly cactus, some of it poisonous, entwined in a hedgelike growth which the natives call *brasada*. The only inhabitants of the Great Plateau of Mexico, where the *brasada* flourished, were Lipan Indians, bandits, and deserters from the French Foreign Legion. It was emphatically no place to be burdened with wagons, teams, and artillery. Shelby accepted Biesca's offer of $16,000.[5]

Biesca did not have $16,000 on hand, but he raised it easily enough by raiding the till of every merchant in town. Piedras Negras had done a booming business with the Confederacy for four years, and its merchants were rich, by Mexican standards.

The usual formula of the *préstamo*, or levy, was carried out. A list of contributors was made up, an adjutant with a file of soldiers called on those whose names appeared, pointed to the figure by their names, and waited, with bayonets courteously at the fix. Given no choice, the merchants paid, and by evening $16,000 in silver had been paid over to Shelby and deposited by him in the Customs House for safety.

With all these matters settled, the men scattered to the cantinas. The day was hot, white glare upon white dust, and no breath of air stirring in the streets. The mood of the brigade was festive, and there would have been no trouble with the inhabitants of Piedras Negras if it had not been for a pair of troublemakers who had enlisted with Shelby somewhere above San Antonio, representing themselves as veterans of Lee's army.

This pair now circulated among the male portion of the population, amazingly fluent in Spanish, declaring that Shelby's men were desperadoes, with a long trail of rapine and slaughter behind them in Texas, who would leave not a virgin unravished or a store unrobbed in Piedras Negras. Furthermore, they declared that their own presence in Piedras Negras was due entirely to the fact that Shelby's men had stolen their horses, back in Texas, and that they had trailed along only in the hope of recovering their mounts, which they prized above their own lives and which were worth a fortune.

The sullen Mexicans, hearing the loud voices of the gringos in the cantinas, and the pealing laughter of the girls, swore a great oath that the horse thieves from north of the river should deliver up every branded horse among them. This would have been a large order, for

Ike Berry and Dick Winship, who had been first into Piedras Negras, each rode a branded horse and so did scores of others.

Afternoon drill, on which Shelby always insisted, was just over, and Ike Berry was seated cross-legged in front of regimental headquarters enjoying the sun and a meerschaum pipe which he had picked up in his travels. His horse was tethered near by. Ike was a low, squat Hercules, with a long yellow beard and unshorn locks, a man free of speech and quick with a sabre.

Directly across from Ike Berry, Captain James Wood was leaning against the door of a café. He had a better view of the street than Ike Berry, and he was the first to see a detail of thirty-five Mexican soldiers approaching Shelby's headquarters. They were trailing their rifles, Mexican style, and at their head marched a smartly uniformed, handsome young lieutenant.

Wood went inside the café and spoke to Martin Kritzer, who had his arm around an Indian girl, beaded and beautiful.

"Looks like Old Joe delivered those guns too soon," Wood said to Kritzer. "Maybe we're going to have to take them back."

Kritzer and Wood walked back to the door of the café, and watched. One of the men who called himself a veteran of Lee's army now approached Berry. Berry knew him and greeted him cheerfully. The renegade pointed to Berry's horse. Backed by the rifles of the Mexican captain's squad, he was arrogant.

"That is my horse, Berry," he said. "He wears my brand. I've followed him to Mexico and these boys aim to see that I get him back."

Ike Berry was taken by surprise. He knocked out his meerschaum pipe. Then he rose and smiled slowly, a frank, disarming smile. It was the kind of smile, full of wonderment and pleasure, which he had been accustomed to wear in battle. He pulled his sabre from its scabbard and with one swift, slicing blow laid open the man's arm from shoulder to fingertips.

At a shouted command from their captain the Mexicans closed in on Ike Berry and overpowered him. Martin Kritzer dropped his Indian girl and ran through the crowd of Mexicans for Shelby.

Shelby was sitting in another café, drinking cognac and discussing the mysteries of the Catalan language with a psycopathic, scholarly Englishman who had joined the brigade at Austin. The Englishman interested Shelby more than any other man in the brigade because he cherished an overweening passion to perish in a train wreck, and had come to Mexico, so he said, in the hope of finding a stray locomotive on a siding with cars attached.

"They are after the horses!" shouted Kritzer as he burst into the café.

"What horses?" asked Shelby.

"All of our horses," said Kritzer.

"We might have known it," said Shelby. "After we have delivered up our arms, too. Well, sound the rally."

Kritzer blew a blast that could be heard in Eagle Pass across the river, and the laughter died in the cafés. Men swarmed out of doorways, flushed but sobered, and when they had taken note of the situation, opened fire on the Mexicans from every direction with their sidearms.

Jim Wood was armed with a short Enfield rifle, and as the Mexicans fell upon Ike Berry he took aim at the young Mexican captain. A beautiful, tawny Mexican girl—perhaps his sweetheart—tried to strike the Enfield from Wood's hand, crying, "Spare him!" but too late. Wood shot the captain dead, and when the revolver smoke had cleared, seventeen Mexican soldiers lay dead or wounded in the plaza. The rest fled back to their barracks.

And now, Major Edwards notes in his diary, "a dreadful commotion fell upon Piedras Negras." The long roll sounded and the entire Mexican garrison turned out. Shelby's men mounted their horses and charged them. At the same time a detachment of the brigade under the command of a Virginian named Langhorne battered down the doors of the Customs House, seized the sacks of silver belonging to them, and made off with it after locking the sentries inside.

Shelby waved his hat, stormed at his men, and threatened, but for once his commands were not obeyed. Governor Biesca also dashed into the plaza amid the milling horsemen and began a passionate speech of apology, but since it was in Spanish it was not too well understood.

"I'm sorry, Governor," said Shelby, "and I don't know what it's all about, but the devil is in the boys, for all that."

He went vigorously to work, however, at the task of quieting his men, and eventually suceeded, although what he was shouting could not have been heard above the crack of pistol shots, the ringing of church bells, and the wailing of women.

When quiet was restored, Biesca ordered all of his men confined to barracks and implored Shelby by all the saints in the Mexican calendar to leave Piedras Negras as quickly as possible. Shelby promised to do so, but it was a promise impossible of immediate performance. His men had seized not only the money, but all of the howitzers which had been sold, and it would require some persuasion to make the men part with them again. Shelby, however, assured Biesca, whom he liked, that he would get his howitzers back, and as an earnest of good faith, again placed the $16,000 in the Customs House for safe keeping.

Shelby's men were never ones to hold a grudge, and incredible as it may seem, a short time after the massacre in the plaza they were back in the wine shops of the bordellos, laughing, whooping, and singing cavalry songs to the girls of those establishments.

The day had been full of surprises, and it was not over yet. Standing in front of his headquarters with three of four officers, and discussing the arrangements for returning the howitzers, Shelby heard a shout like an Indian war whoop. Looking down the street, he saw three men, two of whom he recognized. They were Joe Moreland, brother of James, and William Fell, and they had a prisoner. Though the man looked like anything but a desperate character, Fell and Moreland evidently considered him a great prize, for they were guarding him elaborately with drawn sabres and egging him along with the muzzles of their revolvers.

The prisoner proved to be a shifty-eyed individual, not a Mexican, with a wisp of a beard and with frightened, though intelligent, eyes. A crowd of soldiers gathered around him.

"Who the hell's that?" asked Shelby.

Moreland was in a mood to make a speech. Pointing to his trembling charge, he delivered himself of these remarks:

"Make way, Missourians, and therefore barbarians, for the only living and animated specimen of the Genus Polyglot now upon the North American Continent. Look upon him, you heathens, and uncover yourselves. Draw nigh unto him, you savages, and fall upon your knees. Touch him, you blood drinkers, and make the sign of the cross."

This was Southern platform eloquence, and there was no more appreciative audience for such than the men of the former Missouri Cavalry Division.

"What did you call him?" a voice rang out.

"A polyglot, you Feejee Islander; a living dictionary, a human mausoleum with the bones of fifty languages; a lusus naturae, a royal

nonesuch and a sine qua non; a paragon of perspicacity without a
peer in prolixity; a gringo in the land of garlic and a guardian of the
greaser gold. In short, let me introduce the clerk of the Customs
House."

The prisoner, who by now had stopped shivering, was indeed something of a curiosity. He said that he had been born of Creole parents
in New Orleans, that his name was Dupré, and that he had been
everywhere in the world and seen everything. His knowledge of
languages would seem to bear out at least a part of his story: besides
being able to speak English, French, Spanish, German, and Italian, he
said, he was proficient in modern Greek, ancient Arabic, and a number
of Indian dialects, both Eastern and American. His native language,
he said, was Gumbo French, and his linguistic accomplishments had
earned for him the appointment of clerk of the Customs House in
Piedras Negras.

He charmed Shelby and his entire company from the beginning.
Shelby, who was never so happy as in the company of odd fish, like
the locomotive-happy Englishman, ordered that a party be held in
Dupré's honor immediately, at regimental headquarters. It lasted far
into the night, Dupré matching the stories of Shelby's men with exotic tales of adventure in many lands, of which he himself was the
hero. It must have been one of the greatest lie swaps of all time, and
a credit to the storyteller's art.

The newcomer also proved to have a good singing voice, and Major
Edwards says that "he remained late over his wine, singing songs in
all manner of languages and boasting in all manner of tongues."

As dawn approached, Dupré was invited to stay and share a bunk
with the gringos, but he bowed himself out, in a grave and courtly
manner, expressing gratitude for their hospitality and promising to
return on the morrow for more *aguardiente*. The soothing charm of
his voice, says Edwards, fell upon the bemused Missourians like the
feeling of benediction which follows prayer.

That morning he stole $2,000 of their money. As clerk of the Cus-
toms House, of course, he had the key.

When the money was counted and the loss discovered, Biesca
swore, and Shelby could not believe his eyes; but $2,000 was gone and
the Polyglot was the only man who had the key.

Such was the spell he had woven over Shelby and his followers,
however, that they did not hang him at all, but forgave him; and be-

fore they departed, Shelby gave him a beautiful ivory-handled pistol, worked in gold, as a souvenir.

When the brigade left Piedras Negras, the Polyglot still had their $2,000.[6]

21. *Across the Sabinas*

THE BRIGADE marched south at daybreak, while Piedras Negras slept. There is a ridge in the back of the town, and as the column trotted onto rising ground, Shelby halted his men for one last look backward across the Rio Grande. The day was clear and golden, the river a lazy cattle stream, and the fields of Texas were green in the shimmering haze. Above the fort on the hill, back there at Eagle Pass, a faded Confederate flag hung motionless, dull red in the morning sun. The hats of the brigade came off, and Shelby's hat, no longer decorated with the plume.

Bearded and brown as Mexicans, swathed in cartridge belts and loaded down with all manner of gear, the sun glinting on the handles of their bowie knives and pistols, they gazed silently at the mirage of the flag on the Texas shore. They would not see that sight again. Then, at a command from Shelby, which the platoon leaders echoed, they replaced their hats, swung round in their saddles, and urged their horses forward. They looked back no more. Ahead lay Monterrey and the Great Plateau of Mexico, seven thousand feet up in the invisible distance, and beneath them the broad highway of the conquistadores.

A horseman in a sombrero came panting up to overtake them. Shelby reined in his horse and took the man's extended hand, although he could not remember having seen him before.

"Amigo!" said the Mexican.

"Friend, yes," said Shelby. "*Que va?* You wish to join us?"

The Mexican shook his head. "No, señor," he said. "I wish to warn you. An American saved my life once, in Texas. Perhaps I can repay the favor to his countrymen. You are riding toward the Sabinas. Beware of ambush."

"Ambush?" asked Shelby.

"This is evil country, señor. Beware of the Sabinas." He wheeled his horse and rode away.

Shelby turned to Ben Elliott. "That fellow thinks he knows something," he said, "and maybe he does, at that. Keep your eyes sharp."

The march went on, along the hard rock road. It was desolate country, but within a few miles the flat, square roofs of an adobe village mushroomed in the plain. The village seemed at peace, and undefended. There was no cover as far as the eye could reach. Shelby ruled out the possibility of ambush here. The column would rest, for the day was coming hot, and he would send a few men ahead to reconnoitre.

In the village street, a sight presented itself that caused the faces of the brigade to go white beneath their tan, and their horses to rear and neigh shrilly. The village was a thing of horror. Guerrillas had been there—the bloodthirsty guerrillas of Mexico whose refinements of cruelty would make a Quantrill or an Anderson blench. The entire population of the village had been wiped out in an orgy of sadistic, senseless slaughter. The broken bodies of men, women, and children lay everywhere, attended by dogs and vultures. Many had died in torture. "Men hung suspended from door facings literally flayed alive. Huge strips of skin dangled from them as tattered garments might hang. Under some a slow fire had been kindled, until strangulation came as a tardy mercy for relief. There were the bodies of some children among the slain, and one beautiful woman, not yet attacked by the elements, seemed only asleep." As the brigade rode into the silent street, the vultures flapped away and the carrion dogs backed off, snarling. Hardened as they were to the sights of the Kansas frontier and the rapine and slaughter of four years of war, the men of the Missouri Cavalry felt sick, some of them, and the air was blue with profanity and revulsion as the riders jerked their horses steady.

Pity and horror swept over Shelby, but he ordered the column through the village at full speed: the victims were beyond help, and to halt and give them decent burial might expose the brigade to attack. As he rode beside Ben Elliott he said shortly, "If worst comes to worst, Colonel, keep one pistol ball for yourself." Elliott, "that grim Saul who never smiled," slapped his dragoon's holster in agreement. He had taken away the scalping knives of his Comanches before sending them into battle, but his savages of the reservation would never have been guilty of the butcheries he had seen in this Mexican village.

The men were in a vicious and introspective mood, a new experience for them, as they rode on. They had seen nothing in this God-forsaken country but treachery and sudden death. Plainly the French did not rule in Mexico. No one ruled in Mexico. As a civilized country it was a nightmare; the very earth of Mexico cried out for an iron hand to take over.

The same thought occurred simultaneously to Jo Shelby and John Edwards, riding with Elliott at the head of the column. With 50,000 men from over the border, this country could be had for the taking. Not for a Maximilian or a Juárez, but for the stricken South: the white people of the subjugated states who would welcome the chance the flee from oppression. Once this country could be policed into a semblance of law and order, and the guerrillas hanged, the fertile lands of Mexico could create a Paradise for the Southern people. Let the Yankees have their Black Republic. In Mexico there was land for all: not to be wrested from the wilderness, as in Kansas and the western states, but simply to be scratched with a hoe to produce every sort of agricultural wealth in abundance. That was it! Resettle Mexico with the people of the South, and raise the Stars and Bars again— over the Palace of Chapultepec! Edwards' brain reeled, and a wild light came into his eyes as he rode.

Magruder saw his expression, and mistook his emotion for horror inspired by the sights they had left behind.

"Never mind, John," he said. "Today is the third of July. Tomorrow is the Fourth. Maybe we'll see fireworks."

Edwards nodded. He was thinking of Maximilian, and the throne he could not hold.

Toward evening the brigade encountered two deserters from the French Foreign Legion at Monterrey. They were Austrians, sick of a dog's life in the Legion, and Texas-bound. Shelby questioned them as to the road ahead. They had crossed the Sabinas at the main ford, and they had not seen a living soul. After giving them food and brandy, Shelby bade them good luck, and they tramped off. The brigade pitched camp where it was, and next morning Shelby sent D. A. Williams ahead with twenty men to reconnoitre. As Williams trotted off with his detachment, Shelby called his officers together.

"The logical place for an ambush is beyond the Sabinas," he said. "Williams has gone ahead to smoke them out. We shall have no peace until we scatter them. According to those fellows who were taking French leave, there are fords in the river where the crossing is easy and where we can be shot down like dogs. I shall try none of them. When we have caught up with Williams again, we shall find our own crossing, and when the bugle sounds, form your men in fours and follow me. Our first object is to get across the river; after that we shall have to see."

It was simple cavalry strategy, of the kind that works well. Jeb Stuart had used it superbly when he went on the Chambersburg raid in 1864, while all the North was watching. Stuart traveled home with his hostages so far west of the fords of the Potomac that he was in the Valley of Virginia before the enemy knew he had left Pennsylvania. Shelby did not know where the river might be crossed, but as always he relied on his intuition. He meant to cross at a seemingly impassable point and strike the enemy in his flank, or in the rear if possible. It was the oldest trick in his bag; he had used it to good advantage at Carthage, on his first day of battle, when he had frightened Sigel into running twenty miles to Sarcoxie with all of his artillery, and had almost got the famous Dutchman courtmartialed.

Ten men would go ahead to draw the enemy's fire when the river was reached; and Shelby called for volunteers. So many responded that lots were drawn, and those who drew the short straws were McDougall, Maurice Langhorne, James·Wood, George Winship, Ras Woods, James Kirtley, James Rudd, James Chiles, James Cundiff, and William Fell. Colonel Ben Elliott would command. The main body would follow him.

The plan is set; every man understands it, and the march begins again. It is three o'clock of a hot Fourth of July afternoon, and the dust kicked up by the column settles in the throats of the men. They empty their canteens and clatter ahead toward the river.

Williams has accomplished his mission when they catch up with him again. He has spotted skirmishers in the dense underbrush on the other side of the river. All his horsemen have to do is show themselves: shots from the opposite side ring out at once. Nobody is hit, but the volley has halted Williams. His orders were to uncover the ambush, not to attack it, and he has retreated beyond their range and out of sight to wait for Shelby.

But he has done more than find the enemy. He knows their number. On most of the four hundred battlefields of Missouri his ear has been trained to estimate the strength of the enemy by the volume of his musketry; he knows that there must be eight hundred men over there as well as if he had counted their crouching forms. The guerrilla force is nearly the equal of Shelby's own.

The column comes up through the yellow dust to the green line of the river, and Shelby confers with Williams. Their conversation is brief.

"You found them, it seems."

"Yes, General."

"How many?"

"Eight hundred. Armed with muskets."

"Good. Take your place in the front ranks. Elliott goes ahead with ten men. I shall lead the column."

To Elliott he gives the order to advance. "The sooner over, the sooner done," he says. "Take the water as you find it, and ride straight forward."

Elliott's ten plunge down the bank and into the stream, ten abreast. The Sabinas is a rushing mountain stream and its banks are slippery, uncertain shale. At this point, the current races past jagged pinnacles of rock, upthrust through roiling white spume, and hurls itself downward into a waterfall some distance to the left. It is a rough crossing, full of precipices and quicksands, and a sensible man would ride on here, even without the menace of hidden rifles on the other side.

The Mexicans and Indians, their eyes on the ford, do not see Elliott's ten at first, struggling through the deep water. By the time the commotion has attracted the attention of skirmishers in the woods, and a few scattered shots have been fired, they have gained the other side and scrambled onto a path leading into the brush. A solid blast of musketry now engulfs them, but the Americans ride into the brush with sabres swinging. Not a pistol shot is fired.

Shrieks from the sabred Mexicans echo through the Valley of the Sabinas, to the last outpost of the guerrilla camp. There is a turbulence in the woods as the guerrillas mass to meet the attack. Shelby's men are in the river, their horses churning wildly as they strain their heads for shore. A new volley of musketry breaks out, sweeping the terrain where Elliott's men are at work. For a moment there is such a heavy powder pall on the bank that the men in the river cannot see what is happening to Elliott, but they have no time to speculate. The diversion has not been complete; a murderous fire is suddenly turned on the river, and a dozen saddles are emptied before the men's horses gain the bank, and the bodies are carried away to the falls. Others are wounded, but manage to gain the shore safely, and are helped by their comrades; but the entire brigade is over now and the guerrillas are flanked. There is a path leading into the *brasada*; it is the only escape route of the guerrillas, and it is closed now. A bugle sounds in Shelby's ranks and the brigade swarms into battle formation on either side of the path. Revolvers crash as the attack is mounted. Two-handed now, with sabre and pistol, they ride down the enemy.

Edwards says that "the attack was a hurricane." [1] The surprise had been almost complete, and the result was a massacre. Two hundred bandits were killed, and the rest vanished into the landscape. The Southerners found themselves suddenly alone in the guerrilla camp, except for the dead and wounded and the drifting clouds of revolver smoke. Remembering the villagers flayed alive and the children dead in their mother's arms, the Americans took no prisoners.

Shelby's casualties were thirty-seven wounded and nineteen dead. He paid a high price, but he got across the river safely and routed a force equal to his own; he assured the safety of his march to Monterrey, and did it with revolvers and sabres alone. If he had crossed the river by the ford, his command would have been butchered.

Elliott's volunteers suffered the greatest number of casualties though none were killed. He himself was badly wounded, and had to be dragged from beneath his horse. Cundiff had a flesh wound in his left arm, not serious; Winship and McDougall were down, unconscious, and bleeding badly; Fell had a musket ball in his thigh; and Jim Wood's left wrist was shattered, but he had stayed in the fight, with his bridle between his teeth, using his right hand to fire his revolver until it was empty.

The mad Englishman, he of the locomotives, was mortally hurt. Riding at the side of Shelby and Edwards, he had his horse killed under him, but seized another and caught up with them again. A musket ball struck his ankle and split his leg bone to the knee, but still he drove ahead, firing his revolver. Fifty paces farther on, another ball, striking him in the chest, knocked him from the saddle and put him out of the fight.

Now he is lying on a soft bed of blankets as Dr. Tisdale examines him, blood welling from a great blotch across his chest. He is done for, but he seems to care less for that than for something else. In a racked voice he asks if anyone can speak French.

Governor Reynolds can. He kneels beside the dying man, who whispers something in his ear.

"Get a pencil and paper," Reynolds says, and Major Edwards supplies it. "Why is he speaking French?" asks Edwards.

"He doesn't want the others to understand him," says Reynolds. The Englishman begins to speak, though with difficulty. It was nearly sunset when the guerrillas fled. Now it is getting dark. Reynolds writes rapidly.

The story was the usual sordid one, and straight out of a dime novel: he was a ticket-of-leave man, cashiered from the army for killing a brother officer in a duel, a wanderer over the face of the earth, disowned by country and kin; he did not want to die nameless and unknown, in a no man's land of the Mexican desert. He desired the British minister at Mexico City to notify his parents that he had died a brave man.

The strange and pitiful part of the story is that it may even have been true. There is an old saying that you cannot burlesque life. In this case, the only man who would ever know whether the story was true or not would be Sir James Scarlett, the British minister (wonderful name!). His would be the responsibility of communicating with the dead Englishman's parents, after duly receiving the message from the hands of Governor Reynolds in Mexico City.

One may read the dying man's last words, a good five hundred of them, on page 35 of Major Edwards' book, but they are not among the best of Edwards, and he might have done better if he had had more original material to work with, or if he had understood French. The men of the Iron Brigade buried the Englishman tenderly, reverently, and another cross was added to the forest of crosses in Mexico.

Most of the wounded were up and around in a few days, although weak and sore. Shelby decided to break camp and move on, even though it would be necessary to improvise horse-borne litters for those who could not walk or ride. It would not be practical to send them back to Piedras Negras and the border, for the countryside was still infested with guerrillas. Furthermore, not one of the disabled wished to turn back.

As the brigade kept on its way, the guerrillas, though disorganized, still made their presence felt by taking pot shots at the pickets, attempting to stampede the horses, and firing muskets into the air at midnight. The continual din and the unseen presence of their skulking companions began to get on the men's nerves, especially since Shelby would not permit them to go guerrilla-hunting in the thorny countryside at night. Prodded into a constant state of alertness, they got no sleep, and their tempers grew short. Presently they began to talk of reprisals on the countryside.

For four years Shelby had dealt ruthlessly with this sort of thing, and he was stern now. The time had come to exercise the authority which had been voted him on the plains of Corsicana. He ordered the column under arms and faced the men, the old wrath showing in his countenance. His eyes moved quickly over the line, picking out the malcontents. To them he addressed the ultimatum.

"There are some signs among you of bad discipline," he said, "and I have called you out that you may be told of it. What have you to complain about? That there are those who follow on your track to kill you? Very well, complain of them if you choose, and fight them to your heart's content, but lift not a single hand against the Mexicans who are at home and non-combatants. We are invaders, it is true; but we are not murderers. Those who are shall not follow me. He who robs, who insults women, who oppresses the unarmed and aged, is an outcast to the good fellowship of this command, and upon him a soldier's work will be done. He will be driven forth out of this camp as an enemy to us all."

In guerrilla country, they knew what that meant.

Shelby paused. Then, to show in what affection he held them, he said, "Hereafter, be as you have ever been, brave and true and honorable."

There was no more mutiny.

The marches became shorter and the bivouacs anything but agreeable. They were in mountain country now, with altitude increasing at every step, and the thin air had a razor edge to the lungs. Although the rainy season had not set in, some chill rain fell, and both men and horses suffered. The horses, unused to the higher altitude, did not acclimatize themselves rapidly. They began snuffling and developing a high fever. Dr. John Tisdale,[2] whose fifty years rested on him as lightly as "the night air in the mountains of San Juan Aguilar," turned veterinarian and ordered that the animals be swathed in mountains of blankets, and as the sweat poured out he poured the whiskey in. When the fever broke, the horses were given a few days to convalesce and enjoy such rocky pasture as they could find, while the men sat hunched in their overcoats about the fires, and did not even bother to hunt small game. Shelby frowned on it anyway, as the guerrillas seemed to be quiet, and he did not wish to stir them up. For the time being he did not even send out scouting parties.

The guerrillas had not given up, however. The gringos had silver in their pockets, a thousand serviceable horses, each man an Enfield or Sharpe's rifle, shiny new Navy or dragoon pistols for which a Mexican would sell his soul, and untold wealth of other description in their saddle bags. To loot their camp would be second only to looting Mexico City, and the two leaders of the bandits in this neighborhood, Juan Anselmo and Antonio Flores, lay awake thinking of it at night, and dreamed feverishly of it when they slept. Anselmo was a renegade priest and Flores a young Cuban who had sold his sister to a wealthy *hacendado* and turned robber when the money was spent.

Two days' journey from Lampazos, on the other side of the Paso de Palmas, the brigade halted for the night in a palm grove in the pass. It was a chilly night, but moonlight, and through the two spurs of the mountain range which flanked the pass, the men could see the plain, like a bay of shining silver, stretching away along the highroad to the town. On one side of the road, under the frosty moon, they could see a casual cemetery of white wooden crosses, the inevitable crosses that dotted all the roads of Mexico they had traversed. One could count the deeds of violence in Mexico, says Major Edwards, by the number of crosses which were everywhere.

With this grim reminder of mortality in front of him, Shelby scattered his sentinels a little wider than usual that night as the men bedded down. By midnight, after the fires were out and a mist had replaced the moonlight, a pistol shot rang out. Shelby lifted himself up in his blankets and roused John Thrailkill, the old guerrilla, who shared his outdoor sleeping quarters.

"Who has the post at the mouth of the pass?" he asked Thrailkill.

"Joe Macey," said Thrailkill.

"Something's up," said Shelby. "Joe Macey never fired at a shadow in his life."

He sat upright in the blankets, and the two men listened, as minutes went by, but there were no more sounds.

"Either hit the——or scared the——out of him," said Thrailkill, and rolled over again.

As the silence continued, Shelby soon lay down again, and slept instantly, as he always did. An hour later he was awakened again, this time by a blinding flash, followed by the report of a volley of musketry. The whole camp struggled to their feet this time, cursing and stamping their feet as they shed their blankets.

The volley had been fired by a party of Mexicans who had crept down the side of the mountain to the edge of a stream and had taken point-blank aim at the camp. By a miracle, no one had been hit. The volley had passed over the heads of the men sleeping on the ground.

Unclad, barefoot, and fighting mad, the brigade now surged forward with revolver and sabre. Muskets crashed as they surged up the mountainside in the cold darkness, and many went down, but the rifle flashes served as a guide to the rest. And the Mexicans were trapped—they had tethered their horses on the other side of the mountain until they should return at leisure, after wiping out the gringo camp and gathering up the loot. No match for Shelby's borderers, they went down before the revolver and sabre—those that did not flee. Sixty-nine of them were dead when the revolver smoke cleared and the sabres were dropped. Two prizes were among them—the dead bodies of Anselmo and Flores, the guerrilla chieftains. Eleven Americans were dead, too, and seventeen wounded. But the band that had tried to trap them on the Sabinas was wiped out.

Lampazos was another Piedras Negras, a sizable village on the plain at the foot of the San Juan Range, and exactly half way to Monterrey. Shelby had learned his lesson at Piedras Negras, and he marched his brigade through the town without a halt until he reached a camp site beyond the suburbs.

Lampazos was enjoying a feast day as the bronzed strangers marched through, and Shelby ordered the men confined to camp. His own eye had been caught by the swirl of skirts without petticoats, and the low cut camisas of the laughing girls, as they marched through the celebration, and Shelby's faithful biographer observes that he was "unwilling to trust his men to the perils of so much nakedness."

A large number of Shelby's followers, however, were determined to be exposed to such perils, and after guards had been posted for the night, they managed to slip past them and back into town. The wine shops and the señoritas were waiting. Jealous lovers were waiting too, and three of the men soon wished that they had remained in camp. These three gay caballeros—Walker, Boswell, and Crockett—attended the fiesta and drank sizable quantities of red Catalan wine. As they walked back through the streets in the moonlight, they saw a beautiful, dark-haired Mexican girl standing in the doorway of a house. The men called out to her, and she answered with a laugh. This is nothing in a country where women look at men as boldly as men look at women, but Crockett went up to her and laid a hand on her shoulder. He also asked for a kiss, and when it was refused, attempted to take it. In doing so, the girl's *rebosa*, the garment which serves in Mexico for both shawl and brassiere, fell away, exposing her bosom.

As Crockett attempted to seize her, the girl gave a high-pitched feminine cry of distress, which brought half a dozen Mexican gallants flying. The three Americans were unarmed, or there would have been a repetition of the affair at Piedras Negras; as it was, they did not make their escape until Boswell had been stabbed three times and Walker had been shot through both cheeks and the tongue. Crockett, the cause of it all, was unhurt.

The Mexicans did not pursue them. Fearing reprisals at the hands of the gringos' comrades, they vanished into the shadows of Lampazos. One young Mexican who had taken no part in the melee, but had watched the affair from the sidelines, came boldly up to Crockett, announced that he was the girl's brother, and demanded satisfaction. Crockett now was interested only in getting his wounded companions back to the camp, and he merely snarled at the Mexican to make himself scarce. The Mexican followed them to the camp, his eyes smoldering.

The sound of the shots had roused Shelby and the rest of the brigade, but Shelby checked a torrent of profanity when he saw how badly two of them were wounded—Boswell slashed from throat to waist and Walker dumb from the wound in his tongue, the lower half of his face smeared with blood. Shelby summoned Dr. Tisdale with a roar. Then he saw the Mexican.

"What do you want?" he asked.

The Mexican pointed to Crockett. "This man has outraged my sister," he said. "I demand satisfaction."

Shelby turned on Crockett. "Is this true?" he asked.

Crockett shook his head. "I meant no harm to the girl," he said. "I had a few drinks, and I put my arm around her."

"What business had you to touch her at all?" demanded Shelby. "How many times must I tell you that the man who does such things is no follower of mine? You will give her brother satisfaction."

"Very well," said Crockett sullenly. "Somebody give me a gun."

"No, no, señor!" said the Mexican. "Not the gun. The knife. Is the American afraid of the knife?"

"He has the choice of weapons," said Shelby, but Crockett growled like an animal and waved protocol aside.

"Somebody give me a knife," he said.

A bowie knife was handed him, and the Mexican produced a blade of his own.

"All right," said Shelby, "I tolerate this, but only according to the rules. At first blood, the encounter is over."

Both men nodded, and Shelby gave the signal. The Mexican struck first, a wild thrust aimed at Crockett's ribs. Crockett fended off the blow with only a scratch on his forearm. Then he struck downward, through the Mexican's shoulder, burying the blade some inches deep. The man shuddered, choked, and fell backward into the grass, with the knife protruding from his chest cavity like a cross.

No need for Dr. Tisdale here. Cover him up, and send a litter back into the village, and listen for a woman's scream.

22. *Jeanningros*

IN AN EDITORIAL written in 1887, Major Edwards said, "First and last, forty thousand French soldiers were operating in Mexico at one time, to say nothing of the native forces enlisted in the cause of Maximilian, and yet the very best they could do was hold the towns while the Juaristas held the country. All they ever owned, or occupied, or controlled, or felt safe in, was the extent of the territory which their cannon covered." [1]

Colonel Jeanningros, soon to be General Jeanningros, held Monterrey with five thousand French and Mexican troops, including the four regiments of the Foreign Legion, the Third French Zouaves, and two regiments of the Imperial Mexican Army; he was Maximilian's front line of defense against Juárez and the Republicans in the northern tier of states. In the Legion, which was composed of the finest cutthroats of four continents, he had tough, professional soldiers who could match the Mexican guerrillas in ferocity: Germans, Austrians, Americans, English, Irish, Arabs, Turks, Negroes, Belgians, and Swiss. [2] In the Third Zouaves he had one of the crack regiments of the French Army, which was cut to pieces and passed away from service at Gravelotte in 1870. In the Mexican Imperial regiments he had mercenaries of uncertain dependability, whose loyalty was assured by the presence of the Legion and the Zouaves.

Jeanningros was a career soldier who had been in the French Army for thirty years and looked it. He was addicted to absinthe and his excesses in the name of "discipline" had kept him from promotion after promotion, though he would soon be a brigadier; and the knowledge that he had missed a marshal's baton rankled, driving him to even greater extremes of cruelty. The execution wall at Monterrey was stained with the life blood of French soldiers who had been shot for guardhouse offenses; and Jeanningros had chosen, as his right hand, another sadist, Colonel Achille Dupin of the *contra-guerrillas*, a madman who cut off the hands of male Mexicans so that they might not be tempted to bear arms against the Emperor, and hanged an unoffending *hacendado* because it was a "pity" that a tree in the man's yard had never borne fruit. He had been cashiered once, though subsequently restored to his rank, for his conduct as a looter and murderer in the Peking campaign; and he had "parodied the speech of Warren Hastings" at his trial, sneering contemptuously at the court-martial, "When I saw mountains of gold and precious stones piled up around me, and when I think of the paltry handfuls taken away, by God, Mr. President, I am astonished at my own moderation."

This was the pair waiting for Shelby and the Iron Brigade at Monterrey. Jeanningros had been informed accurately of Shelby's movements ever since he crossed the Rio Grande. Agents had brought him the news of the sale of the Confederate artillery to the Juaristas, and it was on receipt of this news that he had promised to hang them all. He was not under any misapprehension as to the fighting qualities of the Confederate soldier, however, having watched the progress of the Civil War with interest from south of the border, and he counseled restraint when Dupin wished to meet the brigade head-on with his *contra-guerrillas.*

"Wait a while," he said to Dupin. "We must catch them before we hang them."

Meanwhile Shelby had marched to within a mile of Monterrey, in sight of the tricolor waving over the barracks. He pitched camp, fed his horses, and threw out a picket line. Comfortably established, he asked Major Edwards to write a communication to Jeanningros and Governor Reynolds to put it into French; John Thrailkill and Rainey McKinney would carry it in under a flag of truce.

The message read: "General. I have the honor to report that I am within one mile of your command. Preferring exile to surrender, I have left my own country to seek service in that held by His Imperial Majesty, the Emperor Maximilian. Shall it be peace or war between us? If the former, with your permission, I shall enter your lines at once, claiming at your hands the courtesy due from one soldier to another. If the latter, I propose to attack you immediately. Respectfully, Jos. O. Shelby."

As Thrailkill and McKinney rode into the square, a bugle sounded, and the garrison turned out, but the white flag was respected. The messengers were conducted to Jeanningros, who received them not unfavorably. He read the message, as Dupin looked on. Then he smiled. The message had had the effect which Shelby had intended that it should. He had suspected that the Frenchman would appreciate a nose-thumbing gesture; Jeanningros did.

"Tell your general to march in immediately," he roared to Thrailkill and McKinney. "By God, he is the only soldier yet that has come out of Yankeedom. The Emperor will bid him welcome! Tell him he is my guest, he and the members of his staff. Tell him to come in!"

A smile hovered over Thrailkill's childlike guerrilla face, and he glanced at McKinney. Old Jo had done it again. They saluted smartly and went back to their horses.

It was an exultant Shelby, surrounded by his brilliant "cabinet of

Confederates"—Magruder, Reynolds, and others—who heard the message which Thrailkill delivered. They had come a long way to the garrison of Monterrey, and they had fought literally for every inch of the way, but it was over now—the Emperor's commander was their friend and colleague—and Shelby's optimism knew no bounds. They had done right, he pointed out, to choose the Empire. Major Edwards proposed a toast—he never lacked the excuse—to Maximilian and Carlota. The glasses were handed around.

"To king and queen and country."

Neither Edwards nor Shelby had forgotten that they were knights errant, and that their mission was to rescue a lady fair.

If it all seems ridiculous now—the speech, the posturings, and the absurd code of honor—it must be remembered that the Southerner of the mid-nineteenth century is a breed as extinct as that of Quïjote and Sancho Panza; he was a curious, but by no means unadmirable, bundle of characteristics which were typical of an America that has vanished—Mark Twain's America. Twain poked gentle fun at it, and it vanished, but Twain himself spoke its language with a robust bellow when he wanted to, and no man spoke it better, for he was a Missourian. And the Missourian was the Southerner of the West. He loved grand gestures and he loved to make a speech—if you had asked Major Edwards the time of day he would have told you how to make a watch—and he was sometimes hard to get along with, but basically he was a very human fellow, a man of good will, who believed that life could be glorious; and sometimes it was. And when the chips were down, he proved that he was one of the best soldiers in the world, that he could live without food and almost without water, and that he feared nothing in this world or the next.[3] He himself would have been the first to admit that his strength was as the strength of ten, because his heart was pure.

Colonel Jeanningros outdid himself in the entertainment of his guests. They were assigned officer's quarters, and Jeanningros himself led them into the banquet hall for dinner, where a table had been set worthy of the representative of a great monarch, Louis Napoleon, and a soon-to-be brigadier of France. He was a superb host, and "emphatic in all his declarations." The talk was soldier talk, and turned on the Civil War, of course, which Jeanningros discussed intelligently, and on the campaigns of Louis Napoleon in which he had served, in the Crimea, in Italy—where Maximilian had won a regency—in Algeria, and in China in 1860, when the Allies had opened up the Treaty Ports.

The eyes of both Jeanningros and the silver-bearded, bronzed Dupin lit up with pleasure when they spoke of the Chinese Treaty Ports and of Pekin. Pekin! Ah, messieurs, there the greatest loot in history took place, the loot of the Imperial Summer Palace at Pekin!

As Jeanningros waxed eloquent, Shelby and his company found themselves in imagination outside the gate of a fairyland palace, the summer and autumn palace of the Chinese Emperor twelves miles from Pekin, in the splendid autumn of September, 1860—with the British and French caissons of the Joint Allied Forces rumbling past its undefended walls. . . .

. . . Figure to yourselves, messieurs, a Chinese palace fashioned after the Palace of Versailles, and laid out on the exact measurements of Versailles, by Jesuit priests from France, for a Chinese Emperor who wanted nothing but the best. In 1860 we were on our way, with the British, to the capital city of Pekin, to force the Emperor to open the Treaty Ports, in accordance with his word; but there had been Chinese treachery before we reached Pekin, and when we reached the Imperial Summer Palace, where great dragons gaily switched their three-meter tails in the air to support the roofs of the pagodas, we decided to have a look at the residence of the Emperor.

. . . The Emperor had left his palace in a hurry, not bothering even to lock the doors behind him, or to carry anything away. In this palace of his were all the art and treasures of the vast Chinese Empire, the most exquisite products of uncounted generations of artists, gem cutters, and gold and silversmiths; all of the tribute which fear or admiration had drawn from the great and humble; all the gifts of the Kings and Emperors of Europe; all the bric-a-brac and curiosities presented by merchants and ship captains wishing to do business in China. . . .

. . . It was like a one-franc bazaar, messieurs, in which every item, instead of being worth nineteen cents, was worth $19,000. In the apartment of the Empress alone there was enough to dress from head to foot ten thousand princesses of the Arabian Nights, so that it would be impossible for the Caliph of Bagdad, a judge of such matters, to find occasion for changing the position of a single pin or to alter a single arrangement. All is of silk, satin, damask, fur, with embroideries sometimes as delicate as spider's webs, sometimes as heavy as those on a bishop's cope; it is a brilliant display of birds, butterflies, and flowers fresher than those in the sun, with diamond dewdrops in their perfumed calyxes. . . .

. . . Our troops staggered out of the apartments of the Empress half smothered in the folds of brocade and pieces of silk; others stuffed rubies, sapphires, pearls, and jewelry into their pockets and their hats. Silks and fabrics worth twenty millions were trampled into the mud; engraved ivories were ground into the earth by the wheels of wagons and caissons; soldiers lighted their pipes with priceless and beautiful vellum manuscripts.

. . . That night was a nightmare in camp. It was like a New Year's Eve celebration in Bedlam. The French soldier, messieurs, is passionately fond of clocks and mechanical toys, and each soldier had his mechanical bird, his music box, his monkey, his trumpeter, or his rabbit. The night was hideous with the caterwauling of rabbits playing tambourines, cuckoos screeching, mechanical musicians fluting sweetly, music boxes emitting waltzes and quadrilles, cocks crowing, clarionets blaring, horns and cornets sounding, and soldiers guffawing their heads off. . . .

The entranced Shelby nodded. Soldiers were the same the world over. "What a place to loot!" he said.

"So said Blucher of London," commented Jeanningros. "The looting took three days, although some of us," and he looked significantly in the direction of Dupin, "were courtmartialed. However, the Emperor had left his palace unlocked, and the Chinese of the countryside had already attempted to set fire to it in order that what they had stolen should not be discovered. It was better for the Allies to loot it. Those Chinese would have cabbaged everything." [4]

As the cigars and brandy were passed, Shelby took advantage of the genial frame of mind of his host to ask the question that was in his mind. "His Majesty the Emperor Maximilian, what kind of man is he, Colonel Jeanningros?"

"Ah, the Austrian," said Jeanningros. "You should see him to understand him. More of a scholar than a king, good at botany, a poet on occasion, a traveler who gathers curiosities and writes books, a saint over his wine and a sinner among his cigars, in love with his wife, believing in destiny more than in drilled battalions, good Spaniard in all but deceit and treachery; honest, earnest, tender-hearted and sincere. His faith in the liars who surround him is too strong, and his soul too pure for the deeds that must be done. He cannot kill as we Frenchmen do. He knows nothing of diplomacy. In a nation of thieves and cutthroats he goes devoutly to mass, endows hospitals, says his prayers and sleeps a good man's sleep in the Palace of Chapultepec. Bah! His days are numbered, nor can all the power of France keep his crown upon his head, if indeed it can keep that head upon his shoulders."

Jeanningros checked himself abruptly. He had said too much.

"Has he the confidence of Bazaine?" asked General Clark.

"The Marshal, you mean?" repeated Jeanningros. "Oh ho! The Marshal keeps his own counsel. Besides, I have not seen the Marshal since coming northward." He smiled, and changed the subject. "Have you journeyed far, General Clark?"

Clark smiled in return. He realized that the subject was closed. He said that he had journeyed from Texas, and hoped to continue as far as Mexico City.

"Ah, Mexico City! It is not too unlike Paris," said Jeanningros, "save for the great cows at court, who would never be permitted as ladies-in-waiting at Versailles."

It was daybreak before the party broke up—the Americans to sleep, Jeanningros to sign a death warrant.

23. Parras and Encarnación

SHELBY seldom had need for sleep when there was anything important afoot, and as he walked about in the dazzling morning sunshine of Monterrey, his head clearing of the champagne and the brandy, he thought more and more of Jeanningros's contemptuous assertion that not all the power of France could keep Maximilian on his throne. This was precisely his own opinion. If Maximilian was to maintain himself, he must have an army other than French, and he, Shelby, could supply it. The answer to the problem was as simple as that. It was an uncomplicated solution of the kind that appealed to Shelby, and he presented himself to Jeanningros again as soon as the Frenchman was available.

"I don't know what you think of things here, Colonel," he said, "or what the future has in store for the Empire, but one thing is certain and I shall tell you the plain truth. The Federal government has no love for you French or your French occupation of Mexico. If diplomacy can't get you out, infantry divisions will. I left a large army concentrating on the banks of the Rio Grande and all the faces of the men were looking straight forward into Mexico. Will France fight? I think not; if your Emperor had meant to be serious in this thing he would have formed an alliance with Jefferson Davis long ago. Now it is too late. Nevertheless, if you will give me a port as a basis of operations, I can organize an American force capable of keeping Maximilian on his throne, composed of men who would be delighted to fight Yankees again. If left discretionary with me, that port shall be either Guaymas or Mazatlan, on the Pacific coast. The Californians love adventure, and many leaders among them have already sent me messengers with overtures. I am not informed as to the wishes of the Emperor; but the French cannot remain and he cannot rule over Mexicans with Mexicans. The plan I propose is his only hope. You know Bazaine better than I do. What would Bazaine say to all this?"

Jeanningros was equally frank. "Bazaine would say that he is daily expecting orders from Louis Napoleon to reduce the size of the French force in Mexico, with the eventual expectation of getting out of the country entirely. That is, he would say so if he were frank. There is no love lost between Bazaine and Maximilian, but I do not think that he would be adverse to employment of Americans as soldiers of the Empire."

"I have your permission, then?"

"You have my full permission to march to the Pacific, to Guaymas or Mazatlan, or wherever you choose, and to take whatever steps you deem necessary to recruit an army for the Empire." Jeanningros rose and extended his hand.

Shelby shook his hand, and saluted. "Thank you, Colonel Jeanningros. And again, the thanks of my officers for your hospitality."

"It was for my own pleasure," said Jeanningros. "Good luck, and *au revoir.*"

The brigade camped that night on the field of Buena Vista, where Southerners and Northerners had last fought as comrades in '47. It was a beautiful view indeed, with a moon as big as a tent-leaf palm shining down on the field of Mars, and the sierras mist-hung in the distance. For Magruder it was a return to the scene of earlier glory. He had been here in '47, and to the younger men, veterans of another and bloodier war, he pointed out familiar scenes.

Here the left of the American Army had rested; there Bragg's battery crouched in the mesquite ambush; here Santa Anna had sacrificed the best blood of his men in a vain attempt to hold the highway to Saltillo; here the Lancers charged in scarlet and gold; there the Mexicans broke and fled into a ravine, with Hindman and Colonel Jefferson Davis in hot pursuit. Shelby's yellow-haired borderers listened respectfully, in the patient manner of youth toward age, and Shelby in his tent studied a map of the road to Parras, where the next French garrison lay.

The clouds which had hung about the mountains of Buena Vista were rainfilled, and as Shelby's men clanked along the broad highway westward, an inundation like that of the march from Stone Point poured out of the sky. The rainy season had begun with a vengeance. Just beyond Saltillo Shelby pitched camp in a canyon which the heavens seemed bent on turning into a river. Watch fires went out, sleep was impossible, and the wind howled down the canyon in a private war of its own with the rain. Pipes would not stay lit, and the plainsmen grumbled through the night as they waited for the mountain dawn.

No amount of bad weather ever caused Shelby to relax his rule of stationing a picket guard, and he sent four men to the mouth of the canyon, Dick Collins, James Kirtley, George Winship, and James Meadow—four of the toughest soldiers ever to draw a bead. They had Sharpe's carbines which they had picked up in Monterrey and they settled down for a night in the rain with the rifles thrust into their greatcoats. The Confederate soldier, when he was not lousy, was wet, and in the Missouri and Arkansas campaigns he had usually been both; tonight's bivouac was nothing more nor less than what he was used to.

Collins, the old battery commander, was huddled under the lee of a boulder, wide awake and soggy, and as the first light showed above the dark jaws of the canyon he saw two dark objects move. Instantly he was on his feet, the carbine moving like a finger.

Guerrillas were moving about them in the gloom, and the four were ambushed. Musketry rang out in the half light, and all four replied with their Sharpe's, but they were shooting at phantoms and before they could reload, the invisible foe caught them with a volley. Collins took a ragged wound in the shoulder, Kirtley was hit in the left arm, and Meadow and Winship were grazed. The wind was still blowing furiously and the rain was still pelting the camp as the sharp notes of the bugle sounded. The men of the brigade were fully awake, although some of them were hatless and bootless as they struggled out of their blankets. They ran toward the sound of the shots, but as they did so, rifle fire broke out in their rear. The camp was being attacked from two sides and they could see the moving forms of the Mexicans plainly.

This was work for the revolver and sabre, and they threw down their carbines and fanned out in every direction. At such close quarters their casualties were fearful. Slayback and Cundiff held the post in the rear while Shelby pressed ahead to the picket line a quarter of a mile away. He left Slayback and Cundiff fighting desperately with a detachment of twelve men, nine of whom were killed or wounded; Jim Chiles had a sudden thought for the horses and with half a dozen men pressed in that direction. Langhorne and the Kritzer brothers, Martin and John, detailed to guard the mounts, mistook them for guerrillas and opened fire. George Hall's overcoat suffered a shredded collar and he let out a profane yell of self-identification, which halted the shots; Hall's shout gave Jake Connor an idea and he lifted his powerful voice in song, a song they had heard him lead on the march to a hundred prairie battles. *"Tramp, tramp, tramp, the boys are marching!"*

It was the Confederate soldier's song—next to "Dixie"—and several guerrillas went to purgatory with the mad gringo hymn ringing in their ears. They were driven off at last; the close, reckless fighting saved the camp and scattered the desperadoes back to the hills. When Shelby was able to bring reinforcements for Slayback and Cundiff, it was all over. Edwards says that the brief, sharp fight in the canyon was "the most persistent and bloody of the expedition." He took a gallant part in it himself, but no modern reader, turning the musty leaves of his account, would ever know it. Edwards wrote more than a thousand pages on the campaigns in which he served as Shelby's shadow, but as far as the reader can tell, he might have been writing of the Punic wars; not once is his own name mentioned.

It was a sobered brigade which marched on in the rain to the

French stronghold of Parras. More than fifty of their comrades were dead, in the little more than a month since they had crossed the Rio Grande, and more than twice as many had been wounded, some badly. But neither blood nor rain could dampen the lust for life of the Iron Brigade. The plumes and the lances and the gilded ease were there—they were sure of that—just over the horizon at Parras, in the service of the Emperor. They had seen the proof at Monterrey, where Algerines in turbans and Zouaves in baggy trousers swaggered in the sun and preened themselves before the pretty Mexican girls. Soon it would be their turn for a season in the sun.

Colonel Depreuil of the French garrison at Parras was another of the officers of Louis Napoleon's army who was an unwilling exile from the boulevards of Paris. He commanded the Fifty-Second French Regiment of the Line at Parras, and Parras was the key to Sonora and Chihuahua, from which the forces of Juárez had been scattered. Depreuil's vice was brandy, and the monotony of this Mexican outpost afforded him an added excuse to indulge it. He was in many respects a fine soldier, but tyrannical and overbearing, and given to the easy fury of the alcoholic. He had been enraged by the news that the Confederates were taking refuge south of the Rio Grande, and he had sent word to Bazaine that they were robbers and plunderers who would involve the French in trouble with the United States troops on the border.

Bazaine agreed with him. Furthermore, he had heard of Shelby's march toward Sonora, and he sent a message which was lying on Depreuil's desk when Shelby arrived. Bazaine ordered that their march was to be arrested and that if they refused to return to their own country they were to report to him in Mexico City at once. The French commander at Parras was to give them no alternative.

Depreuil was rereading this message with some degree of satisfaction when Shelby and his officers entered, confident of a cordial reception. The Frenchman did not bid him be seated, but Shelby thought nothing of that; he was in too good a mood to notice trifles. He did notice, however, that it was a little early in the day for the barroom aroma which pervaded the place.

"I have called, Colonel," Shelby began, "for permission to continue my march to Sonora."

"Such permission is impossible," snapped Depreuil. "You will turn aside to Mexico."

"May I ask the reason for this sudden resolution?" asked Shelby. "General Jeanningros had no information to this effect when I left him the other day in Monterrey."

The reference to Jeanningros as a general provided the match for the fuse of Depreuil's temper.

"*Colonel* Jeanningros does not command in all Mexico," he roared, "and the devil fly away with you and your information. It is the same old game you Americans are forever trying to play—plundering, plundering, plundering!" His voice rose to a shrill pitch. "You shall not go to Sonora and you shall not stay here. And whatever you do, you shall obey!"

Shelby replaced his hat and spoke deliberately.

"It seems I am mistaken," he said. "I thought an American visiting a French soldier would find an officer and a gentleman. Ah well, one cannot always keep his hands clean; I wash mine of you. You are a slanderer and a coward."

Depreuil's knuckles whitened on his sword; the Confederate officers clapped their hands on their revolver holsters. The French guards outside the door, hearing the inflection of the voices inside, stepped across the doorsill with rifles at attention.

Depreuil pointed to Shelby's hat. "Remove that!" he ordered.

Shelby replied that he removed his hat only to beauty and to God, and that in Depreuil he saw nothing that resembled either.

The officers in the room thought for a moment that Depreuil would strike him, but instead Depreuil, with trembling underlip, said to the guards: "Retire instantly!" When they had done so he walked around his desk and faced the Rebels.

"Get out," he said, "before I outrage all hospitality and dishonor you in my own house. You shall pay for this; you shall apologize. But now, get out."

"Never," said Shelby, referring to the demand for an apology. He nodded to his officers, and they walked out together. They knew what was coming now.

Shelby sought out Governor Reynolds and sent him to Depreuil with his compliments. As the challenged party, Depreuil had the choice of weapons, and he was an expert swordsman; Shelby, on the contrary, still had a stiff right arm where the minie ball had coursed downward from his elbow. He was willing to fight Depreuil with the sword but when Governor Reynolds pointed out to Depreuil Shelby's disability, the latter agreed to pistols. The Frenchman, in fact, was as agreeable to Governor Reynolds as he had been disagreeable to Shelby. He was by no means sober but he had a code of his own, and he and Reynolds chatted for some little time. Satisfied that Shelby would blow Depreuil to Kingdom Come, now that the weapons were pistols, Reynolds was not too discouraged over Bazaine's message; it might be the best thing, after all, for Shelby to see the Emperor. Depreuil couldn't say as to the Emperor. Privately, however, he could have said as to Bazaine: The old goat had made up his mind, or perhaps Louis Napoleon had made it up for him, on the subject of dealing with Confederates.

The projected duel never took place.

At ten o'clock that night, amid a clattering of sabres and galloping of horses, Jeanningros rode into Parras on an inspection tour of the entire northern line of outposts, accompanied by four regiments of Chasseurs d'Afrique, and he found Depreuil in a regrettable condition. He also heard, in no time, that Depreuil had insulted his friend Shelby and that a duel was scheduled in a few hours. Now wearing the epaulets of a brigadier, Jeanningros placed Depreuil under arrest, a violation of which would cost him his life, and sent for Shelby. In Jeanningros's presence Depreuil, sobered now, apologized freely and frankly; by one of those coincidences with which Shelby's career was filled, he was to save Depreuil's life at the hands of the guerrillas a year later. But all the sweetness and light which obtained in Parras did not alter the fact of Bazaine's order. They would march now to Mexico City to see the Emperor Maximilian.

The katydids in the bearded cactus were singing the end of summer as Jim Wood and Yandell Blackwell took their turn at picket duty beyond the camp, the first night out from Parras. The fire had gone out, the soldiers slept, and the earth smelt sweet with grass. Yandell Blackwell's eyes caught the sight of something like a flag waving to and fro not fifty yards away. His carbine snapped to attention as a moving figure approached, and he saw that the flag was a blanket, held aloft on a stick like a flag of truce.

"Who lives?" he shouted in Spanish.

The bearer of the flag came into plain view. He was a Mexican Indian, and he took off his hat.

"*Hola, amigo!*" he said. "You are the Americans?"

"Yes," said Blackwell shortly. He had developed an unneighborly dislike for Mexicans in the last month.

"I come to ask you a question. Do you know the hacienda of Encarnación?"

"No," said Blackwell, still shortly.

"What about it?" asked Jim Wood.

The Mexican crossed himself, being about to speak of the devil. Encarnación, it seemed, was a plantation with royal stables, and acres of corral, with abounding water, long rows of male and female slave cabins, with a veritable Don for an owner, who had music, singing maidens, and pillars of silver dollars. He was Luis Enrico Rodríguez, a Spaniard born and patron saint of all the robbers who lived in the neighboring mountains. A man in league with the devil himself; otherwise his passionate life would have been a brief one at the hands of the French. Their hands had never been laid upon him. Not even the contra-guerrillas had penetrated his mountain fastnesses.

"If you mean the hacienda is a good place to loot, *muchacho*," Wood said, "you may be right, but you're barking up the wrong tree. The French cut off the hands of looters, but General Shelby cuts off their heads and boils them in oil."

"No, señor," said the Mexican. "I am not a robber. Rodríguez is the robber. He has robbed me. Therefore I have come to you. The name and fame of the Americans has spread through this country, as a terror to such as Rodríguez. What will you say that he holds captive an American woman, young and beautiful, against her will?"

"What's that?" said Yandell Blackwell. He looked at Jim Wood.

"Say on," said Jim Wood. "Are you sure you're telling the truth, bub?"

"As the Virgin is true, señor," said the Mexican. He launched into his story, which amounted to this: years ago a California prospector had drifted into the Sonora hills looking for gold, and married a woman of one of the local tribes. They had a daughter, who despite her Indian mother was *muy rubia*, a golden-haired beauty with dark eyes. The prospector struck it rich; he sent his daughter to San Francisco to be educated. When she returned she was American, having nothing of the mestizo about her save her coloring. Even her mother's language was unknown to her. Rodríguez had looked upon her in Guaymas, and though he was a Spaniard, and rich, her father had forbidden him to woo her. The outcome was but natural; to a Spaniard and a millionaire all things are possible, and Rodríguez seized the girl and bore her away to his mountain fastness at Encarnación. But in order to do so, he had to shoot her father dead. To Rodríguez this was nothing; a *bravo* more or less. But his victory was an empty one. The girl was still in his power, but prayers of vengeance for her murdered father still rose to her lips; she would have nothing to do with Rodríguez, despite his magnificent hacienda and his ill-gotten wealth. So said the Mexican goatherd, wrapped in his blanket like a mantle of truth.

The Missourians looked at each other. They were thinking the same thing. Old Jo would skin them if they meddled in anything like this without his permission; but their duty was plain, and it seemed a pleasant duty in prospect. Still, they had warning doubts; if anything went wrong a prison term behind stone Mexican walls would be the least that could happen to them, and the wrath of Shelby might be even worse. It was no time for larking around; but a beautiful American girl in distress, held prisoner by a fat *hacendado* who had murdered her father? They were Missourians, and whatever misgivings they had were brushed aside as unworthy.

"Look here," said Jim Wood to the goatherd. "How far is it to this Encarnación?"

"By tomorrow night, señor, you will be there."

"All right. We'll find out if you're telling the truth. You'll sleep here tonight, and tomorrow you'll go with us and show us the way."

The Mexican muttered something in protest. Wood pointed his revolver at him. "Roll up in that blanket whenever you feel sleepy," he said. "I don't know how much English you understand, but you understand this, so muffle up your ears with that blanket." The Indian shrugged, rolled out the blanket, and lit a cigarette, sitting crosslegged. When he had finished, he rolled over in the blanket.

"You never know when the yellow snakes are asleep," said Wood.

"They never sleep," said Blackwell. "What's the girl's name, did he say?"

"Inez Walker."

"Think we'd better speak to Old Jo?"

"We'll see how he's feeling tomorrow."

"Pass the word for volunteers anyway."

"Think he'll take it as calmly as he did at Lampazos?"

"That was a drunken brawl. This is attacking a peaceful hacienda."

"Not so peaceful with a murderer and kidnapper inside," said Jim Wood. "Besides, the greaser says he's a guerrilla."

"Maybe we'd better do it our own way," said Yandell Blackwell. "Old Jo won't complain after we rescue the girl. I aim to have a word with this Rodríguez and if Jo Shelby don't like it he can lump it."

The second night's camp was pitched in view of the hacienda of Encarnación, which, if it did not come up to the goatherd's description, at least was a plantation of respectable size, tucked into the side of the mountain like an eyrie. The day had passed with no word being spoken to Shelby of the fair Inez; he looked as if he had matters of unusual importance on his mind, and the curt replies he made in ordinary conversation were not encouraging to Blackwell or Wood. They passed the word to a dozen men who could be trusted, no more, and the Mexican marched glumly with them, somewhat to Shelby's surprise. Wood had promised to shoot the man like a rabbit if he stepped so much as a foot in the direction of the towering cactus.

The night was starlit, and Wood and Blackwell reconnoitred the place with a practiced eye. The hacienda was set on the side of a hill, and on the right, like an ornamental fence, stretched a row of cabins, the quarters of the peons. The corral was near the gate. Within, the horses were saddled. Rodríguez was ready for a fight or a flight.

On top of the main building a kind of tower lifted itself up. This was to be expected; where there is a maiden in distress there is a tower. The hacienda seemed to be roomy and could be approached from the outside by circular steps. Perfect, thought Wood and Blackwell; a quick rush up those steps with a battering ram and it would be over. *Once aboard the lugger....*

They were not two shaggy borderers in butternut, standing before a farmhouse in Mexico; they were Galahads about to rescue a lady fair, with all the splendid dash of mediaeval chivalry. Her prison tower loomed before them. They went back to camp and waited for the stars to go in. At midnight the light faded, and the volunteers slipped out of the camp leaving no hole in the dark behind them. They were armed with revolvers, and carried a huge piece of timber which they had wrenched from the upright fastenings of a large irrigation basin.

Wood made a brief speech. The time to turn back was now, if any had misgivings. "We must have the American woman safe out of their hands," he said, "or we must burn the buildings. If the hazard is too great for any of you, step out of ranks. Old Jo will hear the noise soon." No one moved, and a one-armed soldier named Sweeny who had served with Walker in Nicaragua cut short the forensics. "Save the speech, Jim," he said. "We're with you." The names of others have come down to posterity too. Among them were McDougall, Boswell, Armistead, Winship, Ras Woods, Macey, Vines, Kirtley, Blackwell, Tom Rudd, Crockett, Collins, Jack Williams, Owens, Timberlake, Darnall, Johnson, and the two Berrys, Richard and Isaac. Jim Wood stood forward by the right as leader.

Twenty-two men lifted the beam as easily as if it were a log of paperwood and sent it crashing into the gate, ripping its hinges from the adobe wall which enclosed the hacienda. The horses in the corral, masterless and riderless, began milling about and giving shrill neighs of alarm.

As Jim Wood's men poured through the breach in the wall, swarming across the flattened gate like the drawbridge of a moat, the rancheros of Encarnación took alarm too, and a dozen or twenty of them sprang up out of the flagstones of the patio. Shots crisscrossed. There was no light anywhere except in the tower; the men fought now in the dark. Young Tom Rudd was killed, Crockett, the victor of the Lampazos duel, Rogers, Provines the Louisianian, and a German named Matterhorn. He was one of the damned Dutch of St. Louis but he had not fought under the Dutch flag. He was riddled with bullets.

The survivors drove their battering ram against a great door leading into the main hall, and it gave way, like the gate. No lamps lit the hall, but Rodríguez himself was there with half a dozen men, and in the brief flashes of revolver fire Wood's men took aim. In the dark you could not tell who killed Rodríguez, but he fell dead, and Wood's men groped past each other uncertainly in the dark. From within they had no tower light to guide them, and from without came the sound of Shelby's bugle; but the hall was clear now. The whole brigade was advancing on Encarnación and drawing the scattered fire of *rancheros* from the windows and the top of the wall. They withheld the fire of their carbines, knowing that their comrades were inside, but the Mexicans, seeing the awesome sight of the yellow-haired Neanderthal men approaching, stripped to the waist and nearly nude, abandoned their posts and the fire died down. All was quiet in Encarnación.

Shelby's face was quivering as he faced Wood. This went beyond anger, and beyond punishment. It was gross betrayal of the expedition and a death blow to all their hopes, worse than any insubordination or personal disloyalty to himself. It meant that his men were hooligans who would kill for loot, jailbirds and gallows bait; he could not offer such men to the Emperor Maximilian as an elite guard.

"Who among you has done this thing?" he asked in a terrible voice. There was no answer. The men put up their weapons.

"Speak up!" said Shelby. "Let me not find you cowards before I finish the job on you that the Mexicans have done so badly."

Jim Wood, covered with blood and powder stains, came forward and told the story. He told it as the goatherd had given it to him and Yandell Blackwell.

It was, of course, as Yandell Blackwell had said. Shelby could not blame them too much when he knew their motive. But they did not understand how badly they had interfered with his plans for a peaceful march to Mexico City. The Empire would be ringing with condemnation of the invaders for the sack of Encarnación. And four good men of the brigade lay dead for no other reason than the irresponsibility of Wood and Blackwell.

"Why did you not tell me?" he asked harshly. Again there was no answer; Wood could not tell him that during the last few days Shelby had been in such a mood that no man dared approach him.

"Very well," said Shelby, characteristically. No man accepted a *fait accompli* with fewer reservations when it was necessary; and there was still the woman.

"Where is she?" asked Shelby.

Inez Walker was brought. Edwards writes, "Grief-stricken, prematurely old, Inez Walker came into the presence of Shelby, a queen. Some strands of gray were in her glossy, golden hair. The liquid light of her dark eyes had long ago been quenched in tears. The form that had once been so full and perfect was now bent and fragile; but there was such a look of mournful tenderness in her eager, questioning face that the men drew back from her presence instinctively and left her alone with their General. He received her commands as if she were bestowing a favor upon him, listening as a brother might until her wishes were all made known. These he promised to carry out to the letter, and well he did so. For the rest of that night she was left alone with her dead. Recovered somewhat from the terrors of the wild attack, her women came back to her, weeping over the slain and praying piteously for their souls as well."

When the dead had been buried and Dr. Tisdale had seen to the wounded, and Jim Wood had received a warning "which he would remember to his dying day" [1] a guard of honor was detailed to a conveyance which was new to the men. It was a carriage with the blinds drawn, and it moved southward with the soldiers in the morning. No one needed to ask its occupant. [2]

24. *Mexico City at Last*

THE MEN OF THE former Missouri Cavalry Division went into battle as a unit for the last time at Matehuala, Mexico, in August of 1865. Matehuala is north of San Luis Potosí and was a city of 20,000 at that time. It was being held precariously by 500 French of the 82nd Regiment of the Line under a Major Pierron. "A weak detachment for such an exposed outpost," Major Edwards comments.

As the Iron Brigade approached, the sound of cannon could be heard, and as they came down the slope they saw what the situation was. The Juaristas—whom the historian of the expedition persists in calling guerrillas—had got hold of half a dozen cannon (perhaps Shelby's) and with 2,000 men were laying siege to Matehuala.

Shelby sent two scouts into the city—Cundiff and Hodge—and advised Major Pierron that he had a thousand men who would attack the rebels from the rear if Pierron felt that he could attack in front at the same time. The delighted Pierron agreed, and at the signal agreed upon Shelby attacked from the rear—mainly with the revolver —while the French made an unexpected sally against the Juaristas. Probably the element of surprise prevailed, for they scattered, although they outnumbered their foes; still, Shelby's men were bad men to have at your back.

Major Pierron, says Edwards, made Matehuala a Paradise for a few days. Undoubtedly it seemed like Paradise to men who had been sleeping in the rain in cold canyons and fighting in their sleep. What interested Shelby most was that he could get shoes for the men, which they badly needed, and other supplies from the well-equipped French

Army. After three days they marched on to San Luis Potosí, where the commander, Colonel Douay, informed Shelby that he would like to send him on an expedition against guerrillas at once, but that Marshal Bazaine's orders were inflexible: Shelby must march at once to Mexico City, with no more diversions. Bazaine had heard of the participation of the Americans in the affair at Matehuala and was displeased by it. Major Edwards says that he believes the Matehuala battle finally made up Bazaine's mind that he would have no Confederate units in the Imperial Army because of the excuse it would give for United States intervention. It had been his plan, thinks Edwards, to recruit them individually into different units of the French Army and the Mexican Imperial Army, but he now feared that when news of Confederate participation in the battle of Matehuala reached General Sheridan, it would be misconstrued, and so henceforth Bazaine determined to have nothing to do with the Confederates as soldiers.

Whether Major Edwards' reasoning is correct or not—and it would seem to be—his conclusion was eminently correct. From now on the men of the former Missouri Cavalry Division would be nothing but traders and farmers in the Mexican Empire.

There was nothing of this, of course, in their minds as the Iron Brigade approached Mexico City. They were met by a full battalion of Chasseurs d'Afrique sent out by Marshal Bazaine, to guide them into the stone barracks which temporarily would be the home of the men. There is no record that they were asked to lay down their arms; it is highly probable, however, that the French asked every man to register his name and the number of his belongings, including arms. If that register existed today, what a find it would be! It would include some of the finest names in the South.

Although Major Edwards had gone ahead with Magruder and Governor Reynolds, reaching the city two days ahead of the Iron Brigade, he wrote of the feelings of all of them, as the Chasseurs d'Afrique led them in:

"The city of all men's hopes and fears and aspirations—the city of the swart cavaliers of Cortez and the naked warriors of Montezuma, who rushed with bare bosom on lance and sword blade— . . . the city which had seen the cold glitter of Northern steel flash along the broken way of Contreras and wind itself up, striped thick with blood, into the heart of Chapultepec—the city filled now with Austrians and

Belgians and Frenchmen, and an Emperor newly crowned with manhood and valor, and an Empress royal with imperial youth and beauty
—the city of Mexico was reached at last." [1]

In her book, *Ten Years of My Life*, Agnes Salm-Salm, wife of a
German nobleman and soldier of fortune, Prince Felix Salm-Salm,
who had been attached to the Union army under Sherman and was
now an adviser of Marshal Bazaine, describes it thus: "It [the city] is
six leagues in circumference, has four hundred and eighty-two streets
which are mostly straight, paved, and provided with sidewalks. There
are sixty large and smaller squares, fifteen monasteries, twenty-two
nunneries, seventy-eight churches and chapels, three great theatres,
two arenas for bull fights, three principal promenades, and ten
hospitals." [2]

The houses were never more than two stories, and Princess Agnes
found them rather monotonous, but the Alameda she found finer than
the Tiergarten in Berlin and the great Cathedral of Mexico enchanted
her. Situated in the midst of the Plaza de Armas, it inspired her to
remark that the capital of Mexico was a large parallelogram with a
candelabra in the center; and the College of Mines, built entirely of
green porphyry, left her somewhat speechless, as well it might. She
also remarked upon a fact which is remarkable: the city of Mexico
was entirely paved "and kept tolerably clean" in a horse-drawn era
when even the streets of great cities like Washington and London
were not paved.

It was into this wonder city that the men of the Iron Brigade
marched, and for many a country boy from Missouri it must have been
like marching in a dream. They were given quarters in the stone barracks of the French Army while Shelby went to the Hotel San Carlos
to join Edwards and Henry Watkins Allen, the former Governor of
Louisiana who had been a brigadier general and badly wounded at
Shiloh. Allen, Edwards, Magruder, Reynolds, and several others had
been first in conference with Matthew Fontaine Maury and then with
a Monsieur Loysel, who was confidential secretary to the Emperor.
M. Loysel had arranged a conference between Shelby and the Emperor
for the following Thursday afternoon at two o'clock. Magruder had
already spoken to the Emperor and seemed somewhat to have gained
his confidence. In fact, Alexander Watkins Terrell relates this anecdote
about Magruder and the Emperor. Magruder, always a meticulous
dresser, wore a dove-colored top hat and a salt-and-pepper cutaway

for an afternoon meeting with the Emperor; the next time Terrell saw the Emperor, the latter was wearing a dove-colored top hat and a salt-and-pepper cutaway.[3]

The historic meeting between the Emperor and Shelby took place as scheduled in an informal reception room at the Palacio Nacional. Perhaps no single room in history has ever held a more varied array of personalities. Besides the Emperor Ferdinand Joseph Maximilian, descendant of Emperor Charles the Fifth and a long line of Hapsburg kings, there was Marshal Bazaine, the Marshal Ney of Napoleon the Third; Commodore Matthew Fontaine Maury, the first man to chart the currents of the oceans; General John B. Magruder, one of the most colorful generals in an army in which colorful generals abounded; Jo Shelby, who as a cavalry immortal ranked with Jeb Stuart; Count de Noue, the son-in-law of old General Harney back in Missouri, who was to act as interpreter; and Major John Newman Edwards, who although only an obscure aide to Shelby was to become one of the great American editors of the nineteenth century and the Horace Greeley of the West.

This was the first meeting of Edwards with the Emperor and he was impressed, as were all who saw him, by the magnificent appearance of the Austrian Pretender. "In height," recalls Edwards, "Maximilian was six feet two inches. His eyes were blue and penetrating, a little sad at times and often introspective. Perhaps never in all his life had there come to them a look of craft or cruelty. His forehead was broad and high, prominent where ideality should abound, wanting a little in firmness, if phrenology is true, yet compact enough and well enough proportioned to indicate resources in reserve and abilities latent and easily aroused. To a large mouth was given the Hapsburg lip, that thick, protruding, semi-cleft underlip, too heavy for beauty, too immobile for features that, under the iron destiny that ruled the hour, should have suggested Caesar or Napoleon. A great yellow beard fell in a wave to his waist. At times this was parted to the chin, and descended in two separate streams, as it were, silkier, glossier, heavier than any yellow beard or any yellow-haired Hun or Hungarian that had followed him from the Rhine and the Danube." [4]

Maximilian met the Confederates without ceremony and with great friendliness. Although he understood English, he felt more at home in French, and it was in that language that the interview was conducted. Shelby had rehearsed this moment from the day the vote of his soldiers was taken at Piedras Negras, and he made the most of it now. In a confident voice, he laid his plan before the Emperor and before Bazaine, who in the final analysis must approve it. His plan, said Shelby, was to take immediate service in the Empire, recruit a corps of 40,000 Americans, supersede as far as possible the native troops in the Mexican Imperial Army, consolidate the government against the time of the withdrawal of the French soldiers, encourage immigration in every possible manner, develop the resources of the country, and hold it, until the people became reconciled to the change, with a strong and well organized force.

He was proposing to do neither more nor less than Cortez had done, and every man in the room knew it. He was also proposing to wipe out the four years leading up to Appomattox, so far as the Southern people were concerned, and reestablish their Confederacy. That was Joseph Orville Shelby. Throughout his life, from the boyhood days when he rode with Billy Hunter and Johnny Morgan across the fields at Lexington, he made no little plans.

Major Edwards records that "every proposition was faithfully rendered to the Emperor, who merely bowed and inclined his head forward as if he would hear more."

"Shelby," says Edwards, "continued in his straightforward, soldierly manner:

" 'It is only a question of time, Your Majesty, before the French soldiers are withdrawn.'

"Marshal Bazaine smiled a little sarcastically, it seemed, but said nothing.

" 'Why do you think so?' inquired the Emperor.

" 'Because the War Between the States is at an end, and Mr. Seward will insist on the rigorous enforcement of the Monroe Doctrine. France does not desire a conflict with the United States. It would be neither popular nor profitable. I left behind me one million men in arms, not one of whom has yet been discharged from service. The nation is sore over this occupation, and the presence of France is a perpetual menace. I hope Your Majesty will pardon me, but in order to speak the truth it is necessary to speak plainly."

" 'Go on',' said the Emperor, greatly interested.

" 'The matter whereof I have spoken to you is perfectly feasible. I have authority for saying to you that the American government would not be averse to the enlistment of as many soldiers in your army as might wish to take service, and the number need only be limited by the exigencies of the Empire. Thrown upon your own resources, you would find no difficulty, I think, in establishing more friendly relations with the United States. In order to put yourself in a position to do this, and in order to sustain yourself sufficiently long to consolidate your occupation of Mexico and make your Government a strong one, I think it absolutely necessary that you should have a corps of foreign soldiers devoted to you personally, and reliable in any emergency.' "

"On being appealed to, Commodore Maury and General Magruder sustained his view of the case and Shelby continued:

" 'I have under my command at present about one thousand tried and experienced troops. All of them have seen much severe and actual service, and all of them are anxious to enlist in support of the Empire. With your permission, and authorized in your name to increase my forces, in a few months all the promises given here today could be made good.' "

"The Emperor still remained silent. It appeared as if Shelby was an enigma he was trying to make out—one which interested him but at the same time puzzled him. In the habit of having full and free conversations with Commodore Maury, and of reposing in him the most unlimited confidence, he would look first at Shelby and then at Maury, as if appealing from the blunt frankness of the one to the polished sincerity and known sound judgment of the other. Perhaps Marshal Bazaine knew better than any man at the interview how keenly incisive had been Shelby's analysis of the situation; and how absolutely certain were events neither he nor his master could control, to push the last of his soldiers beyond the ocean. At intervals, the calm, immobile face would flush a little, and once or twice he folded and unfolded a printed dispatch held in his hands. Beyond these evidences of attention, it was not known that Bazaine was even listening. His own judgment was strongly in favor of the employment of the Americans, and had the bargain been left to him, the bargain would have been made before the end of the interview. He was a soldier, and reasoned from a soldier's viewpoint."

In the end, Maximilian did not reply directly to Shelby. He arose, beckoned De Noue to one side, and spoke to him earnestly and quietly for several minutes. Then he dismissed his visitors pleasantly and withdrew, in the company of Marshal Bazaine.

De Noue gave Shelby the verdict. The Emperor had refused absolutely to consider the plan. His Majesty, said De Noue, was not willing to trust the Americans in an organization so large and so complete—an organization composed of forty thousand skilled and veteran soldiers, commanded by top-ranking officers of the Confederate Army. Maximilian was a man of immense good will and much woolly thinking—but even he found the thought of such an army in his midst disturbing.

Furthermore, said De Noue, the Emperor had other plans. He wished to establish peace and friendship with the United States through diplomacy, rather than by trying to maintain himself by force of arms. He believed that Secretary of State Seward and the dominant party in the United States would not be adverse to his experiment in trying to bring good government to Mexico—a thing unknown up to now—once it was understood in Washington that that was his sole aim. De Noue shook his head as he repeated this statement. "He reasons with his heart instead of his head, and is furthermore exceedingly stubborn," said the Frenchman. "It is no use, General: the Emperor will not give you employment."

"I knew it," said Shelby.

"How?" asked De Noue.

"Not once could I bring the blood to his face," said Shelby. "He has faith but no enthusiasm, and what a man in his position needs is not only enthusiasm but audacity. You have spoken to me frankly. I shall speak to you frankly. Maximilian will fail at any sort of diplomacy."

"Why do you say that?" asked De Noue.

"Because he will not have time to work the problem out," said Shelby. "I have traveled slowly and in my own fashion from Piedras Negras to the city of Mexico. You have not one foot of Mexican territory in sympathy with you. As surely as the snow is on the brow of Popocatepetl Juárez lives in the hearts of this people and before an answer can come from Seward to the Emperor's Minister of State, the Emperor will have no Minister of State. That's all. Thank you for your kind offices today, Count. I must go back to my men now. They expect me early."

The men of the Iron Brigade had made their own observations on the march from Piedras Negras, and they knew by now that the French did not want them, would not have them under any circumstances, and so perhaps it is not surprising that Major Edwards records the fact that when Shelby informed them of the Emperor's decision they received it with something like apathy or indifference. They had dreamed of a new home, a new flag, a new country—and a full portion of the richness of a tropical land—and while dreaming the useless and unprofitable dream they had gone hungry for bread of late. Money was a commodity they scarcely remembered. Again to quote Edwards, "if all the purses of the men had been emptied into the lap of a woman, the dollars that might have been gathered up would scarcely have paid for a bridal veil."

But if they were indifferent, they were still cheerful, and they laughed—the tension broken—when Shelby, instead of bemoaning their fate, said, "How many of you know enough Spanish to get you a Spanish wife with an acre of breadfruit, twenty-five tobacco plants, and a patch of corn? We cannot starve, boys."

Innumerable plans were discussed, but it was obvious now that every man was thinking of himself as an individual rather than as a member of the brigade. The cohesive agent that had held them together as a unit was gone: the Iron Brigade ceased to exist from the moment that Shelby announced that the Emperor would not have them. They would go their separate ways now, and a majority of them were merely anxious to get out of Mexico. They had not come here to scratch the soil for a living and raise half-Mexican brats.

To do anything at all, however, it would be necessary to raise some money, and the courtly and elegant Governor Reynolds solved that problem for them handsomely. He went at once to Marshal Bazaine and pointed out that at Parras the expedition had turned aside to Mexico City by his inviolable command; that the movement necessarily cut off the brigade from all communication with friends at home; that if they had marched to Guaymas or Mazatlan on the Pacific Coast, return to California would have been easy; and that, in the circumstances, he felt that Bazaine should deal with them as one soldier with another.

Bazaine responded not only generously but extravagantly. Although he headed an army in which men were paid a few cents a day, he drew from his war chest fifty dollars in gold for each of Shelby's men, "and this amount came to each as a rain to a field that the sun is parching." Officers and men got the same amount, and with this sum in their hands they were again masters of their own destiny. Edwards says a little sadly, "Thereafter every man went the way that suited him best."

The few who were willing to remain as colonists prepared to follow Shelby wherever he might settle. "Shelby," says Edwards, "told them all he knew about [the proposed colonization project of] Carlota and advised them briefly to pre-empt the legal quantity of land and give up at once any further idea of service in the ranks of Maximilian's army. Many accepted his advice and entered at once and heartily upon the duties of this new life. Others, unwilling to remain in the Empire as colonists, received permission from Bazaine to march to the Pacific. On the long and dangerous road some died, some were killed, and some took shipping for California, for China, for Japan, and for the Sandwich Islands. A few, hearing wonderful stories of the treasures Kidd, the pirate, had buried on an island in the Pacific Ocean, got aboard a schooner at Mazatlan and sailed away in quest of gold. Those that survived the adventure returned starving, and for bread joined the Imperial Army in Sonora. Perhaps fifty took service in the Third Zouaves.

"A singular incident determined the regiment of their choice," says Edwards. "After authority had been received from the Marshal for the enrollment, a dozen or more strolled into the Alameda where, of evenings, the bands played and soldiers of all arms promenaded. In each corps a certain standard of height had to be complied with. The grenadiers had need to be six feet, the artillerymen six feet and an inch, the cuirassiers six feet, and the hussars six feet. Not being all of the same stature, and not wishing to be separated, the choice of the Americans was reduced to the infantry regiments. It is further obligatory in the French service that when soldiers are on duty, the private in addressing an officer shall remove his cap and remain with it in his hand until the conversation is finished. This was a species of discipline the Americans had never learned, and they stood watching the various groups as they passed to and fro, complying scrupulously with the regulations of the service.

"At last, a squad of Zouaves sauntered nonchalantly by—great, bearded, medalled fellows, bronzed by African suns and swarthy of brow and cheek as any Arab of the desert. The picturesque uniform attracted all eyes. It was war dramatized—it was campaigning expressed in poetry. An officer called to one of the Zouaves, and he went forward saluting. This was done by bringing the right hand up against the turban, with the palm extended in token of respect, but the turban itself was not removed. The subordinate did not uncover to his superior, and therefore would the Americans put on turbans and make Zouaves of themselves. Major Pierron (he of Matehuala) more of an American than a Frenchman, supervised the metamorphosis, and when the *toilette* was complete even Shelby himself, with his accurate cavalry eyes, scarcely recognized his old Confederates of the four years' war. At daylight next morning they were marching on the double-quick to Monterrey."

25. *The Colonization Scheme*

SHELBY was now as poor as the poorest of his *peregrinos*, but he had friends in high places, and even before his rejection as a soldier by the Emperor he had had an alternative plan of campaign mapped out: if he could not serve in the army he would go into the coffee raising business and make another fortune such as he had made in hemp in Missouri before the war. If the country had been at peace, there is not the slightest doubt that he would have done so, for a profit of $16,000 could be realized in a year on an investment of 60 acres,[1] and land could be bought from the government at a price ranging from twenty-five cents to a dollar an acre, under the generous terms which the Empire was now granting to foreigners to encourage immigration.

General Sterling Price was in Mexico City, looking more than ever like a Roman Senator, bringing with him 460 pounds of official documents of the Army of the Trans-Mississippi. He planned to establish an agricultural colony for Southerners somewhere in northeast Mexico, not too far from Vera Cruz and the sea-lanes. Soon Shelby was deep in conference with him and with such top-ranking Confederates as former Governor Isham Harris of Tennessee, Judge John Perkins of Louisiana, Brigadier General Richard H. Maury, and Lieutenant General Dick Ewell, who had succeeded to Stonewall Jackson's command in the Shenandoah Valley. (It was beginning to look as if every surviving Confederate general in the army was either in Mexico or planning to go there soon.) All of them had one objective: to make a fortune in coffee and revive the old South's aristocratic way of living.

In this scheme they had the complete backing of Maximilian. The Emperor had grandiose plans for the colonization of Mexico by both Europeans and Americans in order to stabilize his Empire and he was willing to finance the project to the limit of his treasury. He had uncounted and unsurveyed acres of fertile lands, dotted with haciendas, which he had expropriated from the Catholic Church, and these he was anxious to make available to immigrants, particularly Confederate immigrants.

By imperial decree of September 5, 1865, three classes of lands were offered for colonization. They were—first, "those of the public domain that have never been reduced to cultivation"; second, "those that have been more or less improved as haciendas, the right to dispose of which the Government has acquired by purchase or otherwise"; and third, "private lands and haciendas, the owners of which are disposed to offer them to immigrants on liberal terms for colonization. Many haciendas that are or have been under cultivation may be bought on easy terms and for less than one dollar per acre."

The terms were the most attractive imaginable. Immigrants "who by misfortune have lost all their substance" were offered a free passage by sea to Mexico, with a traveling allowance of ten cents a league to their new homes, for each member of the family;[2] a single man might acquire 160 acres, and the head of a family up to 640 acres, gratis, of uncultivated lands in the public domain. Each settler was to receive "a duly executed title, incommutable, of his landed estate, and a certificate that it is free of mortgage." The land was to be tax-free for the first five years, after which a ground rent of ten per cent would be imposed, based, however, only on the value of the land and not on improvements which might have been added. Those immigrants who had personal effects would be permitted to bring them into the country duty-free, including "work and brood animals, seeds, agricultural implements, machines and working tools."

Slavery was forbidden in the Mexican Empire, persons of color becoming free by the mere act of touching Mexican soil, but the ex-Confederates could bring their former slaves with them to serve as peons, if the Negroes could be induced to come, and such laborers would be subject to "special protective regulations." Under the Mexican peonage system the employer provided food, lodging, clothing, and medical attention for his employees, in addition to a stipulated wage, of which one fourth was held back until the end of the contract period; the peon in return became an indentured servant for five years and was prohibited by law from leaving the service of his master.

The Imperial Decree also exempted new settlers from military service for five years—an attractive inducement for war-weary Confederates—guaranteed toleration of Protestant churches and schools, and even promised endowments of land for the support of schools and colleges.

The first to receive the benefit of the lavish outpouring from Maximilian's treasury was Henry Watkins Allen, Confederate brigadier who had been nearly shot to pieces at Shiloh, and governor of Louisiana during the last year of the war. Allen arrived in Mexico City independently of Shelby, Price, and the rest, with $500 which he had borrowed from friends in Louisiana. As soon as the Imperial Decree was promulgated in September, Allen was granted a subsidy of $10,000 and a salary of $150 a month to establish an English language weekly in Mexico City, *The Mexican Times,* as an organ of the Imperial Government. In this enterprise he was soon joined by Major Edwards as editorial assistant.

In October the Emperor appointed Matthew Fontaine Maury honorary counsellor of state and Imperial Commissioner of Colonization. At the same time, John B. Magruder was appointed chief of the Office of Land Colonization. Another ostensible plum went to Governor Reynolds as head of the American and Mexican Emigrant Company, chartered by Maximilian, which was to establish emigrant assistance offices in the United States.[3]

The emoluments attached to these officers were substantial. The salary paid to Reynolds is not on record, but Maury was paid $3,000 annually, with additional authorizations of $150 for office furniture, $500 annually for expenses, $100 a month for office rent, one clerk at an annual salary of $1,200, and $300 yearly for a private messenger. Magruder received the same except that no provision was made in his office for a clerk.

The Emperor authorized Maury to appoint agents of colonization for certain districts of the Southern United States; Virginia, North Carolina, South Carolina, Texas, Mississippi, California, Louisiana, and Alabama. Officers for the last two were to be established at New Orleans and Mobile. These agents were to receive $100 a month as compensation and the further sum of $300 a year for general expenses.[4]

Secretary of State Seward in Washington crippled this venture from the start by forbidding the agents to enter the country; nevertheless literature was distributed throughout the South telling of the activities of the American settlers in their adopted country and urging others to start life anew by joining them in the Mexican project. Those who may have had any idea of doing so, however, were prevented, in the main, by another Federal decree. General Philip Sheridan, commanding the Departments of Texas and Louisiana, ordered that no one was to leave for Mexico from any Gulf port without special permission.[5]

Despite the seeds of its own destruction which the colonization project carried within itself—the hostility of the United States, the hostility of the Mexicans themselves to any project of Maximilian's, and the hostility of the press of the Southern United States, which objected to the best blood of the South being drained off to a foreign country [6]—there was vast enthusiasm in Mexico for the colonization scheme all through the fall and winter of 1865 and 1866, and a reporter for the New York *Herald* who went there to report on the development wrote a series of articles for his paper which were mostly ecstatic. The *Herald* was unique among American newspapers in giving friendly coverage to the Confederate settlement in Mexico.

There was considerable justification for optimism at this point. First, the land was there, hundreds of thousands of acres of the finest farming country on the entire globe, which Maximilian was either willing to give away or sell so cheaply that it amounted to a gift. Second, Juárez was in hiding in the United States and the Confederates believed that Maximilian was in Mexico to stay. Sterling Price voiced the sentiments of all when he told the *Herald* reporter that "the Napoleon family is not in the habit of backing down in the accomplishment of its schemes." Besides, he added, France was bound to Maximilian by treaties which it could not give up without compromising its prestige and its national honor: before Napoleon would back down he would seek the cooperation of other nations, as he had done in '61, to control the affairs of Mexico; and finally, if the United States intervened in Mexico it would arouse Mexican nationalism and unite the two factions, Imperialist and Juarista.

"Every friend of the Empire," said General Price, "trusts in these considerations, which are, in their estimation, sufficient to discount any appearance of danger on the part of the United States." [7]

General Price selected a colonization site of 500,000 acres of abandoned land in the beautiful Cordoba Valley sixty-five miles from Vera Cruz and a three-day journey by stage from Mexico City. With him went Shelby, Perkins, and Harris, Shelby being accompanied by about fifty members of the Iron Brigade. The prominence of the Confederate leaders associated with the Cordoba Colony gave it the greatest prestige of all the Confederate colonies in Mexico. Lawrence F. Hill, in his "Confederate Exodus to Latin America," says that "the fact that such men proceeded with arrangements to establish themselves and their dearest friends in the community made a powerful appeal. The appeal captured the imagination of all classes: every rank known to the Confederate Army was represented; every sort of politician listed in a dictionary of political science was included; every type of artisan and planter known in the Old South was there; every social position from big planter to lowly slave was included. The total number of persons included varied with the season, with the months, with the moons, even with the suns. One settler said that at one time five hundred emigrants found themselves in the valley about Carlota, the name given a town [built] in honor of the Empress of Mexico." [8]

Carlota was a brand-new settlement. The old Mexican town of Cordoba, which was the focal point for the Confederate colonists, was the capital from which the development fanned out. It lies in the state of Vera Cruz about ninety-two miles from the City of the True Cross. The settlers who came by way of the Gulf of Mexico, and most of them did, in spite of General Sheridan's order, had to make part of their journey by rail and partly by *diligencia*, or Mexican stagecoach. From Vera Cruz, the Imperial Mexican Railway ran sixty-four miles to a terminus at Paso del Macho. From there on, Cordoba had to be reached by twenty-eight miles of winding mountain road. The Cordoba Valley ranges from 800 to 2,000 feet above sea level; and when the yellow jack was not raging, or guerrillas raiding from the mountain passes, it was another Garden of Eden, with equable climate, moderate rainfall, and soil capable of producing four crops a year. As Major Edwards put it, "So impatient is life in that tropic land that there is no death." Orange trees, he found were white with bloom and golden with fruit at the same time.

Experienced farmer that he was, Shelby did not need a second look to know that here in the Cordoba Valley was the earthly paradise which he had been seeking for Betsy and the children. He arranged to buy a magnificent stone *residencia*, surrounded by twelve acres of land suitable for coffee cultivation, the Hacienda of Santa Ana,[9] two miles from Cordoba in the purple heart of the tropics, and he sent a letter posthaste to the Gratz mansion on Mill Street in Lexington, Kentucky, bidding Betsy Shelby leave at once with the children for Vera Cruz. As always whenever the Shelby saga touches Lexington, the record fades; but it requires no vivid imagination to realize that Shelby's letter, full of a glowing account of the rich coffee plantations of the Cordoba Valley, must have brought great joy not only to Betsy Shelby, but to the entire Gratz household, and especially to Anna Gratz: the wandering Confederate black sheep has found a home at last, and of the kind that is suited to him. He has given up the perilous life of a soldier of fortune and gone back to an occupation in which he can, as he has demonstrated before, make not only a living but a fortune. There are tears at parting in Lexington, but they are tears of joy, as Betsy and the two little boys take the steamer for St. Louis and New Orleans. In a money belt around Betsy's waist there is five hundred dollars in gold which Anna and Benjamin Gratz have placed there.[10] We know from *The Mexican Times* that they arrived at the Hacienda Santa Ana in October.[11]

The colony was already growing apace when Betsy Shelby and little Joe and Orville arrived. As early as September 20th, there had been ninety-eight Confederate families seeking homesteads in the region, so that the jump to 500 by the first of the year is probably no exaggeration. In fact, Henry Watkins Allen visited Cordoba just before his death in the spring of 1866 and was astonished by what he saw—and not only astonished, but alarmed, for Allen never had any faith in the colonization project. He alone of the Confederates seems to have had a realistic view of the intentions of the United States toward the colony. Furthermore, he had felt from the beginning that the extravagant inducements would attract an undesirable element— loafers and ne'er-do-wells who expected to live without working—and that they would be a millstone around the necks of their more energetic neighbors. In this he was partly right, although only partly. Following his visit to Cordoba he wrote to a friend, Mrs. Sarah Dorsey of Crockett, Texas, on March 16, 1866: "Immigration is setting in fast in Mexico, *in earnest*. Every vessel brings many passengers as emigrants, from Tennessee, Georgia, Mississippi, Louisiana, South Carolina and Missouri. *There is enough land here for all the South*, but they are slow in surveying it; and all those who come here should bring some money. I fear there will be much misery among the colonists who come here without money. *They had better stay at home.*" [12]

The sentiment was echoed by the New York *Herald* on April 19, 1866. The friendly reporter of that newspaper (he remains unidentified, although he made several trips to Cordoba and Carlota) warned:

"This is no country for drones. A man without money, industry and energy had better go hang himself before he starts for Mexico—he will be glad of it afterwards. Mechanics and farmers are needed here. Such, if willing to work, cannot go amiss. Wages are low, compared to what are paid in the States, laborers receiving seventy-five cents and one dollar a day and board; *but with this a man can soon secure a fortune.* Clerks and professional men should by all means avoid Mexico. . . . There are no opportunities for clerks, ministers and lawyers; and happily for the community a doctor's services are rarely needed in this climate. Forty acres in coffee is a fortune to any man, and there are a dozen other articles that can be raised with little labor, and which will pay 200 per cent more than the best crops that can be raised in the States. But hardships are to be endured that few colonists are prepared to encounter; therefore, unless they have a little money or a trade and are willing to work, they had better remain where they have friends to help them in case assistance is needed."

The drones in the colony of Cordoba appear to have been comparatively few, however, for as the same reporter says, "little more than half of the Southerners who went to Mexico (in the first rush of immigration) remained, and many of them caught the first returning steamer they could reach." Confronted with the necessity of working for a living, even in Mexico, those with a distaste for it left in a hurry. The attitude of the responsible, hardworking settlers towards these people (and towards the land from which they had exiled themselves) is well expressed in a letter written February 9, 1866, by an unreconstructed rebel, Benjamin Crowther, to his friend J. Calvin Littrel of St. Louis:

"I was sorry to see and witness so many Confederates come to Mexico with wrong and improper motives; some imagined that they would be installed forthwith in some fat office, like Commodore Maury, and because they were not, and not being disposed to adapt themselves to temporary inconveniences, would not labor, and to their shame went back to the dis-United States, like a dog returning to his vomit; whereas had they been patient, and not tried to force things whether or no, they would, by settling colonies of twenty-five and fifty families, as is now the case at Cordoba, Rio Verde and other places—they would have all done well and been of mutual assistance to one another. The only temptation that I or any of my family could have to return to the United States would be on the occasion of a war with any other power on earth and that of the federal government, in which event you may expect to see me in the service of that army, whatever army it may be." [13]

Those who prospered, however, prospered exceedingly. The ubiquitous *Herald* reporter commented: "Of all these [prominent Confederates in Mexico] General Shelby is the most energetic and enterprising, and consequently his prospects are more flattering than any American's in the country. Besides working in his hacienda, he runs large wagon trains from the railroad terminus at Paso del Macho to the City [of Mexico]. His wagons are all of Yankee manufacture, are drawn by ten mules each, and every wagon carries a load of six to seven thousands pounds, the freight of which is 300 to 350 dollars." [14]

From Cordoba the *Herald* reporter went to Carlota, in a wagon driven by a one-legged Confederate veteran who pointed out the sights as they went. The village, which was now firmly established with a population of thirty families, was laid out systematically around a large square "which is covered with a natural growth of trees, among which is a grove of mangoes, the most beautiful shade trees, whose interlacing boughs and thick, glossy foliage exclude completely the sun's rays, affording a delightful retreat during the heat of the day. In a few years, Carlota, will be the most pleasant town in Mexico. It will be built after the American style, with a degree of beauty and comfort elsewhere unknown in the Empire and the society there will be formed from the best educated families of the South and West." [15]

At Carlota, the newsman called on Sterling Price and found the portly general seated on the porch of his bamboo house, the finest in town. It was set "amid a grove of mango trees near the *casa* which afford a cool and inviting retreat for the old soldier, and here he may be found at all hours, seated upon a chair of his own manufacture, cracking jokes with old companions in arms, or giving orders respecting the cultivation of his plantation. Everything is of the most primitive description, the tables and chairs being the General's own handiwork. General Price is not a little of a Yank, and is about as ingenious and handy as any New Englander. Governor Isham Harris and the General are inseparable companions, living together until the Governor's house shall be completed." [16]

The reporter sat with General Price for five hours on the porch of his bamboo house while the General discoursed at length on the subject of the war, Reconstruction, and colonization in Mexico. As far as prosperity went, the reporter found that Price was doing as well as Shelby. He boasted that during the winter he had exported coffee to the value of $25,000, in addition to tobacco, beans, cattle, horses, sweet potatoes, and fruits,[17] nearly everyone in Carlota was doing the same thing on a smaller scale. Said Price, "I have six hundred and forty acres here which I would not exchange for twelve hundred anywhere in the United States," and he advised the *Herald* reporter to abandon journalism, "settle down in this magnificent country, and turn farmer." [18]

This was in April, when there were in the lush Cordoba Valley possibly 5,000 inhabitants, including colonists, Indians, Mexicans, and regiments of French and Austrian soldiers. It was the high noon of the colony's existence, and General Price was right in saying that Mexico had everything to offer the industrious settler—everything, that is, except the one indispensable condition of successful colonization: a stable government. Even while Maximilian was dreaming his Utopian dreams and giving away lands that did not belong to him, it was a fact well known even to those around him that the Liberals, the Republican followers of Juárez, would soon be in power; and it was well known to the Liberals themselves. Juárez was in the United States, in contact with top political and military leaders of the administration, and they had given him their assurance that the French would be compelled to withdraw, although given the opportunity to do so gradually. As soon as that happened, the scattered Juarista armies would unite and converge on Mexico City. They would be unopposed except for a handful of troops of the "Imperial Mexican Army" commanded by a bewildered Maximilian—himself no general even if he had had an adequate army.

In the spring of 1866, however, all was peace and prosperity on the surface. The French still held a tight cordon of the toughest troops in Europe—veterans of Algeria and Pekin—across Mexico from Vera Cruz in the east to Mazatlan on the Pacific. The market value of colonization lands cultivated by settlers had quadrupled.[19] Henry Watkins Allen, dubious as he was about the success of the scheme, was able to write: "In a recent trip to Cordoba we were much delighted by this interesting city. It is now the center of much attraction and has been almost Americanized. In fact more Americans are seen on the streets, in the hotels, and public places than any other class of person. They mingle freely with the Mexican population and are universally treated very kindly and hospitably by them."[20] The best of the three hotels in Cordoba was the Confederate, run by W. G. Johnson of Texas, a regular advertiser in *The Mexican Times* who boasted that the Confederate Hotel was the largest two-story building in Cordoba.

Jo Shelby's freight line was doing a thriving business, as already reported, carrying supplies from Vera Cruz to Mexico City and from Mexico City to the French army outposts, in addition to the freight which he hauled for the colonists; he had twelve acres in coffee; he was a vigorous thirty-five years old, reunited with his family for the first time since 1861, and Betsy Shelby was awaiting her third baby, the only one of the eight Shelby children to be born in Mexico;[21] Jo Shelby was as happy as he had ever been in his life, and as busy. He had taken into partnership in the freight line a Major McMurty of whom no other mention survives, and he and McMurty had a monopoly of whatever goods were hauled for the French army other than by rail.

If all of Shelby's neighbors had been as tactful in dealing with their Mexican neighbors as he,[22] the fate of the colony might have been different; but they were not. As a result of one highhanded action by a family of ex-Confederates, disaster befell the Cordoba colony. This family selected some land to homestead, and ordered an Indian family occupying it to clear out forthwith. The Indians left, but laid their case before the leader of the nearest Juarista command, one Colonel Figueroa, who already had an evil record as the murderer in cold blood of a party of prominent Confederates.[23] Figueroa welcomed the opportunity to make a surprise attack on the Cordoba plantations, galloping through a mountain pass which the French had left unprotected, with 1,000 guerrillas. He smashed farming implements, burned cabins, destroyed stock, and carried off thirty settlers as hostages, seizing many of them in the fields, and eventually demanding $10,000 for their release. There are various estimates as to the number of these hostages, but most accounts place the number at thirty. They were kept for a month "in barbarous captivity," stripped, robbed, and beaten, but the ransom was not paid and in the end they were released when it became known that French troops were on their way into the hills to rescue them. Half naked, and half dead from hunger and exhaustion, with "passports" signed by Figueroa, they made their way back to their homes eventually. There they found that their work of nine months had been wiped out. And the village of Carlota had been burned to the ground.

As a result of the attack on the colony, General Price went to Mexico City to see Bazaine. The Marshal sent Dupin and his *contra-guerrillas* to Omealco and Toloquillo, two of the plundered haciendas, with orders to remain there indefinitely; and Dupin at once went to work scouring the hills for Figueroa and his men, with considerable success.

On July 2, 1866, Price wrote to his son Edwin, back in Missouri (a delayed account), "I visited Mexico at the request of our Colony... and to make such arrangments as would prevent such things from occurring again I have succeeded in having done. These robbers, failing to get pay, have released their prisoners, who have returned, and an Imperial military outpost has been established in their midst. The Imperial troops went in search of the robbers a few days since, came upon them in camp and scourged them terribly, killing their commander and about twenty others; six thousand dollars were found upon the person of the commander." [24]

The affair had interesting repercussions over beyond the French lines in the camp of the supreme Juarista commander, General Alejandro Garcia, whom *The Mexican Times* had at first erroneously accused of attacking the colony.[25] Garcia publicly deplored Figueroa's deed and declared that he would have hanged Figueroa as a common robber had he not perished at the hands of the French; and he shrewdly seized the opportunity to let loose with a blast of anti-Imperial propaganda. The colonists, he said, had "brought all their trouble on themselves. In the first place, they had no title to the lands upon which they squatted [the Juaristas of course denied the right of Maximilian to dispose of Mexican territory] and refused to enter into any arrangement for their purchase. Secondly, they had neglected the advice of Maximilian not to be violent imperialists; [26] and thirdly the conduct of the party [of settlers] was such that the Liberals were obliged to break up the colony, some of the men attempting to dispossess old settlers of their homes and two being guilty of worse crimes in connection with native women. Their indiscretions have effectually broken up the settlement for the present and put a stop to American colonization. This is more to be regretted as parties are now engaged in surveying and plotting out land for colonization purposes in the state of San Luis Potosí, and the [Liberal] Government offer to settlers of 21,000 acres on the Hacienda of Michopa near Cuernavaca" [27]—about seventy miles west of Mexico City.

Garcia did not exaggerate. The Figueroa raid ended the settlement of Carlota—the town with the ill-fated name. Those settlers who, like the Shelbys, occupied haciendas on the edge of Cordoba itself, and had escaped molestation, remained. General Sterling Price, however, had lost his home and his investment in Mexico and after his return from the visit to Bazaine he became ill, chiefly from anxiety, so much so that he was unable to bring himself to write the account of the raid to his son until two months after it happened.

Fate was dealing unkindly with the old warrior, and some of his friends back in Missouri proposed to raise $50,000 to reimburse him for his losses in Mexico; when Jo Shelby heard of it, he wrote to a friend in Mexico that instead of raising $50,000 for Price, they ought to raise that amount for the "widows and orphans that were made by his dam'd blunders." [28] Such bitterness was not often characteristic of Shelby; one can only conclude that the pompous Price, in his role as patriarch of the colony, had been getting on Shelby's nerves with his pretensions and the pontifical blasts which he was constantly loosing in the press back in the United States. The papers back home felt somewhat the same way about Price, at least outside of Missouri, where he was still revered; the Charleston *Daily Courier* for June 1, 1867, had this to say about him:

"The General is by no means a favorite with the Liberals, who if the opportunity offers will give the old Missourian short shrift and the benefit of a stout rope. This fact Price fully appreciates, and when he heard the Liberals intended to raid the Carlotta [sic] colony mounted his horse and hied him in haste to Cordoba, where he begged the Americans there to arm themselves and go to Carlotta, excusing himself from going on the ground that if the Liberals caught him they would send him to hell or the United States, and he would as soon go one place as the other." [29]

As long as the French army garrisoned the frontier, which it did through most of the summer, Shelby's freight business held up, but the French were pulling in their lines now, harried as they went by the slowly but relentlessly advancing armies of Juárez and Porfirio Díaz. North of San Luis Potosí the Liberals were commanded by the notorious Escobedo, who was to be the executioner of Maximilian, and who hated all foreigners with a hatred that amounted to loathing,[30] and the Liberals took no prisoners. Remembering the hands and feet of Mexicans cut off by the French *contra-guerrillas*, he visited unspeakable tortures on any of them who fell into his hands.

Appropriately enough, Shelby's last pitched battle in any war was fought with Escobedo's men from behind the barricade of a wagon train which was carrying supplies to the French garrison at Cesnola, above San Luis Potosí. Ironically, the commander at Cesnola was Colonel Depreuil, his old antagonist of Parras, and Shelby was to have the unique opportunity of rescuing Depreuil from the Juaristas, thus heaping coals of fire upon his head. Revenge, as Major Edwards says, is sweet, especially the revenge of returning good for evil.

Shelby's last fight resembled Custer's in many respects except that, through the use of bold strategy, Shelby emerged from it alive, and the rescue party arrived on time. The engagement was fought Indian style, by twenty dismounted cavalrymen of the Iron Brigade, now serving Shelby as waggoners, and the finish was in the best tradition of the Wild West, with three squadrons of cavalry and a section of flying artillery, led by three civilian scouts, dashing to the rescue at the last moment. Nevertheless it was a desperate fight in which men were killed just as dead as at Shiloh, and but for Shelby's delaying action the garrison at Cesnola would have been cut off and massacred.

Shelby had come up to San Luis Potosí from Mexico City with eighty wagons of supplies for the garrison of Colonel Douay, and after reporting to Douay he was sent forward with twenty men and ten wagons toward Cesnola. As he advanced into open country, his advance was led by James Kirtley, Thomas Boswell, and George Hall, as it had been a thousand times, from Missouri to the Gulf. The advance was fired upon, and two soldiers, James Ward and Sandy Jones, were wounded. Shelby countermarched quickly to an abandoned hacienda, encamped his wagons within the walls, formed them into a circle, and awaited an attack. It was impossible to tell how large a force was between them and Cesnola, but it was death to be taken, and Shelby sent Kirtley, Boswell, and Hall back to San Luis Potosí for aid. Their mounts were not of the best, and it was thirty miles to the encampment of Douay. Shelby and his seventeen teamsters were outnumbered ten or twenty or even thirty to one, and the situation would have been hopeless except for one fortunate circumstance: the Juaristas had no artillery. Shelby was able to throw up a formidable breastwork under the wheels of the wagons: sandbags and several hundred sacks of corn intended for Depreuil. A musket ball could not penetrate them, and as long as the Missourians kept their heads down the Juaristas would be wasting ammunition.

The Juarista leader, a Colonel Gutiérrez, realized that this was the situation and sent a soldier across the plain waving a flag of truce. The Liberals had 500 soldiers, explained the *descamisado* who was fighting under the banner of *Tierra y Libertad*, and the Americans were trapped. Colonel Gutiérrez advised surrender.

Shelby had heard of Gutiérrez, a renegade priest with a savage reputation for torturing prisoners. There would be no surrender, but on the other hand no relief could come until tomorrow, even if Kirtley got through. Shelby decided to parley.

As an American soldier, he told the messenger, he could not dishonor himself by surrendering until he was convinced that resistance was hopeless. He would not even discuss surrender until he had seen a show of overwhelming force. The messenger could go back and tell his commander that.

On receiving this message, Gutiérrez surveyed the situation at Shelby's improvised fort. He could see at least fifteen gleaming rifles, with hairy faces above them, thrust across the sandbags and sacks of corn. There might be more, but not many; a show of force would certainly convince the commander of the Americans that they would be slaughtered if they did not surrender.

Gutiérrez therefore wasted some valuable time, until the sun went down, in parading his 500 poorly armed rancheros in front of Shelby. When he concluded that the display had had the required effect, he sent another messenger, demanding Shelby's surrender once more. Shelby replied that the review had not been impressive; Gutiérrez would have come and get him. Gutiérrez decided to do so at about dusk.

Then, says Major Edwards, "with a shrill, short yell, the Mexicans dashed forward to the attack. Had the wave held on its course it would have inundated the earthwork. It broke, however, before it reached halfway across the open space behind which it had gathered for the onset. Those in front began to fire too soon, and those in the rear, not seeing from the smoke what was really in front, fired too, and without aim and object. With unloaded guns they dared not go on—the fire of the Americans was distressing beyond endurance—the wave broke itself into fragments—and the sun sank lower and lower." [31]

As the Mexicans fell back, the full, ringing notes of French bugles were heard, and the siege was lifted. Three squadrons of Chasseurs d'Afrique, led by Scouts Kirtley, Boswell, and Hall, and followed by a battery of horse artillery, rode into the mass of retreating Juaristas and laid about them with the sabre. There was no organized resistance. Gutiérrez' command broke and fled into the cactus.

At Cesnola Shelby found that Depreuil had been unaware of the fact that a large body of the enemy was interposed between him and San Luis Potosí; but he was made aware of it speedily, for Captain Messillon, the commander of the Chasseurs, brought word from Douay that the Juaristas about Cesnola were believed to number several thousand while Depreuil had only several hundred in his command. Messillon brought orders for Depreuil to fall back to San Luis Potosí and join the main French force at once; evacuation of the Mexican state of that name was to begin immediately.

Depreuil was in a state of almost tearful Gallic abjection as he apologized to Shelby "for the rude things said and done at Parras." There was no need, said Shelby, to apologize; Depreuil had been justified in suspecting at first that the Americans were bushwhackers, and bushwhackers should be dealt with sternly. He rode back to San Luis Potosí with the column, paid his respects to Douay, and prepared to leave. Douay wished to reward him, but Shelby would not have it.

"Nevertheless," said Douay, "you are poor, you are an exile, you can have no more refuge in this country when it is learned that you have rescued a French garrison, and I demand the privilege of paying you for whatever losses you may have incurred."

"Very well, Colonel," said Shelby, "you can settle the bill next time we meet in Mexico City."

He knew that for him and Douay there would never be another meeting in Mexico City. The garrison at San Luis Potosí was among the first to be evacuated, and the French troop ships were already on the tide.

Shelby realized that his days as a freighter were over, not because he had rescued a French garrison, but because with the departure of the red-trousered veterans he would have no more customers. Concentrated principally in the large cities now, awaiting their orders of embarkation, the French no longer patroled the roads or attempted to give protection to those who lived away from the garrisoned towns. The highways of Mexico were a bandits' paradise. He must find some other means of making a living. Furthermore, the colony of Cordoba was expiring from the blow dealt it by Figueroa the previous spring. Immigration was at an end. This year's crops had been ruined, and not replanted. There would be no more coffee, bananas, and sugar to haul to the railhead at Paso del Macho, and even if there had been, there would be no chance of getting through the guerrilla lines. He and his partner, McMurty, sold off their stock, and at the end of the rainy season, Shelby took Betsy and the three children to Mexico City.

A farmer at heart, Shelby had not yet given up the idea of establishing his own plantation on the rich soil of Mexico; it was a dream that died hard with him, and furthermore he had no intention of returning to the United States. The war was only fifteen months ended, and the brutalizing effects of four years of war had made conditions frightful in the former Confederacy. From Virginia to Texas, the South had been converted from a garden into a desert. Wreck and ruin covered the land, and with them despair. Such proud cities as Richmond, Atlanta, and Columbia stood in blackened ruins. Railroads had been destroyed and not rebuilt; hordes of idle Negroes lorded it over their former masters while the fields went unplanted for lack of help to work the great plantations; cash money was so scarce as to be nonexistent; a vindictive peace of disfranchisement and humiliation had been imposed upon the whites; and the proud, imperial South, which had been served by proud men like Joseph Orville Shelby and John Newman Edwards, lay prostrate in the dust. In Missouri conditions were perhaps worst of all, for there it had been brother against brother, and neighbor against neighbor; and Jo Shelby, on October first, 1866, could not imagine any conditions under which he would return to the state of his adoption. No matter how bad things were in Mexico, they were worse at home; and besides, on this day the Emperor Maximilian had sent for him.

With the Emperor was a Baron Sauvage, a French financier who had acquired a grant of land from Maximilian as big as the state of Delaware. It was on the Tuxpan River, which empties into the Atlantic between Tampico and Vera Cruz, and dense with rubber and mahogany trees. (The first are described, in the records of this pre-automotive age, as "india rubber trees," the product of which was used mainly for elastic and buggy tires, and they stood on the present site of the great oil wells of the Tampico area.) The climate was tropical, the grant being in the lowlands, and none too healthy. The inhabitants were Toluca Indians, an ignorant and primitive race, but believed to be friendly. Baron Sauvage was dreaming of great wealth from his Tuxpan project, but he had no intention of taking up the life of a pioneer; he wanted a manager and partner who was used to peril and privation and who would be willing to found a colony in such a steaming jungle outpost. The Emperor had recommended Shelby enthusiastically as just such a man.

Shelby was willing, and when the interview was over a scheme of colonization had been formed similar to that which had failed in the Cordoba Valley; but the promoters believed that their chances of success at Tuxpan lay in the remoteness of the colony. Cordoba had failed only, Shelby believed, because of its exposed position; even with Sheridan's ban on emigration, he argued, success at Cordoba would have caused thousands to defy it and flock to Carlota as to another California. At Tuxpan, the colony would have the impenetrable jungle at its back. Its commerce would flow unmolested to the seaport of Tampico for shipment to all the world, and all that was needed was to clear the jungle for a settlement.

Maximilian lost no time in signing the necessary permissive documents. On October 8 *The Mexican Times* announced a decree of the Emperor permitting Baron Sauvage to transfer his rights and privileges of colonization to Jo Shelby in return for stock in the company. Two hundred shares were issued at $500 a share, and these were to be placed in the market at once to raise money for immediate necessities. The price of the land, to colonists, was fixed at $1 an acre up to 320 acres; and two schooners were ordered to be placed on the line between New Orleans and Tuxpan.

"Every emigrant," said the *Times*, "will be landed free of cost

within two days march of his settlement; agents of known energy
and discretion are to be sent through North America, and the stock
of the company will be offered at once in the New York market. The
lands are government, without being obtained by confiscation, and
are among the richest in Mexico. It is impossible to overestimate the
grave political difficulties about to transpire in the United States, and
the great advantages of a colony located near Tuxpan will be to the
government and the friends of improvement and agricultural wealth,
and the great necessity for the immediate pacification of this department is most evident. The destiny of the Government is in its own
hands now. Colonization, unfortunately mismanaged at first, comes
back again to the vision on the horizon of Mexico, and when Shelby
and Laurence Keith Boyle and others of similar energy and intelligence put their shoulders to the wheel success is easy and colonization
already commenced."

The Laurence Keith Boyle mentioned was an American entrepre-
neur in Mexico City, a promoter of a variety of business enterprises,
and his part in the venture was to leave at once for New York and
obtain Wall Street backing for the company.

On November 19, 1866, Major Edwards reported to his readers,
"We have gratifying intelligence that General Shelby has gone to
work with his accustomed hardihood in this really important enterprise. He intends leaving in a very short time [for the Tuxpan colony]
with some twenty or more families, for the scene of his labors, and
he is so happily constituted that he brings to his energy—which is natural and inherent—a faith that is limitless . . . an enthusiasm born of
the army, a diplomacy uncultivated, but pliant as wax and sharp as
caustic, and a courage when all else fails, that would dare everything
and grapple everything.

"We conscientiously believe that had the management of affairs at
Cordoba been entrusted to his keeping today a great and growing
colony would have been stretching browned hands southward from
the Gulf and westward to the gates of Mexico, holding up the white
beacon of cotton bales and beckoning from the world commerce,
enterprise and capital. With him there is no such word as fail,
and the man who went up from captain to major general along a
path illuminated only by the light of his sword and the blaze of his
genius, will find it easier to destroy the obstacles of nature alone than
to overcome the barriers of man and nature combined, as he always

did. When all arrangements have been perfected we will have other and more extended information to offer our readers."

A survey of the Tuxpan lands was undertaken under the direction of a former Confederate engineer, Major R. J. Lawrence of Kansas City, and Maximilian pledged $20,000 as a subsidy to build a railroad from Tampico to Vera Cruz. Shelby hired 200 Mexicans as laborers, acquired a house for Betsy and the children, and went by passenger ship to Havana to buy supplies. There he bought "a seaworthy sail boat" and loaded it with American plows, harrows, railroad tools of all kinds, enough provisions for a summer's campaign, and sailed back to Vera Cruz with a hired crew.

At Vera Cruz Shelby purchased another schooner from the French Coast Guard, and hearing that Marshal Bazaine was in the city, went up to visit him. The marshal of Louis Napoleon greeted him cordially, as always, and Shelby came directly to the point.

"Marshal," he said, "we have taken upon our hands much work. We have plenty of farming implements but no guns. I understand that your army of occupation has been supplied recently with the new *chassepot* rifles, and I am wondering if you couldn't spare us some of your old muskets. With 500 muskets and enough ammunition to protect the colony at Tuxpan for six months, I promise you that we can build a colony as prosperous as the colony of the Emperor Napoleon in North Africa."

Bazaine smiled a rare smile, but he did not hesitate; he signed the order for the 500 muskets just as he had given Shelby's men fifty dollars apiece in gold. It was always said of Magruder that he could charm the birds out of the trees, but Shelby could charm thousands of dollars out of a Frenchman without even promising to pay it back. Bazaine wished him luck, and Shelby sailed out of the harbor of Vera Cruz that night, past the dark battlements of the Castle of San Juan de Ulloa, the possessor of 500 elegant rifles, great stores of ammunition, and a boundless faith in the future. The colony at Tuxpan, like Plato's Atlantis, was to be wiped out "in one dreadful day and night," but as the tropic breezes blew across the Bay of Campeche, and the gentle waves slapped at the sides of the schooner, he turned in on deck and slept serenely in the winking dark, confident that success was at hand.

Back in Tuxpan Shelby put his 200 hands to work, and construction of the Tampico-Vera Cruz railway was actually begun. Meanwhile, Laurence Keith Boyle had been flooding Texas and Arkansas with circulars from his headquarters in New York, and a trickle of immigration began, twenty families at first. No records exist of the Tuxpan colony except the references in *The Mexican Times* and the *Railway Era*, and the account given by Major Edwards in his history of the Mexican expedition. Edwards says, "Through no fault of any Americans there, the colony did not live. Shelby did the work of a giant. He was alcalde, magistrate, patriarch, contractor, surveyor, physician, interpreter, soldier, lawgiver, mediator, benefactor, autocrat, everything. All things that were possible were accomplished. Settlers came in and lands were given to them. The schooners were loaded with tropical fruit and sent to New Orleans. When they returned they were filled with emigrants. The railroad took unto itself length and breadth and crept slowly through morass and jungle toward Vera Cruz. Disease also decimated. The rank forests, the tropical sun, the hardships and exposures of the new and laborious life told heavily against the men, and many whom the bullet spared, the fever flushed. The living, however, took the place of the dead, and the work went on."

The blow fell at Tuxpan just as it had fallen at Carlota. The French garrison at Correzetla, the only troops between Shelby's settlers and the ragtag Indian armies of Porfirio Díaz, was ordered to Mexico City, one of the last French units to go; and word came to Shelby that 2,000 Mexicans were marching to the colony, shouting "Death to the Gringo!" He was forced to give the order to evacuate Tuxpan, although it came too late to save settlers in the outlying districts, who were massacred. Arming all those capable of bearing arms, he set out on a toilsome march for Cordoba, through the mahogany forests. At Tampico he learned that his two vessels had been scuttled, the crews murdered, and their bodies thrown into the sea. Behind him lay the great wreck of the plantation of Tuxpan, soon to return to the jungle, the farming implements buried forever in the strangling vines. He was through with Mexico now.

It was March, 1867, when the disheartened survivors of the Tuxpan expedition returned to Cordoba. The Hacienda Santa Ana still stood, intact, but Shelby's title to it, derived from the Emperor Maximilian, was bogus now. He and Betsy had a choice; they could go home, or they could migrate to Brazil, where Confederates now lived in peace. But Shelby was not disposed to risk any more hardships for his family; he was heartsick at the thought of what his tiny, adorable wife had already been through for his sake. They would go home, no matter what. General Grant was running for President of the United States, and his election was a foregone conclusion; that was good news. The old soldier who had been generous to a fallen foe would not continue to humiliate the South. Jefferson Davis was free, and Horace Greeley had gone on his bail bond. Perhaps the nation's wounds would be bound up, after all. And the Shelby's were homesick for Kentucky and Missouri.

John Edwards was at Cordoba, ready to go home, and Betsy and the three boys could make the trip to New Orleans and St. Louis under his protection.[32] Shelby would remain a few weeks to see what could be salvaged from the wreck, then join them in Kentucky.[33]

Home!

Betsy Shelby divided her jewelry among those of Shelby's men who were still with him, reserving only enough for herself and the children to take passage to the United States.[34] Of cash reserves they had none. When they boarded the ship at Vera Cruz, all that they took with them from Mexico was a little dog which Archbishop Labastida, the Cardinal Archbishop of Mexico, had given the Shelby children.[35]

In New Orleans Major Edwards gave an interview to the Associated Press in which he summed up the situation in Mexico:

"There is no love for the people of the United States, and the only sympathy for them at all is because they are presumed to represent opposition to the French and to have expressed dislike for them.

"The settlement at Cordoba is among the things of the past. The departure of General Price, which has been duly chronicled, will be followed by almost all who associated with him at Cordoba. Judge Perkins has gone to Paris, France. Governor Harris left two weeks ago for Havana. General Shelby still remains in Cordoba, and probably will remain for several months to come.

"Condition of the country is worse than has been known for twenty years. The main thoroughfare between the city of Mexico and Vera Cruz is interrupted about every fifteen miles and everything the unlucky passengers possess is taken with a quiet shrug of the shoulders and the polite declaration: *no me importa*, which means that it makes no matter to me....

"Governor T. C. Reynolds of Missouri will remain in the city of Mexico, and see the issue of affairs there. General T. G. Hindman will leave in two weeks for the United States where it is his intention to practise law in Memphis or merchandise in New York.

"With the evacuation of Mexico by the French, the rest of the foreigners think it best to leave the country; and those of all nationalities are leaving as fast as steamers will bear them from Vera Cruz. The great idea in the Mexican mind is to get rid of foreigners, *nolens volens;* and whether it is the French this year or the people of the United States the next, it makes but little difference to them." [36]

As the news of reverse after reverse came to Maximilian in the Palace of Chapultepec, he turned despairing eyes toward the Americans once more, and sent for Shelby. Although he was exposing himself to great danger in traveling alone in Mexico, Shelby allowed himself to be joggled for three days in a mule-drawn *diligencia* to reach the capital. Then for the last time the blunt and faithful exile stood before his Emperor.

"How many Americans are there in the country?" inquired Maximilian.

Shelby shook his head sadly.

"Not enough for a corporal's guard," he said.

"I need twenty thousand men," said Maximilian.

"I beg pardon," said Shelby, "but you need forty thousand. Not a single regiment in your service is dependable. You cannot now rely upon numbers; only upon devotion. I am but one man, but I am at your service."

Maximilian spoke slowly. "It is refreshing to hear the truth," he said. "I feel that you tell it as one who neither fears nor flatters." He unclasped the Golden Cross of the Order of Guadelupe from his breast, and fastened it upon Shelby's.

"This is all I have to give," he said. "Take this in parting, and remember that circumstances never render impossible the right to die for a principle."

The two men shook hands, and Shelby walked away into the night of Mexico. They were not to meet again, but Shelby watched at a distance as Maximilian evacuated his capital forever, moving northward with a token army—the Imperial Mexican Army—to meet the massed forces of Benito Juárez. Hemmed in and beseiged at Querétaro, he was betrayed by one of his own officers, captured by General

Escobedo, and shot, "the final victim of imperialistic European plots in America."

Shelby returned home to Kentucky during the second week of June, 1867, a few days before Maximilian met his death.

Lexington, which had been a staunch Confederate center during the war, despite the Union sympathies of such leading citizens as the Gratzes, acclaimed him a hero.

26. *"The Mexican Times"*

No history of Shelby's expedition to Mexico would be complete without a day-by-day reading of *The Mexican Times*, the weekly English language newspaper of the exiles established in Mexico City under the patronage of Maximilian by Henry Watkins Allen and John Newman Edwards. Seldom has a livelier and more sparkling record of a Continental capital been left between the covers of bound volumes of newsprint.

Mexico City under the Empire was another Paris, as Jeanningros had said, although with the advent of Shelby's borderers the *paseos* and boulevards began to take on some of the overtones of the Wild West, the American Civil War, and Election Day in Missouri. The effect was pictorial rather than audible, however, for the brigade was under heavy discipline, and virtually in custody of the French army. While not confined to barracks, the ex-Confederates, having not one silver peso to rub against another, found little temptation to range abroad in search of excitement. The people of Mexico City went their way unmolested. They were either very rich or very poor, in their Parisian finery or their Indian blankets, and if the Imperial Court was not a second Versailles, it was no fault of the French. The Emperor and the Empress drove out every evening in the plaza, the military bands played French and Mexican airs, and Juárez seemed far away.

Allen and Edwards, both enthusiastic newspapermen, though only Edwards had professional training, plunged into the colorful life of the capital with avidity, and their newspaper contains a complete record of what they saw and felt. The *Times* was financed by Maximilian himself, and the Empress Carlota smiled on it. She had a warm spot in her heart for the sans-culottes of the South, had the regal Carlota, and they returned her friendship with adoration.[1]

The *Times* was printed on good stock, which has withstood well the ravages of time, and was published every Saturday. Its masthead was set in the same type as that of the New York *Times*, in "Old English" lettering, and the paper consisted of a four-page folder well buttressed with advertisements. The price was two reales per copy or a dollar a month by subscription. The first issue appeared on September 16, 1865, under the chief editorship of Henry Watkins Allen. At the death of Allen, Edwards succeeded him as editor and held that post as long as the *Times* remained an official organ of the Empire; after the subsidy was withdrawn and Edwards resigned, it was owned and edited by one C. B. Barksdale, an American business-man who urged the Emperor to abdicate and was jailed for a month for his pains.

Under the editorship of Allen, however, with Edwards as assistant, the *Times* got off to a handsome start with $10,000 in the bank. Both Allen and Edwards had the ear and confidence of Maximilian, and their devotion to the imperial cause was not wholly self-serving, al-though the subsidy and the weekly paper were a newspaperman's dream come true—and in a paradise of the tropics at that. Both ro-mantic Southerners would have worked willingly for nothing, if that had been possible, for both had succumbed, instantly and irrevocably, to the charm of the Emperor and Empress; and Edwards mourned the Empress all his days, writing, in the Kansas City *Times,* upon her confinement in a European madhouse, the famous editorial, "Poor Carlota," [2] which was reprinted all over the English-speaking world. It was such an editorial as Galahad might have written of Guinevere.

The Mexican Times opened its offices the second week in Septem-ber at No. 17, Hotel de San Carlos, on the corner of Coliseo and San Francisco streets. One of Allen's first acts as editor was to set up a register on which newly arrived Southerners could record their names and addresses for the benefit of their friends. Edwards signed the register as having arrived on August 29th, Jo Shelby on September 3rd, and Commodore Maury and Editor Allen each noted the fact that they had been in the city since June 1st and July 29th respec-tively. The register was reprinted in the first edition of the paper.

The *Times* informed the public that copies were available at the

San Carlos, and at the two swankier hotels, the Iturbide and the Nacional, and that it could also be bought at the newsstand of H. C. Covert on the corner of Second Plateros and San Juan streets. The newsdealer's address caused Editor Allen to complain of the Mexican custom of naming a street more than once; it was confusing, he pointed out, to have a First Plateros Street and a Second Plateros Street.

In the first issue Allen announced that the foreign policy of the *Times* would be the same as that which Marshal Bazaine had announced for Mexico: "indemnity for the past and security for the future." There was also an editorial on the weather: "The Rain—It Raineth Every Day."

Like the editors of many weekly papers, Allen was hard up for front-page material. On the front page of the first issue were two lengthy features, "The Death of Montezuma," dealing with a news event three hundred years old, and a history of the song, "Annie Laurie." There was more than a hint of nostalgia in the second selection. Henry Watkins Allen was never a willing exile, although he wrote in a letter home, "I receive much kindness here; I ought to be grateful. *I am.* My sanctum in Mexico is the headquarters of all Americans. I do not expect to be permitted to return, but *I shall live and die an American citizen.*" [3]

In the issue of the 23rd, the *Times* announced, "It is our pleasure to state that the following gentlemen have been appointed agents of colonization by the Imperial Government: Sterling Price, Isham Harris of Tennessee, John W. Perkins of Louisiana and W. T. Hardiman of Texas. Also Señor Roberts of Texas." On the 19th, Price, Perkins, and Harris had left for Cordoba, Hardiman and Roberts for Tepic. "In a few weeks," says the *Times*, the reports of the agents of colonization will be received, and good lands, in healthy districts, will be apportioned to everyone who wishes to become a citizen of Mexico."

Meanwhile Allen's editorial assistant had been roaming the streets of Mexico City like a delighted child, savoring the Utopian sights, sounds, and smells, enjoying the mild weather and exulting in the heady altitude. John Edwards was a bachelor and there were no ties tugging at his heartstrings, as there were at Henry Allen's. And he loved Mexico City. As the Reverend George Plattenburg, of Dover, Missouri, said of him after his death, "What a strangely romantic period these two years must have been to the dreamy, poetic soldier of the North. The rich, tropical foliage, the skies luminously blue, the warm airs and the voluptuous climate, the romantic people inheriting the glorious traditions of old Spain, memories of the Cid, the songs of Calderón and Lope de Vega, chanted in the sweet Castilian tongue must have been things of ceaseless charm to the imaginative temperament so strongly marked in Major Edwards." [4]

Edwards, in fact, was thinking of exactly all those things, for he was a student of heroic literature of all ages, but he was also a newspaperman and he missed nothing in the current scene. One fact especially enchanted him and he noted it for the paper: "Ice from Popocatepetl is sold on the backs of burros (asses) at one and a half cents in the streets." Editorials were unsigned, but the suspicion is strong that he also wrote the one entitled, "Oh, the Beautiful Flowers!" It read:

"On the corners of the Calles Calisco and Espíritu Santo where they join the San Francisco, the Broadway of Mexico City, are to be seen every morning long rows of Indian boys and girls offering for sale the most beautiful flowers made into the most exquisite bouquets. These flowers grow in the valley around the city and are brought to market by means of the canals, which are still much used by natives. In passing these marts of Flora we always stop and feast our eyes on nature's loveliest work—always excepting woman. Heretofore, seen side by side are all the rare and beautiful flowers known to the tropics. The passion flower and the superb cloth-of-gold, the most delicate cactus and the *flor del paraíso* are also here in great profusion. . . ."

Mexico's Independence Day is September 16th, and on that day Their Majesties attended the opera. It was "Belisario," one of Donizetti's best. The Italian Opera Troupe sang the national hymn on the stage after the performance in honor of the Emperor and Empress. That was a Sunday afternoon. In the morning the editors of the *Times* had attended a military mass at the Cathedral and been greatly impressed by the uniforms.

The influx of ex-Confederates into Mexico City was having a plainly discernible effect on life in the capital, as reflected in the advertisements. Dr. B. M. Rodgers (from California) announced to the public that he kept always on hand not only the best cigars, Havana and Mexican, but the BEST Virginia chewing tobacco, at wholesale or retail. F. Dufere, formerly of the Hotel St. Louis in New Orleans, had opened the National Bar for Americans at the Hotel Nacional, but Ed Daily, new proprietor of the St. Charles Saloon at the San Carlos, warned that his establishment was "the only saloon in the place where London and New York drinks are served."

The San Carlos, host of *The Mexican Times*, advertised "well furnished and arranged and ventilated apartments" and Editor Allen in appreciation gave it a free plug, declaring, "We recommend the San Carlos to the traveling public. This elegant, newly furnished and well kept Hotel is decidedly one of the best in the city. It is the favorite resort of Americans." Shelby was staying there too, although "Prince John" Magruder was at the more fashionable Iturbide in his dove-colored top hat and his pepper-and-salt cutaway.

There was also the National Shaving, Hairdressing and Dyeing, Curling and Shampooing Salon, at the corner of Santa Clara and Third San Francisco streets. For those interested in reading matter, the English Circulating Library, No. 4 Calle San Francisco, offered a collection of 2,000 volumes, "the only one in Spanish America."

The issue of September 23, 1865, also announced that Matthew Fontaine Maury had become a citizen of Mexico, and featured an article on the cultivation of the cacao plant, "of interest to all who are going into the chocolate business." It was to be the first of a series of articles on money crops which could be raised in Mexico. For the benefit of the exiles, two exchanges were headed "Destitution in Georgia" and "The Kentucky Elections a Mockery," designed perhaps to make them more contented with their lot in a foreign land. The following week, the *Times* carried the text of Maximilian's proclamation declaring that since Juárez had left Mexican soil, and was a refugee in Texas, his followers were now bandits and outside the law. This was the famous "Black Decree," which made mandatory the execution of prisoners and cost Maximilian his own life when he himself was made a prisoner.

By October 14 Maury had become Chief of Colonization and Magruder Chief of the Office of Land Colonization. Their friends in the United States will be pleased etc. At the Concert Room in the Palace, the Italian Opera Troupe gave a special performance for their Majesties; "the beauty and the fashion of the city were there"; likewise Major John Newman Edwards.

The American Steamship Mail Company of New York, says the

Times, is now running two modern steamers to Vera Cruz, the *Manhattan* and the *Vera Cruz;* the captain of the *Manhattan,* Captain Turner, a fine upstanding fellow and a credit to the American Merchant Marine, has visited the *Times* office. The Empire is riding high, the rebels are scattered in the north and Porfirio Díaz is cut off in the south; Editor Allen cries, "Give us immigration! Give us the skill and energy of Americans, French, English, German and Irish!"

There is some other important ship news also in the same issue. Mrs. Shelby, wife of the General, and her two small sons, have arrived in Mexico from New Orleans, and the *Times* reports that Mrs. Shelby wrote in a letter that General Sheridan told her, "Your husband outlawed himself in going to Mexico." [5] Editor Allen has been to Cordoba to see the Shelbys, and he comments on the bad roads, especially in the region of the Paso del Macho, which would "literally swallow up stages, passengers, mules and all. The Ministro de Fomento is at work on it."

But Allen found things humming in Cordoba: "There is no limit to the land the company can buy," and the crops that will grow there, at the mere scratch of a hoe, are tobacco, coffee, sugar cane, rice, indigo, cochineal, and all the cereals in great perfection. Also fruits and vegetables. Generals Price and Shelby are doing well and there is still plenty of land left at the twenty-five-cents to a dollar-an-acre figure, with five years to pay. "Cordoba is in fact a paradise ... not like the West which has to be reclaimed from the wilderness. Here the settler has only "to redeem from the ravages of war."

The *Times* wishes "Success to these noble pioneers! Success to the Village of Carlota!"

But it is Christmas time, and not all the cheers for the Emperor nor the good wishes for the village of Carlota can take the place of being home at Christmas. Henry Watkins Allen, he who had been once of that company whom O. Henry called the angels of the earth, could not forget. On Christmas Day he wrote:

"On Last Christmas we were seated in our executive chair, chief magistrate of the great State of Louisiana, the Governor of a noble constituency of lovely women and brave men. The Christmas before that we were a brigadier in the field. On the next Christmas we were confined to our bed, given up to die and suffering all the agonies of terrible wounds. Today we are in this great city, editing this humble paper and coining our brain into our daily bread, but thank God, in good health—as it were rejuvenated—and now enjoying the hospitality of the good people of Mexico. God bless the exiles wherever they may be in this wide world of sorrow and may they on Christmas Day with grateful hearts thank all who have been kind to them in the land of the stranger. That heaven may bless our native land, and bind up the bruised and broken hearts and dry every mourner's tear, is our sincere, fervent prayer."

If I forget thee, O Jerusalem!

On New Year's Day, 1866, the *Times* devotes its whole front page to the message of Andrew Johnson to Congress on the restoration of the Union. The Empress Carlota has returned from a trip to Yucatan, and Major Edwards composes a long poem in honor of the event.

On January 16th Editor Allen welcomed the *Deutsche Presse*, published in German in the city. "It is a highly respectable sheet," he said, "and we hope it will be well and liberally patronized by the public. The German population including the officers and soldiers of German extraction form a large and highly respectable portion of this empire. They should have a newspaper. We welcome Dr. Frederico A. Ludert to the corps editorial."

In the same issue the *Times* said: "We have received letters from Señores Price, Shelby, Perkins and Harris at Cordoba. They are all doing well and delighted with Mexico. We have also heard from Col. Terry of Guadalajara and Col. O'Bannon of San Luis Potosí." [6]

The *Times* also quotes with approval an editorial in the New York *Daily News* which reports that many disaffected Southerners are in Mexico, "all of them in high spirits and expect to make a fortune raising coffee." The same paper carries, too, the letter of General Sterling Price to a friend in New York pointing out that "we are practically as near the markets of New Orleans and New York as are the people of Central Missouri, and the climate is the best in the world." There is also mention of the fact that the Imperial Mexican Railway will be extended soon from Vera Cruz into the highlands, and that the ex-Confederate colony soon will be linked by rail to the sea.

Major Edwards' preoccupation with natural phenomena is seen in two items published about this time. One is an editorial on an earthquake, the other on a sea serpent reportedly seen in Virginia. Even in 1865, the sea serpent was a newspaper standby.

An earth tremor had shaken up the *Times* office. (The editorial rooms had been moved from No. 17 to more commodious quarters in No. 37, Hotel de San Carlos.)

"The cool weather of the last few days," says the editorial, "doubtless has been caused by the earthquake. Why and how we leave to the weatherwise philosophers to tell. What is the primary cause of earthquakes? An intelligent article on this all-absorbing topic is solicited." As any newspaperman can see, Major Edwards was having a very fine time at his job of assistant. An indefatigable reader of exchanges, he also published the report that "the Richmond (Va.) *Times* amuses itself with refreshing stories of the old newspaper canard of the sea serpent. The fabulous monster has reappeared on the coast of Nahant and Willis Creek, Virginia. At the latter place when seen it was reported to be 150 feet long."

In December, 1865, the first of the exiles to return to the United States has gone. The ageing Kirby Smith has left Mexico, and is reported to be in Lynchburg, Virginia. But Jubal Early, "a noble Southern Tacitus," is in town. He and General Sheridan are rumored to be on the verge of a duel because of snide remarks made by the Yankee general in an interview.

The paper was having trouble with one of its advertisers. Under an editorial banner entitled "HOLLOWAY'S PILLS," it complained: "We have published his pills for several months and now he refuses to pay the draft of his agent. Out upon such a swindling, thieving concern! Stephens [a representative of Holloway's Pills] has his price for his pills and we have our price for the paper. Benjamin Holloway Stephens should be condemned to sit in the pillory and swallow his own pills until he has purged himself to death."

In March Editor Allen took a trip to the seaside at Vera Cruz, visiting the colony of Carlota en route, and on St. Patrick's Day, 1866, bathed in the ocean, writing to Edwards in Mexico City, "I have bathed in the briny waters of Old Ocean and laid my hands upon his mane and played familiar with his hoary locks." Allen was one, like Edwards, who scorned to use the copper coin of language where there was so much gold lying about. "When the Imperial Railway to Vera Cruz is finished, what a rush there will be for fresh oysters and fish and sea bathing!"

The gallant Allen was feeling much better than he had in years, and seemed on his way to a full recovery from the ill health that had plagued him since Shiloh; but the hand of death was laid on him at Vera Cruz. That graveyard of Europeans and Americans in the mosquito-infested lowlands, was full of the yellow fever at this season, and Allen came down with it. He died of it in Mexico City on April 22, 1866, in spite of all that Marshal Bazaine's personal physician could do, and Edwards succeeded to full control of the paper.

March was a fateful month. It was during March that the United States inaugurated the moves which were to hasten Maximilian to his doom; and in Allen's last editorial he had written, concerning the rumors that the French troops were to be evacuated from Mexico, "The United States are spoiled children whose pranks old Europe often smiles at; but the statesmen of America should avoid abusing the patience of France and England beyond their endurance. The evacuation of Mexico by French troops will commence the moment that the Government of the United States shall have recognized the Emperor Maximilian."

The French, in fact, had already got their marching orders from Secretary of State Seward. Politely, but firmly, he had told them that they must go. They could take eighteen months to do so, and withdraw gradually, thus saving face; but go they must, for, as General Grant said, the French invasion of Mexico was so closely related to the Rebellion as to be a part of it.[7] Louis Napoleon and Bazaine had already acquiesced, and even though Maximilian was to occupy the throne of Montezuma for a full year longer, preparations were going forward for the withdrawal of the French troops.

To Edwards, withdrawal of the French troops was as unthinkable as it had been to Allen. On May 19, 1866, he wrote: "We do not believe, in the first place, that the French troops will be withdrawn. Eighteen months is a long time and North American insolence and aggression may become insufferable. Mr. Seward's menace of Austria, and the rest of the world, General Sheridan's hatred of emigration, and General Weitzel's conduct on the Rio Grande and other markedly unfriendly acts show that the chronic bullying of that party has not yet exhausted itself, and the only question is how far it can be carried unless it is speedily checked."

When it became obvious, as it soon did, that nothing was going to check the policy of the United States with regard to Mexico, Edwards wrote petulantly: "Since the Emperor [Napoleon] has announced openly his intention to withdraw his forces, why, the sooner they go, the better, that's all. The Emperor Maximilian has possession, which is the nine points involved, and the tenth may be found in the determination with which he intends to strive for his honor and his cause."

None should have known better than Major Edwards that it would take more than mere determination to set at naught the purposes of men like Grant and Seward.

Shortly thereafter the attack on the Cordoba Colony occurred and the *Times* reprinted an account of it from the columns of the *Railway Era*, an English language publication which had been established at Orizaba by George W. Clarke:[8]

"A well mounted column under Col. Figueroa swept down on the unprotected outpost, swallowed up men, stock, implements and provisions, and threw their advance to the gates of Carlota, where they were beaten off. In a night the hard-bought improvements of nine months were swept away, were destroyed totally. Homes were plundered, trunks forced open, mules taken, clandestinely approved by sympathetic neighbors. If they had been Yankee railroad contractors or owners of model coffee haciendas there would not have been a horse stolen or a firkin of lard run into tortillas. They were mostly ex-Confederates, which only means, as we have ever contended, that Southern men are naturally and instinctively supporters of the Empire."

Edwards pointed to the Cordoba raid as an example of the Emperor's need to follow Shelby's suggestion and recruit 50,000 soldiers of the Southern Army to bolster his sagging Empire. Under former C. S. A. commissioned officers, Edwards said, such an army still could replace the troops of Louis Napoleon and secure Maximilian on his throne.[9]

He was having troubles of his own, too. The $10,000 subsidy had been spent, and in August, 1866, the paper suspended publication for a week. "Owing to changes necessary to be made in the paper," Edwards advised his readers, "its publication for one week will be suspended, at the expiration of which time we hope to offer renewed inducements to our subscribers." Business was bad for the Empire, too; the subsidy would not be renewed although Edwards' salary would continue. Juárez was back in the country with a large if ill-trained army and General Sheridan had been in contact with his emissaries in the North, "taking care not to do so in the dark."[10] The

Juaristas were equal at least in numbers to the French and they were in possession of the whole line of the Rio Grande and all Mexico as far down as San Luis Potosí.

Edwards managed to resume publication of the *Times* on August 27, 1866. Throughout the fall and winter his paper reflected the uneasy mood of the capital, although nothing could altogether extinguish his natural optimism. In June he had written: "Life is very brief and commonplace, but crest it with a crown, deck it with the glory and grandeur of royalty illumined by great and heroic deeds, and it floats away in an eternal sea of history and renown." In that sentence was summed up the whole creed of John Newman Edwards, the votary of Sir Walter Scott; but as winter came on, no amount of optimism or imperial tinsel could stay the course of history.

Shortly after Sheridan extended the hand of friendship to the Juaristas, the New York *Times* reported that an agreement had been reached under which the United States was to give military support to Juárez in return for the cession of the rich mining states of Chihuahua and Sonora. Edwards dismissed the report as the foolish rumor that it was, in an editorial entitled "All That Glitters Is Not Gold," but he turned both journalistic barrels on the correspondent of the New York *Times* who had originated the rumor. The mountain, he said, had attracted the attention of a mouse. The mountain was "this goodly city of ours" and the mouse the "Washington penny-a-liner"; but the real RAT was the New York *Times*, "which has gnawed its way into every party and then gnawed out again." Edwards did not like the New York *Times*.

He had good reason not to. The *Times* had been an implacable foe of the Confederates in Mexico. In this case he was perhaps thinking of a particularly infuriating article written by a *Times* correspondent on January 19, 1866, entitled "Interview With Seedy Southern Exiles —Failure of the Southern Emigration Scheme." Since the colony had been barely established at that time, announcement of its failure was certainly premature; yet the New York reporter had written condescendingly: "We had a look at some of those great and mighty Southerners who have sold four thousand Southern families to the Empire. The Emperor, however, begins to smell a rat, and begins to see that Maury, Price and Magruder have humbugged him. The four thousand families have not been delivered according to bargain—not even one thousand, not even one hundred, not even fifty. The poor fellows looked seedy enough ... they had one horse between four. Indeed the ways of a sinner are hard."

As Major Edwards said, if anyone smelled a rat, he could identify the rat.

The Mexican Times was in serious financial difficulties by November; Edwards tried valiantly, after the subsidy was spent, to pay expenses through job printing and advertisements; but he was no business man and after three months the paper's affairs were in such a snarl that there was nothing to do but put it on the auction block. B. C. Barksdale, who had a sewing machine agency in Mexico City, and had made a fortune selling the *máquinas de coser*, bought it for an undisclosed price. Major Edwards laid down his pen and for the next two months visited friends at Cordoba and elsewhere before returning to the United States. He arrived home in Missouri in April, 1867.

The last editorial that Edwards wrote for *The Mexican Times* concerned Carlota. He had received shocking news; the Empress had suffered a nervous breakdown in Rome, whither she had gone to ask the aid of the Pope in keeping her husband on the throne of Mexico. The Pope had been a last, desperate resort; Louis Napoleon had already refused to have anything further to do with Maximilian, and when the full realization of what this meant came to the highly strung, ambitious woman, her mind gave way.

Edwards wrote, "Very weak and pale today at Miramar, surrounded by the unseen wings of angels, lies the proudest, queenliest, noblest woman of the age. Pure and stainless as a heaven-guarded child, she has hazarded life for humanity and sacrificed health for her kindred and her cause. Within the hushed and silent chamber rises up a shrine bright with glorious teachings of nobility—so holy that womanhood all over the earth can bow down and worship there as the Persian bends in wild idolatry to the shining God of his country and his faith.

"Beautiful in the pride and purity of her kingly race; filled inexpressibly with the great longings of heroic ambition; brave unto death and clothed with a mantle of living hope and desire—she vanquished the terrors of pestilence, scorned the dangers of the sea, endured the fatigues of a dreary voyage and entered the palace of the Tuileries as a saint might enter heaven—because she had a right to be there and because she was the equal of any prince or emperor, pope or potentate from the confines of one continent to the confines of another.

"Amid the vastness and age and memories of the Eternal City she was stricken down as a flower when the hoar frosts fall and the north wind comes heavy with the wings of the snow. It is only left to those now who have received from her unbounded charity, help and sympathy; those who have drawn from her immortal example, courage and devotion; those who feel pride in their sex because it has been crowned, and enabled to pray to that God who tempers the wind to the shorn lamb that he will cool her fevered brow with the gentle streams of his everlasting mercy and bless her returning health with wishes gratified and hopes fulfilled and realized."

The same issue also recorded the fact that General Shelby had left for Tuxpan with twenty families. Edwards assailed the immigration authorities, but he lauded Shelby to the sky, saying that if the management of Cordoba had been entrusted to him a great and growing colony would extend southward from the Gulf and to the gates of Mexico City. "With him there is no such word as fail."

With Edwards, however, there was such a word now, and he left his office at the San Carlos for good on December 5th. There would be other newspapers, in Missouri, and an editorial fame that would spread beyond the borders of the state; but there would never be another such venture, for him, as *The Mexican Times*.

Under Barksdale, the paper prospered at once. He was a capable editor and a courageous one and he had in ample measure the business instincts which Edwards lacked. Within a short time the paper was a bi-weekly instead of a weekly and the front page was covered with ads instead of features copied out of the encyclopedia. Henry Allen and John Edwards had used the New York *Times* as a typographical model; under Barksdale the paper resembled the London *Times*, which has published ads on the front page for a hundred years.

From the first, Barksdale was impatient with Maximilian for not packing his valise and going home to Europe where he certainly belonged. When Maximilian went out to the field to look over troops of his "Imperial Mexican Army," Barksdale wrote: "It is our inflexible idea that the Emperor will not return to this capital." The Emperor did return, in brief triumph; but Barksdale quoted Marshal Bazaine as saying, "The Republic has entered into the manners and ideas of a majority of the people." Barksdale remarked: "This is the confession of one who has been for some two years in Mexico, fighting and working to make it his empire. With 40,000 French and 20,000 Mexicans under his command, the marshal confesses the failure of the attempt."

As another not so gentle hint to the Emperor to get out, Barksdale ran this item: "A Significant Notice: The Last Convoy. Col. Napoleon Boyer, Marshal Bazaine's chief of staff, announces through the columns of the *Ere Nouvelle* that the very last convoy will depart from this city on Friday the 1st proximo. He warns all persons who intend to improve the opportunity that there will be no postponement. The date mentioned is farther off than was intended, but on account of the large number of families that are anxious to go to Vera Cruz with the convoy, a postponement has been made from the 27th to the 1st proximo."

All of this was extremely annoying to the Imperial officials in Mexico City, but it was not until Barksdale reported that Maximilian was seeking to make a deal with Porfirio Díaz that they acted. Barksdale was in jail for a month before he was able to make his peace with General Marquez, whom Maximilian had named his *lugarteniente* in the capital.

The suspension of *The Mexican Times* for eight issues seems but to have whetted the appetite of its readers for later issues; the paper picked up right where it had left off and on June 17, 1867, Barksdale announced that "the rapid increases in circulation of the *Times* since the change of management in December 1866 has clearly proved that a newspaper published in the English language in Mexico City is not only a necessity, but that it can be a power in the country."

The next day, the troops of Porfirio Díaz entered the city, and all foreign language newspapers were suppressed.

PART FIVE

The Bluegrass and Missouri Again

———◆◆◆———

27. *Home from the Wars*

IT WAS a changed Lexington to which Shelby and his family returned in June, 1867. His old boyhood friend, John Hunt Morgan, was dead in the war, as were so many of the gilded youth of Kentucky who had been his boon companions in the long-gone days at Transylvania University. The war had killed the hemp industry in the state, and in fact in the entire South.[1] His stepfather, Benjamin Gratz, had been retired since 1861. The ropewalk in the rear of the mansion on Mill Street was idle now, and practically the only business interest in which Gratz was active was the cultivation of the big $40,000 farm outside of Waverly which he had acquired during the war.

The political atmosphere of Kentucky, however, delighted Shelby. In Mexico he had heard grim stories of Reconstruction, but as he walked the streets of Lexington he found Southerners holding their heads up, for the pro-Confederate element had succeeded in doing at the polls in 1866 what they had not been able to do in '61: they had gained control of the state. The Democratic Convention at Louisville in May had adopted a belligerent platform condemning the Federal government for its "usurpations," extending sympathy to the Southern states in their troubles, and demanding the right to regulate the political status of the freed Negroes. The platform praised President Andrew Johnson for his stand on the Freedmen's Bureau and the Civil Rights Bill, and pledged support of efforts to restore the Constitution and the powers of the states.

When the election was held, the candidates of the simon pure Democrats, running on this platform to repeal the Civil War, were elected by an overwhelming majority. The Cincinnati *Gazette*, a Radical Republican newspaper and self-appointed monitor of Kentucky politics, admitted: "It was a straight-cut rebel victory. There is not the least necessity in trying to dodge or evade the issue. . . . The rebel gray has whipped the union blue at the polls." [2]

The reason for this revulsion of feeling in Kentucky undoubtedly was that the Federal occupation authorities, with their harsh rule and their indiscriminate use of firing squads, had alienated even that section of the population which had been staunchly Unionist throughout the war.[3] The emancipation of the slaves, now set over their masters in the Southern states, was a sore point, too. In fact, Kentuckians found the political philosophy of the Radical Republicans altogether too proletarian and exotic, and they flocked back to the banner of what the New York *Herald* called "Bourbon Democracy" with a vengeance.

Jo Shelby found the air of Kentucky sweet to breathe again.

The first reference to Shelby in Lexington after he reached St. Louis aboard the *Great Republic* is to be found in the *Kentucky Gazette* for June 22, 1867, which observes: "General Jo. O. Shelby paid our city a visit on Thursday last and spent the day receiving the congratulations of his friends and the hearty good wishes of those who have differed with him politically. He has no enemies, and it is gratifying to observe that his intercourse with our people was both friendly and cordial. This is right; for there is no sort of propriety in allowing old questions to disturb the equanimity of the present, or add an obstacle to the heartiest reestablishment of those kindly relations that should subsist between the people whose political destiny is so intimately and inseparably conjoined.

"Gen. Shelby did not merely receive a cordial welcome from politician friends, but the greeting extended to those of opposite sentiment, who had known him in brighter and better days, all giving him the right hand of friendship and wishing for him prosperity and happiness. This cordial reception in the capital of his own county must have been gratifying, if not indeed flattering to him. And this is just as it should be. We should not allow prejudice to so far overcome our judgment of propriety and right as to either forget or neglect the genial and pleasant gentleman and brave and intelligent soldier—the hero of a hundred hard-fought battles in the open field against a legitimate enemy, each contending for what they thought right."

The account further records that "in the evening, Gen. Shelby did the ladies present at Arcana Hall the honor of his presence for a short time, where the welcome to him was marked with all the cordiality and respect due to a gentleman and a soldier. We again welcome Gen. Shelby to his old county, and hope that he will find it to his advantage to make Fayette County his home. But should he not do so, our best wishes follow him wherever he may elect to reside."

It was Lafayette County, Missouri, however, not Fayette County, Kentucky, which was home to Jo and Betsy Shelby, and he made plans to return to Missouri immediately, to a farm near Aullville in the hemp country. The hemp industry was in a bad way; in fact it was just as dead in Missouri as it was in Kentucky, but Jo Shelby could not foresee that, and since Missouri had been the nation's greatest hemp-growing state in the late 1850's, it was logical to suppose that the future of the hemp industry still lay in Missouri.

Furthermore, the state had been laid waste by war, and its economy would have to rebuild. In that fact lay the seeds of a mighty prosperity, for in addition to the agricultural wealth of Missouri, there were thick beds of coal under the western ridges, and mountains of iron ore. With the railroads pushing west (the Union Pacific was being driven to California that very year by the swinging picks of the Irish) and with Missouri standing at the crossroads of the nation, a boom was inevitable when political conditions should return to normal. Shelby could not wait to begin spreading hemp again. And of course, as always, he would go into a little of everything to bolster his hemp crop; farming, buying livestock, and turning prairie lands into wheat fields.

Betsy Shelby too was homesick for Missouri and the beautiful countryside from which she had been so rudely banished six years ago. She wanted to go home with the children, and so did her husband.

Thus, with the financial backing of the family, Shelby returned to the Missouri River Valley in the summer of 1867, only a few miles from the spot where he had ridden away as a captain in the State Guard in 1861. Their home was a plain farmhouse, twelve miles from Lexington and the broad Missouri River, situated in a triangle of rich prairie formed by the towns of Aullville, Page City, and Higginsville. Higginsville, six miles away, was the post office. Nathan Parker, a writer from the North who published a book that year, *Missouri as It Is in 1867*, now a gold mine of information on postwar Missouri, says of the neighborhood of Higginsville that "the traveler sees as fine country as there is in Missouri. The landscape is beautiful and imposing. In summer the prairies resemble a vast carpet of green spread out before him, dotted here and there with herds of cattle that crop the luxuriant native grasses, and flowers of every hue and every color of the rainbow, which perfume the atmosphere while they dazzle the eye of the beholder, and he can hardly dismiss the idea that the cattle are trespassers on his artificial parterre, which seems to have been cultivated and carefully dressed, and set in groves skirted along the streams with beautiful parks." [4]

But the beauty of the countryside belied the harsh reality of life for those Missourians who had fought against the Union or supported the Confederacy behind the Federal lines. Hostility against the Southern minority was deeper and more vindictive in Missouri than in any other state, for Missouri had been not only a battleground, but a house divided against itself. Her body politic had been clubbed into a sense-less, bloody pulp by the internecine warfare, and by the atrocities committed, on the one side, by Quantrill, Anderson, and Todd, and by Lane, Jennison, Ewing, and McNeil, on the other. The whole community was seething with hate, hating as only neighbors and kinsmen can hate.

The Union had won, and dire and bitter measures were being taken against the ex-Confederates. The Drake Constitution of 1865, while it could hardly be called a carpetbag Constitution since it was drawn up by Missourians, was nevertheless an instrument of vengeance against the ex-rebels which was not surpassed in any of the "recon-structed" states, not even under Governor Brownlow in Tennessee. Former Confederates were not only disfranchised in Missouri, they were forbidden to teach, preach, practice law, perform the marriage ceremony, or engage in corporate business. To make sure that no state court would interfere with its provisions, the Constitution provided for the removal of judges and other officers of government at the instance of the governor, who could replace them with Radical Republicans at will.

The fanaticism of the Radicals was to prove their own undoing in the end, as it had in Kentucky, and the pendulum was to swing in the other direction by 1870, when Gratz Brown was to be elected governor; but at this time the only occupation open to Shelby was that of farmer. He could not engage in business as he had done in the 1850's, or in any other occupation save that of the soil. In this he was not so fortunate as General Lee, who had become a college president in 1867.[5]

But Jo Shelby was a farmer at heart, and the next two years were happy ones for the Shelbys, after the turmoil of Mexico. In 1868 the disabilities of ex-Confederates were removed, and their fourth child, Webb Shelby, was born. With four small boys Betsy Shelby had her hands full. (It was beginning to look as if there would be no girls in the family.) She was not too busy, however, to keep the open house that Shelby loved. During these years the farmhouse was visited by hundreds of old Confederates, many of whom were homeless upon the roads of Missouri, and for them the latchstring was always out, as well as a good dinner cooked and a clean bed waiting. The Shelby latchstring was out not merely for old Confederates. In his home Shelby entertained almost daily former officers and men of the Blue Armies, especially those who had fought against him and who were impelled either by admiration or curiosity to see the Great Raider of the Rebellion in person. Between old soldiers, naturally, there was no animosity, for as Grant said, if it had been left up to the soldiers, peace would have been restored in a year.[6]

The fame of the Shelby hospitality soon became such that in a short time anybody who needed a meal, or an encouraging word, or help of any kind—such as eloping sweethearts—wound up at the Shelby homestead whether they knew the Shelbys or not. On at least two occasions the romantic Jo and his no less romantic Betsy assisted runaways to get married. One of these was John Newman Edwards and his fiancée, Virginia Plattenburg, who was also his cousin. They were married at the Shelby farm on March 28, 1871. The gallant major was forced to elope with his bride from her home at near-by Dover, for Jennie's parents objected to the union on the ground of the near family relationship of the parties. But it was a love match and highly successful, much more so than might have been expected from a bachelor of the age and disposition of John Edwards. The romantic soldier, now a newspaper editor in Kansas City,[7] made a devoted husband.

Among the visitors to the Shelby homestead in the late sixties and early seventies were Jesse James, Frank James, Cole Younger, and some of their friends. Their business seemed to carry them about the country a good deal, and Jesse always tried to pay for their meals, though Shelby wouldn't hear of it. They were as welcome as the flowers in May, Frank especially, for they were his old boys, and in Jo Shelby's eyes his old boys could do no wrong. There were plenty of stories going around to the effect that they were road agents, but if so, it was up to the law to catch them. And the law in Missouri, at least in the first few years after the war, would get little aid or comfort from Jo Shelby. It was that same law which disfranchised Southern white men and dragged them down to the level of Negroes before the war; if the boys got a little desperate under these circumstances, no one was going to criticize them for it—or interfere with them—in Shelby's presence.

Many of Shelby's admirers have made much of the supposed fact that Shelby always absented himself from home if he knew that the James Boys were coming, but the plain truth of the matter is that he didn't. If he was at home, he stayed and greeted them; if he had gone to town, he had gone to town, and Jesse's and Frank's schedule had no influence on it one way or the other.

As the St. Louis *Republican* said, " It made no difference whether General Shelby was home or not. The latchstring was out just the same; and if it was winter, the big, open fireplace was made to blaze with logs and the table groaned with the bounteous fare which the Shelby family always kept. There were more dainties when guests came and somehow the fire seemed brighter and bigger. But Jesse James was safe and he knew it. Shelby had announced that anyone who surrounded the house would have to take the consequences. It would have been a reckless daredevil of a detective indeed who would have dared intrude upon the Shelby homestead, for with him his home was his castle. A hungry detective might have pulled the latchstring, found food and shelter, but the minute he sought to intrude his mission it would have been a sorry day for him. None were brave enough to try it, although they must have known where the game could be found. Constables and sheriffs knew where Jesse came and went. They knew him by a great fleet-footed gray horse, a pet that he always rode, and yet none of them called at the Shelby homestead for several days thereafter, and then not on business. Jesse made no effort to conceal his identity. He rode along the country highways and through the village streets. . . ." [8]

That was written much later, when the James Gang had attained its national notoriety as robbers of both trains and banks, but it would have made no difference at any time, as events showed. Aside from his unswerving loyalty to the men of his old command, Shelby considered that he owed Frank James a debt that he could never repay, for saving him from capture at Prairie Grove, and that Jesse shared in the debt which he owed to Frank.

Shelby was to repay this debt to Frank James twice over, during the next fifteen years or so, and it was to cost him dear, but where there was a question of loyalty involved, with Jo Shelby there could be but one answer. Frank and Jesse and their companions were welcome at the house between Aullville and Page City. Such loyalty is not unknown in Missouri in our time, around Independence, not far from the Shelbys' neighborhood.

One day in 1872, Frank James rode up to the Shelby farmhouse. Visits from the James Boys were not unusual (Jesse especially had always put himself out to be nice to Betsy Shelby and on one occasion had saved a Negro boy on the place from violence at the hands of white ruffians), but this time Frank was alone. Furthermore, he was in a desperate condition. Shelby said afterward that he was bleeding at the lungs. Whether this was from a bullet wound is not clear. Robertus Love, in his *Rise and Fall of Jesse James*, says that Frank was rumored to have tuberculosis,[9] but at any rate, Frank was as pale as death and unable to ride or walk another step. The Shelbys took him in, and for the next two and a half months nursed him until he was able to be up and about again. As Shelby testified later at Frank's trial, everyone knew he was there, but he was not molested by the officers of the law during all that time. When he recovered, he rode away to Tennessee. That was the last time Shelby saw Frank James until he saw him in the prisoner's dock, on trial for his life, twelve years later.

28. *"The Bloody Bonds": The Gunn City Massacre*

WHEN THE DISABILITIES of the ex-Confederates were removed in 1868, Jo Shelby cast around for some business to go into, aside from farming. The farm prospered, but not sufficiently to support the lavish hospitality which he and Betsy extended to all who chanced their way; and railroads, which were enjoying a postwar building boom, seemed the most promising opportunity for big money.

"Boom" is a mild word for the turbulent revival of railroad spending which was taking place in Missouri. A race was on—a race to be the first county in a given section to have a railroad, and whole communities, stirred by promotion literature and editorials in their local papers,[1] felt that here was the philosopher's stone—transportation. Land values would rise at least five dollars an acre within five miles of any railroad; farmers' market prices would increase fifty per cent; and a flood of immigration, with prosperity in its wake, would follow wherever the magic tracks were laid. Half the counties in the state were mortgaging themselves up to the hilt, and beyond, to build short lines or "feeders" to connect with big railroads, such as the Missouri Pacific, which ran from St. Louis to Kansas City, and thence with main lines in Kansas and Nebraska.

No fewer than eighteen of these short lines were built,[2] and some of them, like the Missouri, Kansas & Texas (the "Katy") grew into major railroads. In some cases, however, where the counties parted with the bonds before the work was done, they found themselves with a large bonded indebtedness and no railroad;[3] but the bonds could not be repudiated if they had come into the hands of "holders in due course"—as the promoters saw that they had—and their grandchildren would still be paying the bill as late at 1934.[4] Most of the trouble arose not from fraud and collusion—although there was plenty of that—but simply from the fact that the counties overestimated their ability to pay.[5]

Enthusiasm for railroads in Missouri was not new. The fever for railway expansion which had gripped the entire nation during the prewar years had been at the top of the thermometer in Missouri in the 1850's, but little had been done. The war had put a halt to all construction except 108 miles of track which represented the efforts of the Missouri Pacific to reach the western boundary of the state.[6] Now that the war was over, and the general tone of business improved, the rosy dream appeared a possibility, and the St. Louis *Republican* found that "never before was the railroad mania in a more intensified condition than at present"[7]—1868.

Shelby had superintended railroad construction in Mexico, and the romance of railroad building had a strong appeal for him. The fabulous profits envisioned by the promoters had an even stronger appeal, no doubt; to a man of Jo Shelby's extravagant needs railroads seemed like an immediate answer to prayer, and the year 1869 found him deep in the affairs of not one, but two, rail transportation schemes. The first was the Lexington and St. Louis, already being built, of which he was elected a director, and the second was the famous, or infamous, St. Louis and Santa Fe, whose bond scandals caused a bloody massacre, and for whom Shelby and a business partner, James Lillis, contracted to lay $75,000 worth of track.

The Lexington and St. Louis, a strictly legitimate enterprise, was a project for which the people of Lafayette and Pettis counties had voted $800,000 in bonds in two elections. Its charter dated from 1859, but war had halted two attempts at construction, in 1860 and 1861. After the war the project was revived, and on April 1, 1869, the directors let a contract to Daniel R. Garrison for the construction of the roadbed. On May 12, 1869, the first spike was driven at Sedalia.

It was a gala occasion. A large body of prominent citizens of both counties assembled and marched on foot to the proposed site of the new terminus, about a mile west of town. President George H. Ambrose led the ground-breaking ceremony and there were speeches by the directors. Unfortunately there is no record of Shelby's speech on this occasion, but he undoubtedly made one, just as he undoubtedly attended the big banquet for 150 guests which followed at the Ives House at Sedalia, "where toasts to the new venture and funmaking ensued."

Shelby's connection with the new road was reported in the Kansas City *Times* with a flourish which leaves no question as to the writer's identity. The style is pure Edwards. Shelby's *fidus Achates* outdid even himself in the bouquet of superlatives which he tossed in the direction of his old commander:

"Gen. J. O. Shelby has been appointed General Superintendent and Financier of the Lexington and Sedalia [*sic*] Railroad. The enterprise will be finished. From a raid to a railroad, Jo Shelby is invincible. He works like he fought—that is to say, 24 hours out of the 24. He is a country farmer, having the power of a king; the leader of 10,000 men, driving oxen; the sower of wheat today, tomorrow sees him upon the market negotiating a hundred thousand dollars worth of county bonds; living in the saddle, ubiquitous at Sedalia and Lexington. It is safe to say that the railroad will be finished by January."

The road was not finished by January, although a creditable amount of work had been done (thirty-six miles of track laid out of fifty-five) and the company reported that its aggregate capital, invested in "rolling stock and appurtenances," amounted to $870,000.

The progress being made on the Lexington and St. Louis, however, did not satisfy at least one resident of Pettis County, who complained about the slowness of construction and the manner in which the finances of the railroad were being administered.[8] Shelby was deeply offended by the criticism and offered to resign if the board would appoint the critic in his place. But the other directors refused to hear of Shelby's resignation, and President George Ambrose of the Lexington and St. Louis called the critic "a vicious man." [9]

The St. Louis and Santa Fe was an iron horse of an entirely different color. Its officials were involved in one of the most celebrated swindles in the history of American railroading, and the manipulation of its securities led to a massacre at Gunn City, Missouri, on April 23, 1872, in which outraged citizens brutally shot to death a judge of the county court, a city councilman, and an attorney for the railroad.

Shelby's connection with the St. Louis and Santa Fe was entirely innocent. He was not a member of the board of directors nor associated with the railroad in any way save as a contractor—a paid employee. He and his new business partner, James Lillis, were hired to construct the roadbed; Lillis was an estimable citizen of Cass County and his son, Thomas F. Lillis, later attained eminence as a bishop in Kansas City. Shelby and Lillis were losers on the Santa Fe deal; of the $75,000 worth of track contracted for, only $17,000 was laid, and the road was never completed. The names of Shelby and Lillis, however, will always be associated with the "Gunn City massacre," for by a stroke of pure coincidence, they happened to be passengers on the train on which the Santa Fe conspirators were murdered. But that is getting three years ahead of the story. In midsummer, 1869, Shelby and Lillis had formed a new partnership, and they were after big game—the contract to build the proposed new road of the St. Louis and Santa Fe, of which R. S. Stevens was president.

Stevens was dangling a big railroad project in front of the rustics of the western Missouri counties. He proposed to build a road from Holden, in Johnson County, westward through Harrisonville, the county seat of Cass, to Paola, Ottawa, and the Cottonwood Valley, and thence to New Mexico. Such a railroad, linked with the east, would mean virtually a transcontinental line through southwestern Missouri, and there was great excitement over the project. Large meetings were held along the proposed route, and the enthusiastic counties went overboard, some of them subscribing one amount and then, on thinking it over, petitioning to be allowed to increase their subscription. Two hundred and twenty-five thousand dollars' worth of bonds were voted at elections held at Coldwater, Dolan, Camp Branch, Grand River, and Index.

The company was organized, the contract let to Shelby and Lillis, and the first section, from Holden to Harrisonville, was scheduled for completion by September 1, 1870. The contract called for completion of construction to the Kansas City line by July 1, 1871. The capital stock of the company was listed at $700,000, of which $225,000 had been taken by the counties, and bonds to the extent of $20,000 per mile were to be issued to contractors for building the road.

So far, so good. Now came the chicanery, in which Shelby had no part. R. S. Stevens, president of the St. Louis and Santa Fe, knew that, before the war, the Missouri Pacific Railroad had been planning to build a road through Cass County, and that $100,000 in bonds had been voted for the purpose. He also knew that the bonds were long overdue, the war having prevented the building of the railroad, and that, since they represented a transaction which had never been fulfilled on either side, they were worthless unless revalidated by court order, and their terms brought up to date.[10]

The bonds were still in existence, in the vaults of the Missouri Pacific up in St. Louis, and Stevens had a bold plan for getting hold of them, having them revalidated by court order, and transferred to the St. Louis and Santa Fe, without consulting the people of Cass County.

Such a highhanded procedure would be possible, under the law, only with bonds issued before the war, and that is why Stevens singled out the Missouri Pacific issue. The Drake Constitution of 1865 forbade county authorities to subscribe to railroad stock without submitting the question to a vote of the people, but in the case of bonds issued before the war, the old railway charters empowered a county court to subscribe to such stock at its discretion, without holding an election. Here Stevens saw his chance, so he thought, to acquire $100,000 worth of negotiable securities by a simple piece of sleight-of-hand.

To do this, of course, he had to have the connivance of the Cass County Court, but this, he felt sure, he could obtain, and, as events proved, he was right. What neither he nor the court reckoned on was the fury of an aroused populace in Cass County when its citizens found that they had been loaded down with an overwhelming bonded indebtedness without their consent.

The year 1869 had started out as a year of great promise, with Shelby director of one railroad and contractor for another, but 1870 was to be a year of double misfortune. Although he and Lillis were negotiating for other contracts,[11] their big customer, the Santa Fe, had bogged down hopelessly in the prolonged litigation over the bonds; and in late March the Shelby farmhouse at Aullville burned to the ground.

Shelby was absent in Lexington that day, and the barns and out-buildings were saved by the neighbors and the hired hands, but the farmhouse in which the family had been so happy was a charred ruin, collapsed upon its foundation, with only curling smoke where the second story had been.

Confident that no defeat could ever be inscribed permanently on the Shelby banner, John Edwards wrote in the Kansas City *Times* on May 1, 1870; "Little he cares about the strokes of fortune. He takes fate as he finds it, and loves to prop a falling house or back a losing horse. About his character is that admirable trait which all thorough soldiers have, and misfortune no more deters the man than would the wind blowing over the billowy wheat from the South. The house he lost was a good house, but in a month he will have a better one, and when it is finished, the welcoming lamps will be hung again in the window, and the guest chambers will be arrayed as of old."

Benjamin Gratz's farm near Lexington now afforded sanctuary for the Shelbys,[12] although it is probable that Betsy took the children back to Kentucky about this time for a visit, while Jo Shelby supervised the rebuilding of the house. Betsy was a prime favorite with the family in Kentucky, and remained so all her life.[13] As Major Edwards had predicted the house was rebuilt in record time—in less than two months—and the Shelbys lived in it for the next fifteen years, until 1885, when they moved to Adrian in Bates County.

There were four boys in the family now, and no girls. (The Shelbys' only daughter, Anna, was not born until September, 1875.) Orville, the oldest, was twelve; Joe, born the first year of the war, was nine; Ben was four, and Webb, the baby, was two. When the family moved into the new house at Aullville, Betsy was expecting her fifth child, who was born in 1871 and named Sam Shindler Shelby for one of Shelby's comrades of the war.

Shelby himself, forty and acquiring a waistline, was leading the busy life of a railroad executive, roadbed contractor, country gentleman, and prosperous farmer, roles which suited him immensely. He had not yet turned his attention to politics, in which he was to figure so prominently in Missouri during Reconstruction, for Reconstruction can hardly be said to have begun at this period. Not until some time after the election of his cousin Gratz Brown as governor in 1870 would political issues become sharp. Up to now Southerners were second-class citizens in Missouri, under the Drake Constitution and Governor Fletcher. It would be left to Gratz Brown to inaugurate the "Liberal Republican" revolution which would bring back the rough-and-tumble days of politics in Missouri, with "mossbacks and Bourbon Democrats"—unreconstructed Southerners—slugging it out with the Progressives, like Jo Shelby, for control of the Democratic party.

In 1871 and 1872 the railroads were the burning issue in Missouri— along with the James Boys and their gang, who robbed the railroads while the railroads robbed the people—and it was during these two years that the final acts in the drama of the St. Louis and Santa Fe were performed. The climax of the melodrama had been long delayed by the tedious progress of litigation through the courts, but when it came, its blood and thunder were real.

On March 1, 1871, the infamous order making the bonds negotiable was issued. The conspirators were tired of waiting, and the swag, with accumulated interest, now amounted to $229,000. March 1 was on a Saturday, and the bonds were made out the night before in the office of Cline and Hines, attorneys. J. R. Cline was the legal representative of the St. Louis and Santa Fe, and J. D. Hines was the county attorney. Judge Jehiel Stevenson acted for the court, normally composed of three judges, and by his order, the bonds were funded and became as good as cash when packed into a suitcase and taken to St. Louis or Kansas City.

Stevenson sent his son, John, in a fast buggy to East Lynne, with the bonds and another conspirator, named Higgins, who committed suicide later. This pair went on to St. Louis with the bonds in a suitcase. They were joined en route by agents of President Stevens of the St. Louis and Santa Fe, and at six o'clock on Sunday morning in the

Southern Hotel in St. Louis, the swagholders divided the spoils. Judge Stevenson was charged with having received $12,000 for his part in the transaction (he had arrived in St. Louis in time for the meeting) and Cline $55,000. The remainder of the bonds were placed in the hands of Stevens' agents.

Attorney Cline and Judge Stevenson were arrested the following week, a great hue and cry, as well as an offer of a $1,000 reward, having followed their flight to the big city. Stevenson had to post a bail of $15,000, and Cline $10,000, to keep out of jail pending trial. Cline posted his bond in cash, but Stevenson had to get several friends to put up the $15,000 bond required of him. One of these was a city councilman, T. E. Dutroe, whose act was to cost him his life.

Back in Cass County, Stevenson and Cline, though facing long prison terms if convicted, showed no evidence of concern, and boasted openly that they would be freed in court. By this arrogant behavior they signed their own death warrants.

On the morning of April 24 they were advised by friends that public indignation was at such a pitch that they had better get out of the county that day. Accordingly, they decided to go over to the depot and take the train to Kansas City. The news of their intended departure soon spread, and a mob began to gather up the line.

T. E. Dutroe, the city councilman who had gone on Judge Stevenson's bond, decided that in the interest of his own safety he had better accompany them. At five o'clock that afternoon the three of them, muffled in overcoats, boarded the train at East Lynne. They were recognized by some of the passengers, who behaved in a menacing manner, and they soon went forward and hid in the baggage car.

At Gunn City the trap had been laid. All afternoon armed men had been drifting into town, and when about fifty had arrived, they donned masks and took control of the entire community. Pickets were established, and no one was allowed to leave or enter Gunn City. Those who had come into town to trade were locked up in Zook's store. Then the masked men began piling rails, logs, boulders and old plowshares across the railroad tracks. When a barricade had been erected, they entered the brush on either side and waited for the train.

When the engineer approached Gunn City he was forced to halt. As he did so, he heard the warning sound of pistol shots fired into the air, and fifty masked men emerged from the brush. They found

Stevenson, Cline, and Dutroe huddled in the baggage car, and without a word, opened fire.

Stevenson fell first, a bullet piercing his jugular vein. At the same time, someone struck him a blow with a sharp instrument which split his forehead to the eyebrow. He was thrown from the coach and left to bleed to death beside the tracks. Cline had time to draw a gun, and escaped momentarily from the baggage car, but was brought down, stone dead, by a fusillade of bullets, three of which passed through his brain. Dutroe was shot in the back of the head, the ball lodging over his left eye.

On this train also were Jo Shelby and Jim Lillis, who were going to Kansas City on business. They had not been in conversation with Stevenson, Cline, or Dutroe, although in all probability they knew they were on the train, since the other passengers knew it. Apparently they had no intimation of the violence which was to take place at Gunn City, or Shelby certainly would have gone forward to the baggage car and confronted the mob; as it was, he remained seated in a rear coach, and the mob confronted him.

The word had spread that Jo Shelby was on the train, and since he was a contractor for the St. Louis and Santa Fe, somebody yelled, "Where's Jo Shelby? Get Jo Shelby!"

Shelby heard the cry. He did not move from his seat as the masked Missourians, thirsting for more blood, stood over him. The bearded lips curled, and in a voice that carried distinctly through the coach, he said, "Well, here I am. Come and get me."

Confronted with those icy gray eyes and that lion glare, the men's pistols wavered, and finally somebody mumbled something apologetic.

"Get out before I recognize some of you," said Shelby, and suiting the action to the word himself, got up, and with Jim Lillis, stalked from the coach.

As a result of the Gunn City Massacre, as it came to be known in Missouri, forty-one men were arrested and brought to trial for the deaths of Stevenson, Cline, and Dutroe. None of them was convicted. "The Bloody Bonds," as they were called, were recovered by court order and burned, all but two, Nos. 1 and 229, the first and the last in the series, which were turned over to the city fathers of Harrisonville and Gunn City respectively. There they were framed and hung in the courthouse, "that the public servants of old Cass may remember, when they trample upon the rights of the people and refuse to hear their prayers, that they will appeal to a higher power and serve an injunction that will stick." [14]

Truly, as the Kansas City *Star* said many years later in a headline over a feature story on the Gunn City massacre, "General Shelby's Turbulent Days Did Not End in Mexico."

29. *Coal Mining: Boom and Bust*

THE TURBULENT DAYS OF SHELBY's postwar career in Missouri had just begun. The first six months of 1872 had seen the collapse of a business venture, a narrow escape from death at the hands of a lynching party, and a wounded bandit, sought by detectives in six states, as a guest for two months in his home. At forty-three he had lived enough lives for a dozen men, and one would think that he would welcome a chance to devote himself to the farm and the prosperity which he now enjoyed.

But Shelby's temperament was such that he could not enjoy life except in the atmosphere of headquarters in the midst of a big campaign, and in 1872 his restless mind was turning to a new business with even more enchanting prospects than railroading. That business was coal mining. The railroads, pushing into every corner of the state, at least on paper, had brought on a boom in the coal and iron industries. In March, 1871, the legislature had limited the amount of aid any city, county, town, or township might subscribe in railroad bonds,[1] and had specified that the bonds must be paid up in two years. It was felt that thereby the railroad industry of Missouri was stabilized and taken out of the realm of speculation; and that henceforth the railroads, sound as a dollar financially, would be good paying customers for the thriving coal and iron industry. Actually, regulation had come too late. The panic of 1873 was just around the corner, and in the Great Crash of that year, a dismal replica of all the Great Crashes before and since, prosperity was to disappear from all Missouri industries alike; but Jo Shelby could not foresee that.

On the face of it, optimism was justified. The coal and iron were there. Central and southern Missouri were popping at the seams with coal, and, if anything, Missouri had more iron than she had coal—mountains of it. Yet Missouri industry was paying fifty dollars a ton for British ore! It was not only good business, it was the patriotic duty of Missourians to develop their mineral resources and resist this imperialist economic aggression. As a Scottish traveler in Missouri wrote, about this time, it was "certainly aggravating to the Americans and especially to the people of that state [Missouri] to have to buy British iron when they have literally mountains of iron ore beside them." [2]

The people of Missouri, as Dr. Lopata says, still "breathed and ate railroads" and the boom showed no signs of diminishing; Jo Shelby was soon in the coal mining business. Exact dates are not available for this period, but sometime in 1872 he leased a "coal bank," or coal mine, at Clarksburg in Moniteau County and moved the family thither. He did not, of course, give up the farm.

Clarksburg was a roaring frontier town in the seventies. Situated on one of the deepest veins of coal in Missouri, it had attracted the usual fly-by-night population of a boom town of the West, except that in place of cowhands there were sooty-faced miners who drank themselves stiff on Saturday nights. The house to which Shelby brought his family stands today in the middle of town, but in those days it was a little to the north of it. The Shelbys drove up in a fine carriage, drawn by a beautiful team of matched bays,[3] and the boys were delighted with the woods near by, which were much thicker than the woods at home.

Shelby's mine was located on a coal bank of "the old Isaac Williams farm" a mile south of Clarksburg and just to the east of a country road which connected with the state highway. Here he sank a mining shaft several hundred feet deep, and a good deal of his available cash. He employed fifty men, miners by vocation, and for them he built a large two-story frame boarding house near the mine, as well as a number of separate dwellings for those with families, so that the settlement at the coal bank had all the appearance of a crossroads town. Shelby also built himself a private office near the shaft, within a few feet of the spot where the Clarksburg railway station now stands, and here he could be found at all hours, ready for a social chat or a business conference.

At first the coal was moved into Clarksburg by large wagons, drawn by the biggest mules Shelby could find, "much larger and better bred than the average mule in that section of the country at the time," but as the work progressed and the mine gave evidence of a large supply of coal, a narrow-gauge track was built on the east side of the public road from Clarksburg. This spur line was elevated at the mine to a point where coal could be dumped directly into the cars for shipment, after it had been brought out of the mine in wagons pulled by smaller-sized mules than those Shelby used for outside transportation.

The output of coal was so heavy that Shelby inaugurated a night shift. According to the Tipton *Times,* he had no trouble finding help, for "to drive a small mule or horse attached to a small coal car was a novelty and provided a thrill, to those thus engaged, heretofore unknown in that day, and naturally there were more applicants for the position, either day or night, than could be accommodated."

The professional miners, however, for whom the thrill and novelty of coal mining had long since worn off, were accustomed to spend their leisure hours in the saloons of the near-by town of California, where they could relax with liquor purchased either by the drink or by the gallon. On Saturdays, according to contemporary accounts, they left for California by local freight early in the morning and returned, if able, in the evening. The Tipton *Times* says that even among those that did return "many of them would be unable to travel on foot without a guide."

To make sure that all of his wayfaring employees should return to their boarding house at the coal bank in safety, if not in good order, on Saturday night, Shelby had one of his large coal wagons, with a big team of mules, wait at the railway station for the freights to pull in. Those who had been able to get into the boxcars at California, but were unable to get out at Clarksburg, because of more nightcaps en route, were hauled home to their boarding house or to their wives. Thanks to this system of Shelby's, says the *Times,* "they were always ready and willing to report for duty on the following Monday morning."

Visitors were brought to the coal mine office in the fine carriage drawn by the matched bays, after they had been given an expense-free tour of Clarksburg and vicinity—possibly that they might contrast the splendor of Shelby's coal mining operation with the dingy and squalid establishments of his competitors. The driver on this free tour was a redheaded youth named George Gay, whom Shelby employed for his conversational talents as well as for his ability to drive a spanking team of bays. George drove the visitors around for an hour or so, haranguing them on the sterling quality of the coal mined hereabouts, and then—and only then—says the *Missouri Historical Review*, were they introduced to the bluff and genial manager, who took them on another tour, this time of the mine.[3]

Young Orville and Joe were growing up to be fine horsemen like their father, and with an older friend, Jerry Warren, they would traverse the country on horseback for miles, in search of small game, both timber and game being plentiful in Moniteau County. There were no hedge and wire fences in the neighborhood in those days, only the kind known as "stake and rider fences," which a horse could negotiate after the top rails were removed. This necessitated crossing private property, but the young Shelbys had been brought up to have good manners, and they always, says the Tipton *Times*, asked the farmer's permission, which was always granted "for the reason that they never molested anything." It was also said of them that they never fired a shot at any game "except while on the run or on the wing." Their father would have tanned them properly if he had heard of their doing otherwise.

During the summer, a blighting middle-western drought settled down on central southwestern Missouri, and all of the wells at Clarksburg, except that at the Shelby home, went dry. The shortage of drinking water was so serious in the fall that school children drank from an old mill pond near the schoolhouse, the water of which was in a stagnant condition. As a result, typhoid broke out. Shelby sent word to the teacher at the school to send the children thereafter to his home for drinking water, and added that if his well should go dry he had plenty of money with which to replace it.

This solvent condition was to be of short duration. The new coal baron was to find his well of money running dry, before long, for, partly because of the extravagant manner in which he had conducted his enterprise, Shelby's mine was unable to weather the financial storms of the year 1873, and his investment was wiped out. This time there were no fraudulent bonds, no absconding officials; but the *déroute*, as the old-fashioned military term had it, was complete. When the customers stopped buying coal, as they did, he sadly closed his mine and drove off in the carriage with the matched bays.

But there was always the farm in Lafayette County, with its acres of waving wheatfields, and back to it the Shelbys now went.

30. *Shelby in Reconstruction*

THE ERA OF BIG BUSINESS was ended for Jo Shelby. He engaged in other commercial ventures, as a commission merchant for a St. Louis firm and as part owner of a store in Lexington,[1] in addition to farming, but his capital was depleted, and there was no more venture money to be had during the depression. For the next eighteen years we find him farming, "politicking," and slipping easily into the role which he played so well in his later years, that of The Grand Old Man of Missouri. During those years he was to suffer new financial reverses which overwhelmed him, so that in his latter years he was to know the harassment of debt, and at the end he did not even own the farm on which he was living; but to measure the postwar years entirely by the yardstick of financial success would be to miss the point entirely.

The Shelby of Reconstruction was to emerge as a much more powerful, much more human and beloved figure than even the hard-riding cavalry chieftain of the war days. Whereas at the end of the Civil War he had been a living legend, by the time of his death he had become a folk god in Missouri. Although rocked by blows, some of them to his pride, which would have embittered a lesser man, he did not, like many old Confederates, become cantankerous in his old age; on the contrary, he grew more courtly and popular. The paradox of his character was that he who in his youth had been at times cantankerous and imperious, grew mellow and tolerant with the years, though he was as good-humoredly tactless as ever. His peculiarities were endearing rather than otherwise, and he remained a public darling.

In the early seventies Shelby's connection with the railroads caused some people to mutter; the scars left by the cruel frauds of the railroad swindlers would not be erased in Missouri in a generation, but when it became cameo-clear that Shelby had had nothing whatever to do with the financial manipulations, the criticism ceased as abruptly as it had begun. It was also known that he had worked for better conditions for workers in the railroad camps, and that he had built what amounted to palatial quarters for his coal miners at Moniteau; but none of this would have sufficed to wipe out the stigma of association with the railroads if it had been anybody but Jo Shelby.

He was not within a thousand miles of being a good business man. His open-handedness and his flair for doing everything on a grand scale far outweighed the element of shrewdness which had been one of his great assets on the battlefield. If it was a choice between what is known as "good business" and doing a favor for a friend, the friend won out. Major Jake Stonestreet, now living in Kansas City, made the apt observation that "it took as much to run him as to run a steamship line." [2]

For the first few years after the return from Moniteau, all went swimmingly. The thousand-acre farm at Aullville was well stocked, and the Shelbys lived high, raising wheat, "spreading hemp," and trading in livestock. (The store was a latter day venture, in 1889.) There are newspaper references to Shelby's raising blooded horses, certainly no occupation for a poor man, and an admiring reporter writes particularly of "Columbus the roan and Niagara the upstanding black," both of a fine Canadian strain.

For a man who had lived as many lives as Shelby, farming, even in the grand manner, was not sufficient outlet for his energies. He was as restless and unruly as his blooded horses, shackled to the routine of the farm. In such a case, it was inevitable that he should turn to local politics, and just as inevitable that, with Shelby mixed up in them, fireworks should result.

Politics in Missouri was always a rough-and-tumble affair, and especially during Reconstruction. Quentin Reynolds once remarked in an article on the Irish that in Ireland every man considers himself an expert on politics, and is. The same thing was true in Missouri. Politics was the poor man's entertainment. It was the one free show which all could attend, the wool hats in the same seat as the aristocrats, with the privilege of hurling ripe fruit at the actors.

Among the boiling political issues in Missouri in the seventies and eighties were railroad regulation, the greenback or cheap money question, the exploitation of natural resources by out-of-state interests, and the war records of the various candidates. The situation was complicated, of course, by the fact that Missouri had just passed through the distressing period of Boom and Bust. As an anonymous writer in the *Missouri Historical Review* points out, "The period up to 1873 in Missouri was a period of boom times and prosperity. Characteristic of the period were rise of prices, great apparent prosperity, large profits, high wages, large importations, a railway mania, expanded credit, over-trading, overbuilding and a tendency to run into debt. There was a willingness to borrow on any terms and confidence that the process would never stop." [3]

When the process did stop, "the farmer found that he was not accumulating but that his interest charges and his debt were increasing. Saddled with debt, he lost his holdings or became a renter. The quickest way to fortune was to be found in combinations or units of industry and fortunes made in this way did not appeal to the masses as being the reward of productive enterprise and were viewed with alarm. Prices were low in depression, money was hard to borrow, and in effect a contraction of the currency was in progress." This brought about a demand for greenback inflation, and the birth of the Greenback party. "The opinion was general that the decline in prices, particularly grain prices, was due to legislation on the currency. It was the commercial east against the agricultural west. If more currency were printed the occupation of the money lender would be gone." It was also a continuation of the old quarrel between the North and the South.

To Shelby's credit be it said that he did not fall for the lure of printing press money, or the proposal to pay gold bonds in greenbacks. That was cheating, in his code. He clung to what he lovingly called "the old Democratic Party" until 1896, when the party embraced Free Silver and William Jennings Bryan. That year he voted for McKinley. He had learned the value of sound money, the hard way.

His first appearance in connection with anything political was his endorsement, in 1869, of a bill introduced into Congress by Colonel Robert T. Van Horn for the relief of John M. Fleming of Lexington. Fleming had owned a beautiful home in Lexington which the Federals had burned during the siege to prevent the State Guards from using it as protection for one of their batteries, although Fleming was known as a staunch Union man. After the destruction of his house, he rented another in which he cared for four wounded Confederate officers as well as Federal wounded. Now an old man, and penniless, he was petitioning Congress, through Congressman Van Horn, for compensation.

Shelby wrote to the Kansas City *Journal* on December 1st, "I see that Colonel Robert T. Van Horn has introduced a bill in Congress for the relief of John M. Fleming of Lexington. I hope it will be passed at once, for it has as much merit as any measure ever presented for consideration of the house. There can be no valid reason why the Government should not pay the amount specified, and there is no reason why any member should hesitate to support that measure. It is the compensation due an honorable man and a noble citizen who had noble qualities that rose above the heat and strife of war days, and made him beloved by both Federals and Confederates."

Although he voted Republican in the last year of his life, the thought of doing so in the 1870's would have been unthinkable. In the files of the Lexington *Intelligencer*, which kept minute tabs on the doings of the great man who lived twelve miles away, we find that such a suggestion has angered him. The *Intelligencer* quotes the St. Louis *Globe* as saying on September 11, 1872, that "Grant was good enough for him [Shelby]—he believed the true friends of the South were the Republicans of the nation. In the Republican Party a Confederate soldier knew where he stood."

"All a lie, was Shelby's reply," says the *Intelligencer* lyrically. General Shelby's admiration for Grant was well known, but it did not extend that far. "The thing for Democrats to do," he advised his constituents through the *Intelligencer*, "is to support the Democratic ticket."

Shelby steadfastly refused to run for public office himself, though he might have had the nomination for any office within the gift of the Democrats. His refusal to make political capital of his war record was rooted firmly in his admiration for the Grand Old Gentleman who had just died in 1870 in his college president's chair over in Virginia, Robert E. Lee, who not only took no part in politics but said that a soldier had no business doing so, even in peacetime.

If he had wished to run for office, as his friends urged him to do, Shelby would have had a powerful ally within the party in the person of his cousin Frank Blair. Nauseated by the excesses of his Republican friends under Reconstruction in Missouri, Blair had become a Democrat. In makeup he was very like Shelby. He had been an abolitionist and a Republican when such an affiliation brought down the anathema of his own class upon his head; now that he could have enjoyed the fruits of power with the Republicans he threw in his lot with the shirtless ones of the Democratic party. That his perverse honesty cost him heavily did not matter to his future, for he had little of that left. He died in 1875, in his early fifties, burned out by years of intense living.

At first, Shelby's political activities seem to have amounted to no more than an outlet for his social nature, a means of escaping the routine of farm life, and a natural desire to help his friends, for before 1876 there is only one account of his presence at a political rally. On August 19, 1875, the *Intelligencer* recorded, "At a picnic at Three Groves, north of Corder, Elisha M. Edwards of Waverly, candidate for State Senator from the 17th District, and Jos. O. Shelby made speeches." Other speakers were A. A. Leseur, who became Secretary of State for Missouri, and Captain Dick Collins. In 1875 Collins was still a bachelor. He was the last of those famous uncatchable beaux of the Waverly countryside to hold out against the blessed estate—even Aldridge Corder had recently succumbed to matrimony, at the age of forty-three.[4] Collins was not to escape forever. He married in 1888, inspiring John Edwards to write an editorial on love.[5] Edwards at the time of the political picnic was finishing his second book at the home of his wife's parents at Dover, and may have been present to hear Collins and Shelby speak.

The spotlight of national political news was turned on Jo Shelby in 1876. It was after the Hayes-Tilden presidential contest, when Rutherford B. Hayes was seated, although Samuel J. Tilden, a Democrat, received the majority of popular votes. There was much resentment in the South, especially in Kentucky and Missouri. Henry Watterson, the fierce, Mark-Twain-like editor of the Louisville *Courier Journal*, announced that there would be 100,000 Kentuckians in Washington on Inauguration Day to see that "the right man was inaugurated." Even more serious, though idle, threats of a new Civil War were made. In this crisis Jo Shelby, in St. Louis at the time, gave an interview to the *Globe Democrat* in which he announced his intention "to stand by President Grant in whatever course he may take regarding the contest." The electoral college was sitting but there was apprehension that the Senate and House, one Republican and the other Democratic, might refuse to abide by the decision and the President would have to step in. Shelby deplored talk of violence and declared that "in the event there is a failure to decide the election in a lawful and constitutional manner, and President Grant is determined to exercise the power of the Chief Executive in favor of the one he regards as duly elected, I propose to support the President in his action whether that action be favorable to Tilden or Hayes."[6]

It was the right note, coming from one of the most famous living

Confederates, and both Republicans and Democrats soon came to look on Shelby as a balance wheel for sanity in Missouri politics. The day after the interview appeared, Colonel Alonzo Slayback and Colonel Clay King, another ex-rebel of note, came out in indorsement of Shelby's position, and there was some reason to believe that the Civil War, in Missouri at least, was over.

Slayback especially let the Northern Democrats have it with both barrels:

"They [the Northern Democrats]" he said, "encouraged the Confederate war. They led the Southern people to believe that Lincoln's call for volunteers and his armed invasion of the South would be resisted by them. They not only falsified these pledges, but wore the blue, and came on to the work of that ravage and bloodshed with that rash zeal which is ever the mark of new converts, trying to prove their fidelity to their adopted loyalty by acts more cruel and military orders more brutal than any that emanated from the lifelong abolitionists. All through the war they fed the South on these vain hopes that either by riots in New York or by release of prisoners in the Northwest or by assassination of leaders in Washington City or by a general uprising of Southern sympathizers all over the Northern states the Government would be forced to suspend hostilities. . . . These flatteries were all delusions. They left the South to starve and bleed and die and sent as the flower of the Yankee Army young Democrats who had been promised as recruits for the Southern army. They talked all the time of what they would do but when the time came they were afraid to commit any act of overt treason, as they glibly learned to call it, and were desperately anxious to commit some act of loyalty when there was no occasion for it. The men who are talking loudest about fight right now won't fight if there should be a war and their braggadocio might as well stop and let honest people attend to their business." [7]

It will be seen that Colonel Slayback would have been quite willing to start another war if he thought he could win it, but was convinced that he could not and that the South should accept the situation gracefully. This was the attitude, in fact, of Shelby and most ex-Confederates at the time. Real loyalty to the Union would come later; in the seventies it was still too soon for that, but the pronouncements of such men as Shelby and Slayback were powerful medicine at the time and there was no more talk of seating Tilden by force.

Missouri was in an irritable frame of mind, nonetheless, and Missourians were looking around for a scapegoat. Since it could not be Yankees, it might as well be Mexicans. Mexicans were making cattle raids on the border. Remembering that six thousand Missourians had volunteered in the Mexican War, a lot of people began talking about another expedition to Mexico. Jo Shelby was on hand; perhaps he could be persuaded to lead it. The rumors flew thick and fast, and soon a first-class tempest in a teapot was brewing in the newspapers. The *Centennial History of Missouri* says that "as the talk of invasion grew, in 1877 [in retaliation for raids and stealing on the Texas frontier], the seeming inability of the Mexican Government to maintain peace seemed to offer an excuse. Shelby's name was mentioned freely as the most eligible leader of it. Rumor was that he knew of the movement; that there was already a secret organization; that Missouri ex-Confederates were actively planning." [8]

It even reached the point where the St. Louis *Times* sent John Edwards to ask Shelby about it. The *Times* knew, and Edwards knew, that the talk was pure foolishness, but it was a good chance to do another colorful feature around Shelby. Shelby denied any further designs on the Mexican Republic but in this interview he disclosed for the first time that, according to Frank Blair, his expedition had the unofficial blessing of Abraham Lincoln. [9]

In 1879 Shelby appears to have had a brief illness, for the *Intelligencer* reports on November 29 that General Jos. O. Shelby "is walking around" again at his farm at Page City; on March 13, 1880, he and his family have returned from a visit to Kentucky; he has also had a stud horse named for him, and in April, 1880, he has just returned from Bates County, where he has bought a new farm near Adrian. "General Jos. O. Shelby," says the newspaper, "who has been in Bates County, returned Monday. The General was overseeing the laborers on HIS NEWLY PURCHASED FARM." He was not moving from Aullville, however, the paper was glad to note, and in July a one-line item makes mention of "General Jos. O. Shelby threshing his wheat crop (Page City Farm) and will ship at once." At the same time the paper reported that J. O. S. is "still a Democrat, but don't like a Democrat he's a-feudin' with."

A year later, "General Shelby and son Orville talk of going to Bates County. John Morgan Shelby has moved his cattle to Barton County."

In the fall of 1882 Shelby supported the candidacy of Alexander

Graves, a Democrat, for Congress. Graves's opponent was one of Shelby's own men of the Iron Brigade, Lieutenant Colonel John T. Crisp, who had the endorsement of the Republicans of the Fifth District, composed of Jackson, Johnson and Lafayette counties. The editor of the Lexington *Register*, a Republican paper and consequently a supporter of Crisp, sought to counteract Shelby's endorsement of Graves by charging that Shelby was "anti-foreign"—meaning anti-German, in that town of large Teutonic population—and "anti-Negro."

Shelby let loose with a blast in which he said, "I was a Democrat when there were only about three hundred here [in Lafayette County] in 1852 to 1854, and there were twenty-seven hundred of the 'Know Nothing' party." He praised Colonel Crisp, saying that he "was part of my command and an important part," but added, in his reply in the *Intelligencer*, "that to lay the blame of everything on the Democrats and Confederates was unjust and untrue."

As for "foreigners," Shelby said, "The issue of slavery was all that ever separated the foreigner from the Democratic party. That is gone and gone forever and we of the South are glad that slavery is dead for all time." This was an unusual instance of soft words from Shelby turning away wrath. He still harbored some of the bitterness of the ex-Confederate on this subject, although he was not being untruthful when he said that he was glad that slavery was no more. His entire feelings on the subject he set forth in a letter to George Lankford, another of his old boys, some time later:

"My dear Lankford,

"Your kind favor of July 27th has been received—The expressions therein contained are well calculated to cause ones thoughts to revert to the good old days when we were battling against the *World* for our independence—We failed but we (the South) have the satisfaction of Knowing that no people on Earth endured or fought more from patriotic desires—We were overcome by the *hirelings* of the World, who were avaricious, Mercenary, ignorant of our people, devoid of honor and patriotic duty. It is over, and as we all surrendered it behooves us all to abide by the terms imposed. As to the institution of slavery, nobody cares that it is obliterated. All the World is opposed to it, and in due time the South would have abolished it—So it was not the loss of it we so much objected to, but the manner in which it was taken from us. The War has demonstrated that so far as the Constitution is Concerned, it amounts to Naught—It is force that frames Constitutions and fanatics When they can exercise the power over the Masses will by force break Constitutions. After all, it is the greatest number of bayonets. As to being with you at Higginsville [Lankford had invited him to attend ceremonies at the Confederate Home] I fear I will be debarred of the pleasure—I am not well, besides circumstances that are of no interest to anyone are of such a nature that will prevent my going on the day designated. As for my presence, you flatter me, a few like yourself would be glad to meet me, but to the greatest number it would be of no moment. Renewing my thanks for your Kind words, I remain your friend, Jo. O. Shelby." [10]

The blue note in this letter was due only to the temporary indisposition; Jo Shelby was not used to being sick, and obviously didn't like it. In the Graves campaign he stumped for his man with all the old-time energy. The Kansas City *Times* reports his activities during this period in the following breathless paragraph:

"It is the same Shelby, whether in the lobby or on the long march. He never sleeps. When other men tire, when other men faint and drop by the wayside, he has just begun to fight. He never forgets a face or loses a man. He knows everybody. About the man there is a personal magnetism impossible to resist. Whether it is a fort or a vote that he wants, he goes straight at it. Baffled, he retreats a little, re-forms his line and returns to the attack with a redoubled effort. He does not understand the word defeat and refuses to learn it. In one week he was at six meetings in Lafayette, he was in Kansas City, St. Louis, Harrisonville, in Jefferson City, in Sedalia, in Chicago, and made eleven speeches, wrote fifty-two letters, sent forty-eight separate telegraphic dispatches, held nine caucuses and slept just thirty-five hours."

Graves won. His opponent was snowed under, and in Shelby's home county of Lafayette his majority was 1,777; a phenomenal record, considering that Frank Blair had been elected to Congress the last time by a majority of only 1,500 in the teeming city of St. Louis.[11] It was a personal tribute to Shelby, of course, and demonstrated that any suspicion which may have attached to his earlier connection with the railroads had long since been forgotten. He was a power in Missouri politics. At this juncture—just before the trial of Frank James in 1883—he might have had anything he wanted, within the power of the electorate. But he declared that he wanted no public office, despite the urgings of his friends to run, and he even pretended, during the whirlwind campaign for Graves, that he was just an obscure worker in the political vineyard. When posters flamed with the announcement that General Shelby would speak, he told a reporter for the *Times*, "O, I never make speeches and the committee should not have advertised me. I expect to do all in my power in other ways, however, to elect Mr. Alexander Graves, having advocated him even before the primaries." Graves carried every ward in Kansas City and rural Jackson County.

Before the election Jo Shelby had made a trip to Washington, to discuss Missouri politics with the state's leaders, and being something of a national figure by now, found himself at a dinner for the *bon ton* in the nation's capital, which was plentifully sprinkled with glittering names in blue uniforms. His companion at dinner was a once wiry, redheaded little man of considerably less than Shelby's own short stature, and like Shelby, inclining to plumpness in his middle years. This personage, to whom Shelby was introduced for the first time, was Lieutenant General Philip Henry Sheridan, sometime scourge of the Shenandoah, and Reconstruction commander in both Texas and Missouri. Soon he would be general-in-chief of the armies and the top ranking general in the United States.

(*"Little Phil Sheridan . . . through the Shenandoah!"*)

What the thoughts of the two great warriors were, as they were introduced, is open to speculation. Sheridan knew Shelby well, though he had never seen him before; Shelby had caused him plenty of trouble in Texas, and even before that, from reports received, he had known him as the only great Confederate commander west of the Mississippi. As for Shelby, though he had never fought against Sheridan, he might have taken some pardonable pride in having given him the slip in 1865, when Sheridan had a force fifty times as great as his own.

Yes, although they had never met, the two had a lot to talk about, and they greeted each other cordially. Eventually, at dinner, as the wine bottles clinked on the thin-stemmed glasses, the talk turned on Mexico.

"I was very anxious to go over into Mexico after you," said Sheridan (according to the New York *Herald*, which had a reporter at the dinner).[12] "In fact," continued the hero of Winchester, "if my request had been granted you would not have gone to Mexico. While I was waiting for orders, you slipped in. The orders to go after you never came, and it was one of my bitterest disappointments."

Shelby might have enlightened him as to why those orders never came, but instead he said gallantly, as he lifted his glass, "I wish you had got them, for we found it mighty lonesome over there for two years."

"Shelby," said Sheridan with characteristic graciousness, "I believe that every man who went through our war felt lonesome for two or three years after it was over."

The conversation turned, too, on politics and Reconstruction, men and books. Sheridan was writing his memoirs; so was Grant. Both men would die within a short time of publication. Both were concerned with the future of the country, and a South not yet reconstructed. Undoubtedly Sheridan congratulated Shelby on his stand during the Hayes-Tilden dispute; undoubtedly he spoke of the difficulties of rebuilding the country, and especially Missouri, where Sheridan had most recently served; and undoubtedly he expressed some such wish as that the Confederates would come back into the Union.

Just what Sheridan's exact words were, makes no difference. Such an appeal could hardly fail to go straight to Shelby's heart. From the time of his visit to Washington, there was discernible plainly in his public utterances a new attitude; from having been an advocate of docile acceptance of the status quo as something that could not be helped, he became a crusader for a genuinely reunited country.

He would have come to it anyway, in the mellowness of time, but the conversation with Sheridan had touched a vital chord. Something that the great Union cavalryman said opened his eyes to the glory of the nation, not as it was, but as it should be; the grandeur of the past, and the promise of the future, of "the best government the sun ever shone on." Confederates had been accustomed to quote that phrase in sarcastic contempt. Shelby saw now how blind they were. Sheridan was right; disunion meant, first of all, chaos and ruin and, eventually, loss of national identity. He, of all people, who had seen the fate of a nation divided in Mexico, twenty years before, should know that better than anyone else.

But for the fortuitous circumstance of its geographical position next to the United States, a disunited Mexico would have lost its independence forever to the conquering armies of a European power. A divided union of the American states would fare no better. The theory of states' rights, carried to its logical conclusion, would result in the formation of three or four weak nations, like Mexico, each an easy prey for the Louis Napoleons of the future.

Up to now, Jo Shelby had been a citizen of the South, under whatever flag might be waving overhead. From now on, he became an American citizen. With the zeal of a convert, he returned to Missouri, determined to show his unreconstructed associates the error of their ways.

In this he had set himself quite a task. Since most of his old friends were of the ex-Confederate persuasion, his stand was not going to be immediately popular. Shelby's own term for the enemies of progress, as he now viewed them, was "mossbacks," but he soon adopted the apt description of the New York *Herald*: "Bourbon Democrats"— meaning those who never learn anything and never forget anything, and his tactlessness, which was characteristically his own, did not improve his approach. He gave out some newspaper interviews in which he advocated the encouragement of more immigration into Missouri— more lop-eared Dutch!—to develop the state's natural resources, and he advised Missourians that it was time to forget the war and their narrow provincialism, in preparation for the New Day that was about to dawn.

These utterances were welcomed by the Republican press, which mistakenly interpreted them to mean a conversion to Republicanism. Over in Lawrence, Kansas, the editor of the *Tribune*, the same who had had dinner with Shelby at the home of Colonel Sam Wood in Lawrence the night before the election of March 30, 1855, wrote:

"The recent position taken by Jo Shelby against 'mossbackism' and his declaration that 'Bourbonism' hung like a pall over the state, impeded her progress and turned immigration from her borders, reminds us of two interviews we had with the distinguished Confederate leader—one in 1855 and one in 1875." After discussing Shelby's activities at Lawrence on that long-gone day, the editor went on to say, "Our second interview was at the Kansas City fair in 1875. As we saw him walking alone across the grounds, we approached him with extended hand, and remarked, 'This is General Shelby, I believe,' giving our own name. 'I do not know whether you will remember me, but I took dinner with you at Sam Wood's house in Lawrence when you came to help us in the little matter of voting.' He was very cordial, shook us heartily by the hand, saying: 'We have all made damned fools of ourselves since those days.' We said: 'General, since Kansas City has extended its hospitalities to Jefferson Davis, I thought I would call on you and extend to you the hospitalities of Lawrence.' He laughed, and said he would really like to visit Lawrence, inquired all about the place, what it had grown up to, and about various persons, including Col. Wood and wife.... There are few more genial, gentlemanly men than Jo Shelby, and if he really wants to join the Republican Party, we cannot see why the liberality of the Methodist hymn may not apply to him:

> " 'While the lamp holds out to burn,
> The vilest sinner may return.' " [13]

There were howls of surprised anguish from the Bourbon Democrats. Among these was John Newman Edwards, now conceded to be the most brilliant and popular editor in Missouri. Edwards was not only a Bourbon Democrat, but a mossback and unreconstructed rebel of the most unalloyed sort. The dye in his Southern wool was so deep that he refused even to believe that Quantrill was a bad man,[14] and as for Republicans—with whom Jo Shelby was now hobnobbing —it was Major Edwards' unshakeable conviction that every Southern boy who lay in a soldier's grave had been shot by a Republican, and he wanted no truck with any of them. After reading Shelby's pronouncements, he wrote one of his most famous editorials, "On Bourbon Democracy," which is a hymn to the ante-bellum South. Although he would never have criticized his old commander by name, out of the love he bore him, he plainly had Shelby in mind when he wrote:

"One hears much of this term [Bourbon Democracy] lately. It is as glib in the mouth of certain Republican men and newspapers as the forked tongue in the mouth of the snake. And just as glibly does it dart in and out, by its rapidity something like a nerve that jumps and throbs under galvanism, and something like a cutthroat in ambush where the hedge is thickest, or the road the most lonely and God-forsaken.

"In their estimation Bourbon Democracy means pull down; burn school houses; retrograde; have here and there a touch of the thumbscrew; the rack also upon occasions; proscription always; guerrillas out in the underbrush; all the better if a few train robbers ride and raid; breaking into the strong place where the public money is kept;

chaos; no more law and order; no more jails; the Rebels in the saddle; and no pitch hot in any available direction.

"The truth about Bourbonism in Missouri is just this. It got its name from the fact that it would not steal in the old days, nor disfranchise, nor break into meeting houses to deprive other denominations of their property, nor confiscate railroads, nor run away with county funds, nor be generally unclean, despicable and dishonest.

"True, a Bourbon Democrat delighted in the past. He believed in the old fashioned way of doing things. He lived in peace with his neighbors. He burnt neither their hay, their wheat, nor their straw stacks. Nor was one ever known to break into a smokehouse. He believed in the family and taught his children to rely upon it as the basis of all society, the foundation upon which the state rested, the bulwark against which all the Cossacks in the world could not prevail when they came to attack civil and religious liberty. He liked his dram and got the best that was going. No Puritanical processes invaded his sanctuary, preaching free love on the one hand and Prohibition on the other. Virtue was a shrine at which all Missourians worshiped. . . .

"The Bourbon Democrat was also a pastoral American. He hunted, fished, plowed, loved the woods, laughed and sang at his work, indulged in much reverie, which is the parent of sadness, did not know how to lie, never knew the road to Canada with his stolen goods and chattels, would have put his wife and daughter to death before permitting either to work or to vote at the polls, . . ." [15]

There was much more, but Major Edwards concluded that "the man who would not take the oath to foreswear his people was a Bourbon Democrat."

None of this indicated a break in the firm friendship of the two cronies. Readers understood that such editorial pyrotechnics from Major Edwards meant merely that he did not agree with the sentiments expressed. They were accustomed to Edwards' style, and would have been disappointed with anything less colorful and vehement. Through long exposure to it, they knew that the Major's bark was much worse than his bite, and that he was congenitally unable to express himself, when aroused, except in the most explosive terms. It was well understood, for example, that when Major Edwards wrote that he hoped to see the day when there would be a jug of free whiskey, with tin cup attached, on every stump in Missouri, he was merely indicating that the editorial policy of his paper was opposed to prohibition. He and Jo Shelby would soon be working hand in glove to secure the acquittal of Frank James, who, as the campaign of 1882 ended, was wanted by the State of Missouri to stand trial for murder.

31. *The Trial of Frank James*

IF YOU DRIVE west on the main street of Lexington, Kentucky, you come to a gray stone pile in the middle of town which is the Fayette County Courthouse. In one corner of the courthouse green, as you approach, is a bronze statue of General John Hunt Morgan, the Confederate raider, seated on a horse, although he never rode anything but a mare in his life. Several blocks behind you, and to the right, is the Morgan home, with a Commonwealth of Kentucky marker advising the passerby that this was the birthplace of John H. Morgan, "The Thunderbolt of the Confederacy."

At the opposite end of the courthouse green from the Morgan statue there is a vacant space which would be a splendid location for another statue, but there is no statue there to Joseph Orville Shelby, although this was his home town and he lived two doors away from the Morgan home, where the "Thunderbolt" marker is.

Inquiry into the history of the family in Lexington discloses that there may be a reason for this which is not altogether the fact that Shelby commanded Missouri troops and is generally thought of as a Missourian. The feeling persists that if Robert E. Lee or J. E. B. Stuart had been born in Lexington there would be monuments erected to them there even though they commanded troops in Virginia. The reason in Shelby's case seems to go much deeper than that. One lady of impeccable connections (including the Shelby one) snapped, when asked about the General, "I heard he had a war career but don't believe it. He was intimate with the James Boys, you know."

There you have it. Lexington, Kentucky, is not Lexington, Missouri.

Now, as to Shelby's having been intimate with the James Boys, that has an ominous ring; but when one considers that he had an opportunity to loot an entire government sub-treasury at Austin and turned it down, it seems safe to say that Jo Shelby would not have robbed a bank if his life had depended upon it. His old boyhood chum, John Morgan, thought nothing of rifling a bank (Yankee) in Mt. Sterling, Kentucky, according to reports; but that is another story and a good one.[1]

The damning fact remains, however, so far as Lexington, Kentucky, is concerned, that the James Brothers and other members of the gang visited the Shelby farmhouse in Missouri; that Frank James, when wounded, had been given asylum in the Shelby home; that the wife of Frank James had once appealed to Shelby to intercede with the Governor for a pardon for her husband; that Jo Shelby gave an interview to the press in which he credited Frank with having helped to save him from capture by the Yankees; that he appeared as a character witness at the trial of Frank for murder, at Gallatin, Missouri, in 1883; and that largely as a result of his support, Frank was acquitted with something like acclamation. As Paul I. Wellman said many years later in a signed article in the Kansas City Star, "When Jo Shelby was a witness, and the Lost Cause an issue, there could be but one answer. Frank James was acquitted." It was, of course, so far as a Missouri jury was concerned, as if General Lee himself had appeared; for Jo Shelby was the General Lee of Missouri and, as one account has it, half the old Confederates in the state would have lifted their hats at the mere mention of his name.

The story of Frank and Jesse James is too well known to need recounting in detail, but a brief résumé of the events leading up to Frank's trial is necessary. After the war, Frank and Jesse, finding ordinary labor unrewarding, took up robbing banks and railroads. They had learned a good deal in the army, and they displayed much of the tactical genius of the Confederate cavalryman; for sixteen incredible years they headed a group of mounted holdup men who were known to newspaper readers throughout the country as "The James Gang" or "The Border Bandits." As a result, Missouri became known as "The Robber State," or "The Outlaw State." The James Boys were heroes to all Missouri, principally for this reason: they seldom robbed anybody but banks and railroads, and both of these institutions were fair game from the Missouri point of view. The banks foreclosed mortgages with villainous elation and the railroads stole hundreds of thousands of dollars from the counties through the sale of worthless bonds. The railroads, as far as most Missourians were concerned, were greater bandits than the James Boys; and some Missouri farmers claimed that the railroad locomotives set fire to haystacks, for which the railroads refused to pay. If it be protested that the James Boys robbed passengers, who were certainly not responsible for the thievery of the railroads, the Missourians had an answer for that, too: the James Boys never robbed Southerners, and especially old Confederates.[2] The James Boys, therefore, were merely getting back some of what the Missourians regarded as their own. They were chastising the capitalists of the railroads and the banks as the border ruffians had chastised the abolitionists in Kansas; in their way they were champions of the oppressed and downtrodden South. Jesse James, as leader of the gang, became the Robin Hood of Missouri.

It seems to be an established fact—at least there is no evidence to the contrary—that Jesse James was in his own way honest. He always paid for food or lodging whenever he stopped, and he stopped at countless farmhouses in Missouri, including Shelby's, during the sixteen years he was on the road. At towns like Waverly the James Boys were never at a loss to find someone to help them "get across the river." Jesse in particular was well liked because of his personality. Frank, being older and more serious, was less popular. But Jesse was earnest, honest, and religious (a well-thumbed Bible always in his pocket); he sang in church choirs, and his blue-eyed good looks were appealing. The people of Missouri knew that he would never have robbed either a bank or a railroad unless he needed the money. For sixteen delicious years they followed his exploits like a modern serial on television.

The fact that they had the people of Missouri behind them—a support which had extended back into the days when they were guerrillas during the war [3]—is the reason that the James Boys were able to continue their career for sixteen years, despite Pinkerton .detectives and rewards offered by the state of Missouri and the railroads themselves. But the inevitable occurred at last, and Jesse James was done in, in 1882, by Bob Ford, a traitorous pal, who hoped to collect all or part of the $10,000 reward which Governor Thomas Crittenden had offered for him.

The story has been told often, of how Governor Crittenden met Bob Ford in the St. James Hotel in Kansas City, after Bob had got himself appointed a detective; how the strangely assorted political pair planned to trap Jesse James in his home; and how Crittenden promised Bob, in addition to the reward, a pardon for his brother-in-law, Dick Liddil; and how Bob Ford then rode off to the home of Jesse James, where his brother Charlie Ford, another member of the gang, also was staying. The next afternoon, as Jesse was wandering about the house coatless—it was a hot afternoon—with a feather duster in his hand, Bob Ford shot him dead just as he was about to mount a chair and dust the picture of a racehorse called "Skyrocket." Charlie Ford had his pistol cocked too, but he testified at the inquest that he did not shoot, as he saw that his brother's shot already had done for Jesse.[4]

A great hue and cry went up in Missouri. Governor Crittenden was accused of having plotted the official murder of Jesse James, for his own political ends, rather than have him captured and tried. Writers on Jesse James disagree; many, including Homer Croy, insist that Crittenden did commission Bob Ford to execute Jesse James. In an interview with a reporter of the St. Louis *Republican* on April 17, 1882, Governor Crittenden denied emphatically that he had ever done any such thing and pointed to the language of his proclamation offering a reward for Frank and Jesse. The offer was for $5,000 for the apprehension of each outlaw and $5,000 additional for the conviction of either in court.

Nevertheless, a large section of the press believed that Jesse James had been the victim of an official murder, and feeling ran high as the Ford brothers were brought to trial for murder. No man in Missouri was more wrathful over the "official murder" than Major Edwards. He was at this time editor of the Sedalia *Missouri Democrat*, and he let loose with an editorial blast which has become a Missouri epic. Of Jesse James he wrote:

"We called him outlaw, and he was, but Fate made him so. . . . Proscribed, hunted, shot at, driven away from among his own people, a price put upon his head, what else could a man do, with such a nature, except what he did do? He had to live. It was his country. The graves of his kindred were there. He refused to be banished from his birthright and when he was hunted he turned savagely about and hunted his hunters. Would to God he were alive today to make a righteous butchery of a few more of them.

"There never was a more cowardly or unnecessary murder in all

America than this murder of Jesse James. It was done for money. It was done that a few might get all the money. He had been living in St. Joseph for months. The Fords were with him. He was in the toils, for they meant to betray him. He was in the heart of a large city. One word would have summoned 500 armed men for his capture or extermination. Not a single one of the attacking party need to have been hurt. If, when his house had been surrounded, he had refused to surrender, he could have been killed on the inside of it and at long range. The chances for him to escape were as one to 10,000 and not even that; but it was never intended that he should be captured. It was his blood the wretches were after—blood that would bring money in the official market of Missouri. And this great Commonwealth leagued with a lot of self-confessed robbers, highwaymen and prostitutes to have one of its citizens assassinated, before it was positively known that he had ever committed a single crime worthy of death."

As Major Edwards contemplated this unholy liaison, it was too much for him, and he wrote with flaming pen:

"Tear the two bears from the flag of Missouri! Put thereon, in place of them, as more appropriate, a thief blowing out the brains of an unarmed victim, and a brazen harlot, naked to the waist and splashed to the brows in blood!" [5]

Edwards' estimate of Jesse James was just about the estimate of the people of Missouri, and Governor Crittenden found himself in considerable hot water. The Cincinnati *Times Star*, which was some distance from the redhot Jesse James country, reflected the opinion of much of the press when it commented: "If Governor Crittenden of Missouri reads the newspapers extensively, he has discovered that public opinion severely condemns assassination by law, even in the case of a notorious desperado and outlaw. Not a single reputable paper in the land justifies the part he plays in the conspiracy to murder James."

The unalterable fact remained, as Edwards pointed out, that Jesse could have been captured easily; but the point that seems to escape even latter-day writers on the subject is that a man like Bob Ford would not have missed for all the world the chance to go down in history as the man who shot Jesse James.

When the Ford brothers were brought to trial, largely on account of popular opinion, they were sentenced to be hanged. Two hours later Governor Crittenden gave them an unconditional pardon and they walked forth from the penitentiary at Jefferson City as free men. By this act Crittenden committed political suicide. He was never again even nominated for an office in Missouri.

The killing of Jesse James and the fact that his killers went scot-free had a profound effect on Frank James. The old guerrilla and retired bank robber was living a sequestered life in Baltimore at the time, and he read about Jesse's death in the newspapers. Jesse had been reported killed a number of times; but this time Frank believed it.[6]

"I think this time it's true," he told his wife. "I think they've got Jesse." It was something for a man to think about; Jesse shot down while peaceably dusting a picture in his own home. It could happen just as well to Frank James in Baltimore reading a newspaper. Furthermore, the fact that the newspapers were mourning Jesse as a great man made Frank wonder whether he might not be wise to stand trial, and get an acquittal from a Missouri jury. The James Boys had plenty of friends in Missouri and, with the right lawyer, twelve of them would be sitting on the jury.

Governor Crittenden received a letter asking whether, if Frank James surrendered, he would be given a fair trial. Frank O'Neil, a reporter on the St. Louis *Republican,* acted as go-between. Crittenden assured O'Neil that Frank would get a fair trial but that if convicted he would have to pay the penalty. Frank James would risk that. He took a train from Baltimore to Jefferson City, and at Sedalia he was joined by the redoubtable Major Edwards, who accompanied him to the capital.

At one o'clock in the morning the sleepy night clerk of the McCarty Hotel in Jefferson City was aroused by two guests who wished to sign the register. One of them he knew. Everybody in Missouri knew Major Edwards. The other was a stranger who signed the register as B. F. Winfrey. The two slept in the same bed at the McCarty that night, the two veterans of diverse and bloody campaigns, the friend of the Emperor and Empress and the common bank robber. They ate breakfast together and spent the day greeting people on the street in Jefferson City. Not until five o'clock in the afternoon did Edwards escort Frank James into the office of Governor Crittenden at the Capitol and introduce his companion. Frank reached under his coat and laid a six-shooter on the table.

"I want to hand over something that nobody but myself has touched in twenty-five years," said Frank James. "I've taken out the cartridges." He showed Governor Crittenden the cartridge belt; it was old United States army issue and the brass buckle was stamped with the letters "U. S."

"I got it off a dead Federal soldier in Centralia, Missouri," said Frank James. "We had killed him."

That was one killing for which he would not be tried.

Great excitement spread through Missouri when it was announced that Frank James was surrendering; it reached an even greater pitch when it was learned that Jo Shelby would appear as a character witness for Frank. It was a fact known to all Missouri that the James brothers had stopped frequently at the Shelby farm, and it was also known that Old Jo had befriended Mrs. Frank James when she had come to the Shelby home with her baby, seeking shelter; and all Missouri applauded that. These facts were, as a matter of fact, so well known that a short time before the killing of Jesse, when Shelby was stopping at the St. James Hotel in Kansas City, the *Journal* sent a reporter to interview him on the subject of the James Boys.

With characteristic forthrightness Shelby said that he believed Governor Crittenden would pardon them both if they surrendered. The entire interview is worth quoting, as it gives not only Shelby's reason for going to the assistance of Frank James later, but also throws a good deal of light as to what he was doing in Missouri in the spring of 1883.

GENERAL JOE SHELBY

Interview With This Celebrated Confederate Cavalry Leader
Yesterday Afternoon

What He Knows About Jesse, and the Remainder of the Outlaw
Gang. Why He Is Their Friend

They Have Visited Him

Some New Incidents and Adventures in the Career of Jesse James

"The famous Confederate cavalry leader, General Joe Shelby, was in the city yesterday, stopping at the St. James, where he was found by a Kansas City *Journal* representative engaged, in his bluff jovial way, in a running conversation with a group of friends. Gen. Shelby was on his way to Bates County, where he has large farming interests, having a farm of 320 acres sown in wheat alone. He also owns a tract of 640 acres of land in the same county under the surface of which large coal beds have been discovered of a compact and excellent quality. His visit to Bates County is for the purpose of putting in force plans for the development of these coal beds to the fullest extent, and attending to other important business interests. The general is one of the largest wheat raisers in the state, having a farm of 1,000 acres in Lafayette County, where he resides, devoted exclusively to the production of this valuable staple.

" 'To change the subject, general, is there any truth in the rumors circulating around to the effect that you are a friend of the James Boys?'

" 'I can answer that question by relating an incident,' General Shelby then said. 'A cavalry company under command of Dave Pool, among the most prominent members of which were Jesse and Frank James, were ordered to report to me at Prairie Grove in 1863, when Generals Herron and Blunt were in command of the federal forces and General Hindman the confederate commander. My forces being in the advance, I was ordered to attack Herron at daylight. I charged his lines at the foot of the ridge, drove his outposts back on the infantry lines, and carried 700 prisoners to the rear. The federal line rallied, counter-charged, and I was captured by a troop of cavalry. Captain Pool, under Quantrill, was on the left of our line, and seeing the situation, with the Jameses and the rest of the company, dashed to my relief, driving the enemy back and rescuing me. For this and the [other] past associations of the war I do not feel it incumbent on me to betray a set or class of men who offered to sacrifice their lives in defense of mine. Therefore I haven't volunteered any information to officers in hunting these now notorious outlaws.'

" 'Under what circumstances would you aid the authorities in their capture?'

" 'When indictments are found and responsible witnesses are found who will attest to the guilt of these persons, I'll not hesitate to be of the number to place them in the hands and the fangs of the law.'

" 'Is it true that you have seen them lately?'

" 'No. I haven't seen them in a year.'

" 'It is intimated that certain officers have harbored these men.'

" 'Why, certainly. These men being with me during the war, I might say belonged to my command. It is not my purpose, when everybody is turned against them, to betray or give evidence against them. Before the robbery on the Chicago and Alton Road I notified President T. B. Blackman and General Manager J. C. McMullin of that road that I had seen the James Boys in this section of the country and that they could take action accordingly. I did not consider that my duty extended farther.'

" 'Have the Jameses ever given you any evidence of friendship since the Battle of Prairie Grove?'

" 'Well, yes. I think it was about eight years ago that Jesse James rode to Lafayette county to see Robert Cox on business for his step-father in regard to breeding stock, and stopped at my house, although I was away at the time. There was a negro boy in my employ at that time named Joe Miller. My wife sent this lad over to Aullville on an errand and he got into a fight with a white boy about his own age, fifteen years, by the name of Catron. This boy fired at the negro three times and followed him on horseback to my front gate when he got behind the gate post just in time to save himself from a load of buckshot. Before Catron had time to reload, Joe rushed out, pulled him from his horse, and had nearly overcome him when a crowd of white men came down the road for the purpose of mobbing the negro, who, seeing his danger, ran into the house and told my wife the men were going to kill him. This so alarmed her that she knew not what to do, and while thus agitated Jesse James stepped up and told her not to be uneasy, he would stop that mob. Mounting his horse, Jesse rode to the Davis Creek bridge between my house and the town, and there stationing himself with a revolver in each hand, he told the advancing crowd that if they harmed the negro there would be enough business around there to amuse the county undertaker for several days. They waited not upon the order of their going, but went. . . .'

"During the few hours Gen. Shelby remained in the city he met a number of old comrades in arms. Among those who greeted him at the St. James Hotel was Major J. F. Stonestreet, who rather prides himself on being a moss-backed Bourbon of the straightest type. He listened to his old commander's fierce denunciations of Bourbonism with amazement, and, unable to control himself, said, 'General, I have known you since you were a boy. I followed you all through the war, and never had a more gallant leader. You made us fight every day in the month and every month in the year, until we were almost worn out with fatigue, but when you rode along in front of our lines and with flashing eyes commanded us to follow you in the charge, we never faltered. We will follow you anywhere now except into the Republican party, where you are certainly headed for, and going with that speed and dash with which you always went for the foe on the field of battle. We can't desert the old Democratic party. As a soldier, none was ever braver or more chivalrous; as a man none was ever more honorable; as a friend, none was ever truer; but politically you are the damndest humbug I ever knew. You could have thousands at your back, who would give you any position you want, if you would only stand by the Democratic Party.'

"This aroused the General to a still more fierce denunciation of Bourbonism, which he declared hung like a pall over the state of Missouri, blighted her progress and turned immigration from her borders. He wanted people to come from the North and East and from Europe to settle among us, and he didn't want them ostracised socially and politically. Missouri, he said, could only be great and powerful when universal toleration of opinion prevailed—when men could vote as they pleased, and have their votes represent their will. About this time Major Stonestreet's indignation cooled down, and he entered a carriage to accompany his old commander to the depot. As a parting word, Gen. Shelby said he meant to return from Bates County on Tuesday (Election Day) to put in a word for Lew Eveland, the only man on the Democratic ticket whose election he could favor. Eveland he said was a federal soldier and the cleverest conductor who ever ran a train. He had 'passed' hundreds of poor Confederates as well as Union soldiers, and he desired to help him."

From the last sentence in the interview it is evident that Shelby's attitude toward the railroads was, in its own way, identical with that of the James Boys and about ninety per cent of the rural population of Missouri.

Frank James, however, was accused of something far more serious than train robbing. He was accused of murder, and not only that— he was accused of shooting an unarmed railroad worker, one Frank

MacMillan, in the back, during the course of a train robbery. The murder of MacMillan had taken place aboard a train of the Rock Island Railroad near Gallatin, and it was at Gallatin that he would be tried. Appropriately enough, the trial was to be held at the opera house, that being the only auditorium in town large enough to accommodate the crowds expecting to attend.

The trial took place during the last week of August, 1883, some three months after the interview which Shelby had given to the Kansas City *Journal*, and it need scarcely be remarked that the members of his aristocratic family back in Lexington, Kentucky, must have thought that he had taken leave of his senses. What passed between them in the way of communications is not known, and never will be, but there can be little doubt as to their attitude. The newspapers, meantime, had been keeping up a great foofooraw about Shelby and the Jameses, and by the time he arrived in Gallatin, he was in a foul humor about the whole thing. To make matters worse, an officious town marshal arrested him on a charge of carrying weapons. He was fined, but promptly appealed, and the matter was not settled for a long time, Shelby fighting it out to the bitter end.

The next day, his disposition no whit improved, Shelby met Edwards for lunch and Shelby, at least, lunched rather too well.

In the afternoon of August 30 General Jo, smelling strongly of Bourbon, took the witness stand. His entry and conduct are described in the St. Louis *Republican:*

"The afternoon session opened with the testimony of Gen. Jo. O. Shelby, who came into court with the stride of a dragoon, and with a savage glare in his eyes which promised trouble. He was shown to the witness chair, which is located a couple of feet below the elevated stage on which the judge sits, surrounded by gaily dressed ladies and less gaudy correspondents. When asked by Col. Philips (the defense attorney) to state his residence the general maintained a silence, turned his fierce glare to the various attorneys' tables, and to the jury box, in evident search of something. Finally he announced that he desired to see and know the court before he answered any questions. It was suggested that if he would look back over his head he would see the gentleman he was looking for, and following the directions he discovered Judge Goodman; smiled blandly on him and assured his honor that while he had not had the pleasure of meeting him, he was glad to know him now, and entertained the most kindly feeling toward him. All this was in a loud, bluff, genial voice, and it was apparent that the general was disposed to shake hands with the court if he could just get at him. Judge Goodman fidgeted rather perceptibly as a titter ran through the court, and then with a quizzical expression of countenance intimated the witness to defer formalities and answer the question. General Shelby next inquired, from another survey of the opera house, where the jury were, and when that body was pointed out he bestowed upon them a friendly bow and settled himself to answer the question of his residence."

The prosecuting attorney, William Wallace, was himself a Confederate veteran, and for this reason Shelby felt a personal antagonism toward him; no ex-Confederate should be assisting at the prosecution of one of the James Boys. Ironically enough, Judge John F. Philips of Kansas City, the attorney for the defense, was a Union veteran who had fought against Shelby and later, as a Federal judge, was to become Shelby's boss when Shelby was appointed United States marshal for the Western District of Missouri.

In response to Wallace's opening question on cross-examination, as to his place of residence, Shelby replied that he had lived for thirty-four years in Lafayette County. "Live nine miles from Lexington and nearer Page City. Remember Jesse James, Dick Liddil, Bill Ryan and Jim Cummings coming to my place in November, 1880." In response to another question he added, "Was spreading hemp at the time, working some twelve or fifteen men, and when I returned home that evening found four men with horses in my yard. Jesse James was there. Young Cummings (Jim Cummings) I knew before, and this man Liddil passed as Mr. Black that time." [7]

Asked by the prosecutor what they were doing there and what conversation, if any, he had with them, Shelby said, "In the morning had a conversation with Jesse James in the presence of Dick Liddil, in which I said that a couple of young men had been arrested for supposed complicity with the alleged bank robbery at Concordia, and that I didn't think they had anything to do with it; and asked Jesse James if he knew anything about that affair to tell me, and he said, pointing to Dick Liddil, 'There is the man that hit the Dutch cashier over the head.' Remember, in November, 1881, meeting Liddil and Jesse James in my lane, and when I asked Jesse who was ahead of them he replied, Jim Cummings and Hite. [8] Remember meeting Jesse James and Liddil again in the fall of 1881, and of asking Jesse where Frank was, and of his announcement that Frank's health was such that he had been south for years, and that when I asked the same question of Liddil he announced that he had not seen him for two years. Reckon I know Cummings better than any man except Ford's and his own people. He was at my house a dozen times. He was with me in the Confederate army. Have not seen Frank James since 1872. Believe he sits there right now. With the permission of the court, can I be tolerated to shake hands with an old soldier?"

THE COURT. No, sir, not now.

SHELBY. Did not see him in jail. Have not seen him since about 1872. Am correct about it, sir, when I say that the four parties I have alluded to by name did not include Frank James, who was not with them. Mrs. Frank James came to Page City in the spring of 1881. She sent for me and said, I am in distress. This man Liddil and others are committing depredations in the south, and they are holding my husband amenable for it, as he has been charged with being connected with them. I have come over on purpose to ask you to intercede with the Governor. I told her there was no necessity for that, and no hope of success. I told her further that Governor Woodson had talked with me at the Planter's House. For Hardin I had no respect at all. She wanted me to intervene in her husband's behalf with the Governor. I told her it would be folly to do so, and advised her to go home to her father. She didn't stop at my house. She could have stopped there if she had desired.

As to the sewing machine, don't know what time the sewing machine arrived there. She simply gave it to Mr. Birch, the agent at the depot, directions for shipping it, and I don't know where she directed it to be shipped at all. Was only assisting a woman in distress, and would have done the same if she had been Jennison's wife, the most obnoxious man in the country. Mrs. James left orders with the agent for the movement of the sewing machine. She was a lone woman, with a little child, and crying, and any man who would have faltered in giving suggestions or aid ought to be ashamed of himself. Have known Frank James since 1862. Got acquainted with him in our army.

WALLACE. This sewing machine you didn't see at all?

SHELBY. Nobody knows better than yourself that I didn't see it.

THE COURT. Answer the question in a straightforward manner.

SHELBY. I did not.

WALLACE. You didn't have anything to do with it at all?

SHELBY. Nothing in the world.

WALLACE. You are just as sure of that as you are of anything else? (The transcript of the testimony evidently is not complete at this point, for newspaper accounts say that this remark by Wallace caused Shelby to demand fiercely whether the prosecutor was insinuating that he was lying; and whether he would like to make a "personal matter of it." The newspaper account was undoubtedly correct, for the judge alluded to Shelby's challenge when he rebuked him later on. At this point, however, the record merely quotes Shelby as saying to the Court: "I should like to know if the Judge is going to permit a lawyer to insult an unarmed man, who is a witness in this case?" The Court responded that "Every witness comes in here unarmed, sir!" and Prosecutor Wallace resumed his questioning)

WALLACE. What are your initials?

SHELBY. If you are desirous of knowing go to the bank here and find out. Jo O. Shelby is my name.

WALLACE. Then your initials would be J. O. S.?

SHELBY. Go to the banks in this town and you will find it to be J. O. S.

WALLACE. Look at the way-bill and see if that has J. O. S. as the consignor of that sewing machine! There may be a great many J. O. S.'s who in that section have those initials beside you.

SHELBY. You had better go and inquire.

THE COURT. I won't have any more nonsense of that kind. You will have to answer the questions as they are put.

SHELBY. You are not protecting me at all.

JUDGE PHILIPS. I suggest to the court that under the circumstances this examination perhaps had better be deferred.

SHELBY. Not at all. Better let it go on. Now is the time for it to go on.

THE COURT. General Shelby, you are a man that I respect and a man with a state-wide reputation as a gentleman. We did not expect such demeanor in this court room. I must admonish you that I can not permit this to go on any further.

SHELBY. Very good, Judge. He has forced it on me. If I am guilty of a misdemeanor, correct me or punish me for it.

THE COURT. I shall do it.

WALLACE. You saw Liddil down at Captain Ballinger's house afterward, didn't you?

SHELBY. You don't propose to invade the household of Captain Ballinger, a soldier of the Federal Army? It is very wrong for a rebel soldier to make remarks about what occurred in a Federal soldier's home.

WALLACE. The war is over, General Shelby.

SHELBY. I don't like to allude to a visit to a gentleman's home. That is indelicate and improper.

WALLACE. Did you see Liddil there?

SHELBY. I did sir. I saw him like a viper, curled up in a rocking chair.

WALLACE. You saw him again at the hotel the other night, or was that a drummer that you took for him?

SHELBY. No sir; by no means.

WALLACE. Were you not about to kill the drummer, thinking he was Dick Liddil?

SHELBY. I have lived thirty-four years in this state and never killed anybody yet.

WALLACE. Answer the question.

SHELBY. I was not. This gentleman was seated at the table opposite to me, and he dropped his knife and fork and looked at me. Have his card in my pocket. He is a Michigan man, not one of your people at all, but a better man than yourself for instance. He was staring at me. Am not in the habit of staring at men on the street, especially ladies anyway, and I must have made some casual remark about it.

WALLACE. Did you get your pistol out?

SHELBY. No sir.

WALLACE. Didn't the marshal of Lexington see you draw your pistol?

SHELBY. No sir; he is a liar, or anybody else, if he says so.

THE COURT. I want no more such remarks as that, General Shelby, or I will fine you $50.

SHELBY. Dick Liddil had partaken of my meals and I had fed my corn to Liddil's horses. That was in 1880, and Jesse James was with him and Cummings and Ryan. Did not know that Jesse James was wanted by the officers. Knew it was asserted that he had been guilty of misdemeanors. Never told any other officer where they could find him, but did once notify the Chicago and Alton and Missouri Pacific people that if they were under the apprehension that George Shepard had killed him they were being misled, and that he was not dead. The last time I saw Jesse was at my house in Page City, in the fall of 1881, where I saw Frank James in 1872, which is the last time I saw him. He was bleeding at the lungs, and Dr. Orear was attending him. Didn't know that he was an outlaw then or that he is one today. Don't know that he was fleeing from the officers. He was at my house some sixty or eighty days that time and everybody knew it. When the four men came to my house, as I have already stated, I told them I could accommodate only two of them for the night. Bill Ryan and Jesse James stayed all night with me. The others stopped with a man from Illinois named Graham, who had been in the Federal Army. Am certain that Ryan was not pointed out to me as the man who hit the Dutch cashier over the head.

This concluded Shelby's testimony, although the record at this point adds: "As the witness started to leave the courtroom he asked permission to go over and shake hands with the defendant. This the Court refused, saying, 'You can call on him some other time'. Whereupon General Shelby spoke to the accused as he walked out, and said, 'God Bless you, old fellow.'"

Shelby's brush with Prosecutor Wallace and with the Court did not end that day, however, although he was not again called to the witness stand. The next day, Defense Attorney Philips arose at the beginning of the session and said, "Your Honor, General Shelby is at the door and desires the privilege of making a statement to the court." Judge Goodman said that it would be permitted.

Shelby entered, and without preliminaries, said, "If anything I said during my examination yesterday offended the dignity of the court I regret it exceedingly, your Honor. As to what I said in regard to others, I have no regrets to express."

The rest of the conversation between Shelby and Judge Goodman is also upon the record:

JUDGE GOODMAN: The court has been both surprised and mortified that a gentleman who was so highly respected as General Shelby, and who had a national reputation—for there was scarcely a man in the West who had not heard favorably of General Shelby—should be guilty of such conduct. Nothing of this kind has ever been attributed to him before. He should have reflected that to enter a court of justice in such a condition as he was in on Thursday was not only an insult to the court, but was an act of the greatest injustice toward the man who was on trial for his life, and in whose behalf he had been summoned, for the reason that it prejudiced his interests before the jury. He (the Court) asked no apology from any man so far as he himself was concerned, but this assault on the rights of the defendant had been so flagrant that the court would not overlook it, and the clerk would be instructed to enter up a fine of ten dollars. The general's conduct had been reprehensible in more than one particular, as the testimony showed that he had drawn a revolver almost at the verge of the court room in one of the hotels of the city.

"General Shelby said he had listened attentively to the court and was very glad His Honor had spoken so fully as it gave him an opportunity to refute a slander. I am charged with drawing a revolver; it is false and the man who said so said what was false."

THE COURT. The information came from the Marshal of Lexington, who had given it under oath.

GENERAL SHELBY. He has lied if he said so.

JUDGE GOODMAN. While on the stand you threatened to call the attorneys of the state to account for what was said by them in your examination. The attorneys are officers of the court and must be allowed to conduct the case in the interest of the state, in their own way. Any intimidation or threat was in the nature of an obstruction of justice.

GENERAL SHELBY. You use the plural, Your Honor. It is not the attorneys, but the attorney (pointing to Mr. Wallace).

JUDGE GOODMAN. Had General Shelby been an unsophisticated backwoodsman and had persisted in disobeying the directions of the court he would simply have administered a rebuke and committed him to jail. Such a course, however, would seem to be hardly necessary in the case of a man with the refined sensibilities which characterized General Shelby and the court disliked to resort to harsh measures with him. So far as the Court was concerned the General's apology was ample, but he felt he had no right to condone the offense of which the General had been guilty in prejudicing the interests of a man who was on trial for his life, and in whose behalf he had been summoned.

GENERAL SHELBY. So far as the term backwoodsman is concerned, I have been a Missouri farmer for thirty-four years.

JUDGE GOODMAN. Yes, but you do not claim immunity on that account.

GENERAL SHELBY. No, sir; I never sail under that flag.

JUDGE GOODMAN. That is sufficient.

Shelby paid the fine of ten dollars and left the courtroom. The next day Judge Philips made a masterly address to the jury. In discussing Shelby's relations with the James Boys and "the fugitive, panting, little wife of Frank James," he said: "Shelby's testimony is worthy of all credit. It is but frank in me to admit that the General's deportment on the witness stand was improper, as a matter of propriety. It hurt no one so much as himself and I know he regrets it. But he spoke truth. His high character needs no defense and no eulogy by me. His name is a household word in Missouri. As splendid in courage as he is big in heart, his home is a model of hospitality. No man, however poor and outcast, was ever turned from it hungry. Truth and chivalry are to him as modesty to the true woman, azure to the sky.

"He has been denounced in public and private as a friend of Frank James. Smirking Puritans and lugubrious Pharisees have shrugged their shoulders at the fact that Shelby gave a bed and a glass of water and a pinch of salt to the defendant when he chanced to pass his door; and for extending the hand of assistance and a word of sympathy to Frank James's wandering heartsick wife. In the midst of so much moral cowardice and starveling charity in this age, I rather admire the quality of heart which prompted Shelby."

So did the jury, and Frank James walked forth from the opera house a free man. But there was still one more act to be played out in the drama at Gallatin which had been attended by "gaily dressed ladies and less gaudy correspondents," as well as by all of the wool hats in Missouri who could manage to be present.

During the afternoon, someone handed a note to Prosecutor Wallace in which, Wallace revealed later, a "friend" warned him that General Shelby had threatened to shoot him on sight as soon as he left the courtroom. In view of the fact that Shelby had just asked him, from the witness stand, whether he desired to make a personal matter of their differences during the cross-examination, and had been balked in this challenge, Wallace may be excused for being somewhat apprehensive as he left the courtroom. He was unarmed, of course, and he was carrying an armful of law books which he intended to study that night at his hotel.

It had rained, and the streets of Gallatin were muddy. Across one mudhole, directly in front of the opera house, a plank had been laid for pedestrians to cross to dry land. As Wallace stepped on one end of the plank, someone else stepped on the opposite end, and the prosecutor looked up from the plank-covered mudhole straight into the eyes of Jo Shelby. Shelby was wearing a long black coat, over the sleeves of which his white cuffs were turned back in the old-fashioned manner.

Wallace did not flinch, for he was a brave man and had served honorably in the same army with Shelby, but the thoughts that flashed through his mind at this moment could not have been pleasurable. It is quite likely that he expected to die on the spot, for directly in front of him was one of the most dangerous men, when angered, in Missouri; and he had seen a fine display of the Shelby temper on the witness stand not an hour before.

General Shelby removed his broad-brimmed black hat and stepped back with a courtly bow. "You pass first, Mr. Wallace," he said, with a Southern gentleman's courtesy.

The gaily dressed ladies and the open-mouthed wool hats who had been watching this scene with exquisite expectation breathed a sigh of relief. They knew now that Jo Shelby had never threatened to shoot Prosecutor Wallace. If he had done so, he would have shot him then and there, for all Missouri knew that Old Jo was a man of his word.

32.   *A Friend Is Gone*

IN THE SPRING OF 1889, the Shelby household was saddened by the news of the death of John Edwards. The legislature was in session at Jefferson City and the Major had gone, as had been his wont for eighteen years, to cover the proceedings in person. He was staying at the McCarty House, where he always stayed in Jefferson City, and with him were Mrs. Edwards, a Negro servant, and his little daughter Laura, now eight years old.[1]

Edwards had been suffering from a heart condition, but his death was sudden and unexpected. A few minutes before he was stricken, he had been teaching Laura to blow soap bubbles from a pipe, and as if he had a premonition of his death, he said to her, "Laura, always remember that your papa bought you that pipe." [2] He was alone when the end came. Mrs. Edwards entered the room, bringing a friend,

Major J. L. Bittinger, and they found him slumped in his chair, beyond medical aid. The gallant heart had given up quietly.

The news soon spread throughout Jefferson City and there were expressions of profound sorrow. No man in Missouri was better known, or better liked, than Major Edwards. At the time of his death he was at the height of his fame as editor of the Kansas City *Times*, which he had left in 1874 and to which he returned in 1887. The thirteen years between had been a whirlwind career on the St. Louis *Times*, the Sedalia *Democrat*, the Sedalia *Dispatch*, and the St. Joseph *Gazette*. In every case his burning pen had lifted the paper out of the humdrum routine of newspapering and kept his readers at a high pitch of enthusiasm or indignation on a variety of public topics.

Always a partisan in politics, and always a die-hard Southerner, he nevertheless had friends in all camps, and when news of his passing reached the State Capitol, half the members of the Senate and the House left their seats and gathered in the lobby and the adjoining rooms. When the afternoon sessions were resumed, both houses adjourned out of respect to his memory.[3]

Officials of the Missouri Pacific Railroad came forward with an offer of a special train to carry his body to Dover, where he would be buried. From the moment of his death until his body was taken to the train at noon the following day, a Sunday, there was a constant stream of visitors passing in and out of the hotel corridor to extend sympathy to Jennie Edwards and to look for the last time upon his features. At 12:30 Sunday afternoon the funeral procession formed at the hotel to go to the depot, where the train was waiting. Secretary of State A. A. Leseur, who was one of the pallbearers, records that "first came a long line of gentlemen on foot, led by Governor Francis, and composed of senators, members of the house of Representatives, and many others. By the side of the hearse were the pallbearers—Dr. Morrison Munford [owner of the Kansas City *Times* and a devoted friend of twenty years], Col. W. D. Marmaduke, J. Frank Merriman, Major John L. Bittinger, Capt. T. P. Hoy and A. A. Leseur; after them came the family and other friends in special carriages."[4] The train arrived at Dover Sunday evening and burial took place the following morning from the home of Mrs. L. C. Plattenburg, Jennie's mother.

As soon as the news of Edwards' death had been telegraphed to

Kansas City, a reporter for the *Times* went to Adrian and informed Jo Shelby. The reporter quoted Shelby as saying, "The news of Major Edwards' death is a great shock to me. I have known and loved him since he was a boy. It is hardly within the power of language to portray or describe Major Edwards as his noble character merits. God never created a more noble, magnanimous and truer man than John N. Edwards." [5]

Among the old Confederates who filed beside his casket when it was opened for the last time at Dover, Shelby, as he turned away with tears in his eyes, said to a friend, "He was the bravest man in war and the gentlest man in peace I ever saw." That summed up the character of John Edwards. He was a man, as Robertus Love says, of "violent convictions and gentle habits." [6]

Simple services were conducted at the grave, as Edwards had requested. He is buried in the old cemetery in the outskirts of Dover. A reporter for Edwards' paper wrote, "It is a quiet, secluded spot, where the rumble of the wagon wheels in the road nearby are the only sounds, save the singing of the birds, heard from one year's end to the other—just the place where Major Edwards' love of nature and the beautiful would desire to lie in his last long sleep. And it was his wish, frequently expressed, that he should be buried there. It is within easy view of the old Plattenburg homestead, where his wife spent her girlhood and he wooed and won her, and from which his body was carried to its last resting place this morning."

The entire press of Missouri mourned the passing of its most colorful and beloved editor. No fewer than 128 editorials in Missouri and Kansas newspapers appeared after his death. [7] They totaled more than a hundred thousand words. Robert M. Yost, writing in Edwards' old paper, summed it up best in a sentence. "There will be tears in every household in Missouri over the death of John Edwards." And he added, as a fitting epitaph, "After life's fitful fever, he sleeps well."

A quarter of a century had passed, and the lines of the Iron Brigade were beginning to thin, but at the Confederate reunions you would not have known it, for most of Shelby's men whom he recruited as striplings were now in their vigorous fifties (Edwards had been fiftyone), and when, once a year, a bugle blew throughout the South, they still responded with firm tread and undimmed eye, to live again for a few brief days their lost years.

But Shelby was older. He would be sixty years old his next birthday, and the chestnut beard, which had resembled the waved mane of a circus horse, was gray now and the shoulders not quite so straight as of old. Those of his men who saw him at reunions in the nineties also saw for the first time that Shelby was not seven feet tall, as many had supposed. He was, in fact, just a courtly little old gentleman with a gray beard.

The family was living in Bates County, at Adrian, not far from Butler, and Shelby had given up all occupations except that of farmer. His sons were able to help him run the farm, and Anna had grown out of pigtails and into lovely teenhood. The scarcity of family records makes it impossible to throw much light on Shelby's finances at the period, but that they were at low ebb for a time there is no doubt. He did not even own the farm in Bates County. The will of Shelby's mother, Anna Boswell Gratz, written in 1886 and filed for probate on August 26, 1892,[8] indicates that Shelby's business reverses of the seventies and eighties had used up all of his fortune and left him in debt, for Mrs. Gratz acquired the Bates County farm, presumably to save him from losing it, and gave the deed, not to her son Jo, but to Betty Shelby.

The terms of the will left no doubt as to the low esteem into which he had fallen with the Gratzes, as the result of his flamboyant postwar career in Missouri. In the second clause of her will, Anna Gratz wrote:

"I devise to my daughter-in-law Betty N. Shelby, the wife of my son J. O. Shelby, the farm in Bates County, Missouri, whereon she now resides, containing about 400 acres to have and to hold to her sole and separate use and estate free from the control or debts of her husband, during her natural life. At her death, if her husband the said J. O. Shelby shall survive her, I wish him during his life to use and control said farm for the support and maintenance of himself and those of his children who shall live with him; but he shall have no interest or estate therein which shall be subject to his debts either past or future; and if any creditor of his should attempt to subject any supposed estate or interest of his in said property to· payment of his debts and the courts should deem the same liable, then all such interest shall at once cease . . . and become vested in those who would take the property in case of his death. After the death of both my said son and his said wife, the said land shall pass in fee simple to the descendants of my said son and his said wife or to such of them as the said Mrs. Betty N. Shelby shall by last will appoint; or in default of such appointment to all their children; and if any of their children be then dead leaving issue the descendants of such deceased child shall take the share the parent would have taken if living." To other members of the family Mrs. Gratz made substantial bequests.

The disinherited Shelby brought suit in the Fayette County Court to upset this will, and spent some time in Lexington at the Phoenix Hotel during its trial in the latter part of 1893.

The testimony at this trial is missing from the files of the Fayette County Courthouse. The explanation may be that Shelby's attorney took the record from the courthouse to have it copied for an appeal, and never brought it back. In law, as distinct from chancery, attorneys are permitted to take papers out of the courtroom for such a purpose. However, the testimony is not on file in Lexington, nor do newspaper files of the period yield any reference to it.

Apparently Shelby based his suit on the allegation that undue influence had been exercised over his mother, and against him. (The appeal papers contain a sample copy of depositions sent to a member of the family then in Kansas City in which the questions indicate that this was the basis of the suit.)

Defeated in the lower court, Shelby noted an appeal on February 16, 1894, in which he alleged "irregularities in the proceedings of the court, by adjournment from time to time, and by the adjournment of the Court for one week which was over the protest of the contestant and an abuse of the discretion of the court by which the contestant was prevented from having a fair and impartial trial." He also claimed that there was misconduct on the part of the jury in that "one of the jurors proclaimed to the jury that he didn't intend to set the precedent of breaking wills by breaking this will," and that another told his fellow jurors that he "didn't believe in breaking wills." Shelby further charged that one of the jurors had been influenced by the promise of a job.

The appeal never reached the higher court, though first papers were filed with the Fayette County Court and the courthouse books show that Shelby paid $150 to have the record copied. The reasons for his failure to pursue the contest into the Court of Appeals are not clear, although a guess may be hazarded that he was not very confident of success on the grounds set forth. Even a layman can recognize the fact that proving bias on the part of the court, or the bribing of the jury, would be extremely difficult, no matter how excellent such grounds might be for a reversal of the decision.

33. *The Great Pullman Strike*

IN THE FALL OF 1892, just after the probation of his mother's will, Jo Shelby allowed his name to be put up for political office. He needed a job. The man who could have been governor or United States senator, and who had refused to trade on his war reputation, as hundreds of lesser men had done, now allowed his friends to nominate him for the office of United States marshal for Western Missouri, which was vacant. Grover Cleveland was President, and Jo Shelby had been one of his most active supporters.

Ex-Governor Fletcher, who had fought against Shelby in the Union Army, made a special trip to Washington to urge Cleveland to appoint him. Fletcher told the President that appointing Shelby would be the most popular thing he could do in Missouri. A recommendation from Fletcher carried weight, for Fletcher had had the thankless task of being governor from 1865 to 1869 and knew better than any other man how hard it had been to bring peace to Missouri. He also knew better than any other man how great had been the contribution of Jo Shelby in finally achieving it.

"Although he was the most dangerous man we had to deal with during the war," Fletcher told Cleveland, "no man was so widely instrumental in helping us bring order out of chaos when the war was over. His influence with the people of Missouri was inestimable and he worked night and day to restore peace by appealing to them to accept the new order of things in a spirit of resignation." [1]

Cleveland nominated Shelby as marshal, a nomination which had to be approved by the Senate as a matter of routine. As always in the career of Jo Shelby, however, what was ordinarily a routine matter turned out to be an occasion for fireworks of one sort or another.

The opposition press indulged in delicious shudders at the thought of the old rebel as United States marshal, and soon found a handy club with which to beat him. An enterprising reporter went to the Official Records of the War of the Rebellion, which were then in process of being assembled, and dragged out Shelby's battle reports, written, of course, after 1862, by John Edwards. All of the florid prose of Major Edwards was paraded before the public as Shelby's, in an effort to make him look ridiculous, to discredit him as a soldier, and to picture him as a posturer infatuated with delusions of his own greatness.

Among the dispatches quoted from the Official Records were those in which Edwards had described Shelby's men as turning like lions at bay, and the enemy as "mongrel soldiers, Negroes and Yankee schoolmasters imported to teach the young idea how to shoot." He was quoted as saying that his own victories were "a beacon light of hope and help reared in the dark night of despotism and oppression," and cited such Edwards masterpieces as the report of the capture of the *Queen City*, which begins, "It was a beautiful moonlit night. White fleecy clouds hovered over the sleeping river, over the doomed craft with all her gala lights in bloom, and over the crouching lines of infantry and the yawning cannon. . . . Just as the white hand of morning put away the sable clouds of night four pieces of artillery sent their terrible messengers crashing through the boat." The newspaper accounts hurled at Shelby the charge of quoting poetry in his dispatches; and the charge was true, except that Shelby had not written them.

Not only had Shelby not written them, he had not read them. The task of writing reports was one that he had been glad to leave to his adjutant. Nevertheless, he could not say so, and as the guffaws arose in the Republican newspapers, the graying Shelby was acutely embarrassed.

The attack boomeranged, as it deserved to. Letters and telegrams began to pour in to the United States Senate denouncing the newspapers for their buffoonery. These came not mainly from old Confederates, but from soldiers of the Blue Armies who had been outridden and outfought by General Shelby during the war, and who knew what manner of man he was. The substance of the messages was that if there was a better man in all Missouri for the post of United States marshal than Jo Shelby, they would like to know about it.

Shelby's nomination was confirmed. He took up the duties of his office in the old Federal Building in Kansas City in January, 1893. He was still able and energetic at sixty, as his handling of the Pullman strike in Kansas City the following year was to show, and the Shelby flair for doing everything with a gracious gesture soon made itself manifest in the conduct of the marshal's office.

On the first day that he reported, naturally, there was a stream of visitors in and out of his office—all sorts of prominent people, but chiefly old soldiers of both armies who came to congratulate him. So congenial did they find the atmosphere that many of them began to make the visit to Shelby's office a daily ritual. The United States' marshal's office became a clubhouse for veterans wearing the Confederate gray of the Old Soldiers Home or the bronze button of the Grand Army of the Republic, who otherwise might have been spending their time sunning themselves on a park bench. There was good talk at all times, and hospitality in the afternoons. George Creel, then a young reporter covering the Federal Building for the Kansas City *World* (a Yankee paper, for working on which Shelby chided him) dubbed them "the Colonels," and he says in his autobiography, "The Federal Building was on my beat and when I dropped in to see the General, it was usually an hour before I could get away. As a rule, members of his old command sat with him, and when dispute occurred as to date or incident, they turned to their Bible, John N. Edwards' chronicle of the expedition." [2]

The eastern press, as well as the press of Kansas City, had been in something of a stir when Shelby was appointed marshal, and there was more of a commotion when he appointed a Negro as one of his deputies. This deputy, named Bob, was of the aristocratic Negro manservant type, a representative of the vanishing race of majordomos who had ruled autocratically in the plantation "big houses" before the war. He carried out his duties with the bearing of a Senegambian prince. The New England press, says Creel, cheered that "at last . . . the 'man and brother' had been given recognition, and by a former slaveholder and great Confederate leader. It was a good thing the New England editors never visited the General's office, for while Ol' Bob did have the title of United States deputy marshal his real job was to wait on Mars' Jo and see to it that the mint juleps were properly frosted." [3]

About this time Shelby got word that Billy Hunter was working as a bricklayer in Indianapolis, and he sent one of his deputy marshals, C. C. Colt, to bring him back, if he would come, to the Shelby household at Adrian. Billy was glad to come back to the home that had always been his, and he spent the rest of his life with the Shelbys. He was with his old master when Shelby died.

Shelby's notorious tenderheartedness, which had made him a soft touch for every old soldier, now made him a soft touch for everybody. For the first time, he came in contact with human misery as it is seen only in a courtroom. As Judge Philips said in his last tribute to his friend, "The angels alone have recorded the sums of money he has given for bread and raiment to the wives and little ones of convicts in court. He gave so often that recently one foolish woman came to the notion that the government furnished the money and wanted me to require him to do more." [4]

One day, hardboiled attorneys were moved as Shelby stood and listened while the judge pronounced sentence upon a young man convicted of a petty postoffice theft. Having spoken the fateful words, the judge directed Marshal Shelby to remove the convicted youth. Thereupon Shelby stepped to the side of the prisoner, but instead of catching him roughly by the arm, he laid his own over the young man's shoulders and spoke to him in a low voice, full of understanding. The boy looked up at the sympathetic touch, buried his face in the marshal's shoulder, and burst into tears. Thus they left the courtroom, while spectators gazed in astonished silence. [5]

When two thinly clad newsboys came into the office on a bitterly cold day in Kansas City, Shelby gave them jobs on the inside where they would be warm. He could not quite get away with appointing them his deputies, but he surmounted the difficulty. Thereafter, says the Kansas City *Star*, "visitors to the courtroom could not fail to observe what could not be found elsewhere in the land: two small boys filling the important posts of bailiffs. They were so small that, at the opening day of term, when they approached the clerk's desk to take the constitutional oath of office, they barely reached over it. Shelby admitted to the judge that they hardly came up to 'the most ancient standards for bailiffs,' but explained that they were two newsboys whose aged mother was dependent upon them for support and he would like to give them a better job." [6]

Advancing years had not lessened Shelby's gallantry toward the fair sex, and down the corridor in the Federal Building worked a pretty young woman of whom he was extremely fond. Two or three times a day, reporters at the Federal Building recall, he entered her office and talked to her in "his knightly and courtly fashion." If he found any man there wearing a hat, he would instantly pluck it off. "Sir," he would say, "do you know no better, sir, than to remain covered in the presence of a lady, sir?" [7] Shelby had become a character, and of course he knew it; no man could be the object of as much public adoration as he had been in Missouri for thirty years without acquiring a few royal mannerisms, but to Shelby's eternal credit it must be said that the pampering had not spoiled him. Only the petty become spoiled, and Shelby, whose eyes were always on horizons which other men could not see, had no time for pettiness.

In July, 1894, occurred the great Pullman boycott and strike of the railroads, one of the bloodiest labor wars in American industrial history. Hundreds of thousands of dollars' worth of railroad property was destroyed, dozens of persons were killed and wounded, the militia was called in twenty states, and the Federal government finally intervened with troops and injunctions to bring an end to the chaos. In Missouri there was little violence, as compared with such areas as Chicago, the storm center of the strike. That the trains ran and the mails were delivered in Missouri was due in large part to the swiftness with which United States Marshal Shelby acted when the Federal government stepped in.

The basic cause of the strike, which originated in the little Chicago suburb of Pullman, a "company town" of the Pullman Palace Car Company, was the panic of 1893. The economic disruptions of that year launched one of the bitterest depressions of the nineteenth century. More than 16,000 business firms had gone bankrupt, including fifty companies with a capital of more than half a million dollars each. The bottom dropped out of wholesale prices, making it difficult to produce goods at more than the barest minimum of profit, and companies repeatedly slashed the pay of their workers. Especially hard hit was the village of Pullman, Illinois, which the company had built for its workers, and in which it was the only employer and landlord. Even in prosperous years the wage standards of Pullman had been lower than union wages for similar work in Chicago, but the rents for the company cottages were 20 to 25 per cent higher. Labor being a drug on the market in 1894, there were no other jobs to which the Pullman workers could go; it was work for Pullman or not work.

Although the company had on its books an undivided surplus of $2,320,000 at the end of the fiscal year in July, an amount which exceeded its total wage outlay for six months, the wage cuts and lay-offs continued, but rents were not lowered. One skilled mechanic worked ten hours a day for twelve days and received a pay check of seven cents. His wages were $9.07, but he owed the company $9.00 rent.[8]

On May 7, 1894, the employees presented their grievances to Pull-man executives, but were not satisfied with the result. On May 11, 9,000 workers left their jobs and the remaining 300 were quickly laid off by the Pullman Company. The walkout was orderly, and Eugene V. Debs, president of the American Railway Union, with which some of the strikers were affiliated, undertook to arbitrate, al-though the ARU had neither caused nor authorized the walkout.

The Pullman Company refused to arbitrate, and on June 22 an ultimatum was issued by the American Railway Union: unless the company agreed to enter into negotiations within four days, the Pull-man shops at Ludlow, Kentucky, and at St. Louis would be struck, and the ARU would refuse to handle Pullman cars. Again the com-pany was adamant, and the boycott was voted to begin on June 26 unless the company changed its mind in the meanwhile. It did not. At noon on the date set, the ARU ordered all Pullman cars cut from their trains and sidetracked.

The railroads now stepped in. The General Managers Association, representing twenty-four railroads having their terminus in Chicago, which operated 41,000 miles of track and had 221,000 employees, an-nounced that they could not move trains without Pullman cars because of their contracts with the Pullman Company. To move them with Pullman Palace Cars attached meant hiring strikebreakers. That touched off the fuse which exploded in twenty states.

There had been strikes aplenty in the United States since the Civil War, but never one like this. More than 100,000 men had gone off their jobs, and between Chicago and the Golden Gate only the Great Northern Railway was maintaining a semblance of its regular schedule.

The Federal government was now involved whether it liked it or not, for the delivery of the mails was affected. On July 2 a Federal court in Chicago issued an omnibus injunction prohibiting officials of the American Railway Union from aiding the boycott in any way. It was a sweeping injunction, and it cut the ground from under the feet of the strikers. Debs and his fellow ARU leaders were eventually indicted for conspiracy, refused bail, and imprisoned. On July 2

President Cleveland ordered Federal troops to Chicago. Riots, blood-shed, arson followed. In Chicago alone $300,000 worth of property was destroyed on July 6, and the soldiers fired into the mob. (A dis-patch in the Kansas City *Star* said on July 12 that ten lives had been lost in Chicago and forty-one persons injured.) Losses to the Pullman Palace Car Company throughout the country were estimated after the strike at twice the value of the Pullman holdings.

Shelby swore in 700 deputies in Missouri at the beginning of the strike, which began at noon on July 2. The Kansas City *Star* reported on that day that "at the Union Depot a force of deputies of Marshal Shelby is guarding Santa Fe Trains and everything sent out yesterday had deputies on the coach platform as far as Argentine [Shelby had 61 men on duty at Argentine]. Even the backups, local trains that stop here, are backed into the Union station and are guarded by deputies."

The Chicago and St. Louis Limited Express was held up at Slater, Missouri, and Shelby sent Chief Deputy Marshal C. C. Colt to Slater with a force of deputies to see to it that trains moved unmolested. At this point he found himself involved in a controversy with Governor William J. Stone. Stone, along with Governor Altgeld of Illinois, viewed with alarm the use of Federal troops as police, holding that it was a usurpation of the power of local and state authorities and an invasion of states' rights. He addressed a letter to Shelby in which he set forth this view. Shelby did not make the letter public, but the *Star* reported on July 3, 1894, that "Governor Stone wants to know by what right the United States court and marshal presume to interfere with the free action of the people of Missouri at Slater and other points where trains are stopped by strikers. The letter," continued the *Star*, is "full of suggestions that the United States has gone beyond its authority when deputy marshals were placed at stations within the state of Missouri to protect trains."

Shelby took only the curtest notice of this communication from the Governor. He replied that "in protecting trains he was carrying out the orders of the United States courts for the protection of property in their hands,"[9] and he suggested that Governor Stone apply to Washington for further information.

Stone wrote a letter to his brother, John B. Stone, in Kansas City, in which he complained that the newspapers were trying to involve him first in a quarrel with General Shelby, which he said did not exist, and secondly with President Cleveland. Nevertheless, he said, he opposed "the dangerous policy of making the protection of the mails or inter-state commerce a mere pretext for supplanting state authority." "Even in recent decisions of the Supreme Court," he said, "the line between the state and federal government has been well drawn by the constitution and by repeated and even recent decisions of the United States Supreme Court."

The Governor's brother showed this letter to Shelby, as he doubtless was intended to do, and Shelby replied, as quoted in the *Star* on July 12, "If the Governor had been through what we have he would have known that the question he thinks is still open was long ago settled in blood." [10]

But Shelby, now incensed with the Governor for interrupting him on a busy day, did not let the matter rest there. In the same letter to his brother, Governor Stone had said that he had received complaints from the local authorities at Slater that Shelby's deputies were roughnecks who were making themselves obnoxious to the public at Slater. Shelby was as quick to defend his deputies against this charge as he had been to defend his men against the charge of looting during the war. He sent a telegram to Mayor R. T. Brightwell of Slater asking what the conduct of his deputies had been at that place, and received this reply, signed by Brightwell and three other city officials: "THE CONDUCT OF THE UNITED STATES DEPUTY MARSHALS AT THIS PLACE WAS DIGNIFIED, POLITE AND GENTLE-MANLY THEY ATTENDED TO THEIR DUTIES AND THEIR OWN BUSINESS." Shelby did not fail to send this down to the city room of the *Star* which published it, and also commented editorially:

"General Jo Shelby has very decidedly the best of the correspond-ence in which Governor Stone attempts to call Shelby down for ordering United States deputy marshals to Slater to preserve the public peace. The Governor looks upon this as an impertinent inter-ference with the authority of the state and enforces this opinion in a letter which shows a plentiful lack of courtesy for General Shelby and of respect for the General Government. There is a tone about the communication which suggests that if Mr. Stone could have his way he would pitch the United States Marshal of Missouri and all of his deputies into the river.

"In reply to Governor Stone's offensive letter General Shelby states that he acted on the authority and instructions of the attorney general of the United States and adds that if the Governor desires to obtain any further light on the question of Mr. Olney's (the United States Attorney General) right to maintain the dignity of the Government against violent and unlawful interference with the mails he (Stone) should apply to Washington.

"General Shelby writes like an old soldier—Governor Stone like the small-bore politician that he is. Shelby fought in the war on the Confederate side, but was so thoroughly reconstructed that he knows there is nothing left of the heresy of state sovereignty. While Shelby was fighting for the Lost Cause and dodging bullets on many a hotly contested field, Governor Stone, as a beardless youth, was hanging around the Seventh Cavalry camp in Kentucky. That is as near as he ever came to smelling powder. But no rebel who ever took up arms against the Union flag ever had a braver mouth than Governor Stone, who is always ready to rush to the front as the champion of States' rights and 'gallant' defender of the cause which perished without hope of resurrection when Lee surrendered to Grant at Richmond [sic]. The quiet but effective manner in which Jo Shelby has scalped Mr. Stone ought to suggest to the latter some idea of the value of modesty and patriotism in a public officer but it is almost too much to hope that it will have that effect." [11]

By an ironic twist of circumstance, Governor Stone was forced to accept a personal favor from Shelby's deputies at Slater just two days after he had protested that they were roughnecks and exceeding their authority. The State militia staged a sham battle at a Fourth of July celebration at Marshall, at which Stone was present, and when the day's festivities were ended, it was discovered that strikers had made off with the engine of the special train which had brought Stone and the militiamen from Jefferson City.

In a huff, the Governor telegraphed the strikers at Slater that if they did not return the engine he would send the militia after it, a suggestion which the Kansas City *Star* says evoked only horselaughs.

"If it had not been for General Jo Shelby and his deputies," says the *Star*, "the Governor might have been at Marshall yet. General Shelby didn't say anything about it and it was not until the deputies came home that the facts were known. The Governor had a train at Marshall, which is twelve miles from Slater, and no engine. His telegram threatening to send the militia after the engine and strikers was sent to a druggist at Slater. The latter showed it to some of the strike leaders, who laughed a loud horselaugh. The thought of the militia coming after them struck the strikers as funny and they began to debate the question as to how they should entertain the Governor if he should visit them. They said they would receive him as becomes his dignity and high position, though some of the more noisy agitators were for capturing him.

"Meanwhile Chief Deputy United States Marshal C. C. Colt, having been notified by the superintendent of the Alton that the Governor wanted an engine, took four deputy marshals, one of them a fireman, summoned an engineer and went in person with the party and engine to Marshall. After seeing the Governor safely started with the militia-man acting as fireman, he took his own fireman and deputies and went back to Slater on a handcar. The strikers were disappointed at not having a chance to receive a distinguished visitor but it is not recorded that the governor thanked the deputy marshals for their services." [12]

All of Shelby's deputies, however, were not gentlemanly and well-behaved, as the contemporary newspaper accounts show. With a force of 700 special officers, recruited in haste, it is not surprising that there should be some roughnecks among them. No one knew this better than Shelby and every morning when the deputies reported for work he passed in review before them in a "weeding out" process. Any deputy on whom there was a bad conduct report was dismissed immediately. On July 11 the *Star* reported, "His orders to men in charge of details are to discharge any men found drinking intoxicating liquor, if only a single glass, or misbehaving.... One deputy whipped his wife Sunday. She reported it and an order was sent to find the man and dismiss him at once. The wife was instructed to have him prosecuted and how to proceed. This morning City Attorney Walker had a dozen deputies who had been drinking last night." Another item recorded that "Louis Page, one of Marshal Shelby's deputies, wandered across the state line into Kansas City yesterday afternoon and on his way home accumulated a considerable jag. He was arrested and fined $5 for drunkenness by Kansas City police. He could not pay the fine and was sent to the rock pile."

By July 15 the strike was over, and Shelby went back to his Colonels and his mint juleps. There had been only one instance of serious violence in Kansas City during the two weeks of the strike, a fire set on July 6 in the yards of the Chicago and Alton which was extinguished before it could damage the 800 cars standing on the tracks. The *Star* congratulated the community on the law-abiding behavior of its citizens and pointed out that such rowdy centers as Chicago would do well to emulate the example of Kansas City.

In July, 1896, the combined armies of the Confederacy marched again in the Great Reunion held at Richmond. It was only the sixth time since the war that a general reunion had been held, and the occasion would be marked by the laying of the cornerstone for a magnificent monument to Jefferson Davis in the capital of the Confederacy. Shelby made the journey east to Richmond, although in that proud stronghold of the eastern armies he was a little overshadowed by the great figures of the Army of Northern Virginia who were present. The silver-voiced John B. Gordon was chairman of the meeting of the Confederate Veterans Association, Longstreet was among those present, although he rode in a carriage instead of marching, and Shelby led the Missouri Veteran Division, which assembled at the northeast corner of Eighth and Broad on the morning of July 2 for the great parade which preceded the laying of the cornerstone. Among those who marched with him were Maurice Langhorne, Dick Collins, and A. A. Leseur.

The Richmond *Times* published an ink sketch of Shelby and commented that "few of the veterans in Richmond are better known than J. O. Shelby," but reporters did not interview him, and he made only a brief speech at the main session of the veterans' convention.

The pen of John Edwards, which would have risen to heights on such an occasion, was laid aside forever, these six years, but Shelby made a simple, heartfelt statement. "Like many from Missouri," he said, "I have come here to mingle with you for the love and affection I entertain for you. We are here, as ex-Confederates, to watch the laying of the cornerstone for a monument to the memory of Jefferson Davis, whom we all love and revere, and I stand here as a representative of the Confederate cause west of the Mississippi, and I speak for the Missourians when I say that this for all time shall be our Mecca and we shall ever do him honor."

It was his last public appearance. While in Richmond he attended a reception tendered the veterans by Governor O'Ferrall, himself a veteran, and another at the White House of the Confederacy for Mrs.

Jefferson Davis. Then he and his comrades took the "cars" back to Missouri.

34. *Missouri's Farewell*

THE WINTER OF 1896 was blustery, rough and damp in Kansas City. Early in February, 1897, his fellow workers noticed that Marshal Shelby had a bad cold and urged him to go home and go to bed. He would not hear of it, and although it got no better, he insisted on serving summonses personally, as he had always done, despite the sleety weather. On his return from one of these trips, during the first week in February, he was suffering from a fever, and he was ordered to bed by the family physician, Dr. F. G. Henry. Within twenty-four hours he had pneumonia. A short time after being put to bed he had become unconscious from the fever and unable to recognize any of the family.

Dr. Henry sent for the best physicians in Kansas City, and they hurried to Adrian by train, but when they arrived, there was little they could do for the patient, although for a time, during the examination, it seemed as if he were struggling back to consciousness. When the doctors had concluded their visit and had gone into the next room to give Betsy Shelby their verdict, Shelby aroused himself and said in a lucid voice which could be heard through the doorway, "Betsy, don't let the doctors go without their supper."

Those were his last words. They reflected better than any eulogy could the spirit of knightly hospitality of the man who, as William Elsey Connelley said, "was one of the bravest and truest men ever to shoulder a musket in America." His last thoughts, which had been of a courtesy to others, drifted back into the dark chaos, and his breathing became heavier and more painful as the disorder of silent delirium closed in. The doctors had told Betsy there was no hope, and all of the family, except Anna, knew it, as they watched at the bedside through the night. Two hours before daybreak, the spirit fled.

At dawn in the newspaper offices the telegraph keys broke their robot silence of the night to click out the sentence from Adrian beginning, "Gen. Jo. O. Shelby died this morning...." [1]

And on the copy desk of the Kansas City *Star,* a blasé desk man was stirred to feel for, and to write, the appropriate headline. He wrote three words, in capitals which look like handset type: "THY WAR-FARE O'ER."

When C. C. Colt reported for work that day, he received a telegram from Joe Boswell Shelby: "Father died at 4 o'clock this morning."

The deputy marshal walked into the outer office, where the staff was assembled. They saw the telegram in his hands.

"He's gone," said Colt. The girls in the office wept; the deputy marshals gathered in Shelby's office to discuss the matter of what they should do first. Judge Philips was in Colorado Springs on a vacation. Colt sent two telegrams, one to Washington and one to Judge Philips; then he went out to a drygoods store and bought some crape. When the "Colonels" appeared to inquire after the General, as they had done every day during his illness, they saw the crape over the door of the marshal's office, and they filed in silently.

Soon the crowd had increased beyond the normal complement of old soldiers who had been accustomed to visit the office at least once every day, health and weather permitting; the news had spread to the street, and men and women who had known the General, one way or another, came in, ostensibly to inquire if the news were really true, but actually with some awkward idea of paying their respects. With the crape on the door, it was not necessary to ask.

As mid-morning passed, Captain Stephen Carter Ragan came in.[2] He had a newspaper in his hand. He sat down in Shelby's old chair, as one entitled to do so, and unfolded the paper, which he handed to C. C. Colt. The usually keen eyes in his rugged Celtic face were filled with tears. His collar button showed beneath the close-cropped goatee and his chest was rising and falling with emotion as he passed the paper over. Colt read the dispatch from Adrian aloud to the assembly in the office.

"General Joseph Orville Shelby died at his country home, eight miles from this city, at 4:20 o'clock this morning. The end came peacefully. The patient had been unconscious since early Monday morning and had been slowly dying since that time. At a consultation of physicians last night it was given out that death must come before morning, and the family had been constant watchers at the bedside. Gen. Shelby was taken seriously ill ten days ago with pneumonia, and gradually grew worse. Funeral arrangements are not yet perfected."

Captain Ragan spoke up. He was a member of the committee of the Ex-Confederate Association in charge of the plot of ground set aside in Forest Hill Cemetery, near the site of the battle of Westport.

"He wanted to be buried with his men," said Ragan.

Major Stonestreet was present, and he nodded. "He told me three weeks ago he wished to be buried in the Confederate Cemetery," he said.

"It was about three weeks ago he told me the same thing," said Ragan. "I came in here and asked where the General was, and they told me he was in there—" pointing to the closed door of a side room. "I went in and the General was talking with Colonel Hunt. As soon as I opened the door he looked up and said, 'Captain, have you room in that burying ground at Forest Hill for me?' I thought he was joking, and I said there was room for all us old fellows. 'Well, when I die I want to be buried there among my old soldiers,' the General said to me, and I said, 'General, I want to be buried there too, and I want the honor of being buried near you.' That is all that we said, but I am sure that the General meant it, and I am sure that he wished to be buried there."

W. H. Draffen, assistant United States Attorney, said that he had been at Shelby's home the day before and that Sam Shelby had told him that when his father died he would probably be buried at Butler. Someone else remarked that the people of Lexington, Missouri, would probably want him to be buried there.

"It's up to us," said Stonestreet. "I think that Captain Ragan, here, should go to Adrian and tell the family of General Shelby's wishes."

There was general assent, and a telegram was written out and signed by Captain Ragan: *Do not decide on place of burial until you see me.*

It was found that Ragan could catch a train in a few minutes. A letter to Betsy Shelby was composed for him to take with him. It read: "We beg to assure you of our condolence in the great grief which has come upon you and also of our keen regret and grief over the death of General Shelby. Without wishing to intrude upon your opinion as to the proper place of burial for him, we yet feel that he should be buried at Forest Hill Cemetery in this city. This is in consonance with his expressed desire, and it seems to us fitting that he should rest among those who fell about him in the brilliant battles he fought during the war. His public record has endeared him to the people of the state, and in burying him at this place an opportunity would be offered to the people at large to visit his grave from time to time that would not be if he should be buried at Butler."

The letter was signed by John R. Walker, United States District Attorney; W. M. Draffen, the Assistant District Attorney; C. B. Anderson, United States Pension Agent; C. C. Colt, Chief Deputy United States Marshal; Milton Welsh, Surveyor of the Port; Dr. F. G. Henry, Surgeon to United States prisoners; Webster Withers, Internal Revenue Collector; Major Jacob Stonestreet, and Major Charles Carples.[3]

When Ragan had gone, Major Carples said, "I'm glad I've got his picture. One day I took him by the arm and forced him into a gallery and had his picture taken, and it's framed and on the wall at my home. I wouldn't take a million dollars for it." Carples was a Union veteran. He had been one of the Union troops under Pleasanton who had chased Price and Shelby on the last great raid into Missouri in 1864. His eyes were red-rimmed from weeping.

"He was heart; all heart," said Dr. Henry, who was seated now at the dead General's desk, the newspaper clutched in his hand, his felt hat pulled down low over his eyes. He pushed back the hat and laid the newspaper on the desk. "Gentlemen," he said, "he was the Chevalier Bayard of America."

In the doorway, a footstep sounded, and those present in the marshal's office looked up. Framed in the doorway was a silent man in a faded white hat, a Confederate campaign hat. He had gray hair and a gray mustache, with a sharp thin face; but he stood straight and he was every inch a relic of the Missouri Confederate cause. His hands were deep in his overcoat pockets as he gazed at the rosette and streamers of crape. For a moment he stood with his underlip beneath his teeth. Then out came his red bandanna and he pressed it to his eyes, as he leaned his elbow on a high desk near the door and wept silently. For several minutes he stood, and then without a word turned and went down the stairway. The crape on the door had confirmed the news he had heard on the street.

When Ragan arrived in Adrian, another telegram had preceded him—this one from Major Will Warner, Jo Shelby's close friend. Warner, now a resident of Kansas City, stood in the same relation to the Union Veterans' Association of Kansas City as Ragan to the Ex-Confederate Association. Major Warner wanted to know the family's plans for the funeral, so that the men of the Blue Armies could make preparations to pay their last respects.

Under these circumstances Betsy Shelby and the children could not refuse to hold the funeral in Kansas City, although they would have wished him closer home in his last sleep. A mass meeting of Adrian citizens was held, and it was decided after consultation with the family that the body should rest in state for an hour at the Methodist Church, before being placed on the train, so that his friends and neighbors might say goodbye.

The bleak prairies about Adrian were mantled with snow, and the almost impassable condition of the roads made it necessary for the funeral party to leave the Shelby home early in the morning for the slow ten-mile drive to Adrian, with time enough at the church before the train left for Kansas City. The hearse was followed by a carriage, in which were Captain Ragan, Ben Shelby and Joe Shelby. A single horseman, with frayed overcoat turned up against the cold, completed the cortege of the man who had led ten thousand cavalry in battle. The lone rider beside the hearse, as it crawled across the prairie no faster than a man could walk, was Billy Hunter.

The train left Adrian at twenty minutes past one in the afternoon and arrived at Kansas City at four. This was on February 15. At the station an honor guard of ten old Confederates and ten members of the Missouri National Guard met the train. The procession wound through Main Street to Eleventh, thence eastward to Walnut and northward to the Federal Building. There the casket was placed in the courtroom, to lie in state for thirty-six hours.

All day long on the 16th, mourners filed past the coffin, and at the Union station the trains were bringing in people from all over the state, and from across the border in Kansas.

The funeral was held at 10 o'clock on Wednesday morning, February 17, in the auditorium of the Armory, the largest in town, but not large enough by half to accommodate those who attended. There were two thousand people seated inside, and as many more outside, as the Reverend Dr. Neel, pastor of the Second Presbyterian Church, preached the sermon.

Of Shelby's family, only his sons were present. Both Betsy and Anna Shelby were prostrated by grief, and the ordeal of attending the services in Kansas City was out of the question. The seven stalwart sons of the dead general sat together, an impressive sight, in the front row of the auditorium.

The armory was decorated with long festoons of evergreen, hung from the center of the high ceilings and reaching out to the corners and sides. Walls were trimmed with sprigs of evergreen and holly. On the south side of the auditorium a platform had been erected, on either side of which stood a field piece that had been used in actual combat. A stand of arms was stacked on either side, and behind it was draped a bright new flag, the Stars and Stripes. The front of the platform was a solid bank of floral offerings, among them a broken column and sabre that stood six feet high, and a wreath of artificial flowers sent by the United Confederate Camp in St. Louis. The column with the sabre was the gift of U. S. Government officials. One of the handsomest of the wreaths was of hyacinths, roses, carnations and lilies, a remembrance from the Daughters of the Confederacy of St. Joseph, Missouri. At either end of the platform stood tall palms. The coffin rested on a small stand in front of the platform, covered with roses, lilies, and a small silk Confederate flag.

At 9:30 Shelby's sons, and other relatives, took a last look at the face of their dead. It was a touching farewell. There had never before been a death in the family—in twenty-nine long and crowded years—and theirs was a grief for which no words came. They had been close to one another, the Shelbys. They would be closer now.

Dr. Neel took as his text: "War the Good Warfare." One newspaper account says that his "burning words swept the audience like magic and despite the fact that it was a funeral three times the audience broke into applause."

Judge Philips spoke next, and everyone in the audience knew that he had fought for the Union and against Shelby. Referring to Shelby's postwar battle to help restore the Union, he recalled that "this manifestation of patriotic zeal for the Republic in his later life has been greatly misconceived and unjustly criticized by some well-meaning people, some good-meaning people, as well as by some exceedingly narrow persons of provincial tendencies. May I be indulged, in the presence of his speechless tongue, to vindicate him?"

And without hyperbole, or flattery, "which would be an offense," he proceeded to do so. It was a moving speech, portions of which have been quoted in previous chapters, but the conclusion is worth quoting again, for it is the best estimate of the character of Joseph Orville Shelby ever put into words:

"He was not what might be termed a round man, uniform and regular in his mental and moral composition. On the contrary, he was angular to acuteness. It was the sharp angles, the abrupt curvatures in his character that created the constant surprises in his career and lent to his life its singular attractiveness and picturesqueness. There were no dead planes, no monotonous levels in his journey through life, and it ran along rugged mountains, cataracts and varying scenery, much of it exciting, and much of it beautiful." At the end of the service, the congregation sang "My Country 'Tis of Thee."

Four hundred members of the United Confederate Veterans and the Grand Army of the Republic stood bareheaded as the casket was lifted into the hearse in front of the Armory. Among them was a thin, rugged-faced man named Frank James. The procession, which moved through streets filled with snow and ice, was led by the band of Company A of the Third Regiment of the Missouri National Guard. Next came the Third Regiment itself, in full-dress uniform, next the veterans of the Confederate and Union armies, next a group of honorary pallbearers, all members of the Iron Brigade, and then the hearse. In the rear of the hearse, Uncle Billy Hunter, his black face mournful, led a horse belonging to Shelby. It was a wiry, nervous bay (Shelby had a fondness for bays as well as sorrels) bearing Shelby's cavalry saddle, boots, and spurs, the traditional memorial of the dead cavalryman. Following the ex-slave were members of the Shelby family, in carriages, the Kansas City High School Cadets in uniform, United States officials in carriages, county officers, and hundreds of plain citizens on foot, who walked all the way to the gates of Forest Hill Cemetery at 69th and Troost—a distance of fifty blocks.

At Forest Hill the casket was placed in a receiving vault, and the vault filled with flowers. A squad from Company A fired a salute, a bugler sounded "Taps," and the honors to General Shelby had been done. His funeral was the largest Confederate funeral in the postwar South, with the exception of the funeral of Jefferson Davis in Richmond.

Thus they buried Joseph Orville Shelby, the Last of the Cavaliers, and the greatest cavalryman of them all, according to those who should know best—his enemies. But the South, which he served, has forgotten him.

A simple stone ammunition box marks his grave. The lettering reads only:

"Gen'l. Jo. O. Shelby. Dec. 12, 1830. Feb. 13, 1897."

But his real epitaph is to be found in the injunction which he gave his men in the flare of the torches on the steps of the Confederate sub-treasury in Austin, when he refused to touch a dollar of the government's hoard of gold and silver:

"We are the last of our race. Let us be the best as well."

Notes

———◆◆◆———

1. LINCOLN'S CONFEDERATE GENERAL

1. In 1864 Shelby commanded a division; thus his responsibilities were those of a major general. But it was May 16, 1865 (retroactive to May 10) before Gen. Kirby Smith, commander of the Trans-Mississippi Department, gave him the long-delayed commission.—*War of the Rebellion, Official Records of the Union and Confederate Armies* (Washington, D.C., Gov't Printing Office, 1881), Ser. I, Vol. XLVIII, pt. ii, p. 1307. Hereafter cited as *Official Records* or *O.R.*

2. Unless otherwise noted, all facts of Shelby's Mexican sojourn are from the works of Maj. John Newman Edwards of Lexington, Mo., Shelby's adjutant during the war and in Mexico. His *Shelby's Expedition to Mexico, An Unwritten Leaf of the War* (Kansas City, Mo., Kansas City *Times* Publishing Co., 1872) is the only day-by-day chronicle of the expedition ever published. Hereafter cited as *Expedition to Mexico*.

3. Shelby disclosed, in a newspaper interview in 1877, that his cousin, Federal Gen. Francis Preston Blair, Jr., whose father was a friend and confidant of Lincoln, wrote him just before the end of the war that Lincoln would be glad to see ex-Confederate soldiers migrate to Mexico, join Juárez, and depose Maximilian.—Interview quoted in W.B. Stevens, *Centennial History of Missouri* (St. Louis and Chicago, S.J. Clarke Publishing Co., 1921), pp. 297-98:

"You led an expedition in Mexico once, general."

"Yes, an expedition of a thousand men. It could have been fifty thousand just as well."

"Tell ... something about your expedition then."

"There were several things which led to that. Some have been told and some haven't. Perhaps the time is as good as any to make them known.... There were a thousand men in my division who did not want to surrender. If there had been but two I would have felt it my soldierly duty to stand by those two and have gone with them into the unknown. Then again I had ideas, or dreams, or ambitions. I saw, or imagined I saw, a great empire beyond the Rio. This river they call the great river.

"Through General Frank P. Blair I had received, long before the killing of Lincoln, some important information. It was to the effect that, in the downfall of the Confederacy and the overthrow of the Confederates of the East, the Confederates of the West would be permitted to march into Mexico, drive out the French, fraternize with the Mexicans, look around them to see what they could see, occupy and possess lands, keep their eyes steadfastly upon the future and understand from the beginning that the future would have to take care of itself. In addition, every disbanded soldier in the Federal army in the Trans-Mississippi who desired the kind of service I have indicated would have been permitted to cross over to the Confederates with his arms and ammunition. Fifty thousand of them were eager to enlist in such an expedition.

On my march south from San Antonio to Piedras Negras I received no less than 200 communications from representative Federal officers, begging me to wait for them beyond the Rio Grande."

"Do you mean to say that President Lincoln was in favor of the movement you have outlined?"

"I do mean to say so most emphatically. I could show nothing official for my assertions, but I had such assurances as satisfied me, and other officers of either army had such assurances as satisfied them. There was an empire in it and a final and practical settlement of the whole Mexican question."

History offers some support to Shelby's statement in the mission of Frank P. Blair, Sr., to Jefferson Davis in Richmond early in 1865. According to Davis, Blair seems to have had something in mind concerning a face-saving device for the Confederate armies whereby they could be used, in the event of the termination of the war by agreement, to enforce the Monroe Doctrine in Mexico. See Jefferson Davis, *The Rise and Fall of the Confederate Government* (2 vols. New York, D. Appleton Co., 1881), II, 612-18.

There is still other supporting evidence. Gen. Philip Sheridan telegraphed Washington for orders to go after Shelby when it became known that Shelby was moving toward Mexico with an unsurrendered portion of his army; the orders never came.

4. Stevens, *Centennial History of Missouri*, p. 296.

5. Edwards, *Shelby and His Men, or the War in the West* (Cincinnati, Miami Publishing Co., 1867), p. 448. Hereafter cited as Edwards, *Shelby and His Men*.

6. John W. Thomason, Jr., *J.E.B. Stuart, the Portrait of a Cavalryman* (New York, Charles Scribner's Sons, 1930), p. 360.

7. William Elsey Connelley, *Quantrill and the Border Wars* (Cedar Rapids, Ia., Torch Press, 1910), p. 289. Hereafter cited as *Quantrill*.

8. Edwards, *Expedition to Mexico*, p. 4.

9. News of Shelby's march to Mexico soon reached Sheridan in New Orleans. On July 4, 1865, he wrote the news to Grant.—*O.R.*, Ser. I, Vol. XLVIII, pt. ii, p. 1077.

2. BOYHOOD IN KENTUCKY

1. Published genealogies of the Shelby family contain a number of errors. Many biographical references assert that Joseph Orville Shelby was a lineal descendant of Isaac Shelby, which is not correct. The author is indebted to Cass K. Shelby, of Hollidaysburg, Pa., author of *The First Three Generations of the Shelby Family in America* (Hollidaysburg, 1941), for supplying a complete genealogical chart of the family. The line of descent of Joseph Orville Shelby is also settled conclusively in a letter written by his mother on May 22, 1881: "Genl. Jo. O. Shelby was the son of Mr. Orville Shelby, Sumner Cy., Tennessee, his mother (my maiden name was Anna M. Boswell of Lexington, Ky.) eldest daughter of Dr. Joseph Boswell. The grandfather of my son Jo on his father's side [was] Mr. David Shelby of Sumner Cy. Tenn. His grandmother on the same side Miss Sarah Bledsoe of the same county and state.... My son Jo is a descendant of John, and the Shelbys of Kentucky of Evan."—Letter owned by the Filson Club, Kentucky Historical Association, Louisville.

2. Zella Armstrong, *Notable Southern Families* (Chattanooga, Tenn., Lookout Publishing Co., 1922), pp. 305-6.

3. Most famous members of the early Shelby family aside from Governor Isaac Shelby were Isaac's father, Brigadier Evan Shelby, Jr., and his cousin, Dr. John Shelby of Nashville. Evan, Jr., was a noted Indian fighter in Pennsylvania before removing to Virginia and subsequently to North Carolina. He served with the British Gen. Forbes in the attack on Fort Duquesne and was well known to George Washington. He was too old to fight at King's Mountain, as some accounts assert he did, although he had seen service against the border Indians of Virginia and North Carolina. Dr. John Shelby founded the first medical college in Tennessee, Shelby Medical College at

Nashville, later merged with the University of Nashville, now a part of the Peabody Institute. Shelby Avenue in Nashville is named for him. He was a brother of Orville Shelby and consequently an uncle of Joseph Orville Shelby.

4. This John Shelby, great-grandfather of Joseph Orville Shelby, is not to be confused with Dr. John Shelby, who was grandson of the first John Shelby.

5. Robert B. McAfee, *History of the Late War in the Western Country* (Lexington, Ky., Worsley and Smith, 1816), p. 131.

6. Morgan was born in Alabama but spent his boyhood in Kentucky.

7. Edwards, *Shelby and His Men*, p. 42.

8. Executor of the estate was Samuel Grant Jackson, wealthy Kentuckian, father-in-law of Governor Thomas C. Crittenden of Missouri.—H.H. Crittenden, comp., *The Crittenden Memoirs* (New York, G.P. Putnam's Sons, 1936), p. 478. Hereafter cited as *Crittenden Memoirs*.

9. Dated Jan. 21, 1826; published Feb. 6.

10. James Franklin Hopkins, *A History of the Hemp Industry in Kentucky* (Lexington, Ky., University of Kentucky Press, 1951), p. 97.

11. *The Western Farmer and Gardener*, Vol. II (1841), quoted in Hopkins, *History of the Hemp Industry in Kentucky*, p. 102.

12. Record in Fayette County Courthouse, Lexington, Ky. Orville's acres are now part of the Madden Farm.

13. Newspaper files (late 1820's to mid-1830's) tell of cholera epidemics in Lexington.

14. Mr. C.R. Staples of Lexington supplied facts of Dr. Boswell's death.

15. Ann's mother was Judith Bell Gist, daughter of Col. Nathaniel Gist of the Revolution, and granddaughter of Christopher Gist, friend of George Washington.

16. The legend was that Benjamin Gratz's sister, the beautiful Rebecca Gratz, was the original of Sir Walter Scott's "Rebecca" in *Ivanhoe.—Letters of Rebecca Gratz* (Philadelphia, Jewish Publication Society of Philadelphia, 1929), Foreword.

17. *Ibid.*   18. *Ibid.*

19. Today the residence of Mrs. Anderson Gratz.

20. *Letters of Rebecca Gratz*, Foreword.

21. The nature of this misdemeanor is not known. The minutes of the board of visitors show that he was suspended Jan. 20, 1843. He never went back.—Cecil Fletcher Holland, *Morgan and His Raiders* (New York, The Macmillan Co., 1942), p. 23.

22. The Morgan home is still one of the showplaces of Lexington.

23. This child died in infancy.

24. Wilfred R. Hollister and Harry Norman, *Five Famous Missourians* (Kansas City, Mo., Hudson-Kimberly Publishing Co., 1900), p. 339. Hereafter cited as *Five Famous Missourians*.

25. Issue of Feb. 15, 1897.

26. *Ibid.*

27. Kansas City *Star*, Feb. 16, 1897.

28. F. Garvin Davenport, *Ante-Bellum Kentucky* (Oxford, O., Mississippi Valley Press, 1943), p. 28.

29. Told the author as a cherished tradition in the Gratz family.

30. Holland, *Morgan and His Raiders*, p. 23.

31. *B. and M. Gratz, Merchants in Philadelphia, 1754-1798: Papers of Interest to Their Posterity and the Posterity of Their Associates*, edited by William Vincent Byars (Jefferson City, Mo., Hugh Stephens Printing Co., 1916), p. 311. Hereafter cited as *Gratz Papers*.

32. *Ibid.*, p. 263.

33. *Letters of Rebecca Gratz*, p. viii.

34. *Ibid.*, pp. 327-28.

35. Biographical sketch of Jo Shelby in *Five Famous Missourians*, pp. 328-29.

36. *Ibid.*

37. In 1864 it was occupied by the adjutant and was the printing office for *The Mailbag,* Federal soldier newspaper.—*Lexington City Directory.*

38. Morgan frequently slipped into Lexington under the noses of the Federals to visit his mother.

39. In a letter to the author, July 16, 1952, Miss Roemol Henry, Librarian of Transylvania, wrote: "We have no material on Joseph O. Shelby in our library. Our records, though not complete, do not even show that he was a student here."

40. Letter to the author from the late Mrs. J.C. Bryant of Wheatridge, Colorado, niece of Shelby, who as a girl visited the Shelbys in western Missouri. Hereafter cited as Letter from Mrs. J.C. Bryant.

3. WAVERLY: THE GOLDEN YEARS

1. Holland, *Morgan and His Raiders,* p. 7.

2. Howard Swiggett, *The Rebel Raider* (Indianapolis, Bobbs-Merrill Co., 1934), p. 15; Holland, *Morgan and His Raiders,* p. 26.

3. Most biographical sketches of Shelby, including that in the *Dictionary of American Biography,* state that he attended college in Philadelphia *after* leaving Transylvania. An examination of the records of all of the institutions of higher learning in the Philadelphia area in existence in the 1840's and 1850's has disclosed that there is no record of his having been a student at any of them. The Historical Society of Pennsylvania also found no record of it. The original papers on which the *D.A.B.* sketch is based have also been examined in the Library of Congress, and these cite no authority other than the published references given, all of which contain many errors. The Rebecca Gratz letter of March 24, 1846, plainly fixes the date of Shelby's Philadelphia schooling. At this time he was fifteen years old and hardly of college age.

4. See Hopkins, *History of the Hemp Industry in Kentucky,* pp. 131-32.

5. *Missouri Historical Review,* XXVI (Jan., 1932), 190.

6. Gratz Moses was a St. Louis physician, cousin of Benjamin and Rebecca Gratz; later professor of obstetrics at the Missouri Medical College, president of the St. Louis Obstetrical Society, and doctor for the St. Louis Board of Health.—*Gratz Papers,* p. 279.

7. *Letters of Rebecca Gratz,* pp. 327-28.

8. William Ernest Smith, *The Francis Preston Blair Family in Politics* (New York, The Macmillan Co., 1933), I, 292. Hereafter cited as *Blair Family in Politics.*

9. The Lexington *Reporter,* Jan. 9, 1850.

10. Hopkins, *History of the Hemp Industry in Kentucky,* p. 109.

11. Edwards, *Shelby and His Men,* p. 82.

12. *Crittenden Memoirs,* p. 479.

13. Morgan founded the Lexington Rifles, a fashionable organization of young bloods.—Swiggett, *The Rebel Raider,* p. 18.

14. Seven-page manuscript entitled "The History of Waverly," by J. M. Motte, in the Western Historical Manuscripts Collection of the University of Missouri. Original owned by Q.W. Brickin. Hereafter cited as Motte's "History of Waverly."

15. *Ibid.*

16. Fred Erving Dayton and John Wolcott Adams, *Steamboat Days* (New York, Frederick A. Stokes & Co., 1935), p. 356.

17. Motte's "History of Waverly."   18. *Ibid.*

19. Facts on the firm of Gratz and Shelby through 1835 quoted from files of Lexington newspapers.

20. Shelby operated a packet line to Lexington; one of his trim little steamers is known to have been the *Winnie Belle.* The other boat with which his name is associated was the *A. B. Chambers,* a larger craft. (Steamboat lists give names of captains rather than owners.)

21. Louis C. Hunter, *Steamboats on the Western Rivers* (Cambridge, Harvard University Press, 1949), p. 661.

22. Quoted in letter to the author by Drury Tillman Boyd of Joplin, Mo., as having been made in a letter by his father, a sergeant in 34th Arkansas Volunteers.

23. Letter from Mrs. J.C. Bryant.

24. Claiborne Jackson was a Kentuckian who had come to Missouri at eighteen and become a wealthy merchant and banker.—W.L. Webb, *Battles and Biographies of Missourians* (Kansas City, Mo., Hudson-Kimberly Publishing Co., 1900), pp. 294-304.

25. One of Shelby's Kentucky friends, Col. William Warner of Lexington, named his daughter Shelby Warner, at Shelby's suggestion, according to Col. Warner's great-granddaughter, Mrs. Shelby Warner Steger of Bear Camp Hollow, Mo.

26. Charles P. Deatharage, *Steamboating on the Missouri River in the Sixties* (Kansas City, Kansas City News-Press, 1924), pp. 12-13.

27. *Ibid.*

4. THE BORDER WARS

1. An unidentified writer in the St. Louis *Republican* in 1898 recalled in an article, "Fruitful Missouri," that the farm of Howard Gratz and Jo Shelby was one of the finest in Lafayette County. Reprinted in the *Kentucky Gazette*, Lexington, Nov. 9, 1898.

2. The promise was not kept.—Thomas Hughes, *The Struggle for Kansas*. Published as an appendix in J.M. Ludlow, *A Sketch of the History of the United States from Independence to Secession* (London, The Macmillan Co., 1862), p. 330. Hereafter cited as Hughes, *Struggle for Kansas.*

3. This statement is not an exaggeration. Eli Thayer, president of the Massachusetts Emigrant Aid Society, who more than any other man was responsible for the colonization of Kansas, says in *The Kansas Crusade* (New York, Harper and Brothers, 1889) that it was a holy war and that the society was formed for no other purpose than "to put a cordon of free states from Minnesota to the Gulf of Mexico and stop the forming of slave states."

4. The best description of the Blue Lodge is contained in *Report No. 200* of subcommittee of Committee on Elections of 34th Congress (Washington, D.C., Gov't Printing Office, 1856). Hereafter cited as *Report No. 200.*

5. Speech quoted in Connelley, *Quantrill*, p. 294.

6. Thayer, *Kansas Crusade*, p. 31.

7. Testimony of Samuel N. Wood, *Report No. 200*, p. 140.

8. Testimony of F.P. Vaughan, *ibid.*, p. 130.

9. Testimony of Ira W. Ackley, *ibid.*, p. 156.

10. Hughes, *Struggle for Kansas*, p. 325.

11. Unidentified writer in Lawrence, Kan., *Tribune*, Apr. 12, 1882.

12. Testimony of Lyman Allen, *Report No. 200*, p. 138.

13. Hughes, *Struggle for Kansas*, p. 333.

14. Wood said, "I never saw any of the strangers before."

15. Quoted in Charles Robinson, *The Kansas Conflict* (New York, Harper and Brothers, 1892). Robinson was first governor of Kansas.

16. Quoted in Thayer, *Kansas Crusade*, p. 237.

17. Quoted in Robinson, *Kansas Conflict*, p. 133.

18. *Ibid.*, p. 158.   19. *Ibid.*, p. 329.

20. Connelley, *Quantrill*, p. 286.

21. Lexington, Ky., *Observer and Reporter*, Dec. 19, 1855.

22. The Eldridge House was opened in March, 1856.—G. Douglas Brewerton, *et al., The War in Kansas, or a Rough Trip to the Border* (New York, 1856), pp. 351-52.

23. Connelley, *Quantrill*, p. 287.

24. Robinson, *Kansas Conflict*, p. 265.

25. St. Louis *Republican*, Sept. 15, 1856.

26. D.W. Wilder, *Annals of Kansas* (Topeka, T. Dwight Thacher, 1886), p. 138.

27. Connelley, *Quantrill*, p. 288.

28. *Ibid.*, p. 291.
29. Kansas City *Star*, Feb., 1897.

5. STEAMBOAT WEDDING

1. Howard Gratz edited the *Gazette* for many years.
2. *Gratz Papers*, p. 268.
3. See his "Reminiscences of Famous Americans," *Gratz Papers*, Chap. XX.
4. Letter from Mrs. Louise Davis Brown of Waverly.
5. Zeiler's band (four brothers) was famous on river boats.
6. Shelby kept "a steamboat tied up at the wharf all day to take his wedding party to St. Louis."—Motte's "History of Waverly."
7. Marriage Record Book No. D (Lafayette County Courthouse), p. 367.
8. Letter, July 6, 1857, *Letters of Rebecca Gratz*, p. 405.
9. *Crittenden Memoirs*, pp. 4-5.
10. Recollection of Miss Elizabeth Corder.
11. Now in the possession of Mrs. H.K. Thomas, Marshall, Mo.
12. The Blair Family Papers, Library of Congress, contain no mention of Jo Shelby, but Frank's father wrote that Frank owed $85,000.
13. Newspaper references here are from files of the *Express* or the *Caucasian*, only ones that survive.
14. Thomas Shelby not identified in Shelby genealogical record.

6. MISSOURI AND THE UNION

1. A correspondent in the *Anzeiger*, St. Louis German language newspaper, chided Blair during the 1858 campaign for owning slaves while advocating abolition of slavery. Blair replied in the *Daily Republican*, Oct. 4, 1858: "I am the proprietor of some slaves, of whom most were purchased to prevent separation of families, and the number of slaves to whom I have given freedom is greater than the number I possess. The principle I represent contemplates ... giving freedom to all the slaves in Missouri, mine as well as the others.... Our free Negroes should be colonized in Central America under the protection of the Government and equal social and political rights guaranteed them."
2. Tom North, *Five Years in Texas* (Cincinnati, Elm St. Printing Co., 1867), pp. 88-89.
3. The Census showed 30,000 Irish, 5,500 Germans, 5,200 French, 4,500 Swiss, 2,800 Canadians, and 2,000 Scotch in St. Louis as against 56,780 of native Missouri stock.— Figures quoted in *Blair Family in Politics*, II, 30.
4. Edwards, *Shelby and His Men*, p. 42.
5. *Blair Family in Politics*, II, 21.
6. *Ibid.*, p. 23.   7. *Ibid.*, p. 28.   8. *Ibid.*, p. 37.
9. Edward Conrad Smith, *The Borderland in the Civil War* (New York, The Macmillan Co., 1927), p. 229.
10. Quoted in *Blair Family in Politics*, II, 46.
11. *Personal Memoirs of U.S. Grant* (Cleveland, O., reissued by World Publishing Co., 1951), p. 119.
12. *Blair Family in Politics*, II, 17.
13. Letter from Mrs. J.C. Bryant, who heard the story from "Aunt Betty."
14. John McElroy, *The Struggle for Missouri* (Washington, D.C., National Tribune Publishing Co., 1909), p. 90.
15. Price was chairman of the convention which affirmed Missouri's loyalty to the Union.
16. *O.R.*, Ser. I, Vol. III, p. 374.

17. Smith, *The Borderland in the Civil War*, p. 247.
18. *Ibid.*, p. 50.
19. Major H. A. Conant of Lyon's staff.
20. Thomas L. Snead, *The Fight for Missouri* (New York, Charles Scribner's Sons, 1886), pp. 199-200.

7. BOONVILLE AND CARTHAGE

1. Lyon asserted that it was the other way around (*O.R.*, Ser. I, Vol. III, pp. 11-12). Nevertheless Lyon's statement to Price, "This means war," preceded the Governor's proclamation and was the direct cause of it.
2. McCulloch's original assignment was simply to guard the Indian Territory against invasion from Kansas (*ibid.*, p. 575) and to obtain the active cooperation of the Indian nations with the Confederacy. But he was to give "only such assistance to Missouri as will subserve the main purpose of your command." Secretary of War Walker at Richmond pointed out in a letter to McCulloch on July 4, 1861 (when McCulloch had already disregarded orders and moved to join Price), that "the position of Missouri as a Southern state still in the Union requires, as you will readily perceive, much prudence and circumspection," and added that only when "necessity and prudence unite" might McCulloch proceed into Missouri. Thus it will be seen that McCulloch acted solely on his own initiative.
3. R.S. Bevier, *History of the First and Second Missouri Confederate Brigades, 1861-1865* (St. Louis, Bryan Brand & Co., 1879). Hereafter cited as Bevier.
4. *O.R.*, Ser. I, Vol. III, p. 14.
5. Mrs. J.C. Bryant recalled that Shelby did not join his command until after the Shelbys' second child was born.
6. Bevier, pp. 35-36.
7. Sigel's report, *O.R.*, Ser. I, Vol. III, p. 17.
8. Rains's report, *ibid.*, pp. 20-22.
9. *Ibid.*
10. Rains passed over his own cavalry commander, Col. R.L.Y. Peyton, to assign Shelby to the task of flanking the enemy.—*O.R.*, Ser. I, Vol. III, p. 28.
11. Rains's report, *ibid.*, p. 17.
12. Letter from Brig. Gen. J.M. Schofield to Maj. Gen. Halleck on Feb. 13, 1862: "Sigel retreated all day long before this miserable rabble, contenting himself with repelling their irregular attacks, which he did with perfect ease whenever he ventured to make them."—*Ibid.*, p. 94.
13. *Ibid.*, p. 19. Lyon thanked Sigel for his "brilliant service."

8. WILSON'S CREEK: THE FACE OF WAR

1. Pearce commanded the Arkansas militia, McCulloch the troops of the Confederate Provincial Army.
2. Snead, *Fight for Missouri*, p. 238.
3. *Ibid.*, p. 242.   4. *Ibid.*, pp. 245-46.   5. *Ibid.*, p. 245.
6. Hardee to H.M. Rector, president of the Arkansas Military Board, Aug. 8, 1861: "If General McCulloch intends attacking Springfield, he has already done so."
7. For a full account of this military fiasco, the first in a long series of major blunders in the Trans-Mississippi region, see correspondence on pp. 607-40 of the *Official Records*, Ser. I, Vol. III, between Pillow, Polk, Hardee, Thompson, etc.
8. Shelby acquired an entire "battery" of such "guns."—Edwards, *Shelby and His Men*, p. 33.
9. Shelby never permitted a captured steamboat to be destroyed.—*Ibid.*
10. And far more savage, being fought Indian style.

11. Recollections of Mrs. Lavonia Ray Bruton (1938), Western Historical Manuscripts Collection, University of Missouri. Hereafter cited as Bruton MS.

12. *O.R.*, Ser. I, Vol. III, p. 76.

13. Cary Gratz's body was reinterred in the family plot in Lexington Sept. 11, 1861.

14. Not, however, his routine report to Adj. Gen. Cooper in Richmond but a supplementary report quoted in the *Missouri Historical Review*, XXVI (July, 1932), 354. The supplementary report, setting forth McCulloch's defense of his actions before and after Wilson's Creek, appeared originally in the *Historical Magazine* in New York, March, 1872, contributed by none other than Gen. Franz Sigel, who had somehow come into possession of it.

15. This decision was born of exasperation and desperation on McCulloch's part. He felt that he had to strike a blow with his army before it fell apart. Although he had assumed supreme command, with the consent of Price, he found that he could do little or nothing with the individualistic Missourians. "There was left," says McCulloch, "only the choice of a disastrous retreat, or a blind attack upon Springfield." He chose the latter.

16. Lyon to the Adjutant General's office at St. Louis, Aug. 4, 1861.—*O.R.*, Ser. I, Vol. III, p. 47.

17. Although McElroy quotes Schofield as saying that Lyon gave Sigel credit for the plan of battle at Wilson's Creek (*Struggle for Missouri*, pp. 158, 161), it is not likely that Lyon trusted blindly to Sigel's judgment.

18. Sigel's report, *O.R.*, Ser. I, Vol. III, p. 86.

19. Snead, *Fight for Missouri*, p. 271.

20. Bevier, p. 46.

21. Snead, *Fight for Missouri*, p. 272.

22. Joseph A. Mudd, "What I Saw at Wilson's Creek," *Missouri Historical Review*, VII, 99. Mudd was a private in Company B, Jackson Guards.

23. Snead, *Fight for Missouri*, p. 275.

24. Totten's report, *O.R.*, Ser. I, Vol. III, p. 75.

25. Snead, *Fight for Missouri*, p. 275.

26. Report of Lieut. George L. Andrews, First Missouri Volunteers, *O.R.*, Ser. I, Vol. III, p. 76.

27. Sigel's report, *ibid.*, p. 86.

28. Bruton MS.

9. A STAR ADDED, A STATE LOST

1. See McCulloch's supplementary report cited in n. 14, Chap. VIII, above.

2. Edwards, *Shelby and His Men*, p. 41.

3. *Ibid.*

4. Letter of Shelby to Col. White, in collection of Missouri Historical Society, St. Louis.

5. Waverly *Morning Visitor*.

6. Webb, *Battles and Biographies of Missourians*, p. 100.

7. Quoted in a souvenir booklet of Lexington, by A.L. Maxwell, *Sixty Days in Sixty One; the Siege and Battle of Lexington* (Lexington, Mo., 1952), p. 12.

8. Clement A. Evans, ed., *Confederate Military History* (Atlanta, Confederate Publishing Co., 1899), IX, 65. Hereafter cited as *Confederate Military History*.

9. How methodical it was is described thus by an anonymous newspaper correspondent: "An old Texan, dressed in buckskin and armed with a long rifle, would go up to the works every morning about seven o'clock, carrying his dinner in a tin pail. Taking a good position, he banged away at the Federals until noon, then rested an hour, ate his dinner, after which he resumed operations until six p. m., when he returned home to supper and a good night's sleep."

10. Webb, *Battles and Biographies of Missourians*, p. 107.

11. The sword was returned eventually to a G.A.R. post by a descendant.

12. *Missouri Historical Review*, III, 9.

13. Maxwell, *Sixty Days in Sixty One*, p. 15.

14. Carl Sandburg, *Abraham Lincoln, the War Years* (New York, Harcourt, Brace & Co., 1936), I, 349.

15. Maj. Charles Zagonyi, chief of Frémont's bodyguard, describes a "rout" that allegedly took place at Springfield (*O.R.*, Ser. I, Vol. III, pp. 251-52), but Moore says, "As Zagonyi and his resplendent command came dashing in [the State Guard] fired a volley that emptied a third of the saddles and sent the remainder of the command back pell mell upon the main body." Nevertheless the Confederates retreated through Springfield.—*Confederate Military History*, IX, 80.

16. *Report of Joint Committee on the Conduct of the War* (Washington, D.C., Gov't Printing Office, 1861), III, 1 ff.

17. See testimony of Zagonyi before committee, *ibid.*, p. 192.

18. Joseph Mills Hanson, in *U.S. Cavalry Journal*, Sept.-Oct., 1933, p. 15. Now published as *Armor* by the U.S. Armor Association. Hereafter cited as *Cavalry Journal*.

19. Webb, *Battles and Biographies of Missourians*, p. 97.

20. Recalled by Mrs. J.C. Bryant.

21. Also recalled by Mrs. Bryant.

22. The family tradition in the British Isles was that the first Shelbys came from Scandinavia, according to Miss Minerva Shelby of Parkersburg, W. Va.

23. The Kansas City *Star* recalled, the day after Shelby's funeral, that Billy Hunter "liked to tell of his experiences at the battle of Pea Ridge."

24. *O.R.*, Ser. I, Vol. VIII, pp. 428-29.

25. *Confederate Military History*, IX, 76.

26. See correspondence of Pike with the Richmond government.—*O.R.*, Ser. I, Vol. XIII, p. 893.

27. About 17,000.—*Confederate Military History*, IX, 78.

28. Moore (in *ibid.*), places the Federal strength at 18,000. For once a Confederate estimate would seem to be correct, for Halleck says that he had sent Curtis 16,000 or 17,000 men (*O.R.*, Ser. I, Vol. VIII, p. 555) and to Curtis's forces were added those of Sigel.

29. *Ibid.*, p. 328.   30. *Ibid.*, p. 191.   31. *Ibid.*

10. A COLONEL OF THE CAVALRY

1. For Price's address see McElroy, *Struggle for Missouri*, p. 40.

2. E. M. Violette, *History of Missouri*, (Ramfre Press, Cape Girardeau, Mo., 1951), p. 375.

3. Edwards, *Shelby and His Men*, p. 53.

4. *Ibid.*, pp. 54, 71.

5. Davis was particularly irked by criticism leveled at the West Pointers whom he appointed.—McElroy, *Struggle for Missouri*, p. 295.

6. *Confederate Military History*, IX, 92.

7. Edwards, *Shelby and His Men*, p. 57.

8. *Ibid.*   9. *Ibid.*, p. 58.   10. *Ibid.*

11. Jake Stonestreet to reporter, Kansas City *Star*, Feb. 14, 1897.

12. Edwards, *Shelby and His Men*, p. 59.

13. *Ibid.*, p. 80.   14. *Ibid.*, p. 62.

15. Violette, *History of Missouri*, p. 380.

16. David Porter, *Incidents and Anecdotes of the Civil War* (New York, D. Appleton & Co., 1885), p. 180.

17. Edwards, *Shelby and His Men*, p. 69.

18. *Ibid.*, p. 70.

19. Hanson, in *Cavalry Journal*, Sept.-Oct., 1933, p. 14.

20. Violette, *History of Missouri*, p. 384.

21. For operations of Home Guards against rebel bands around Shelby's property in May, see *O.R.*, Ser. I, Vol. XIII, pp. 80-81-82.

22. Edwards, *Shelby and His Men*, p. 72.

23. Violette, *History of Missouri*, p. 379.

24. Hanson, in *Cavalry Journal*, Sept.-Oct., 1933, p. 18.

25. Many writers on Shelby, including Maj. Hanson, have missed the fact that Shelby did not write his own reports. Hanson says: "Had he [Shelby] done nothing else than contribute his amazing reports to the 128 volumes of the Official Records ... history in its lighter vein would owe him a perpetual debt of gratitude. They seem too good to be true."—*Cavalry Journal*, Sept.-Oct., 1933, p. 12.

26. Shelby's report of the recruiting at Waverly (the style shows that he wrote this one himself) says that he assembled 1,000 men in four days.—*O.R.*, Ser. I, Vol. XIII, p. 97.

27. Hanson, in *Cavalry Journal*, Sept.-Oct., 1933, p. 14.

28. Edwards, *Shelby and His Men*, p. 73.

29. Literally true. The Gold City (Mo.) *Democrat*, March 15, 1953, reprinted in its "News of Bygone Days" the 1890 obituary of a member of Shelby's brigade whose mind had become unhinged as a result of his experiences during the war, and who never recovered.

30. Edwards, *Shelby and His Men*, p. 75.

31. *O.R.*, Ser. I, Vol. XIII, p. 978.

11. THE IRON BRIGADE: FIRST NEWTONIA

1. McElroy, *Struggle for Missouri*, p. 255.

2. The boundaries of the Trans-Mississippi Department embraced the states of Missouri and Arkansas, the Indian Territory, the state of Louisiana west of the Mississippi, and the state of Texas.—*O.R.*, Ser. I, Vol. XIII, p. 829.

3. *Ibid.*, p. 702.   4. *Ibid.*

5. Schofield's report, *ibid.*, p. 17.   6. *Ibid.*, p. 702.

7. E. Merton Coulter, *The Confederate States of America* (Baton Rouge, Louisiana State University Press, 1950), p. 359, says that the Trans-Mississippi Department was set up in early 1863. This Department had an official existence before 1863.—*O.R.*, Ser. I, Vol. XIII, p. 829.

8. Edwards, *Shelby and His Men*, p. 108.

9. Douglas Southall Freeman, *Lee's Lieutenants* (New York, Charles Scribner's Sons, 1942), I, 614.

10. *Ibid.*, pp. 582-84.   11. *Ibid.*, p. 518.

12. See n. 5, Chap. X, for Davis's views on West Pointers.

13. Freeman, *Lee's Lieutenants*, I, 584.

14. Counting Indian troops and units scattered over three states, Holmes had at his disposal 50,000 troops or more. For list of Confederate troops in the Trans-Mississippi Department in 1862 see *O.R.*, Ser. I, Vol. XIII, p. 883; but there is no indication as to which divisions and brigades were up to official strength, so that an accurate estimate of the number cannot be made, but it was certainly 50,000 or better. Over against this force, Gen. Schofield says that he had only 17,360 troops in Missouri, counting regulars, volunteers, and militia. With Curtis's 3,000 at Helena, the Federal strength did not greatly exceed 20,000.

15. *O.R.*, Ser. I, Vol. XIII, p. 883.

16. On Oct. 26, 1862, Gen. Holmes wrote to Richmond: "Colonel White, C.S. Artillery, has reported to me for duty, but the painful disease with which he is afflicted disqualifies him for any trust at all commensurate with his rank. His mind, I think, is seriously impaired."—*Ibid.*, p. 899.

17. Hanson, in *Cavalry Journal*, Sept.-Oct., 1933, p. 14.

18. Edwards, *Shelby and His Men*, pp. 85-86.

19. *Ibid.*, p. 83.   20. *Ibid.*, p. 87.
21. Report of Shelby to Marmaduke, *O.R.*, Ser. I, Vol. XIII, p. 978.
22. *Ibid.*   23. *Ibid.*

12. THE IRON BRIGADE: CAMP AT CROSS HOLLOWS

1. David Y. Thomas, *Arkansas in War and Reconstruction, 1861-1874* (Little Rock, Arkansas Division, U.D.C., 1926). Hereafter cited as *Arkansas.*
2. *Ibid.*
3. Proclamation quoted in *ibid.*, p. 140.
4. *Ibid.*   5. *Ibid.*
6. It was the policy of the Confederate government not to create new regiments until those already in existence were raised to full strength.
7. Thomas, *Arkansas*, p. 147.
8. The Richmond government refused him a commission.
9. Thomas, *Arkansas*, pp. 141-42.
10. Schofield's report, *O.R.*, Ser. I, Vol. XIII, p. 22.
11. *Ibid.*, p. 16.
12. Edwards, *Shelby and His Men*, p. 109.
13. Rains and Col. Coffee were both intoxicated on duty, Hindman said.—*O.R.*, Ser. I, Vol. XIII, p. 48.
14. *Confederate Military History*, IX, 103.
15. Interview with Jake Stonestreet, Kansas City *Star*, Feb. 14, 1897.
16. Connelley, *Quantrill*, p. 277.

13. THE IRON BRIGADE: CANE HILL

1. Edwards, *Shelby and His Men*, p. 95.
2. *Ibid.*, p. 96.
3. Blunt to Schofield, Nov. 26, 1862.—*O.R.*, Ser. L, Vol. XXII, pt. i, p. 38.
4. Shelby's report of Battle of Cane Hill, *ibid.*, p. 55.
5. For figures of the Arkansas brigade, see Carroll's report, *ibid.*, pp. 53-55.
6. Blunt's report of Battle of Cane Hill, *ibid.*, p. 43.
7. *Ibid.*   8. *Ibid.*, p. 44.   9. *Ibid.*   10. *Ibid.*
11. Edwards, *Shelby and His Men*, p. 99.
12. *Ibid.*, p. 80.
13. Thomas, *Arkansas*, p. 160.
14. Carroll's report, *O.R.*, Ser. I, Vol. XXII, pt. ii, p. 55.
15. *Ibid.*
16. Blunt's report, *ibid.*, p. 44.
17. Carroll's report, *ibid.*, p. 54.
18. Blunt, *ibid.*, p. 45.
19. *Ibid.*
20. Edwards, *Shelby and His Men*, p. 102.
21. Edwards, Webb, Hollister and Norman, etc.
22. Blunt, *O.R.*, Ser. I, Vol. XXII, pt. ii, p. 46.
23. *Ibid.*
24. Blunt to Curtis, Dec. 2, 1862.—*Ibid.*, p. 43.
25. *Ibid.*, p. 82.

14. THE IRON BRIGADE: PRAIRIE GROVE

1. This permission was so qualified as to make it of little value.—*O.R.*, Ser. I, Vol. XIII, p. 917.

2. Blunt clung to this delusion even after he fought Hindman at Prairie Grove.
3. *O.R.*, Ser. I, Vol. XXII, pt. ii, p. 807.
4. Edwards, *Shelby and His Men*, p. 111.
5. Moore says Hindman took the Cove Creek Road because he had determined to fight Herron instead of Blunt (*Confederate Military History*, IX, 107-8). This is erroneous, as Hindman's report shows.
6. Hindman's report, *O.R.*, Ser. I, Vol. XXII, pt. ii, p. 139.
7. Monroe's report, *ibid.*, pp. 153-54.
8. Shelby's report, *ibid.*, pp. 148-49.
9. *Ibid.*, p. 149.
10. Hindman's report, *ibid.*, p. 140.
11. Quoted by Thomas in *Arkansas*, p. 169.
12. Hindman's report, *O.R.*, Ser. I, Vol. XXII, pt. ii, p. 141.
13. *Ibid.*, p. 140.
14. Capt. Amos Burrows, of the First U.S. Missouri Cavalry, who was immediately in rear of Bunner's company, says that Bunner's were running so fast before Shelby's cavalry that they could not be halted (*ibid.*, p. 137). This corroborates the Confederate claims of the completeness of the rout.
15. Hindman's report, *ibid.*, p. 141.
16. Edwards, *Shelby and His Men*, p. 118.
17. Shelby's report, *O.R.*, Ser. I, Vol. XXII, pt. ii, p. 150.
18. *Ibid.*, p. 153.
19. Hindman's report, *ibid.*, p. 141.
20. *Ibid.* 21. *Ibid.* 22. *Ibid.*, p. 142.
23. Edwards, *Shelby and His Men*, p. 125.
24. *Ibid.*, p. 127. 25. *Ibid.*, p. 129.
26. Holmes to Joseph E. Johnston, Dec. 29, 1862, *O.R.*, Ser. I, Vol. XXVII, p. 811.
27. Holmes to Hindman, *O.R.*, Ser. I, Vol. XIII, p. 917.

15. THE IRON BRIGADE: MARMADUKE AND SHELBY

1. Thomas, *Arkansas*, p. 173.
2. Hanson, in *Cavalry Journal*, Sept.-Oct., 1933, p. 14.
3. Marmaduke's report of his first raid into Missouri, *O.R.*, Ser. I, Vol. XXII, pt. i, p. 196.
4. *Ibid.*, p. 179.
5. Edwards, *Shelby and His Men*, p. 139.
6. Report of the adjutant general's office at Springfield, Jan. 8, 1863, *O.R.*, Ser. I, Vol. XXII, pt. i, p. 181.
7. Report of Col. B. Crabb of the 19th Iowa to Curtis, on the battle of Springfield, *ibid.*, p. 186.
8. The "Tournament" was played with long wooden lances used at full gallop to spear a wooden ring.
9. Edwards, *Shelby and His Men*, p. 255.
10. For Marmaduke's own statement of intentions, see *O.R.*, Ser. I, Vol. XXII, pt. i, pp. 285-88.
11. After a savage letter to Braxton Bragg saying he would resign rather than serve under Holmes (*O.R.*, Vol. LIII, Supplement, p. 848), Hindman was transferred to Vicksburg on Jan. 30, 1863.
12. See letter of Jefferson Davis to Holmes on January 28, 1863 (*ibid.*, p. 847).
13. *O.R.*, Ser. I, Vol. XXII, pt. i, p. 288.
14. Letter of Davis to Holmes (see n. 12 above).
15. *O.R.*, Ser. I, Vol. XXII, pt. i, p. 259.
16. Marmaduke's report of Cape Girardeau expedition, *ibid.*, p. 288.

16. HELENA: DISASTER IN THE WEST

1. Porter, *Incidents and Anecdotes of the Civil War*, p. 92.
2. The events leading up to the Battle of Helena and the account of the battle itself are based on *O.R.*, Ser. I, Vol. XXII.
3. Interview in Kansas City *Star*, Feb. 14, 1897.

17. SHELBY'S GREAT RAID

1. Henry Clay McDougal, Missouri writer, says in his *Recollections, 1844-1909* (Kansas City, Mo., Hudson Publishing Co., 1910), p. 205: "During the Civil War I served in the eastern army [Union] and came west and located at Gallatin, Mo. Then one night soon after my arrival, I heard one of his soldiers singing 'Shelby's Mule.'... In my day I had done some tall marching, after Jackson, Mosby, Imboden, Jenkins and other Confederate commanders in Virginia; had been startled by their bugle calls, alarmed by the Rebel Yell, but never heard anything like 'Shelby's Mule.'"
2. Edwards, *Shelby and His Men*, p. 197.
3. Webb, *Battles and Biographies of Missourians*, p. 193.
4. *Five Famous Missourians*, p. 365.
5. *O.R.*, Ser. I, Vol. XXII, pt. ii, p. 586.
6. *Ibid.*
7. For the hundred pages of correspondence on Shelby's raid, which do not include any of the official military reports, see *ibid.*, pp. 585-683.
8. Grant was just as mistaken as Lincoln about the condition of things in Missouri.—*Ibid.*, pp. 673-74.
9. Edwards, *Shelby and His Men*, p. 200.
10. *O.R.*, Ser. I, Vol. XXII, pt. ii, p. 627.
11. *Ibid.*, p. 609.
12. *Ibid.*, p. 622.
13. Bennett H. Young, *Confederate Wizards of the Saddle* (Boston, Chapple Publishing Co., 1914), p. 214.
14. *O.R.*, Ser. I, Vol. XXII, pt. i, p. 670.

18. THE END OF THE WAR IN THE WEST

1. Grant had little faith in Banks, and he was more interested in assembling troops for Sherman's campaign than he was in invading the Trans-Mississippi, which was already sealed off.—*O.R.*, Ser. I, Vol. XXXIV, pt. i, p. 203.
2. *Ibid.*, p. 659.
3. *Five Famous Missourians*, p. 367.
4. *O.R.*, Ser. I, Vol. XXXIV, pt. i, p. 660.
5. The volume of Reports dealing with the Camden expedition (*ibid.*) lists many actions as "skirmishes" in which a study of the casualty lists reveals that, from the standpoint of the troops involved, at least, they were battles.
6. *Ibid.*, p. 663.
7. Hanson, in *Cavalry Journal*, Sept.-Oct., 1933, p. 14.
8. Banks got no further than Alexandria, La. Grant ordered his removal from command as a result of the Red River campaign.
9. See Steele's report, *O.R.*, Ser. I, Vol. XXXIV, pt. i, pp. 667-71.
10. See Edwards, *Shelby and His Men*, pp. 299-319, for account of Shelby's cleanup in northeast Arkansas.
11. Though consistently passed over for promotion, there is no record that he ever complained about it.

12. But not more than was usual in the Confederate army, and Shelby was usually careful of his language. He would never swear in the presence of a Methodist divine, Brother Mobley, whom he had appointed his aide.—Edwards, *Shelby and His Men*, p. 303.

13. No regular troops at all were in St. Louis. Rosecrans wired frantically to Gen. Paine in Illinois, who could promise only some 100-day volunteers whose terms were expiring (*O.R.*, Ser. I, Vol. XLI, pt. i, p. 308). The slowness of Price's movements, however, gave Rosecrans ample time to gather an army.

14. Kirby Smith Papers, Southern Historical Collection, University of North Carolina Library.

15. Rumors were flying through the Southern Confederacy (outside of Georgia, of course) that Hood had smashed Sherman at Atlanta. Shelby's letter of July 27, 1864, states it as fact.

16. Jefferson Davis made the comparison in a speech at Macon.

17. Rosecrans' report, *O.R.*, Ser. I, Vol. XLI, pt. i, p. 307.

18. Col. John F. Philips' report on the battle of Marais de Cygnes. The Confederates wearing Union uniforms were "executed instanter" on the battlefield (*ibid.*, p. 352).

19. Ewing's report, *ibid.*, p. 448.

20. See account of Rev. Galusha Anderson, St. Louis pastor, in his *The Story of a Border City during the Civil War* (Boston, Little, Brown and Co., 1908), pp. 328-30.

21. Price's report, *O.R.*, Ser. I, Vol. XLI, pt. i, pp. 625-40.

22. Edwards, *Shelby and His Men*, p. 417.

23. He did it during the pursuit of Price. See Rosecrans' report, *O.R.*, Ser. I, Vol. XLI, pt. i, p. 314.

24. Because Shelby retreated after fighting his rearguard action at Newtonia, the Union reports call it a Union victory; but Gen. Sanborn, who came up on Blunt during the fight to assist him, says that Shelby had driven him back and was attacking him on his flanks. Shelby retreated while still victorious; he had smashed the pursuit.

19. REVOLT AGAINST SURRENDER

1. Edwards, *Expedition to Mexico*, p. 4. Maj. Edwards describes the retreat without mentioning his own part in it. After Edwards' death, Maj. Stonestreet said: "What heroism he displayed in that awful retreat from Westport! Smallpox broke out among the men. John Edwards feared it as little as he did the bullets of the enemy. He would take a soldier with smallpox in his arms, carry him to the most comfortable place that could be secured, and nurse him with the care of a woman ... it was he who cheered and encouraged them and held them together."—*John N. Edwards, His Writings and Tributes* (edited by his wife, Jennie Edwards and published by her, Kansas City, 1889), p. 15. Hereafter cited as *John N. Edwards*.

2. The charges were brought by Gov. Reynolds of Missouri. For an account of the controversy see Edwards, *Shelby and His Men*, pp. 466-84.

3. This figure was not such wishful thinking as it might seem. Smith had 36,000 well fed, well armed troops. A revival of Confederate hopes through such a campaign as Shelby proposed might easily swell the Army of the Trans-Mississippi to double that number. The exact strength of Kirby Smith's forces is set forth in a hitherto unpublished letter to Jefferson Davis dated March 7, 1865, in which he declared: "The effective strength of this department is 19,000 enlisted men of infantry and artillery; 17,000 enlisted men of cavalry, of which 17 regiments (6,000 enlisted men) are being dismounted; in addition 4,000 enlisted men are to be sent on furlough, 10,000 absent on details; 6,000 reserve corps in Texas, 2,000 in Louisiana and 2,000 in Arkansas."— Letter in Kirby Smith Papers, Southern Historical Collection, University of North Carolina Library.

4. State governors in their capacity as commanders-in-chief were frequently at odds with the Richmond government over the disposition of troops.

5. Reynolds carried with him to the governors' meeting a brief document headed "Memorandum for the Marshall Conference" and signed by himself, Shelby, and Colonel L.M. Lewis of Shelby's division. It declared that the Missourians would fight to the last ditch if such were the decision of the conference but added that "if it [the war] is to be discontinued, we desire time, facilities and supplies to leave the country with our personal property." Shelby and Reynolds, this communication makes it clear, meant to take refuge in Mexico whether they had an armed force at their back or not.–Memorandum in Kirby Smith Papers.

6. J.C. de Polignac, distinguished French soldier of fortune, had also served under Stuart in Virginia.

7. Western Historical Manuscripts Collection, University of Missouri.

8. Arndt M. Stickles, *Simon Bolivar Buckner, the Borderland Knight* (Chapel Hill, The University of North Carolina Press, 1940), p. 273.

9. Western Historical Manuscripts Collection, University of Missouri.

20. FROM TEXAS TO MEXICO

1. As stated in n. 2, Chap. I, the entire account of the march to Mexico, except where otherwise indicated, is based upon the only detailed account ever written: *Shelby's Expedition to Mexico, an Unwritten Leaf of the War*, by John N. Edwards. Edwards was a participant in all of the adventures described. With the exception of the fragmentary Memoirs of Thomas Westlake (Manuscript in Western Historical Manuscripts Collection, University of Missouri, Colombia, Mo.), there are no diaries for the historian to consult.

2. The Menger is still a landmark in San Antonio.

3. The *Harriet Lane* was a Federal blockade vessel off Galveston in 1863. In Jan., 1863, Magruder captured Galveston and broke the blockade. The *Harriet Lane* was boarded by Confederates from the *Bayou City,* on which cotton bales had been stacked to protect the engines and wheelhouse, thus earning for the *Bayou City* and her sister ship, the *Neptune,* the title of "cotton-clads."

4. Edwards, *Expedition to Mexico,* p. 24. For an excellent account of this episode by George Creel, who as a young newspaper man in Kansas City heard it told by Ben Elliott in Shelby's office, see *A Rebel at Large* (New York, G.P. Putnam's Sons, 1947), p. 27. Elliott and Thomas Westlake left the expedition at Monterrey and went to join the Liberals.–Memoirs of Thomas Westlake, p. 136. Edwards states in an Appendix to *Shelby and His Men* that Shelby left Monterrey with fifty of his men, evidently referring to those remaining in Monterrey after other parties had left.

5. Creel also says that when Elliott told him this story in Shelby's presence, he exclaimed to Shelby, "But General,...when the Juaristas got your artillery, what was to prevent them from taking back your money and annihilating you?" Shelby replied icily, "You forget, sir, we still had our sidearms."–*A Rebel at Large,* p. 28.

6. According to Thomas Westlake, each man's share was sixty silver dollars. Westlake says: "I never knew just what...our artilery sold for, but have always been satisfied that General Shelby saw to it that all were delt fairly with."–Memoirs of Thomas Westlake, p. 134.

21. ACROSS THE SABINAS

1. Edwards, *Expedition to Mexico,* p. 34.
2. Afterward a physician in Platte, South Dakota.

22. JEANNINGROS

1. Kansas City *Times,* May 22, 1887.
2. Traditionally Frenchmen may not enlist in the Foreign Legion.

3. Admiral David Porter, in his *Incidents and Anecdotes of the Civil War*, wrote: "Who could help admiring such men even though fighting against them? ... In point of endurance they set us an example that would have been hard to follow.... Our commissary department was the best in the world and the waste of our provisions would have supplied a European army."—p. 180.

4. Edwards says that Jeanningros talked on the French campaign in the Orient. His conversation here has been supplied by the author from "The Loot of the Imperial Summer Palace in Pekin," *The Diary of an Interpreter in China*, by Maurice D'Irisson, Comte d'Herisson, translated in the *Annual Report* of the Smithsonian Institution for 1900 (Washington, D.C., Smithsonian Institution, 1901), pp. 601-35.

23. PARRAS AND ENCARNACIÓN

1. Edwards, *Expedition to Mexico*, pp. 52-62.
2. Inez Walker was placed under the protection of the Empress when Mexico City was reached and was seen frequently driving in a carriage with her during the Empress's public appearances.

24. MEXICO CITY AT LAST

1. Edwards, *Expedition to Mexico*, p. 83.
2. Agnes Salm-Salm, *Ten Years of My Life* (Detroit, Belford Bros., 1877), p. 140.
3. Alexander Watkins Terrell, *From Texas to Mexico to the Court of Maximilian in 1865* (Dallas, Texas Book Club, 1933), p. 45. Hereafter cited as *From Texas to Mexico*.
4. Edwards, *Expedition to Mexico*, p. 85.

25. THE COLONIZATION SCHEME

1. Figures quoted by the New York *Daily News*, Dec. 9, 1865.
2. It soon became necessary to abandon the proposal to pay transportation costs. See Savannah *Herald*, May 31, 1866.
3. The American and Mexican Emigrant Company established offices in St. Louis, despite Secretary Seward's order, but never sent a settler to Mexico.
4. Figures quoted in George Harmon, *Confederate Migrations to Mexico*, Circular No. 137 of the Institute of Research, Lehigh University, *Publications*, XII, No. 2 (1937), 460-61-62.
5. Philip Sheridan, *Memoirs of P.H. Sheridan* (New York, Charles L. Webster & Co., 1888), II, 218. Hereafter cited as Sheridan's *Memoirs*.
6. Chief among the Southern newspapers which opposed the exodus were the *Richmond Enquirer*, the Charleston *Daily Courier*, the Raleigh *Standard*, the New Orleans *Times*, the *Daily True Delta* and the *Crescent* of New Orleans, the *Alabama State Journal*, and the *Daily Register* of Mobile.
7. Harmon, *Confederate Migrations to Mexico*, p. 469.
8. Lawrence F. Hill, "The Confederate Exodus to Latin America," *Southwestern Historical Quarterly*, XXXIX, 309-26.
9. Edwards, *Expedition to Mexico*, p. 104.
10. Letter from Mrs. J.C. Bryant.
11. Issue of Oct. 14, 1865.
12. Quoted in Sarah A. Dorsey, *Recollections of Henry Watkins Allen* (New Orleans, James A. Gresham, 1866), p. 340.
13. Quoted in Harmon, *Confederate Migrations to Mexico*, p. 474.
14. New York *Herald*, Apr. 19, 1866.

15. *Ibid.*   16. *Ibid.*

17. *Ibid.*, Supplement, Jan. 12, 1866.

18. *Ibid.*, Apr. 19, 1866.

19. *The Mexican Times*, Apr. 29, 1866.

20. *Ibid.*, Mar. 31, 1866.

21. Benjamin Gratz Shelby, born at the Hacienda Santa Ana in July, 1866, exact birthdate unknown.

22. Edwards, *Expedition to Mexico*, pp. 104-5.

23. Gen. M.M. Parsons, leader of one of the many small parties of Southern exiles who crossed the border independently of Shelby, was captured by Figueroa north of Monterrey in the summer of 1865, and he and five companions were executed under particularly revolting circumstances.–Edwards, *Expedition to Mexico*, p. 45.

24. Letter from Price to Col. Edwin Price, Western Historical Manuscripts Collection, University of Missouri.

25. *The Mexican Times*, June 16, 1866.

26. Maximilian in his Imperial Decree establishing the colony had adjured the newly naturalized immigrants not to mingle in politics.

27. Harmon, *Confederate Migrations to Mexico*, p. 481.

28. Letter written by Shelby, in MSS collection of the Missouri Historical Society, St. Louis.

29. Quoted in Harmon, *Confederate Migrations to Mexico*, p. 482.

30. *Ibid.*, p. 484.

31. Edwards, *Expedition to Mexico*, p. 118.

32. On March 30, 1867, the *Kentucky Gazette*, Lexington, reported: "The wife of Gen. Joseph O. Shelby has reached New Orleans from Mexico. A letter from her to a friend in this city says Gen. Shelby will return in a few weeks to the United States, as it is impossible for an American to live in that country. He is the last of the Confederates to leave."

33. The same newspaper on June 8, 1867, quoted the St. Louis *Times* as saying, "Gen. Jos. O. Shelby, one of the most distinguished, gallant and popular of all brave sons of Missouri who fought in the armies of the Confederacy during the late war is now, we learn, a passenger on the steamer Great Republic and will arrive here from New Orleans this morning. He has been living in Mexico since the surrender of the Southern armies."

34. Mrs. Bryant says that "Aunt Betty" told her many years later at the Shelby home in Bates County, Mo., that none of the recipients ever repaid her for her jewelry.

35. This pet dog lived to a great age. "He was so old," wrote Mr. Motte in a letter to the author, "that when he lay down, he just fell down."

36. Quoted in Harmon, *Confederate Migrations to Mexico* from the Charleston (S.C.) *Daily Courier*, March 15, 1867.

26. "THE MEXICAN TIMES"

1. For Confederates' appreciation of Carlota see Terrell, *From Texas to Mexico*, and Dorsey, *Recollections of Henry Watkins Allen*, p. 334.

2. Kansas City *Times*, May 29, 1870.

3. Letter from Allen to Mrs. Dorsey, from Vera Cruz, March 17, 1866.–Dorsey, *Recollections of Henry Watkins Allen*, p. 342.

4. *John N. Edwards*, p. 17.

5. Evidently Betsy Shelby applied to Gen. Sheridan at New Orleans for permission to leave the country and join her husband.

6. See also Harmon, *Confederate Migrations to Mexico*, p. 459.

7. Sheridan's *Memoirs*, II, 228.

8. Was this the old Indian agent who was charged with the murder of Thomas Barber at the beginning of the Kansas-Missouri border warfare? The name is a com-

mon one and may be a coincidence. Nevertheless the Missouri Clarke was a die-hard Southerner and may well have followed Shelby to Mexico.

9. Harmon, *Confederate Migrations to Mexico,* p. 482.

10. Sheridan's *Memoirs,* II, 218.

27. HOME FROM THE WARS

1. In 1861 Kentucky farmers raised a bumper crop of hemp, but could not sell it. Federal law placed an embargo on Southern hemp (U.S. Statutes 12, 257). Most of the producers, like Gratz, went out of business, although in his case he had reached an age of retirement. Jute largely replaced hemp by the end of the war, and the hemp industry in Kentucky never staged a recovery. Some farmers continued to grow hemp, but sent it to New England to be processed.

2. Cincinnati *Gazette,* Aug. 10, 1866.

3. E. Merton Coulter, *The Civil War and Readjustment in Kentucky* (Chapel Hill, The University of North Carolina Press, 1926), pp. 232-34.

4. Nathan Parker, *Missouri as It Is in 1867* (Philadelphia, J.B. Lippincott, 1867), pp. 293-94.

5. Washington College at Lexington, Va., now Washington and Lee University.

6. Stickles, *Simon Bolivar Buckner,* p. 327.

7. Edwards was editor of the Kansas City *Times* from 1871 to 1874, and from 1887 until his death. From 1868 to 1871 he was associate editor, with Col. John C. Moore as editor.

8. Reprinted from the St. Louis *Republican* in the *Kentucky Gazette,* Lexington, Nov. 9, 1898.

9. Robertus Love, *The Rise and Fall of Jesse James* (New York, G. P. Putnam's Sons, 1926), p. 299.

28. "THE BLOODY BONDS": THE GUN CITY MASSACRE

1. Edwin L. Lopata, *Local Aid to Railroads in Missouri* (New York, Parnassus Press, 1937), p. 65. Hereafter cited as Lopata.

2. They are listed in Margaret Louise Fitzsimmons, "Railroad Development in Missouri, 1860-1870" (thesis, Washington University, St. Louis, 1931), p. 329.

3. Laclede County found itself in this predicament.—Lopata, p. 102.

4. *Ibid.,* p. 7.   5. *Ibid.*   6. *Ibid.,* p. 62.

7. St. Louis *Republican,* May 13, 1869.

8. Kansas City *Star,* May 24, 1942.

9. *Ibid.*

10. For details of the St. Louis and Santa Fe bond history and the Gunn City massacre, see *A History and Directory of Cass County* (Harrisonville, Mo., Cass County *Leader,* 1908), pp. 177-204, and in *A History of Cass and Bates Counties* (St. Joseph, Mo., 1883), pp. 205-6.

11. Newspaper items indicate that Shelby worked as a sub-contractor for various railroads.

12. It was sold shortly thereafter. The Lexington *Caucasian* reported on June 29, 1870, under the heading, "BIG LAND SALE," that "The farm on which Gen. Jo. O. Shelby has been residing, belonging to Benj. Gratz of Lexington, Ky., was sold the other day to Mr. James B. Clay (Sr.) and a grandson of the great orator and statesman, Henry Clay."

13. Mrs. H.H. Gratz, widow of Shelby's early partner, told the author at her home in Lexington, Ky., that Betty Shelby, whom she recalled meeting in Lexington in 1894, was much beloved of all the family.

14. *History of Cass and Bates Counties,* pp. 205-6.

29. COAL MINING: BOOM AND BUST

1. Lopata, p. 37.
2. Gordon Macrae, *The Americans at Home* (New York, E.P. Dutton and Co., reprint edition 1952), p. 421.
3. This and the following information is from the *Missouri Historical Review*, XXII, No. 1 (Oct., 1927), 135.

30. SHELBY IN RECONSTRUCTION

1. Unless other sources are cited, the account of events in the 1870's and 1880's is derived from files of the Lexington *Intelligencer*.
2. Interview with Stonestreet in the Kansas City *Star*, Feb. 14, 1897, the day after Shelby's death.
3. *Missouri Historical Review*, XXIV (Oct.-July, 1929-1930). p. 385.
4. Data on Aldridge Corder supplied by Miss Elizabeth Corder, Marshall, Mo.
5. The marriage took place in Aug., 1888.
6. Quoted in *Centennial History of Missouri*, p. 150.
7. *Ibid.*, pp. 152-53.
8. *Ibid.*, p. 297.
9. See n. 3, Chap. I, above.
10. This letter to George Lankford, who was one of his aides, dated Aug. 2, 1885, is in the Western Historical Manuscripts Collection, University of Missouri.
11. Telegram from Frank Blair to his brother Montgomery in Washington after the election, Blair Family Papers, Library of Congres.
12. Quoted in Kansas City *Star*, May 24, 1942. Date of publication in the *Herald* not given.
13. Lawrence *Tribune*, Apr. 12, 1882.
14. In his book *Noted Guerrillas* (St. Louis, Bryan, Brand and Co., 1877). Edwards accepted the fanciful tales told by Quantrill as to his early background, citing the alleged persecution of the Federals as an excuse for his excesses.
15. Quoted in *John N. Edwards.*

31. THE TRIAL OF FRANK JAMES

1. William H. Townsend, Lexington lawyer and Lincoln authority, author of *Lincoln's Wife's Home Town* (Bobbs-Merrill Co., 1929), told this story to the writer in his office in Lexington in July, 1952: When Townsend's book was published, Miss Nellie Morgan, a niece of the great John Morgan, met him on the street and denounced him for recording the Morgan incident in his book. "Mr. Townsend," said Miss Nellie, "you know that Uncle John never took any money from a bank in Mount Sterling, Kentucky! And you shouldn't have said such a thing!" Townsend replied that he had not said so, but that the newspapers had. Miss Nellie spied an old Confederate across the street, one of Morgan's men, and hailed him. "Come here, Captain Keller," she commanded, "and tell Mr. Townsend that you and Uncle John never took any money from a bank in Mount Sterling, Kentucky." "That's right," obliged Captain Keller. "John Morgan and I blew the durn safe open, Miss Nellie, but there wan't nothin' in it. The Yankees had got there ahead of us."
2. Love cites an instance of this legend in *The Rise and Fall of Jesse James*, p. 131.
3. See also Homer Croy, *Jesse James Was My Neighbor* (New York, Duell, Sloane and Pearce, 1949).
4. Love, *The Rise and Fall of Jesse James*, p. 350.
5. Quoted in *John N. Edwards*, p. 163.

6. Croy, *Jesse James Was My Neighbor*, p. 202. Frank's conversation with the Governor is as quoted by Croy on p. 205.

7. Transcript of testimony appears in *American State Trials* (St. Louis, Thomas Law Book Co., 1916), II, 661 ff. Lent to author by Robert E. Hickman, attorney of Benton, Ill. Also quoted in *Crittenden Memoirs*. The original testimony is on file in the courthouse at Gallatin, Mo., but the author has not had an opportunity to examine the entire record there.

8. Wood Hite, member of the James gang, to whose slaying Dick Liddil confessed.

32. A FRIEND IS GONE

1. The Edwardses had three children. The elder boy, John, seventeen, was a student at St. Mary's College. The second son, James, was fourteen.—*John N. Edwards*, p. 26.

2. *Ibid.*   3. *Ibid.*, p. 27.   4. *Ibid.*, p. 29.   5. *Ibid.*, p. 188.

6. Love, *The Rise and Fall of Jesse James*, p. 293.

7. *John N. Edwards*, pp. 196-228.

8. In records of Fayette County Courthouse, Lexington, Ky.

33. THE GREAT PULLMAN STRIKE

1. Press dispatch sent from Adrian, Mo., on the day of Shelby's death. Quoted here from the Richmond, Va., *Times* of Feb. 13, 1897.

2. George Creel, *A Rebel at Large*, p. 26.

3. *Ibid.*

4. Kansas City *Star*, Feb. 14, 1897.

5. Hanson, in *Cavalry Journal* (Sept.-Oct., 1933), p. 12.

6. Kansas City *Star*, Feb. 14, 1897.

7. *Ibid.*

8. From history of the Pullman strike in Ray Ginger, *The Bending Cross; A Biography of Eugene V. Debs* (New Brunswick, N.J., Rutgers University Press, 1949), pp. 108-52.

9. Kansas City *Star*, July 3, 1894.

10. There are many newspaper versions of this statement of Shelby's, but the *Star's* quotation would seem to be the correct one since its reporter interviewed him.

11. Kansas City *Star*, July 4, 1894.

12. *Ibid.*, July 7.

34. MISSOURI'S FAREWELL

1. Details of Shelby's death and funeral are taken from contemporary newspaper accounts.

2. Capt. Ragan was a Kentuckian who had served with Texas militia during the war at Farmington, Corinth, Chickamauga, and against Sherman on the march to the sea. At this time he was a deputy county marshal in Kansas City.—Webb, *Battles and Biographies of Missourians*, p. 366.

3. Maj. Carples was one of the "Colonels" who was a Union veteran. He served in the brigade of General A.J. Smith, who looted "The Bloody Bonds" at Harrisonville.

Index